Diaries of Girls and Women

Diaries of Girls and Women

A Midwestern American Sampler

Edited by

Suzanne L. Bunkers

The University of Wisconsin Press

The University of Wisconsin Press
2537 Daniels Street
Madison, Wisconsin 53718

3 Henrietta Street
London WC2E 8LU, England

1   3   5   4   2

Printed in the United States of America

Library of Congress Cataloging-in-Publication Data

Bunkers, Suzanne L.
Diaries of girls and women : a midwestern American sampler / Suzanne L. Bunkers.
pp.   cm. — (Wisconsin studies in autobiography)
Includes bibliographical references.
ISBN 0-299-17220-1   ISBN 0-299-17224-4 (pbk.)
1. Girls—United States—Diaries. 2. Women—United States—Diaries.
3. American diaries. I. Title. II. Series.
CT3260 .B86   2001
977'.0082—dc21   00-012231

The following diary excerpts have been reprinted in this volume by permission:

Excerpts from the diaries of Jennie Blair Andrews and Gertrude Cairns by permission of the University of Wisconsin–River Falls, Area Research Center.

Excerpts from the diary of Etta Luella Call by permission of the Kossuth County Historical Society, Kossuth County, Iowa.

Excerpts from the diaries of Majorie L. Bullard, Polly Caroline Bullard, Lillian S. Carpenter, Abbie T. Griffin, Jane F. Grout, Alice Gortner Johnson, and Antoinette Porter King by permission of the Minnesota Historical Society.

Excerpts from the diaries of Maranda J. Cline, Elspeth Close, Mary Griffith, Sarah Gillespie Huftalen, Sarah Jane Kimball, Edythe M. Miller, and Pauline C. Petersen by permission of the Manuscript Collections, State Historical Society of Iowa, Des Moines and Iowa City.

Excerpts from the diary of Margaret Vedder Holdredge by permission of the Berlin Historical Society, Berlin, Wisconsin.

Excerpts from the diary of Maud Hart Lovelace, copyright © 1999 Estate of Merian Kirchner. All right reserved.

Excerpts from the diary of Martha Furgerson Nash by permission of the Iowa Women's Archives, University of Iowa Libraries.

Publication of this book has been made possible in part by the generous support of the Anonymous Fund of the University of Wisconsin–Madison.

When you keep a diary, you want to create
a memory for the future.
—Philippe Lejeune

For those who keep diaries
and for those who read them.

Contents

Contents

Contents

Acknowledgments

Many individuals and organizations deserve thanks for their contributions to this project, which could not have come to fruition without their efforts. William L. Andrews, General Editor of the Wisconsin Studies in Autobiography Series at the University of Wisconsin Press, encouraged me to initiate and persevere with this project. Former and present press staff Raphael Kadushin, Mary Elizabeth Braun, Sheila McMahon, Elizabeth Steinberg, Juliet Skuldt, Carla Aspelmeier, and Sheila Leary guided the book through the publication process.

Primary thanks go to the diarists whose writings appear in this collection. I wish to thank all the living diarists who gave permission for their diary excerpts and photographs to be part of this collection. In addition, I wish to thank these family members and estates, who gave permission to include diary excerpts and photographs: Paul and Juanita Ahrens, Susie Aldrich, Thomas M. Barland, Karen Brindley Christenson, Pauline A. Dallner, Dorothy Errett, Lona Falenczykowski, Ruth King Freymann, Judith and Samuel Gerrish, Pearl Stephens Ginthner, Dee Ginthner, the late Lucille Hutchinson, Lydia E. Kohler, Ronald Langston, Jean G. Linton, Patricia Lorentzen, Marion and the late Horace (Sam) Merrill, Eve von Erdmannsdorff, and Jerome Zuckerman. Excerpts from the diary of Maud Hart Lovelace (copyright 1999 Estate of Merian Kirchner, all rights reserved) appear courtesy of Andrea Shaw, literary executrix.

I am very grateful to state, regional, and local archives throughout Wisconsin, Iowa, and Minnesota for making diary manuscripts and supporting materials available to me. A number of archivists and genealogists provided valuable assistance with this project: Mary Bennett, Coordinator of Special Collections, State

Historical Society of Iowa, Iowa City; Becky Plunkett, Special Collections, Iowa Historical Building Library, Des Moines; Karen M. Mason, Curator, Louise Noun–Mary Louise Smith Iowa Women's Archives, University of Iowa Libraries, Iowa City: Kathryn M. Neal, Curator, Givens Collection of African American Literature, Special Collections and Rare Books, University of Minnesota Libraries, Minneapolis; Mark Greene, Curator, Manuscript Acquisitions, Minnesota Historical Society, St. Paul; Deborah Miller, Research Director, Minnesota Historical Society, St. Paul; Ruth Bauer Anderson, Archivist, Minnesota Historical Society; Harold Miller, Reference Archivist, State Historical Society of Wisconsin, Madison; Susan Ginter Watson, Director, Area Research Center/University Archives, University of Wisconsin–River Falls; Larry Lynch, University Archivist, Special Collections, McIntyre Library, University of Wisconsin–Eau Claire; Paul Beck, Special Collections/ARC, Murphy Library, University of Wisconsin-La Crosse; Sister Mary Elvira Kelley, Sisters of the Third Order of St. Francis Archives, Dubuque, Iowa; Sister Irene Feltz, School Sisters of Notre Dame Archives, Mankato, Minnesota; Denise Hudson, former director of the Blue Earth County Historical Society, Mankato, Minnesota; Brad Linder, Mary Jane Schmitt, and Beverly Hermes, Olmstead County Historical Society, Rochester, Minnesota; William Farnham, Kossuth County Historical Society, Algona, Iowa; Robert H. Selbrede and Eldora Shober Larson of LaCrosse, Wisconsin.

For much-appreciated assistance in the transcription of diary entries, I would like to thank Christy Steele and Kathleen Schultz.

Over the past fifteen years, I have been grateful for research support from the National Endowment for the Humanities, the American Council of Learned Societies, the Iowa Humanities Board, the Women's Studies Research Center at the University of Wisconsin–Madison, and Minnesota State University. Most recently, a work-in-progress grant from the Minnesota Humanities Commission helped me bring this project to fruition.

I have appreciated invitations to present papers at the Modern Language Association Convention, the Midwest Modern Language Association, the Congress of Historical Associations Convention, the National Women's Studies Association Conference, the Rural Women's Studies Association Conference, the History of

Women Religious Conference, the Women's Culture in the Great Plains Symposium, the Mid-continent American Studies Association Conference, and other venues. The First International Conference on Auto/biography, held at Peking University in Beijing in June 1999, and coordinated by Professor Zhao Baisheng, gave me the opportunity to present my research on diaries to an international audience.

I especially appreciate having had opportunities to discuss diaries in the following venues: "Diaries as a Window into Women's Lives," a workshop hosted by Ann Baumgarn, Trudee Svaldi, and the Friends of the Library in Manchester, Iowa; "Two Iowa Women and Their Diaries: A 100-Year Perspective," a performance at the Iowa Sesquicentennial Chautauqua in Manchester, Iowa; "What Do Women Really Mean? Thoughts on Women's Diaries and Lives," an address sponsored by the Minnesota Historical Society's "Have Lunch with a Historian" program; "Writing Your Own Story," a workshop coordinated by Elizabeth D. Cohen as part of the "Writers Live at the Library" series, Middleton Public Library, Middleton, Wisconsin; "Women's Day Out," an address sponsored by Immanuel-St. Joseph Mayo Hospital in Mankato; "Telling Your Story Through Journal Writing," a short course sponsored by the Minnesota State University for Seniors Program; and "Our Grandmothers' Stories," a presentation hosted by Judy Krause and the American Association of University Women in Fairmont, Minnesota.

I would like to thank James Olney, director of the 1983 National Endowment for the Humanities summer seminar, "Forms of Autobiography," who first encouraged me to consider the diary as a form of life writing. I would like to thank Philippe Lejeune for his research on the diary, especially his address entitled "How Diaries End," presented at the "Autobiography and Changing Identities" Conference at the University of British Columbia in July 2000. The book's epigraph comes from this presentation. In addition, I am grateful for the work of many scholars, especially those cited in the introduction to this collection; and I appreciate the support of colleagues, students, and friends who share my interest in diaries.

Finally, I offer a very special thank you to my mother, Verna Klein Bunkers (who knew my first diaries were worth saving); to

Acknowledgments

Bunkers, and Dan Bunkers (who knew my diaries were worth
reading); and to my daughter, Rachel Susanna (who knows why I
keep writing in them).

Diaries of Girls and Women

Introduction

My journal was and is the safe and cherishing container in which I
can be any part of myself that needs to voice whoever she is in whatever words.

—Marion Woodman

Marion Woodman's observation about the value of keeping a diary
or journal speaks to me on two levels. First, it resonates with my
knowledge of diaries kept by midwestern girls and women living in
Minnesota, Iowa, and Wisconsin during the past 150 years. This
book is based on my study of more than four hundred such
diaries—some kept only briefly, others kept during an entire lifetime; some written as the intensely private record of a life, others
written to tell the story of an entire family—stories meant to be
saved and appreciated by future generations.

Second, Woodman's observation resonates with my own
experience as a diarist during a forty-year period. In my attic study
are approximately one hundred volumes of diaries that I have been
keeping since 1970. Before then I wrote in three earlier diaries
that I kept between 1960 and 1968, from my tenth to eighteenth
years, when I was growing up in Granville, Iowa. When I found
my girlhood and adolescent diaries in my mother's attic several
years ago, I sneaked them downstairs and locked myself in the
bathroom, where (just as I had done many years before) I spent
hours poring over individual diary entries I had made.

My first diary is still my favorite. It is a one-year diary, about
four inches by six inches, with one page (of nineteen lines) per day,
and with each day's date printed at the top of that page. Even
though it was a one-year diary, I quickly subverted that format and
made it last for a number of years by writing only half-page entries

one year, then writing the next year's entry for that same date on the bottom half of each page. I didn't write in my diary every day, however. Sometimes a week or a month would go by without my making a single entry. A few years later, even though I was officially keeping a five-year diary, I would go back to my original one-year diary and use its blank pages to write about experiences whose recounting required more space than the four lines allocated for each entry in my five-year diary.

The words, *My Diary,* are imprinted on my first diary's aqua faux leather cover, which features an illustration of a teenaged girl and boy strolling arm in arm past a football stadium. The boy, who wears royal blue slacks and a white sweater, carries a tennis racquet. The girl, who wears white shorts, a red sweater, and chartreuse knee-highs that match her chartreuse blouse, bounces a tennis ball. They smile, serenely in love. As a girl, I found this cover illustration romantic and exotic, for I lived in an Iowa town of fewer than four hundred. We had no tennis courts, let alone a football stadium.

My first diary has a clasp with its own lock and a key. Today, however, the key has disappeared, and the clasp is held together with masking tape, not because it has worn out but because once, more than thirty years ago, a younger sibling (rumored to be my sister Linda) took our mother's scissors and snipped the clasp of my diary.[1] When I tell people about this desperate act, they usually gasp (unless they have done the same thing themselves). Then I hasten to mention that I could hardly hold this act against my sister because (truth be told) I used to read her diary, too. We had identical diaries; mine was blue, and Linda's was red. We received our first diaries for Christmas in 1960, when I was ten and she was eight. My first diary entry reads: "December 24, 1960. Dear Diary, Am very happy with all my gifts. Some are Diary, Barbie Doll, nightgown, slippers, scarf, Bad Minten set, pencil sharpener, candy from Dad's patrons on the mailroute, & perfume. All for now. —Susie." My sister's first diary entry is a bit more somber. It reads: "December 24, 1960. Dear Diary, today I got colorforms, Barbie doll and more things. I began to get the Christmas spirit after all."

Throughout our girlhoods my sister and I shared a bedroom, and each of us kept her diary in her underwear drawer. It wasn't unusual for us to lie on our double bed at night, writing in our diaries before putting them away, saying our prayers, and going to sleep. Sometimes we recorded daily events, noting birthdays and anniversaries along with school assignments and visits with friends. Other times we recorded our trials and tribulations. At the end of her first week of diary keeping, Linda complained: "December 30, 1960. Dear Diary, Today Kathy and Christy will come. Mommy says get up and work. You didn't help once a week. But Mommy just makes it up. We are rilly working hard." As the new year began, Linda wrote a series of short descriptive entries that reflect events in the daily life of an eight-year-old:

January 17, 1961. Dear Diary, Today I saw a satellate out side. It looked just like a star. The satellate was called Echo.

January 18, 1961. Dear Diary, I wrote a pome in school today. Sister said it was very good.

January 19, 1961. Dear Diary, today I will get my pome up on the board by 5ed grades room. It's very cold and I got to stay up till 10:30 because there was no school.

January 20, 1961. Dear Diary, today I am going to watch the inauguration. It begins at 10:00 and last to 3:00 this afternoon. I think she [Jacqueline Kennedy] is over done.

January 22, 1961. ~~I like Frank now.~~ Not for real!

After penning these entries, Linda stopped writing in her diary for six months; when she resumed, it was summer, and her life had a different rhythm: "July 30, 1961. Dear Diary, Today I went to Mary's farm and got some cattails. We played with the cats and rode ponys. There dog came with us everywhere. We had a gay time in the playhouse. I plan to invite her in soon." As the next year drew to a close, Linda wrote this entry: "December 15, 1962. Dear Diary, Today Santa came to town. I got some candy and M & M's. Also I got a apple. I was just watching Leave It to Beaver. Sandy was at her grandma's so I went over & we had a small show. So long. Linda."

From mid-December 1962 through February 1963, Linda

5

made no entries in her diary. She resumed writing in early March 1963 and made fourteen entries that month. Then she did not write again until late May 1963, when our family marked an important event: "May 25, 1963. Today it was Patti Ann's, Kathy's, and <u>my</u> new brother's birthday. We (Rose V. and I) ate dinner at Pat's house. After dinner Denny came over and told me I had a new brother. <u>Boy</u> was I happy. Me again, Linda."

Like my sister, I used my diary to record the same happy event: "May 25, 1963. Today, at 10:04 A.M., a baby boy was born into the Bunkers family. He was weighed in at 7 lb. 12 oz. And will be called Daniel James & Jim Klein & I will be sponsors. Our new little boy looks just like Dad & I'll be surprised if we don't start calling him 'the little Tony.' Mom will be able to bring Danny home next week. So till then, Ta Ta. Sue." More often, however, I used my diary as a sounding board when things were not going my way. As a twelve-year-old eager to be with friends, I sometimes complained heartily about my lot in life:

January 31, 1963. Today was the worst day of my life. Jeanie was sick so we couldn't go to Alton. I had a chance to go to Le Mars game with Mary Mc. but I had to babysit at Angies. Linda was supposed to, but she chickened out & I was all dressed to go—but she made me go babysit because she bawled till Dad gave me Hell & called me 'asshole' & made me go babysit. and what does Linda get out of it? She goes along to the farm & now it is 10:00 & I'm sitting home alone. I am sure mad at her & everyone was growlling at each other & all I got out of it is a damn good headache & a desire for revenge (which I shall get, believe me).

A year later my diary entry reflected that I was suffering from adolescent angst: "February 2, 1964. Today we will go to Worthington to visit Grandma. Nothing will happen & it will be a dull day. I just don't care about anything anymore. I don't have anything to live for. Last nite I cried myself to sleep. I can't go anyplace & I planned on seeing Gary at Alton over the weekend. Why doesn't God let me have some fun? Or good Luck?" But a week later I had recovered enough to write in my diary about what was, for me, a major historical event: "February 9, 1964. Today I was with Sheila, Pat & Gisela. We goofed around & watched the Beatles on T.V. Wow! I like!" The same day, Linda wrote this entry in her diary: "Dear Diary, went to Minnesota today & saw Grandma

& Ray. Got home in time to see the Beatles for the first time. Paul, George, John & R I N G O." When the Beatles made their second appearance on the *Ed Sullivan Show*, Linda waxed enthusiastic, even including stick-figure drawings of the lads from Liverpool as part of her diary entry: "February 16, 1964. Dear Diary, Went to Lemars today for a baptism. Got home just in time for the Beatles. Linda WHOOOOOOOOOOOOOOO YA YA YA."

Although we had little privacy in actuality, the ideal of privacy was important to my sister and me as we continued writing in our diaries. I kept my diary locked, and I hid the key in ingenious places, such as under the pincushion in my sewing basket. Linda, on the other hand, left her diary lying unlocked in her dresser drawer, which made it easy for me to sneak her diary off to the bathroom (the only room in our house with a door that locked) so I could browse through it. My sister had to be more enterprising if she wanted to read my diary.

Both Linda and I used the "Memoranda" sections at the back of our diaries to record special kinds of information. There Linda listed these important events in her life:

1. I was born October 23, 1952.
2. I received my first communion on March 23, 1960.
3. In second grade ~~year of school~~ I have one of the main [parts] in a play called The Little Blue Angel (I was it).
4. Soon I will recive Confermation.
5. I recived Confirmation April 25.

The Memoranda section is also where Linda expressed her feelings about one of her brothers ("Denny is a baby & a dirty pig") and her friends ("Lois and Patsy and Patty Ann are my best, very best friends. Lois is my best pal and buddy forever"). In the autumn of 1963 Linda, who had just turned ten, added this bemused observation about her diary: "By hook by crook I got a mixed up book."

In the Memoranda section of my diary, I wrote an entry pointing to the future: "To my children, I started writing in this diary at the age of 10. I am 12 now and the date is Dec. 15, 1962. Some of the things I have written are crazy, but I was then too.—Suzanne (Suzy) Bunkers (now but not forever)." More important, the Memoranda section of my diary was where I could safely record my secrets. In mid-January 1963, my father's older brother, Dick, died. My mother, pregnant with my youngest brother at the time, traveled to Minneapolis for Uncle Dick's funeral. My father was ill with an inner ear disorder (and was, as I now realize, grief stricken) and was too sick to accompany her. In my mother's absence, I stayed home from school to take care of my father and three younger siblings. On the evening of my uncle's death I wrote this entry on the final Memoranda page in my diary:

Jan. 16, 1963. Today we learned that our uncle Dick Bunkers died of a heart attack in Minneapolis. No one even suspected he was sick. Granma Bunkers wrote in her letter to us that Dick would take her back to Worthington on Sunday. Dad is just sick over it. He lost his sense of balance a couple of days ago and has to stay in bed. He thought he will be well enough to go to the funeral but Dr. Murphy says no. So mom has to go. I really feel bad too, because he was so nice, and his family must not have loved him much. I hope his soul is in heaven because it should be.

A few days later, after my mother had returned from Uncle Dick's funeral and confided to me how he had actually died, I wrote a second entry and hid it on an unused page midway through my diary: "~~July 1~~ Jan. 19, 1963. Mom told me this morning that Uncle Dick committed suicide because he felt so bad because [his wife] didn't care about him. We each got one of his holy cards & I asked mom why they were given out because Dick's soul was in hell. She said that because he was so good all his life that he would suffer in purgatory for it."

As I reflect on these diary entries nearly four decades after writing them, I realize how taboo it was in our staunchly Catholic family to think about, much less write about, the subject of suicide. I couldn't talk about my uncle's death at St. Joseph Catholic School; our religion teacher had told us that, if a person committed suicide, his or her soul would go straight down to hell. I couldn't even discuss the subject with my sister because my mother had warned me to keep silent. My second diary entry concluded, "So now I will try and get everyone to pray for him so he can go to heaven. I wish I could ask Mom more, but I'm afraid to. No one, not even Linda, is supposed to know how Dick died."

Later that year I wrote a series of diary entries that dealt with another, even more incomprehensible, event:

November 22, 1963. Today Pres. Kennedy was killed in Dallas, Texas by Lee Harvey Oswald. Funeral Monday. No skating tonite.

November 23, 1963. Long weekend ahead. No school Monday because of funeral. Everyone is really shocked & sorry.

November 24, 1963. Today we stayed home. . . . Lee Oswald, Kennedy's killer, was killed by Jack Ruby in Dallas.

November 25, 1963. Today we all stayed home & watched Kennedy's funeral. It was so sad. All for now. . . .

December 24, 1963. I'm just sitting here writing this cause I don't know what to do with myself. It's Xmas Eve but no one is excited about it. I guess its because of Pres. Kennedy's death. We didn't send or get as many Xmas cards this year as others, & I guess that's the reason.

Yet even as I wrote the December 24, 1963, entry, my attention was not focused solely on the national tragedy of a presidential assassination. This diary entry concluded, "I can't wait till Jan. 17 for the Floyd Valley–Spalding game. I plan on seeing Gary, but I have the strangest feeling that he won't be there. I'm keeping my fingers crossed."

Looking back, I see that my sister's and my early diaries resemble those kept by many young girls. We wrote about family and school activities, household chores, and religious devotions. We told of babysitting for neighbors' children, weaving and selling hot pads, and starting a lucrative nightcrawler business. We wrote about squabbles with siblings, school activities, and adolescent crushes. We wrote about historical events and, on occasion, about the need to keep family secrets. Although my sister and I were keeping our diaries simultaneously, our diary entries often differed from one another in terms of themes and styles. Linda began by making short, sporadic entries in her red one-year diary during 1961. Then, like many young diarists, she used blank pages to record entries from 1962 through 1964. Her grasp of sentence structure and spelling developed as she grew from age eight to eleven and a half.

I wrote slightly longer, but just as sporadic, entries during my first year or two of diary keeping. Then, as a Christmas present in

December 1962, I received my second diary—the five-year diary. Beginning on January 1, 1963, I wrote daily entries until this five-year diary was filled and, as I mentioned earlier, I would return to the one-year diary for longer entries. Both my sister and I found ways to subvert printed diary formats, and our entries reveal that neither of us used a set formula in the practice of keeping a diary.

When I reopen my first diary, I do so carefully, not only because its pages are brittle and its cover fragile but also because it is *my* diary, my "safe and cherishing container," as Woodman has characterized it. Nearly forty years after I first opened the pages of that diary, I recognize the central role it played in my growing-up process, in my coming of age, in my evolving perceptions of myself and my relationships with others. Mary Pipher's perceptive analysis of the role that journals play in the lives of girls echoes my experience: "In their writing, they can clarify, conceptualize and evaluate their experiences. Writing their thoughts and feelings strengthens their sense of self. Their journals are a place where their point of view on the universe matters" (1994, 225).[2]

I invite you to join me in examining my diary and those of many other midwestern American girls and women. First, we will consider the premises underlying this anthology. Next, we will look into frequently asked questions about the diary and consider useful frameworks for studying diaries as life writing. Then we will examine themes common to many of the diaries in this collection, and we will note editorial principles for this book. Finally, we will read excerpts from the diaries themselves. As we set out on this journey, I hope you will keep in mind the lighthearted (and helpful) advice that Jessica Wilber, an adolescent diarist and author, offers to novice diarists: Remember that there are only two rules for keeping a diary: "(1) Date every entry, and (2) Don't make any more rules" (1996, 4).

Stitching this sampler

All you my Friends that now expect to see
A Piece of Work thus perform'd by me,
Cast but A Smile on this my mean endeavor
I'll Strive to mend and be Obedient ever.

—Nineteenth-century sampler

My study of diaries kept by girls and women living in Wisconsin, Iowa, and Minnesota since the mid-nineteenth century has resulted in this anthology of selections from forty-six diaries. My purpose is twofold: to explore the ways in which diaries can document the diverse experiences of individuals and families, and to understand the ways in which diaries have functioned as forms of life writing. I draw on the metaphor of the sampler, which is appropriate for several reasons. First, the term *sampler* can refer to a decorative piece of needlework that usually has letters or verses embroidered on it in various stitches as an example of the stitcher's skill. The word comes from the Latin word *exemplum*, meaning something that serves as a pattern for imitation or record. The word found its way into English via the French word *exemplaire*, meaning model, pattern, copy, specimen. Girls and women in many cultural settings have created samplers, and the sampler found its way into early American life as a demonstration of various stitches, designs, and motifs that girls and women could study and then imitate in future sewing tasks. It is no coincidence that women and girls created most samplers because they traditionally have done the sewing and fine stitchery in their families. As a form of material culture, girls and women typically designed and preserved samplers as evidence of their skill.

Today the word *sampler* has additional connotations. One can buy a Whitman's Chocolates Sampler or send a Wisconsin Cheese House Sampler as a holiday gift. *Sampler* is also used to represent part of or a single item from a larger whole or group. The term can also refer to the person doing the collecting, as in one who collects or examines samples, and it can be used to refer to that which has been collected, that is, the sample. All these definitions apply to the selections from diaries that appear in this anthology. The act of keeping a diary involves the sampling of one's experiences, followed by the selection of particular details and the shaping of each diary entry. The act of editing a diary, whether it be one's own diary or another person's, involves sampling diary entries, then selecting particular entries, often for an edition or a collection such as this.

Over the years several questions have guided my study of diaries: Why do diaries have such staying power? What makes them appealing to writers young and old? What can diaries help us appreciate about the lives and experiences of those individuals who kept them? What can diaries tell us, not only about why individuals write in diaries but also about why they (and others) preserve those diaries and make them available for others to read and appreciate? Although I do not claim that this collection will provide definitive answers to these questions, I hope that it will open the door for further study of the issues they raise.[3]

Considering the Diary

What is a diary? When I began my research, I made a distinction between the diary as a form for recording events and the journal as a form for introspection, reflection, and the expression of feelings. Like many others, I have found this to be an artificial distinction, both as the result of my research and as the result of my own diary keeping. I found as many kinds of diaries as I found diarists: a diary might be kept in a cloth-bound book with lock and key, but it might just as easily be kept in a spiral notebook, looseleaf paper, or on the back sides of envelopes. A diary entry might be a brief one-line report of events, such as those entries found in diaries kept by Maranda J. Cline or Ruby Butler Ahrens. A diary entry might contain a five-page analysis of one's beliefs, attitudes, and desires, such as those entries found in diaries kept by Sarah Jane Kimball, Emily Quiner, or Ada James. A diarist might write daily entries, as Lillian Carpenter did; a diarist might write periodic entries, as Martha Furgerson Nash did; or a diarist might write sporadic entries, as Maria Morton Merrill did.[4]

Diaries also reflect different kinds of authorship. Some diaries, like those of Mary Griffith and Elspeth Close, have individual authors and appear to have been written for the diarist alone. Some diaries, like those of Sarah Gillespie and Ada James, also tell us that the diarist permitted certain family members (Sarah's mother, Ada's cousin) to read entries in the diaries. The Hamilton and Holton family diaries illustrate multiple authorship of diary entries over years and generations. "The Chronicle of the School Sisters of Notre Dame" as well as the "Annals of the Sisters of the Third Order of St. Francis" illustrate the communal, or group, diary—written as a community record and preserved in community archives. It bears repeating: we find as many kinds of diaries as we do diarists.

A growing scholarly interest in the diary has resulted in a number of critical studies that explore the nature of the diary. Rebecca Hogan analyzes the diary as a "text composed of 'fragments' which nevertheless flow continually through the days," creating a text that "is by its very nature open-ended, unfinished and incomplete, in some cases ending only with the life of the writer" (1991, 100). She describes the diary as a "paratactic form" [a string of clauses without connectives] that is "both repetitive and cumulative, each entry discrete (and discreet), and each entry an addition to the flow of days" (100). Finally, Hogan defines two kinds of parataxis in the diary: the "even, horizontal, metonymic flow of events and entries into the diary" that creates its continuity, and the "series of related items, events and entries without the use of connecting links" that creates the sense of "discrete, separate entries" (104).

The concept of dailiness is useful in characterizing the diary's form, especially when taken in the sense that Bettina Aptheker uses it:

By the dailiness of women's lives I mean the patterns women create and the meanings women invent each day and over time as a result of their labors and in the context of their subordinated status to men. The point is not to describe every aspect of daily life or to represent a schedule of priorities in which some activities are more important or accorded more status than others. The point is to suggest a way of knowing from the meanings women give to their labors. The search for dailiness is a method of work that allows us to take the patterns women create and the meanings women invent and learn from them. If we map what we learn, connecting one meaning or invention to another, we begin to lay out a different way of seeing reality. (1989, 39)

In her recent in-depth study of the diaries of six nineteenth-century American women, Amy Wink defines the paradox inherent in the diary: "Because the diary is, when we read it, a completed work, it can be comprehended as a whole. However, it is only by recognizing the significance of each individual moment of writing that the larger frame may be understood; conversely, it is in seeing the whole text, the life represented, that the individual moments show their importance. What we read is as complex as the chambered nautilus turning upon itself until its opening" (1996, 14). Margo Culley emphasizes the importance of the diary as text—a verbal construct characterized by the "process of selection and arrangement of detail," one that uses such literary strategies as "questions of audience (real or implied), narrative, shape and structure, persona, voice, imagistic and thematic repetition, and what James Olney calls 'metaphors of self' " (1985, 10).

Kathryn Carter, whose recent work on unpublished diary manuscripts confirms their importance as a form of life writing for Canadian women, explains: "In addition to foregrounding a woman's relations to the material conditions of writing, and the discourses available to her at specific moments in history, diaries also highlight the role of audience, issues of publicity and privacy, and their effect upon the act of writing" (1997, 20). In examining not only the material conditions of diarists' writing but also their uses of such strategies as indirection, silence, and euphemism, Carter stresses the importance of the manuscript diary as "currency in a social exchange about history, about community and communication, about family and friendship" (21).

What makes the diary so intriguing to readers? I believe that the diary's appeal can be traced to its expansiveness and flexibility. The diary can incorporate a variety of writing styles; it can range from being formal and stylized to conversational and idiomatic. The diary can envelop a variety of themes; for example, the need for self-affirmation, the conflict between duty and desire, the quest for knowledge, the wish to make one's mark on the world, the coming to terms with change and loss. Because it is expansive and flexible, the diary can be studied simultaneously as a historical document, a therapeutic tool, and a form of literature.[5] The diary can provide valuable insights into individuals' self-images, the dynamics of families and communities, and the kinds of contributions that individuals have made, past and present. The form and content of a diary are inevitably shaped not only by its writer's personality but also by her experience of race, ethnicity, class, age, sexual orientation, and geographical setting. Circumstances influence both what a diarist writes and when and why she writes—and what she does not write.

What strategies are central to the act of keeping a diary? Joan

N. Radner and Susan S. Lanser's research on coding in women's folk culture provides a useful framework for analyzing strategies that diarists use.[6] Radner and Lanser define *code* not only as "the system of language rules through which communication is possible" but also as a "set of signals—words, forms, behaviors, signifiers of some kind—that protect the creator from the consequences of openly expressing particular messages" (1993, 23). They emphasize that "because ambiguity is a necessary feature of every coded act, any instance of coding risks reinforcing the very ideology it is designed to critique" (3). A diarist's encoding strategies might include the use of irony, sarcasm, indirection, substitution, omission, and trivialization, all of which create ambiguity in the text. Excerpts from the diaries of Emily Quiner and Gertrude Cairns illustrate the varied ways in which diarists can use such rhetorical strategies to reveal and conceal meaning.

Sometimes a diarist's encoding strategy consists of creating short, simple sentences—diary entries that conceal as much as they reveal. The diary of Iowa farmer Maranda Cline illustrates conscious and unconscious encoding, both in the entries she made and in those made in the same diary by her daughter, Bertie Shellady, in the days after her mother's death.[7] Patricia Lorentzen, the granddaughter of Maranda J. Cline, describes the diary's paratactic structure this way: "The 'Journal' is a cloth-bound book with leather corner tips on the cover. . . . Some of the pages are ragged and worn on the edges with some of the text missing. The diary is basically a line-a-day matter of fact recitation of events, and there appear to me to be no indications of emotion. Births, deaths, killings, etc. all seem to be mentioned in equally non-colored language" (personal communication, 1987).

What kinds of themes appear in diaries? Six primary themes, often overlapping and interlocking, appear in the diaries of midwestern girls and women in this collection:

1. The need to view the use of one's time and energies as worthwhile. As I have noted elsewhere, "it might, of course, be argued that simply by recording her activities, any writer asserts the belief that what one does is important, yet the tone of many of these diaries and journals reveals that their writers felt the need to explain their activities in detail, not so much as a means of filling pages but as a way of justifying to themselves that they were using

their time well and that their activities were appreciated by others" (1988, 195). For instance, Abbie T. Griffin's diary entries often detail all the sewing and embroidery work she completed on a given day, whereas Maria Morton Merrill's diary entries outline farm tasks such as threshing, harvesting oats and potatoes, and butchering hogs. In their diaries Emily Quiner and Agnes Barland McDaniel catalogue the daily work of the nurse; Pauline Petersen describes the work of a teacher; Maud Hart Lovelace tracks her work as a writer; Lillian Carpenter describes the difficulties of getting and keeping a job during the Great Depression.

2. The need for meaningful connections with other human beings. For many the diary becomes a place where they can write about relationships with others, thereby validating themselves as members of families and communities. Often this need for meaningful connections leads a diarist to fashion a text that members of her family or community, as well as future generations, can read. Speculating on the role that keeping a diary may have played in the life of her husband's grandmother, Marion Merrill asks, "Could it be that some of Maria's loneliness and critical nature, that are shown in the words of the diary, resulted from finding little companionship in the community and from being cut off from those she would have enjoyed, because her illness made it impossible for her to maintain ties with neighbors?" (personal correspondence, 1987). Like the diary of Maria Morton Merrill, the diaries of Sarah Pratt, Sarah Gillespie, Sarah Jane Kimball, and Carol Johnson illustrate how the diary can help the diarist recognize and perhaps fulfill this need for meaningful relationships. In many cases, as a diarist continues to write, her diary itself becomes a trusted friend and confidante. Emily Quiner's final entry, for instance, addresses the central role that her diary has played in her life for more than two-and-a-half years: "It is true, soon I shall bid you adieu, faithful friend, after having gone in your company for nearly two years and a half, laying you away among the relics of my <u>dead past</u>, no more to look upon your pages, save as reminders of what I have been, as chronicled, in you, and what I shall be no more forever."

3. The need for an outlet for intense emotions like grief and anger, emotions not usually deemed appropriate for public expression, particularly by a female. At times the diary functions as a friend or confidante whom the writer can trust with her innermost

feelings and secrets at turning points in her life.[8] Such is the case with the diaries of Margaret Vedder Holdredge, who writes of her loneliness in her husband's absence; Martha Smith Brewster, who grieves the death of her young son; Gertrude Cairns, who recounts the details of her physical and emotional collapse and recovery; and Sandra Gens, who grieves the death of her father.

4. The need for a forum for commentary on religion, politics, and world events. Contrary to popular myth, midwestern girls and women have not been isolated and unaware of world events; in fact, many have used their diaries to express strong opinions on social, political, and religious/spiritual issues, as well as the ways in which such issues are intertwined. Entries in the diaries of Eliza and J. Talmai Hamilton, Edythe Miller, Gwendolyn Wilson Fowler, and Martha Furgerson Nash, among others, illustrate the ways in which the diary can provide a safe place for expressing such points of view.

5. The need to launch a quest that may involve leaving the home or the homeland, going out into the larger world, and making one's way there. Isabella McKinnon's diary, which recounts the story of her family's emigration from Scotland to Wisconsin, illustrates this theme, as do Jane F. Grout's diary of her family's migration from Wisconsin to Minnesota, Alice Gortner Johnson's diary of her trip to the Boundary Waters Canoe Area, and Ruth Van Horn Zuckerman's diary of her and her husband's travels in England. Sometimes the diarist launches a quest without ever leaving her home as she searches for self-identity. Along with many others in this collection, the diaries of Sarah Jane Kimball, Sarah Gillespie Huftalen, Ada James, and Gertrude Cairns—all kept throughout their writers' lifetimes—illustrate the central role that the quest plays in girls' and women's diaries and lives.[9]

6. The need for a vehicle for sending specific messages to one's intended audience, especially when the diarist expects others to read her diary. "The Chronicle of the School Sisters of Notre Dame" and the "Annals of the Sisters of the Third Order of St. Francis" fulfill such a function because in each case the diarist knew that what she wrote would become part of the archival records of her religious order and might be read by others as well. Similarly, the Hamilton and Holton family diaries, written to record the history of several individuals within a family unit, illus-

trate the ways in which a diary can serve as a vehicle for transmitting family history and values from one generation to another.

What does a reader of diaries need to keep in mind? I need to consider the range of interpretations that an encoded text can yield. I also need to note that what is not said in a diary entry can be every bit as important as what is said and that shaping and selection are integral to the diarist's task. In *Read This Only to Yourself,* her influential study of the letters and diaries of North Dakota women, Elizabeth Hampsten puts it this way: "[P]rivate writings of women ask of us, if we wish to read them knowingly, a special inventive patience. We must interpret what is not written as well as what is, and, rather than dismiss repetitions, value them especially. 'Nothing happened' asks that we wonder what, in the context of a particular woman's stream of days, she means by something happening" (1982, 4).

In her recent study of the diary, Alexandra Johnson reinforces the importance of this view: "Invisible sentences, blank spaces, a line suddenly breaking off. Often these are a diary's most intriguing places, the spot where the eye lingers longest" (1997, 107). By attending to what is not there as well as what is, a diligent reader can easily dispel the stereotype of the diary as a series of fragmented, haphazard scribbles. Diaries are forms in which their writers' exacting work cannot always be seen. This does not mean, however, that selection, shaping, and structuring have played no role in their creation. As I have noted elsewhere, many diaries are so skillfully "invisibly mended," to use Jane Marcus's phrase, that only a very close reading can reveal what Elaine Showalter has called "ragged edges"—those bits and pieces that defy tidy inclusion in traditional literary schema (1993, 245). To become a careful reader of diaries, one must scrutinize the physical formats of diaries as well as the kinds of entries they contain.

What about privacy and secrecy in a diary? Although the diary has traditionally been viewed as a "private" rather than a "public" text, actual diaries reveal that this is a false dichotomy and that the diary is often both public and private. For many midwestern girls and women writing since 1850, diaries have not necessarily been the intensely secretive texts that come to mind when most present-day readers imagine diaries with little locks and keys. Although many diaries were private in the sense that they were not published, the writers often intended to share these texts with family members and/or close friends. Ada James shared her diary with her cousin Ada Briggs; in fact, the two young women periodically exchanged and read one another's diaries, then wrote "prophecies" for the coming year in them.[10] Sometimes a diary functioned as a collaborative text, with more than one person writing in it, or with one family member (often a female) writing what was intended as a family chronicle as well as an artifact of material culture to be read and treasured by successive generations. The Hamilton and Holton family diaries illustrate this type of communal text, as do the chronicles/annals kept by orders of women religious.[11] Because the form is so flexible and adaptable in terms of purpose and audience, the diary occupies a unique place in literature and history as a text that can be both personal and communal.

What characterizes the narrative structure of the diary? Like other forms of narrative, a diary tells a story; unlike many other forms, however, a diary need not be plot driven. Many diaries are not, as Helen M. Buss points out in her study of diaries by nineteenth-century Canadian women. Buss notes a phrase that she has come across in several diaries: "as they say in novels." She emphasizes the irony in a diarist's use of this phrase, given "all the ways in which this and similar accounts are different from novels, all the ways in which they do not fulfill the novelistic assumptions of the reader, all the ways in which they demand a different relationship with the reader" (1993, 57). Some publishers and readers, however, expect that a diary must be plot driven to have literary merit, an expectation that can result in its being forced into a traditional narrative frame, with an artificial emphasis on "literariness" to the exclusion of other concerns. The problem, as Kathryn Carter explains, is this: "The concept of a literary tradition fits uncomfortably with diary writing because it implies literary motivations and standards which are erroneously applied to the writing found in diaries. Holding diaries up to literary criteria not only diminishes our understanding of their writing, it also serves to limit the range of diary writings made public" (in press).

Judy Nolte Temple discusses the related issue of whether a published edition of a diary needs to follow traditional narrative patterns (i.e., rising action, conflict, climax, dénouement) in order to succeed as a narrative version of a diarist's life. Temple defines three criteria that publishers often deem necessary for gauging the potential worth of a manuscript diary: plot, setting, and character. She observes: "These three conventional criteria, right out of high school freshman English, exclude more diaries than they include. Only if the writer is among the literary elite—Woolf, Nin—do readers accept more fluidity within the text and its persona" (1989, 77).

Certainly, in its subversion of traditional narrative techniques and forms, in its uses of interruptions, eruptions, resistance, and contradiction, the diary reflects its author's presence in the text, as evidenced in diverse strategies of self-representation. Based on my work with unpublished manuscript diaries, I can affirm that most do not follow a traditional narrative pattern. Rather, a diary reflects its writer's sense of purpose and audience as well as its writer's choice of narrative strategies (e.g., characterization, setting, dialogue) appropriate to purpose and audience. When pondering the ways in which diarists use diverse formats and narrative structures in their texts, I am mindful of what the artist and writer Wanda Gag wrote in one volume of her adolescent diary, as she reached its final pages on September 18, 1909: "Poor diary; nearly done with you, am I not? I'd write piles but I have to save space, because I'd hate to quit writing for a time and I don't know whether I can get another book right away" (1984, 33–34).

How might cultural mores influence diary writing? Since the mid-nineteenth century, many diarists have witnessed and recorded stages in the evolution of cultural norms, expectations, and opportunities for girls and women. Many diaries have served as "staging areas" from which diarists can question as well as conform to gender roles. For instance, in her diary, which she kept from 1876 to 1880, Blanche Brackenridge, an adolescent from Rochester, Minnesota, listed what she called "Knife and Fork Flirtations" in a playful yet subversive look at "ladylike" behavior:

Drawing the napkin through the hand	I decline to converse with you
Holding it by the corners	Is it agreeable?
Playing with the fork	I have something to tell you privately
Holding up a knife and fork in each hand	When can I see you?
Laying knife and fork together on left of plate	After the meal

Clenched right hand on the table	To night
Napkin held with three fingers	Yes
Napkin held with two fingers	No
Holding napkin to chin	Cease signaling
Standing knife and fork (facing left)	Can I meet you
Laying knife and fork (facing right)	I am displeased
Balancing fork on edge of cup	Are you engaged tonight?
Striking fork with knife	Meet me or can I meet you
Placing knife over the glass	Will you be alone?
Balancing spoon on edge of cup	I have an engagement
Stirring the spoon in cup slowly	Will you be late?
Holding the spoon over the cup and gazing meditatingly on it	We are suspected or we are discovered

Like Blanche Brackenridge, many diarists in this anthology used their diaries to acquiesce to and rebel against such culture-bound notions as the "doctrine of separate spheres" and the "cult of true womanhood," which scholars now acknowledge are complicated by issues of race, class, sexuality, age, region, religion, and other variables.[12] Cathy N. Davidson refers to the "metaphoric and explanatory nature of the separate spheres" because, as she explains, it has never been clear to her "that these spheres actually existed in anything like a general, definitive, or, for that matter, 'separate' way in nineteenth-century America or that they existed in America any more than in other countries or in the nineteenth century more than in earlier centuries" (1998, 445). Davidson continues, "[T]he binaric version of nineteenth-century American history is ultimately unsatisfactory because it is simply too crude an instrument—too rigid and totalizing—for understanding the different, complicated ways that nineteenth-century American society of literary production functioned" (445).

How does the diary function as both text and artifact? Diaries are things—artifacts of material culture as well as texts.[13] As Kathryn Carter explains, "Diaries foreground the material conditions of their making and thereby locate the writer as a bodily presence in a particular time and place. . . . Like a photo album or a scrapbook, the diary is the material trace of a human attempting to place herself in the context of her immediate culture" (in press, 32–33). When a diary is considered from this dual perspective—as

Blanche Brackenridge. From the Collection of the Olmstead County Historical Society, Rochester, Minn.

text and as artifact—a thorough exploration requires not only analyzing individual diary entries but also analyzing the size and shape of the diary in an effort to determine how its physical format might have influenced what was or was not written and how it was or was not written. It means examining entries in a five-year diary that refuse to stay within the four tiny lines allotted to them to determine why the diarist might have needed to circumvent the prescribed diary format. It means considering how the use of statements such as "I was unwell today" (which could mean "I had the flu today" but which could also mean "I was having my menstrual period today" or "I was in labor, about to deliver a baby today") simultaneously affirms and subverts notions of "domesticity" and "femininity." It means attending to how all sorts of "ragged edges" might offer clues about the diarist, her writing process, her intended audience, and the purpose(s) for which her text was written. It means "no longer starting from the assumption that I am working with 'odds and ends,' 'fragments,' 'bits and pieces' of women's experiences—everything that has traditionally been relegated to the dustbin of *man*kind's experiences." It also means that "as I read and interpret forms of women's 'private' writing, I choose interpretive pieces; and I cut and shape them—arranging them into intricate, carefully wrought designs, both consciously and unconsciously" (Bunkers 1993, 217).

Setting Boundaries

Why is it worthwhile to study diaries from this three-state area? This anthology is not the first collection to include excerpts from diaries by girls and women; several scholarly and popular studies have, to varying degrees, included such excerpts. With the exceptions of Glenda Riley (who has studied Iowa women) and Elizabeth Hampsten (who has studied North Dakota women), these studies have focused on the writings of English women, American women in the eastern and southern United States, and American women on the Overland Trail and in the American West. Moreover, the primary emphasis in some collections has actually been on retrospective life writing (e.g., memoirs and reminiscences) rather than on diaries.[14] To date, insufficient attention has been paid to manuscript diaries kept by girls and women in Iowa, Wisconsin, and Minnesota, three midwestern states where social, political, and geographic change has been swift and pervasive. Iowa became a state in 1846; Wisconsin followed two years later; and Minnesota joined the Union a decade after that, in 1858. In each state, changing demographics have been a function of communities formed and opportunities available (or not available) to individuals and groups. Many girls and women in my sample were born in one of these states; some arrived with their families; others came on their own and supported themselves as teachers, nurses, and domestic workers. Scores of their descendants continue to live in the midwestern United States today.

Factors that have especially influenced the demographics in these three states include, but are not limited to, the pre– and post–Civil War influx of European immigrants; the post–Civil War migration of African Americans to the Midwest, particularly to larger cities (Milwaukee, Minneapolis/St. Paul, Des Moines, Waterloo) in the three-state region; the forced "removal" of members of Native American nations from western Wisconsin as well as from most of Minnesota and Iowa to reservations in the Nebraska and Dakota Territories; the emphasis on attaining suffrage and property rights for white women; the effects on individuals and family units of wars and economic depressions; and the social and political movements of the mid- to late twentieth century. While I do not assert that the three states of Wisconsin, Iowa, and Minnesota constitute a special geographic or cultural region, I believe that diaries describing the lives of girls and women in the three-state region can contribute to a broader perspective on what is called "midwestern life."[15] After all, not everyone in this part of the world was (or is) living in a little house on the prairie.

What kinds of diaries have I included in this collection? Quite a variety. Some diaries were kept by girls and women who have died and whose families kept their diaries or donated them to historical society archives. A number of modern diaries remain in the possession of the diarists. Several of these contemporary diaries are kept by diarists who know me and who, as the result of our acquaintance, have developed a trust in my ability to present their diary excerpts accurately and empathetically. My intent in compiling this collection has been to create a sampler, not to complete a scientific study. Subjectivity and empathy have been and continue to be cornerstones of my work. As I have noted elsewhere, "My work on women's 'private' diaries and journals does not take place in a vacuum. It occurs within the context of my own daily journal keeping, my own letter writing. It occurs within the context of enduring and not-so-enduring relationships, changes in daily responsibilities, alterations in mind-set and habit" (1993, 219).

Since 1985, when I began to collect diaries for this book, I have made several modifications and refinements in my initial research plan. During the early stages I planned to limit the scope of this book to diaries written from approximately 1840 to 1900 and already donated to historical society archives. As my study continued, however, I recognized the arbitrary nature of that plan. Twentieth-century diaries by midwestern American girls and women are as compelling and revealing as those by nineteenth-century diarists. For this reason I expanded the collection to include a number of recent, even contemporary, diaries. Moreover, many girls and women who began their diaries during the late nineteenth century continued writing in their diaries into the twentieth century (e.g., Maranda J. Cline and Ada L. James). Some diaries were begun in one geographical setting and completed in a different setting (e.g., the diaries of Sarah Pratt, Isabella McKinnon, and Gwendolyn Wilson Fowler). Several diaries were begun by girls and became lifelong autobiographical enterprises (e.g., the diaries of Sarah Jane Kimball, Sarah Gillespie, and Gertrude Cairns).[16] All these realizations required that I expand my initial plan. The result is, I believe, a larger and richer collection than I had first anticipated.

Whose diaries are included in this collection? I found that the woman most likely to have kept a diary in the years since 1850 was a third-, fourth-, fifth-, or sixth-generation Euro-American with adequate economic resources and some access to education. Several diaries in this collection were written by girls and women who had the time and resources accorded by family wealth and white privilege (e.g., Etta Call, Gertrude Cairns, Margaret Vedder Holdredge). At the same time a number of the diaries were written by white working-class girls and women (e.g., Jennie Andrews, Abbie Griffin, Lillian Carpenter); one diary was written by a Euro-American immigrant (Isabella McKinnon) and another by the daughter (Pauline Petersen) of two immigrants. Two diaries (those by Gwendolyn Wilson Fowler and Martha Furgerson Nash) were written by middle-class African American women. Poor and wealthy farm girls and women (Sarah Gillespie Huftalen, Jane F. Grout, Antoinette Porter King, Jennie Andrews, Ruby Butler Ahrens), a group that has traditionally defied categorization by class, wrote several of the diaries.

Whose diaries have been saved and preserved, either privately by family members or publicly in historical society archives? Whether a diary was saved and deemed worthy of inclusion in historical society archives, I found, often depended not on who the diarist was but on whose mother, wife, daughter, or sister she was. Several diaries that I have studied (e.g., those by Emily Quiner, Dorothea Barland, Agnes Barland McDaniel) are not catalogued under the diarist's name but under the name of the family of which she was a member. Certainly, the politics and procedures of manuscript acquisition, cataloguing, and accessibility have constituted an important concern in my research and have led to my determination to make little-known diaries by midwestern girls and women more readily available to students, teachers, and the general reading public. That is one reason I have included several diaries (such as those of Ruby Butler Ahrens, Ruth Van Horn Zuckerman, Carol Johnson, and Sandra Gens) that remain in the possession of family members, friends, or the diarists themselves.

What is useful about studying today's as well as yesterday's diaries? A new strand of my research is the study of diaries being kept right now, at the beginning of the twenty-first century. The growing popularity of diary keeping among adolescent girls has resulted not only from their writers' wider access to historical diaries but also from the introduction of diary/journal writing to elementary and middle-school curricula.[17] This collection includes excerpts from the diaries of seven girls who kept diaries during the 1990s. Some excerpts are intensely introspective, while others are descriptive and/or analytical. While not intended to present a comprehensive picture, these seven diaries by midwestern American girls provide timely glimpses into the world of today's adolescents.

Today, diaries can be found not only in libraries and archives but also in restaurants and coffee shops. Consider, for instance, the "Coffee Hag" in Mankato, Minnesota, where the proprietors, Patti

Ruskey and Lisa Coons, set out blank notebooks in which customers are encouraged to write down their thoughts. For several years customers have filled volumes of these communal texts, penning observations on daily life, love and friendship, social and political issues, and even service ("I wish the Coffee Hag was open on Mondays. That's when I need my caffeine the most!"). The volumes of the "Hag Bible," as it is called, are kept lying on tables, and customers are invited to read and/or write (or sketch) as much or as little as they wish. After penning an entry on June 24, 1999, one customer added, "Thanks for being my journal for the day."

The recent explosion of communication via electronic media has resulted in hundreds of diaries being kept on the World-Wide Web. When one analyzes what it means to keep one's diary on the Web, thereby making each entry accessible to a potentially huge international readership, reconceptualizing the diary and the act of diary keeping itself becomes even more important. Questions of purpose and audience inevitably become far more complex. Why? Because time-worn assumptions that the diary is being kept only for the diarist and that it is an intensely secretive and private enterprise are unworkable when exploring the phenomenon of the on-line diary.[18]

Thoughts on Theory

Since the mid-1970s, we have seen an intensive reexamination of the lives and writings of nineteenth- and twentieth-century American girls and women. Central to this reexamination is the acknowledgment that autobiographical texts can offer one of the most reliable sources of information about what individuals' lives were like and how individuals viewed themselves, their relationships with others, and their experiences. Clearly, the traditional definition of autobiography as a "coherent shaping of the past," offered by Roy Pascal in 1960, has proved inadequate because it has failed to take into account such forms as the diary, letter, memoir, and personal essay—all forms of autobiography commonly used by girls and women.[19] Contemporary theoreticians in the burgeoning field of life studies emphasize the need to cast a wider net when studying forms of life writing, and the examination of diaries is a central part of the formulation of a more inclusive and useful definition of autobiography.

The intersections of poststructuralist literary theory, feminist theory, social history, and ethnographic theory continue to shape theoretical frameworks for studying the diary as a form of life writing and add texture to questions posed earlier in this introductory essay. Marlene Kadar defines contemporary life writing as a evolving continuum influenced by the reader's as well as the writer's perspectives: "Life writing comprises texts that are written by an author who does not continuously write about someone else, and who also does not pretend to be absent from the [black, brown, or white] text himself/herself. Life writing is a way of seeing, to use John Berger's famous phrase" (1992, 10). According to Kadar, life writing can present simple or complex narratives and subvert traditional narrative strategies. The goal of the life writer is to minimize distance between writer and reader. The diarist often crosses generic boundaries and disciplines, with the result that life writing becomes "the playground for new relationships both within and without the text, and most important, it is the site of new language and new grammars" (152).

Like Kadar, Liz Stanley emphasizes experimentation in contemporary life writing, underscoring the ways a writer's and theorist's concern with the details of particular lives debunks the notion that there is one version of Woman's Life and Experience. Stanley continues: "Both biography and autobiography lay claim to facticity, yet both are by nature artful enterprises which select, shape, and produce a very unnatural product, for no life is lived quite so much under a single spotlight as the conventional form of written auto/biographies suggests" (1992, 3–4). By emphasizing the selective nature of what is included and what is excluded, Stanley highlights the necessary role of narrative conventions as well as experimentation with such conventions: "A concern with auto/biography shows that 'self' is a fabrication, not necessarily a lie but certainly a highly complex truth: a fictive truth reliant on cultural convention concerning what 'a life' consists of and how its story can be told both in speech and, somewhat differently, in writing" (243).

Along with Liz Stanley, Evelyn Hinz uses the term *auto/biography* to describe a text that is both biography and autobiography.

Introduction

The appeal of auto/biography today, explains Hinz, "is best understood through an awareness of its ritual nature and in terms of how it answers to spiritual needs: the need for role models who inspire feelings of 'pity and fear' by reason of the limited stage upon which they perform, the need to face mortality and the need to establish a living connection with the past" (1992, 209).

Leigh Gilmore uses the term *autobiographics* to describe both a process of self-representation and a reading practice that focuses on "interruptions and eruptions, with resistance and contradiction as strategies of self-representation" (1994, 42). This term highlights "those elements that mark a location in a text where self-invention, self-discovery, and self-representation emerge within the technologies of autobiography" (42). Gilmore acknowledges that there *is* a subject in the text, not a simple nor a unified one, but an evolving one.

As a form of life writing, the diary crosses that often-blurred (and sometimes imaginary) border between the public and the private, the literary and the historical. The diary also crosses generic boundaries and, although it is not bound by gender, the diary provides an especially congenial form of personal narrative for girls and women.[20] The diary offers a prime illustration of what Susan Stanford Friedman and others refer to as "border talk" (1998, 3). Friedman explains, "Borders have a way of insisting on separation at the same time as they acknowledge connection . . . borders also specify the liminal space in between, the interstitial site of interaction, interconnection, and exchange" (3).

Recent editions of women's diaries affirm what diary scholars have been asserting for years: the diary often functions as a form of autobiography for its writer. Constance Fulmer and Margaret Barfield's *Autobiography of a Shirtmaker* (1998) the diary of Edith J. Simcox (1844–1901), tells the story of an independent Victorian woman who was a businesswoman, social reformer, scholar, and journalist—and who kept a detailed diary from 1876 to 1900.[21] Marcus Rosenbaum's *Heart of a Wife: The Diary of a Southern Jewish Woman* (1998) is the diary of his grandmother, Helen Jacobus Apte.[22] Julia Hornbostel's *A Good and Caring Woman* (1996) draws extensively on the diaries of Frances Cornelia (Nellie) Norton Tallman (1839–1924), who lived in Janesville, Wisconsin, and whose twenty volumes of manuscript

29

diaries tell the story of her family and community.[23] Vladimir A. Kozlov and Vladimir M. Khrustalev's *The Last Diary of Tsaritsa Alexandra* (1997) reproduces the recently declassified 1918 diary of Alexandra Fyodorovna, the last Tsaritsa of Russia.[24] Victor Klemperer's *I Will Bear Witness: A Diary of the Nazi Years, 1933–1941* (1998) is an English translation of the secret diaries, kept in German, by a Jewish professor of Romance languages who lived through the war in Dresden, Germany.[25]

In the prelude to *Memory and Narrative: The Weave of Life-Writing* (1998), James Olney explores the question of what to call the kinds of writing that he has spent decades reading and analyzing. Olney muses, "Although I have in the past written frequently about autobiography as a literary genre, I have never been very comfortable doing it, primarily because I believe that if one is to speak relevantly of a genre one has first of all to define it, and I have never met a definition of autobiography that I could really like" (xv). Drawing on a term used by Count Gian Artico di Porcia in his "Proposal to the Scholars of Italy" in the early 1700s, Olney explains:

What I like about the term 'periautography,' which would mean 'writing about or around the self,' is precisely its indefinition and lack of generic rigor, its comfortably loose fit and generous adaptability, and the same for 'life-writing' . . . For by whatever name we call the literature—autobiography, life-writing, or periautography—there exists a particularly intriguing kind of writing, to be considered for which any one of the terms mentioned might be a fair enough designation, the crucial tactic, in my view, being not to insist on strict definitions and rigid lines of demarcation." (xvi)

Perhaps the concept of the diary as periautography is an idea whose time has come.

Editorial Principles

My objective in editing this collection has been to produce a clear, readable text that reproduces as accurately as possible the original selections from each diary and that interferes as little as possible with the reader's interaction with each diary. Toward this end, I have relied on the following editorial principles:

1. I have retained the original spelling used by each diarist, with the exception of correcting a few misspellings that appear to have been the result of a slip of the pen and which are words that the diarist has consistently spelled correctly elsewhere in her text.

2. I have retained the original punctuation and capitalization used by each diarist, including the use of dashes in lieu of commas or periods and the use of lowercase letters at the beginning of sentences.

3. I have used ellipses at the end of an entry to denote the deletion of one or more entire entries. I have used ellipses within an entry to denote the deletion of a portion of a specific diary entry.

4. I have consistently dated each entry, replicating the style used by the particular diarist and placing this information directly before each diary entry.

5. I have used brackets within diary entries to clarify dates and to note illegible words. Information that appears in brackets between diary entries represents my effort to interpolate biographical information necessary to an understanding of the text.

6. To minimize disruptions of the diarist's text and keep the focus on the diary itself, I have usually not intervened to define terms or add surnames of individuals mentioned in each diary.

7. A brief biographical and thematic sketch, based on archival and family records, precedes the excerpts from each diarist.

Plan for the Collection

In her introduction to *A Midwife's Tale: The Life of Martha Ballard, Based on Her Diary, 1785–1812*, Laurel Thatcher Ulrich muses: "Opening a diary for the first time is like walking into a room full of strangers. The reader is advised to enjoy the company without trying to remember every name" (1990, 15). As a reader and editor of diaries, I have appreciated Thatcher's observation as I have pondered how to select and present selections from the forty-six individuals' diaries included here. First, given that none of the diaries in this collection is presented in its entirety, I have had to consider how much of each diarist's story could be told through the excerpts that I had chosen. At the heart of my consideration is this question: can any diary, edited or unexpurgated, tell

31

the whole story of an individual's life? I do not believe so, for the simple reason that no text can tell the whole story of an individual's life.

Instead, each chapter presents selections from, or moments in, a wide range of diaries. I have selected examples that I believe demonstrate the range of each diarist's interests and feelings and that will give readers a good feel for the overall nature of the entire diary. At the same time I ask readers to remember that no excerpt from a diarist's work is intended to represent either an entire diary or an entire life.

And now, the diaries themselves. As you journey through this collection, the voices of individual diarists may delight, move, puzzle, and/or exasperate you. If so, this collection will have accomplished its purpose.

Notes

1. After reading this introduction, Linda asserted that she had not snipped the clasp of my diary. The culprit, we determined, must have been one of our three younger brothers—Denny, Dale, or Dan. I surmised it had been Denny, but Linda fingered a different suspect: "I would certainly say that the person who did it appears to be Dale!!! If this were 'Clue,' I would say Dale did it, with a scissors, in the bedroom! And once again, poor Linda got blamed for it!!!" When confronted with the evidence, our brother Dale confessed and offered this explanation: "These were the years that Dan was becoming curious with dirty magazines. Being the good brother I was, I did not want him to be exposed to such smut . . . So, I figured he could probably get all the juicy stuff he desired from another source."

2. Sarah Shandler's book, *Ophelia Speaks* (1999), draws on Mary Pipher's *Reviving Ophelia* (1994) as its starting point, noting that Pipher's "portrayal of young females was accurate, but her representation was limited by her role as a psychologist, as a parent, and most importantly, as an adult" (xii). Shandler draws on the struggles of American girls by presenting their personal writings on such topics as family, relationships, religion, and health issues. In characterizing contemporary adolescent American girls, Shandler explains: "We are not dyed in just one color. Rather, we are made from a complex pattern, intertwining weakness and strength, sadness and joy, pleasure and pain. Still, given this opportunity, invited to write what we are encouraged to hide, most girls, but certainly not all, opened the door on dark and disturbing times. Still others allowed light, instead of darkness, to glitter in their contributions" (xvi).

3. Some ideas I present here had their genesis in essays that I have published since the mid-1980s. See the bibliography.

4. Like many diarists whose texts are excerpted in this collection, my mother, Verna Bunkers, who has kept diaries off and on for years, recognizes the unfinished nature of her diaries, which embody process rather than product: "My diaries are never completed—as I see going back over the years—I do half the diary, grow tired

and impatient, and never complete the last half! In a fortune cookie note I found pasted in one diary, it says, 'You should be able to undertake and complete anything'-I'm not so sure about that!" (Personal communication, 1999.)

5. Bunkers and Huff comment: "The diary's flexibility and adaptability enhance its uses in our lives and academic disciplines. Its form, simultaneously elastic and tight, borrows from and at the same time contributes to other narrative structures. Its content is wide-ranging yet patterned, and what is excluded is as important as what is included. Because the form and content of the diary are so adaptable and flexible, the study of diaries brings into play issues of historical, social, and self-construction; exchanges between reader and text; and connections between, and differing effects of, published and manuscript diary records" (1996, 1).

6. Much research on encoding and decoding has been influenced by Basil Bernstein's landmark study, *Class, Codes and Control* (1971). Bernstein's research involved studying codes and speech variants among speakers of different classes in England to determine what influences socialization might have on language codes. Bernstein hypothesized that working-class individuals would be more likely to use what he defined as a "restricted code" while middle-class individuals would be more likely to use what he defined as an "elaborated code": "A restricted code is generated by a form of social relationship based upon a range of closely shared identifications self-consciously held by the members. An elaborated code is generated by a form of social relationship which does not necessarily presuppose such shared, self-consciously held identifications with the consequence that much less is taken for granted. The codes regulate the area of discretion available to a speaker and so differently constrain the verbal signalling of individual difference" (108). Based on his research, Bernstein posited that the change from the restricted to the elaborated code involves a shift from authority/piety to identity (165). Although Bernstein's research is provocative, it is limited in several respects: it presupposes class as static, not dynamic; it is based on a research sample comprised entirely of adolescent boys in London; and it explores spoken but not written language.

7. As Jane DuPree Begos explains, "Many people consider this type of diary dull because there is so little of the diarist in them. But these 'dull' diaries can be chock full of information for social and public historians. They deserve a careful reading, because they can tell us very much indeed about how people lived in earlier times. They give us a sense of the seasons and how time was used. They tell us about place, either a specific house or a locale, both important in historic recreations" (i).

8. Paul Rosenblatt explores this question in his study of the grieving process as reflected in the diaries of fifty-six individuals, tracing the varied ways that men and women use their diaries to write about their responses to deaths and separations. Rosenblatt has found that diaries have "especially great promise in the study of loss" because they "can provide not only more detail, but more accuracy, as well as reactions less distorted by subsequent experiences and thought," providing "a record uncontaminated by a framework imposed by the researcher" (1983, 5).

In *Opening Up*, James W. Pennebaker examines the question of whether writing in a diary can help an individual come to terms with emotions that might otherwise be inhibited or repressed. He explains that not every diarist uses that medium for the expression of deep emotions. In acknowledging the selectivity and shaping that are part of the diarist's process, Pennebaker observes: "Among the people I have interviewed who have kept intimate and emotional diaries, two distinctly different patterns have emerged in the ways they maintain their diaries. One group—of which I am a member—only writes during periods of stress or unhappiness. If life is plodding along in a fairly predictable way, people in this group simply have no interest in writing. The second group, which is less than half the size of the first, writes almost daily. That is, until traumas strike. During massive stressors, people in this group stop writing" (1990, 192–93).

9. Books based on the metaphor of the journey or quest offer valuable suggestions for diary and journal writing. Four of the best examples include Tristine Rainer's *The New Diary*, Richard Solly and Roseann Lloyd's *Journey Notes*, Kathleen Adams's *Journal to the Self*, and Christina Baldwin's *Life's Companion*.

10. In her essay, "'I Write for Myself and Strangers': Private Diaries and Public Documents," Lynn Z. Bloom notes that "not all diaries are written—ultimately or exclusively—for private consumption. Very often, in either the process of composition over time, or in the revision and editing that some of the most engaging diaries undergo, these superficially private writings become unmistakably public documents, intended for an external readership" (1996, 23). Her observation parallels other observations made by Kathryn Carter, Margo Culley, Cinthia Gannett, Minrose Gwin, Rebecca Hogan, Cynthia Huff, Philippe Lejeune, Judy Nolte [Lensink] Temple, and Trudelle Thomas—critics who recognize the complex nature of context that inevitably underlies, encircles, and permeates the text.

11. The concept of the diary as an intensely private text is a relatively recent development. As Margo Culley notes in the introduction to *A Day at a Time*, her study of diaries by American women, "It is only relatively recently (roughly in the last one hundred years) that the content of the diary has been a record of private thoughts and feelings to be kept hidden from others' eyes. Many eighteenth- and nineteenth-century diaries were semi-public documents intended to be read by an audience" (1985, 3).

Similarly, in her collection, *Capacious Hold-All*, Harriet Blodgett notes that we should not presume that all diaries by women are private texts; by the seventeenth century in England, diaries were much more likely to be public than private texts. By the mid-eighteenth century, the letter-diary, which consisted of "daily entries to be sent to a recipient with the writer keeping a copy to serve as a diary," was increasingly popular with Englishwomen (1989, 5).

In his work on the Holocaust diary, David Patterson explains that it is "characterized by the human being's effort to bring the soul to life through an engagement with the self, not just to get in touch with one's feelings but to establish some contact with a truth that may sustain the life of the soul" (1997, 37). According to Patterson, the Holocaust diarist, who "writes at the risk of incurring grave dangers," senses "a necessity to write" and has a stake in creating a text that "goes beyond a concern for inner equilibrium to include a communal salvation—or, failing that, a testimony to and for the sake of the life of a human community" (37).

12. A number of nineteenth-century books of conduct took a prescriptive approach to the question of "woman's proper sphere," laying out rules of proper behavior as the pathway to virtue. For example, the cover page of Mrs. A. J. Graves's *Woman in America* (1841) states the theory underlying the book:

"Woman's empire is *Home*; and, by adding spirituality to its happiness, dignity to its dominion, and power to its influences, it becomes the best security for *individual integrity*, and the surest safeguard for *national virtue*." Similarly, the title page of Mrs. L. G. Abell's *Woman and Her Various Relations* (1853) offers this information about the book's content: "The best methods for dinners and social parties—a chapter for young ladies, mothers, and invalids—hints on the body, mind, and character—with a glance at woman's rights and wrongs, professions, costume, etc., etc." How widely such manuals of conduct were distributed and read by American women depended, of course, on such variables as degree of literacy, economic class, geographical location, race and ethnicity, to name only a few mitigating factors. Many girls and women whose diaries are included in this collection lived in circumstances that would not have permitted them the leisure time and level of education necessary to ponder the question of "woman's proper sphere."

In 1966 Barbara Welter, in her early work on the Cult of True Womanhood, outlines four cardinal virtues that nineteenth-century fiction and prescriptive literature (e.g., conduct books) associated with proper womanhood and with what was termed "woman's proper sphere": piety, purity, submissiveness, and domesticity. In *The Bonds of Womanhood* (1977) Nancy Cott explores the ideal of domesticity as a social ethic, using women's personal documents to understand the relation between changes in material circumstances of women's lives and their outlooks on their place as women (3). The "cult of domesticity," as Cott found it outlined in nineteenth-century New England, emphasized the home as oasis and woman as at the center of this "separate sphere of comfort and compensation" (69).

During the 1990s, a number of scholars re-evaluated these prescriptive concepts in light of ethnographic evidence, determining that class and race were key determinants in whether a woman had the freedom and leisure to contemplate, much less enact, "proper womanhood" and "domesticity." In 1988 Linda Kerber defined the concept of the "sphere" as a figure of speech, a metaphor or trope "on which historians came to rely when they described women's part in American culture" (1997, 161). According to Kerber, three stages characterized the development of this metaphor: the effort to identify separate spheres and place the ideology in an antebellum context; the effort to refine the definition and identify complexities; and the embedding of women's experiences in "the main course of human development" and the conscious criticism of historians' rhetorical constructions in an attempt to "unpack the metaphor" of separate spheres (169–70). Kerber concludes, "One day we will understand the idea of separate spheres as primarily a trope, employed by people in the past to characterize power relations for which they had no other words and that they could not acknowledge because they could not name, and by historians in our own times as they groped for a device that might dispel the confusion of anecdote and impose narrative and analytical order on the anarchy of inherited evidence, the better to comprehend the world in which we live" (1997, 199).

The late Lora Romero's 1997 exploration of this subject goes further, systematically exploring what she calls the "plurality of political positions that representations of middle-class home life supported in the antebellum period" and dispensing "with the familiar polemics of twentieth-century literary criticism by arguing that domesticity was neither simply conservative nor simply subversive" (vi). By moving beyond the binaries that have characterized past analyses of the question, Romero offers a new paradigm for the examination of primary texts such as diaries.

Carol Coburn and Martha Smith, authors of *Spirited Lives*, explain that the doctrine of "separate spheres" and the "cult of domesticity" were cultural directives that had only limited applicability in the lives of women religious: "Although historically almost invisible, American sisters were some of the best educated and most publicly active women of their time. Talented and ambitious women from working-class and middle-class backgrounds, regardless of ethnicity, advanced to teaching, nursing, administration, and other leadership positions in Catholic religious communities" (1999, 3). Coburn and Smith add that, like many other American women, "nuns also utilized religious traditions and symbols to subvert gender limitations and expand their possibilities" (81).

13. Thomas Schlereth offers this working definition of "material culture": "[M]aterial culture is that segment of humankind's biosocial environment that has been purposely shaped by people according to culturally dictated plans" (1985, 5). Material culture includes objects, artifacts, cultural landscapes; according to Schlereth, studying material culture "comprises several disciplines, among them the triad of art, architecture, and decorative arts history; cultural geography; cultural anthropology, as well as cultural and social history" (6).

14. John Mack Faragher's *Women and Men on the Overland Trail* (1979), Glenda Riley's *Frontierswomen* (1981), Joanna Stratton's *Pioneer Women* (1981), Lillian Schlissel's *Women's Diaries of the Western Journey* (1981), and Elizabeth Hampsten's *Read This Only to Yourself* (1982) were among the first book-length studies to draw on memories, letters, reminiscences and (occasionally) diaries of nineteenth-century American women in an attempt to explore individual lives and contribute to the ongoing strands of historical and cultural analysis. More recent collections based on women's personal writings include *Western Women* (1988), edited by Lillian Schlissel, Vicki Ruiz, and Janice Monk; *Women's Voices from the Oregon Trail* (1994), edited by Susan G. Butruille and Kathleen Petersen; *Women's Voices from the Western Frontier* (1995), edited by Butruille; and, most recently, Riley's *Prairie Voices* (1996). Although each study draws on diaries as one type of primary source, only Schlissel's study focuses completely on diaries, with special emphasis on diaries by four women (Catherine Haun, Lydia Allen Rudd, Amelia Stewart Knight, and Jane Gould Tourtillott).

The collection edited by Philip Dunaway and Mel Evans, *A Treasury of the World's Great Diaries* (1957), is one of the larger diary anthologies published; this collection includes excerpts from the diaries of such famous historical and literary figures as John Quincy Adams, Ralph Waldo Emerson, Queen Victoria, Henry David Thoreau, Franz Kafka, Arnold Bennett, and Virginia Woolf. Of the eighty-five individuals whose diaries excerpted in this anthology, twenty-one are women; the only midwestern American woman included is Wanda Gag (1893–1946), who grew up in New Ulm, Minnesota, and whose diary was published as *Growing Pains* (1940).

Recent diary anthologies include the following: Margo Culley's *A Day at a Time* (1985), a collection of excerpts from the published diaries of twenty-nine American women, 1764 to 1985; Penelope Franklin's *Private Pages* (1986), a collection of excerpts from the diaries of thirteen American girls and women, 1832 to1979; Steven Kagle's *Late 19th Century American Diary Literature* (1988), a study of the diaries of twenty-six Americans, nine of whom are women; and Blodgett's *Capacious Hold-all* (1991), a collection of excerpts from the published diaries of thirty English women, 1571–1970. Daniel Halpern's collection, *Our Private Lives* (1988), includes excerpts from the texts of thirty-nine "accomplished writers of prose and/or poetry," ten of whom are women (5). Charlotte Cole's collection, *Between You and Me* (1998), includes excerpts from the personal diaries and letters of young British women who have gone on to become successful writers. As these anthologies indicate, there is clearly a need for this collection, which contributes to the published literature on diaries of girls and women and which focuses specifically on diaries written by girls and women living in the three midwestern states of Iowa, Wisconsin, and Minnesota.

15. The Midwestern United States, sometimes referred to as the Middle West, has been defined in many ways, depending on who is doing the defining and from which perspective the definer is looking at this geographic region. A century or more ago, many considered Minnesota, Iowa, and Wisconsin to be part of the Great Northwest. Wilbur Zelinsky (1994) defines the "Middle West Extended" as the eleven-state cluster of Kansas, Nebraska, Iowa, Minnesota, Wisconsin, Missouri, Illinois, Indiana, Michigan, Ohio, and Pennsylvania. I do not posit a hard and fast definition of the American Midwest, nor do I assert that Minnesota, Iowa, and Wisconsin are the only midwestern states. But I do assume that these three states are in the Midwest and that the diaries I have included represent a "sampler" of such texts produced in this region.

16. Robert Fothergill characterizes this third kind of lifelong diary as the type of serial autobiography that he labels the "Book of the Self": "[A]s a diary grows to a certain length and substance it impresses upon the mind of its writer a conception of the completed book that it might ultimately be, if sustained with sufficient dedication and vitality" (1997, 44). Fothergill goes on to explain that, for some individuals, a diary may well become an autobiography: "Instead of an ad hoc jotting down of impressions, the writing of the diary entails a continual negotiation between comprehensiveness and digested relevance" (154).

17. Judy Stow, who teaches seventh-grade English classes at Dakota Meadows Middle School in North Mankato, Minnesota, explained to me by e-mail how journal writing works in her classes: "Students use response journals in English class in three ways: to develop old or new ideas based on their reading of novels or on their lives; to possibly use those ideas in understanding and making connections to other short stories, novels, etc.; or to find topics or different forms (poetry, letters to editors) for writing workshop projects. I also encourage students to keep these journals so they can someday look back to see who they were, what/how they were thinking when they were twelve or thirteen. Wonderful (and hoped-for, but not verbalized to them) results have included remarks by some students who realize they like to write and who start personal journals. In addition, I have found out more about their opinions and interests. I can then use that information to establish more of a rapport with the students and/or be able to suggest a writing topic if they can't come up with one."

18. The premise of the on-line diary or journal is that it will be viewed and read by others, especially by individuals who are surfing the Web specifically to read

diaries. Search engines such as Yahoo and Google allow one to type in a keyword and find hundreds, if not thousands, of Web sites to visit. When I searched Google for the keyword "Diaries," it gave me over 15,000 web sites. After surfing for an hour, I had visited an intriguing range of diary-related sites: Travel Mag's Travel Diaries, First Response's Diaries of Hopeful Moms to Be, Madonna's Private Diaries, The Bordello Diaries, Eric Boutelier-Brown's Photo Diaries, Ingrid on Ice Antarctic Diary, The University of Tennessee Lady Vols Diary, United States Olympics Diaries, Macalester College's Neuroscience Diary Directory, Power-Students Network Graduate Student Diarists, and Found: the Lost Diaries of Noah.

"Clearinghouse" Web sites offer compilations of and links to other Web sites developed for and devoted to on-line diary-keeping. For instance, The Diary Registry indexes more than twelve hundred Web sites keeping a diary on line: <http://www.diarist.net/registry/>, and The Open Diary, which calls itself "the first interactive online diary community on the Internet," currently lists more than 127,000 on-line diaries from 76 different countries:

< http://www.opendiary.com/>. The Diary Project Web site features on-line diaries that address topical questions such as discrimination, body image, substance use, violence, and loss. Over 24,700 on-line diaries are indexed there: <http://www.diaryproject.com/> Finally, My Dear Diary invites visitors to create their own on-line Web sites and read the site's on-line weekly newsletter: <http://www.mydeardiary.com/

"Gingko," who lives in Brookfield, Wisconsin, keeps her diary on line: "Dreaming Among the Jade Clouds," is at <http://www.jade-leaves.com/journal/jounal_index.shtml> When I asked her how she began keeping a diary on line and what motivates her to do it that way, she replied: "I saw a journal an online friend had and figured that if she could do it, so could I. At that point I'd been completely unaware of the large number of online journals in existence and thought people might think me rather strange for doing it, but the idea of keeping a journal in a digital medium fascinated me, and it seemed like a cool way to share my journal with friends again without having to mess with the post office. Because I've always loved including images in my journals and because my handwriting is truly atrocious, an html journal struck me as the ultimate blank notebook. (That 'ultimate blank notebook' was the main reason for starting it, and it seemed to make sense to use it on my website instead of keeping it hidden just for myself on my hard drive)." All Web sites above were last accessed on 15 August 2000.

19. Pascal's work, now superseded by theoretical views that provide a more inclusive perspective on what might constitute autobiography, was nonetheless influential for decades. Pascal defines "autobiography proper" as a narrative which "involves the reconstruction of the movement of a life, or part of a life, in the actual circumstances in which it was lived" (1960, 9). According to Pascal, the goal of an autobiography is to render a "coherent shaping of the past" (5) and to establish a "certain consistency of relationship between the self and the outside world" (9). A diary, in Pascal's terms, cannot be defined as an autobiography because it "moves through a series of moments in time" and "its ultimate, long-range significance cannot be assessed" (3).

20. For in-depth discussions of this point, see Bloom, Carter, Culley, Gwin, Hogan, Huff, Lejeune, Lensink/Temple, Thomas, and Wink.

21. In this diary, which Edith Simcox entitled *Autobiography of a Shirtmaker,* she recorded daily activities, personal reflections, and her devotion to George Eliot. Simcox's diary, written over twenty five years, became the "authorized" version of her life story; today, it represents her only extant writing. This new edition of Simcox's diary includes the entire text of the manuscript diary, which is housed in the Bodleian Library at Oxford. Fulmer and Barfield's dedication to seeing Edith Simcox's diary/autobiography published in its entirety provides a much wider perspective on the diarist than previously available in the work of such scholars as K. A. McKenzie, whose analysis emphasizes Simcox's "pathological obsession" with George Eliot (xv).

22. In his introduction Marcus D. Rosenbaum describes his grandmother's diary as "the story of a woman coming of age with the world around her, a world moving from Victorian times into the twentieth century" (1998, xvi). Rosenbaum traces several themes throughout the diary, which runs from 1909 to 1946: his grandmother's ongoing struggle between duty and desire, the dynamic nature of love, changing times and mores, and her life as a Jewish woman in the U.S. South. He concludes that "her legacy is her writing, and this is fitting. Her protests to the contrary notwithstanding, my grandmother was a writer" (xvi).

23. Julia Hornbostel explains that she has studied the diaries of Nellie Tallman in relation to several periods of the diarist's life: her years as a young daughter-in-law with no children, as a mother of young sons, as a mature woman, and as a widow (31). In her conclusion Hornbostel evaluates the importance of Tallman's diaries in this way: "On first reading, Nellie's diary entries seem objective notes of trivial details, daily activities, errands, etc., which are not fascinating insights into her life, nor do they bear complete reprinting as a text in themselves. However, overall, they do provide a picture of nineteenth and early twentieth century life in a growing Midwestern town, an upper-middle class socially conscious family, and reflect many broader issues of American life during Nellie's lifetime. Together, her notes are like the threads of a woven fabric, needing other threads, other sources, to create the whole" (250).

24. In their introduction, the editors of Tsaritsa Alexandra's diary recount the history of the diary's creation, disappearance, and recent reemergence; they describe how the diary functioned for its writer: "Alexandra's diary brings the inexorable, predetermined succession of days, anniversaries, hours, and minutes—numbers following one another seemingly without end—into relation with the daily, unpredictable contingencies of the weather, her children's temperatures, and the chaotic events of the Revolution. We see the empress presiding over a world within a world, which is given simple form in her daily observations" (liv).

25. In the preface to his recent translation, Martin Chalmers notes that the "German edition of the diaries Victor Klemperer kept during the Third Reich appeared without fanfare in 1995" and that they soon "had become a runaway publishing success (over 140,000 copies of the 1,500-page hardback edition have been sold)" (Klemperer, 1998, xix). Chalmers goes on to describe the importance of diaries kept during the 1930s and 1940s: "People wrote down in the privacy of their notebooks what they dared not say openly, although even in them there was circumlocution and self-censorship, the effects of the fear of denunciation and discovery. In Germany, as elsewhere, many diaries and memoirs were published in the

years immediately after 1945, the number increasing once more in the 1980s and 1990s, as survivors of the earlier period were able to take stock of their lives" (xix). Chalmers notes that the diaries of Victor Klemperer are unique in that "they were not written with publication in mind and were never reworked to iron out contradictions and repetitions, to make them stylistically more appealing, to revise judgments or to make retrospective justifications" (xix). Rather, they were written to "reflect Klemperer's own need to settle accounts with the events of the day as they affected his own life" (xix).

American Girls

1

Excerpts from diaries kept by thirteen girls aged eight to sixteen address many aspects of development from childhood to girlhood to adolescence. As is often typical with diaries written by children and adolescents, sentence structure, spelling, and punctuation are fluid and changeable. Some diarists (for example, Mary Griffith and Megan Kennedy) write primarily about daily events. Other diarists (such as Sarah Gillespie and Etta Call) write about events, relationships, and feelings. Several contemporary diarists include poetry, letters, narratives, and imagined dialogues, either on their own initiative or in response to suggestions from their teacher.

The thirteen girls have one important thing in common: they are all writing about growing up. As these excerpts from their diaries reveal, it is not always an easy process. Girlhood and adolescence have been, and continue to be, challenging times for American girls. As Joan Brumberg points out in *The Body Project*, her study of adolescent girls and body image,

[D]iaries persist, providing generations of girls with a way to express and explore their lives and feelings. Old diaries are a national treasure, providing a window into the day-to-day routines of family, school, and community. They also recapture the familiar cadences of adolescent emotional life, and they provided authentic testimony to what girls in the past considered noteworthy, amusing, and sad, and what they could or would not talk about. (1997, xxvii)

The Diary of Sarah Gillespie Huftalen, 1877–1879

"Keep well this book and bear in mind/A constant friend is hard to find." Sarah Gillespie wrote this epigraph on the first page of the diary that she began keeping on January 1, 1877. Eleven years old, Sarah had begun keeping a diary four years earlier, while she was living on the family farm a mile west of Manchester, Iowa, and fifty miles west of Dubuque. She would continue to keep a diary for more than seventy-five years. She would live to see 1955, and her diary would truly be her "constant friend" throughout her life.

Sarah Gillespie was born to James and Emily (Hawley) Gillespie on July 7, 1865. Her twin brother was stillborn. Her older brother, Henry, was almost two when she was born. Growing up on a farm in northeastern Iowa meant that Sarah learned to work hard at an early age. All four family members contributed to the daily operation of the farm. Her father and Henry were responsible for crops, livestock, and farm repairs. Her mother was responsible for child care, household matters, and the poultry operation. Sarah's early diary entries tell of feeding the chickens and turkeys, pulling weeds, digging potatoes, sewing a dress, piecing a quilt, and studying her lessons. Like many other farm families, the Gillespies were struggling financially during the depression that gripped the Midwest during the 1870s. On at least two Christmases, Sarah wrote in her diary that there were no presents.

As youngsters, Sarah and Henry were tutored at home by Emily, who had been a country schoolteacher before her marriage. On November 10, 1879, Sarah and Henry began attending the newly established Manchester Academy. There they studied arithmetic, reading, grammar, and spelling. The siblings continued their studies at the Manchester Academy for two years, until a measles epidemic forced its closure in the spring of 1882. As this early volume of her diary reveals, Sarah had a playful as well as a serious side; she liked doing well at school, worked hard at home, enjoyed a rivalry with her brother, and struggled with the growing unhappiness in her parents' marriage. Sarah's girlhood diary, which she called her "con-

Sarah Gillespie Huftalen, 1880. By permission of the State Historical Society of Iowa, Iowa City.

stant friend," reveals what farm and family life were like for one Iowa girl during the latter part of the nineteenth century.

January 1877 New years. I commence to keep a journal to day.

> 'Tis better far to learn while we are young
> Than to wait till we get old, for our
> Learning is better than gold.
> Sarah

Mon. 1. I have not done very much to day. I whittled a little. Henry went to town and got five cents worth of herring for our New Years supper. Ma washed and Pa chopped. Henry and I worked some examples. Cold. . . .

Wed. 3. It was so cold we could not go to school. making a whip stalk. Henry, Pa, and I took some hay down to Uncle Jerome's and saw the new bridge. It is a very nice one and rests on bars of iron. I got a spool of black thread for ma. Henry got the papers. Ma worked on her Sofa Cushion. Warmer.

Thurs. 4. We did two pages of examples. Pa fixed the whippletree to the cutter. Ma do usual work. I pieced nearly a block of my quilt. . . .

Sat. 6. In the forenoon George Trumble was here, he did not come in went down town in the afternoon. Ma got Henry a new suit of clothes, & ribbon necktie. Me a new comb & hair ribbon. Pa a necktie & herself one, they are very nice. we went down to Willie Scanlans in the evening. The tree's were covered with snow or mist. Chilly. . . .

Friday. 12. We went over to the north schoolhouse to visit the school where Nettie Barnard teaches they have from 23 to 25 scholars. the scholars whisper a little more than what is necessary, and make considerable noise for such large scollars as they are. they wrote Essay's the most of them were copied, either out of their books or News-Papers, I know the most of them. Cold. . . .

Mon. 22. We are not going to School any more it is so lonesome up there with only 4 or 5 scholars. Ma worked, she has got a very sore toe, we are going to study at home the rest of the winter. ma says as soon as we get through this arithmetic she will get us another one. Pleasant but Cold. . . .

February 1877. Fri. 2. Calamus day fair and clear there will be 2 winters in this Year. Nellie and Mary Tyler were here we had a splendid good time. They came here about ten oclock and went away a half past five. Do two pages of examples. Pleasant. . . .

Sun. 4. One of the hogs bit a hen so we had to kill her. Foxy is a great deal better. Ma has got a lame neck. Foggy. . . .

Wed. Feb. 14. To day is St. Valentines day. I did not send any Valentines nor did not get any. To day was the last day of our school. there were a good many there. Mr. & Mrs. Chapman, Mr. & Mrs. Van Alstyne, Mr. & Mrs. Sellens, Mrs. Morse & Pa, Henry & myself. Ma did not go. . . .

Sun. 18. lonesome! All day alone. Henry is writing to Grand pa. Pa went down to Mr. Doolittles stayed five hours. There was been some-one here every day this week. All but to day. Pleasant. . . .

March 1877. Ths. 1. To day is Pa's 41st anniversary, we did not have any Party. I made a cake for supper. Pa go to mill. we got our lesson. Pleasant. . . .

Fri. 16. get our lesson. go up to Mr. & Mrs. Morse's in the evening on a Surprise. it is their fifteenth Anniversary. we had a good time. there were 16 Persons, we gave them a set of glass dishes. they were very much pleased with their presents, it was a surprise they did not have the work done up at all. We had them married over again. we had a splendid good time. Pleasant. . . .

Wed. 21. Get our lesson, we had a dance to night. They came on a surprise, but we found it out. It is Poor Sleighing. . . .

April 1877. Tues. 3. I done 24 examples to day. Henry done 19, we go to town, it is very muddy. Sunday evening Barrs livery Stable, the Agricultural Depot & the Blacksmith shop was burned. they saved all of the horses but none of the carriages, he says that his loss is about $3000.00. Mr Barr feels pretty bad over it, all that was left was a buggy-wheel & cook stove & they were all burnt, the stove was cracked & broken, too, it is to bad, me & I thought shure we would tip over in one place. Mud, Mud, Mud. . . .

Wed. 11. to day is ma's birthday. I went up to Mr. Morse's to spend the afternoon. had a good time. Ella & Victor Esty were here. Victor rented 10 acres. Warm.

Ths. 12. get our lesson. ma said her 39th Anniversary was yester-day. Pa says it was a lucky thing that she kept it to her-self begin to wear sun-bonnets. Warm. . . .

Tues. 17. go to school we had 12 scholars, the boys act real mean. the teacher said that there was not but 1 boy in the whole school that tended to his own business. Warm. . . .

Fri. 20. Go to school. The teacher says she wont have only three scholars that would be marked perfect, & they were Susan Stewart & Henry & I, we had 9 scholars. . . .

Ths. [26]. Go to school & have 18 scholars. Ma go to town, she heard that Nellie & Mary Tyler had not got up & that they thought that Mary would die. I hope not, for she is my favorite friend. Warm. . . .

May 1877. Sat. 5. Go fishing & get 28 in all. Henry caught 14. ma caught 12 & I 2. We've go[t] some little chickens. Warm. . . .

Fri. 10. Go to school. kill 2 snakes. a beggar was here. . . .

Sat. 26. Commence going barefoot. Henry go to town, get the papers. Uncle stopped. Warm. . . .

June 1877. Sat. 9. Made some cakes got supper washed the dinner & supper dishes. Make Henrys shirt-sleeves & work the button holes. It is Rain, Rain, Rain. . . .

Tues. 14. Make me a pair of drawers didn't go to school. Rain.

July 1877. Sat. 7. To day I am 12 years old. Warm. . . .

Mon. 9. Help ma all day. pick 19 strawberries. Warm. . . .

Sun. 15. I will write Now see here ma is going to write in my journal. I wonder what she's going to write. I guess I shall have to ask her. Warm. . . .

August 1877. Wed. 1. Henry is makeing him a stand. Help pa. Warm. . . .

Mon. 6. Help ma & pa pull weeds in the strawberry patch. I just touched a little young Bird in the nest & all the rest jumped out. I am so sorry. If it would do any good I'd cry. Cool. . . .

Sat. 11. Uncle fetch a big sheep down here so that we could raise some lambs like him. He is a great big nice fellow & is about half as high as I am. Help pa build fence. Warm. . . .

Mon. 26. Go to School. have 4 scholars. get wet. Miss McCormic teacher. Rain. . . .

September 1877. Sun. 2. Go up to Uncle's & over to Aunt Harriets. we got a letter from Uncle Dennis. "He says he is going to the far west across the Missouri into Nebraska.." Cold. . . .

Thurs. 13. Go to school. Pa hit ma under ~~the~~ her eye with the little end of the whip stalk (by accident) & cut a great gash but nothing Serious. I am so sorry. Pleasant. . . .

Tues. 18. Go to school. Ma has been married 15 years to day. We have a surprise party here this evening there were 23 in all. they were married over again. we had supper all kinds of cake pie & best of all water mellons & musk mellons. they presented ma & pa with a set of glass dishes a real nice time we had. moonlight evenings now. Warmer. . . .

Thurs. 27. we all go to the fair. we had a good time. I got 2 premiums 1 on cake & 1 on bread. Ma has the first premium on a great many things but a few in town are trying to make a fuss about it & say they are not worthy of a premium. ma is a little spunky about it. Foggy. . . .

October 1877. Thurs. 4. Go to school. Pa & ma go to town ma got me two new gingham dresses & a covering for a cloak. They are all very nice. Pa got Henry & I each a saddle. . . .

Sun. 14. Go and take a ride. pa is quite mad about something. I do not know. Beautiful. . . .

Fri. 19. Go to School to day is the last day. speak dialogues pieces & read essays. we had a good time, we went up to Mr. Berry Smith's 25th Anniversary. There were over 50 there. (their silver wedding). we presented them a silver Cake Basket—sugar shell & Castor. they were well pleased with their presents. uncle married them said the ceremony. Rain. . . .

November 1877. Sat. 3. Go to town. Buy me a Combination Pen Holder. There is a pen lead pencil & Eraser. 15 cts. Piece. Long Henry

50 cts due 25 cts. Mr. E. Conger has got some very beautiful presents & toys. Cold. . . .

Mon. 26. Go to School. Someone stole our turkeys & we caught them at it. In the flight pa told them they had not better come back again. Cold. . . .

December 1877. Fri. 17. Go to School. Pa get a barrel of apples. We had a nice slide on the ice. Quite Cold, but Pleasant. . . .

Tue. 25. got a motto on CardBoard & a pair of slippers, but the slippers were too small, ma is going to exchange them. Henry got a purse pair of clippers & perforated motto. Ma got pa a book "The Royal Path of Life," & ma got herself a morocco pair worth 2.00. they were very nice & a perforated board motto. We (H & I) got a small Christmas tree (a limb of our plum tree) & we hung the presents on it, it looked quite nice. so we did not hang up our stockings. work on my Motto. "What is a home without a mother." Foggy, Rainy. . . .

Mon. 31. To day we bid good bye to our old year & wish that our journal will be filled with pleasant & bright hopes. Pa chopped. we started to go to school, but when we were about half of the way we met Charlie Chapman & he said there was no school until Wednesday, so we turned around & came home. so Henry came home & I stayed at Mr. Morse's until about an hour then I came home. Henry went to town in afternoon. peace on my calicoes. I help ma some & read etc. froze some last night. Colder. . . .

March 1878. Fri. 1. Pa is 42 years old. Henry give him a whipping piece. Help ma. Pleasant in the day in the night Rain. Pleasant. . . .

Fri. 8. Help ma. Got the first goose egg we ever owned. Ma made me a new hat it is the nicest one I ever had. Made of green & black silk a white doves wing & part of a peacock feather on one side . . . .

Sun. 17. I am perfectly ashamed of my journal there are so <u>many</u> blob & goose tracks (or as pa calls them hens tracks) all the way through. I <u>must</u> write better. Last night the moon had a golden ring
    To-night no moon we see.

Mon. 18. help ma. work on motto. It looks very nice. I think I will take it to the fair. I forgot yesterday we went to sabbath school we (that is Henry & I) joined the school at the Universalist Church. Henry went in one class & I in another. Henry looked as if he wondered what was coming next & when it did come he looked as if he took a short breath. I know I felt so & to take it all into consideration we were perfect greenies, we each got a book to read until next sabbath. Pa is setting trees along the garden fence & plowing the garden in fact—cleaning up generally. Warm. Pleasant. . . .

April 1878. Th. 11. do not feel very well. make syrup. ma & pa went to town leave H & I at home. a beggar stop & a tin smith. I got awful lonesome. ma get some licorice. ma's 40 years old. Windy. . . .

Fri. 18. got our lessons. Pa go to town, get a letter from Mrs. Wood wanting me to learn a piece to speak next Sunday. Easter we are to have kind of Exhibition get some herring, hog Cholera Medicine, the papers, and a 10 cent piece changed into pennies for ma get caught in a rain storm. Saw Mr. H. D. Wood. I took off my hat & then my Apron & covered up so as to keep it dry, just as I got home it began to just pour down & then hail (this large around 0) If I had not run about 3/4 of the way I would have got soaked through & through. X X X X Rain. . . .

May 1878. Thr. 9. get lessons. our nice little colty died. pa cried. Betsy felt very bad. we are all so sorry. Warm. Forgot to say all our little goslings were taken this morning very sudden. pa said they were just going down to the slough & all of a sudden the old goose flew up in the cow yard & made a great fuss. pa looked out of the stable but didn't think much about it, until we looked & looked & looked again, but could not find them. too bad. Henry & I went up to Morses to see their little wolves. (6) they look quite crabbed. Warm. . . .

Fri. 31. well I have had a pretty good time this month & hope the next I shall have no worse. help ma, etc., my legs ache. Rain.

June 1878. Mon. 3. I am so sorry. those poor old Robins sit on the fence & cry for their little ones, which we think were killed in the hard rain. ma said in the night she thought she heard her turkeys but it must have been those poor little robins. I climbed the tree & ever one was gone. I think it is too bad, did not get lesson. Rain. . . .

Mon. 18. Get all but 1 lesson. Help ma. I mowed down one of those little evergreens. Pa was mad about it & when I told him he said thunderation, & said that we must not touch that scythe again & if we did we would know what we don't it for, I felt real sorry about it Henry mowed most of the grass in the dooryard. Warm. . . .

Sat. 22. get part of lessons. help ma. I am tired ma is ironing & I cannot write very good. Henry go fishing. Quite warm. I forgot to say that pa fell out of the Carriage & hurt his head. . . .

July 1878. Sun. 7. I am 13 years old to day. go to Sabbath school wear my new Pink Chambree dress. in the evening we all take a ride & drive way over to Maggie McCormicks, & this is the way I have celebrated my 13th birthday. Very warm. . . .

Sun. 28. we did not go to sunday-school. pa got mad at a cow this morning & hurt her very badly & got dragged around through the brush by her it did not hurt him very much. He took & tied a rope around her under jaw & thence her leg so as to bring then very nearly together & then chased her it made her very lame. Willie was here most all day & had a good visit. Cloudy. . . .

Wed. 31. To day is the last day of July. I help ma. Willie Scanlan commence to cut oats just as we got the turkeys & ducks in under some boards & in a box it began to hail & rain I tell you it rained so hard that we could hear it over two miles. pa said if it was a tornado that we must go down cellar. it is blowing real hard & raining now. Rain. . . .

August 1878. Sun. 4. did not go to Sunday School but I wanted to. ma gave me a back-comb. it is made of horn & is very pretty. Ma done my hair up very nice. ma has got the blues. . . .

Thr. 8. go blackberrying. A wolf caught one of the little lambs but he had to let go of it & pa caught & carried the little lamb down here. he was sure that it would die but we (ma & H & I) in got him & put some tar on every place that it was bitten, & washed the blood off its little head & eyes. the wolf bit it in the places that is where the teeth went in. the worst places were very near the throat & on the eyelid. we tried to feed it some milk. when the sheep came in the yard we carried it out & it found its mother & tried to eat but he acted as if it hurt him & he is so very weak too by losing so much blood. but I guess that he will get well. I hope so anyhow. go to town & get a chance to ride both ways. Warm. . . .

Sun. 11. Ma, Henry & I go to sunday school afoot & we thought that we would go unbeknown to pa, (for he was watching Sheep), but just as we started he saw us & said: I think that that is great, Mr. Wood is minister. Warm. . . .

September 1878. Wed. 4. Henry is 15 years old to day & Ma make a jelly cake & a common cake & put the candles on the motto was this: "When first I saw your face so fair; my heart was filled with anxious care." I think it was very good. some movers were here to stay all night. 2 men is all. I go to town & get drawing paper, & walked both ways every step. Very warm. . . .

Mon. 9. work on Handkerchief. get part of lesson. ~~get~~ help ma, etc. etc. Ma & Pa & I go up to Uncles & get some butter. there were some movers here & so Henry stayed. when we got home Henry had gone to bed & is asleep. it's 10:15 P.M. Now I must go to bed. good night My Journal. Cold & Windy. . . .

Tue. 24. help me make a necklace to take to the fair. a flea has got onto me & I am just covered in blotches & they itch so I cannot hardly stand it. A wolf came right down to the slough & caught a sheep & I saw the wolf jerk the sheep until he got it down & then we hollowed & made just all the noise we could & he left it but he stopped every 2 or 3 rods & look around as if he were very much disappointed. Henry go a fishing. I help pa sort out sheep & lambs to take to fair. . . .

Fri. 27. We all go to fair. I took 2 mottoes. straw-work Lamp-net & handkerchief. get the 2nd premium on my handkerchief & on my straw-work. my Lampnet & all my things but the mottoes were the only ones there I think I had right to have the 1st premium on them all. ma got quite a no. of Red & blue Cards. we entered Betsy in the wrong class or else we would have got the Red Card = $6.00. we entered her as a horse of all work & it ought to have been draft-horse's because she is so slow. . . .

October 1878. Wed. 2. ma go to town leave me all alone do up all the work in the morning. . . .

Sat. 5. A wolf caught another lamb he caught it in the left side & tore the skin off in a very large place as large as Pas hand. Pa & Ma took it down & let Mr Thorp see it & the butcher would not buy so they brought it back & done it up ma put the skin that was torn down back in place & sewed the wool together then she sewed 2 thicknesses of cloth over it & sewed it to the wool. it looked like this as near as I can draw. I hope it will get well. Henry took the sheep up above the railroad & watched them for 2 hour's. while Pa & Ma were gone G. Trumble came & stayed an hour & the other hour I was alone. I done the morning work they gone just 2 hours the Wolf came right down east of the house. Help ma. Warm. . . .

Sun. 27. we all go up to Aunt Hatties, she cried because she was so glad that we came. I believe that she & John will separate. he wants to go to Nevada & she will not go & if he goes she says she will never live with him again. we went by way of uncles. Chilly. . . .

November 1878. Sun. 10. ma got me a new cap yesterday it is real nice. I put on my new shoes dress & cap & I think they look very nice. I have got my books put up ready to go to school to-morrow all day. Rain. . . .

Thr. 28. Uncle, Aunty Preston, Aunt Hattie & John & the children we had part of a baked pig for thanks-giving dinner. we expected Dan Ryan & his family but they did not come. it was a very beautiful day just like summer. beautiful. . . .

December 1878 Pledge signed by Sarah L. Gillespie in the village of Manchester Delaware Co. Iowa.

Dec. 5 1878 God—Home—Country. Our Pledge. I solemnly promise to abstain from the use or sale of all intoxicating liquors as a beverage & I invoke the blessing of god and the considerate judgment of my friends and neighbors to help me keep this pledge. —Sarah Gillespie

Wed. 25. Christmas. go up to Uncles. Uncle John Aunt Hattie & the children Mr & Mrs Libby & Lizzie (their girl) & we were all there & Susie & all 4 of the children. we had a good time. I got a Cocoanut, China candle-stick, wax candle (red) A yard of satin Ribbon & some crackers. Santa Claus was very good this time. Henry got the same. Cool. . . .

Tue. 31. to day is the last day of the year. go to town get 10 cents worth of paper & 10 cents worth of envelopes & 3 cents worth of candy & a 10 ct salt cellar. I gave Henry & May each 6 sheets of foolscap & 6 envelopes for New Years, & Divided the candy equal. get a ride both ways. Warmer. good bye old year I am ready for the new. Amen. I hope I will have as pleasant a time in 1879 as I had in 1878.

January 1879. Wed. 1. Henry got me a very nice tooth brush & ma a tack hammer, & I gave what I said & got yesterday. I heard that Florence & Bertha Bailey were to be married to day. Loring R. Loomis son of A. R. Loomis & his nephew were here. the little boy was very cold & stopped to warm. pa bought a black cow of Mr. Loomis. Cold. . . .

Wed. 22. go to school. Henry & Pa & Ma go to town get some oysters & crackers. I walked all the way home, & got so very warm & tired I could hardly stand up. We had some oysters for supper & I found a very hard round kind of stone or something like this O & just about as big. these are the first oysters I have tasted in over a year. pa made ma a present of a pair of kid gloves. Warm. . . .

February 1879. Sun. 16. stay at home all day. play ball with Henry. I forgot to say that last mon. a creature stepped on one of the ducks legs & it is very sore it could not walk so I brought it in & put it in a basket with some straw in it, & kept it in the house all last week. let go with the rest Thr. evening. our cow had twin calves while we were gone yesterday & the hogs broke in where she was & ate one of the calves & the other died this morning. Ma & Henry are ciphering. Pa is out doing the chores & I am writing. . . .

March 1879. Sun. 2. Pa is 43 years old to day & pa had a lame side all day. Pa & Henry go to Baptist meeting. ma & I stay at home all day. Rain. . . .

Wed. 12. To day is the last day of school there were scholars & visitors 48 in all. we had a good many pieces. the north school (part of it) came over, & some of the south school. Hattie Beal & Luella Morse read a paper that teacher composed. Cloudy in the forenoon. Cool. . . .

Fri. 28. help ma. Pa went up to uncle Johns when he came back fox (our horse she has been very sick & lame a long time) was lieing down broad side right by the straw stack & was breathing very hard, but after pa went up to A.P. Co. with the milk, we (ma, H, & I) got some hay & some water & bran & fed her it was pretty hard work for her to eat being down so flat but she did. then we went to the house when pa came in at night he said she would be dead in 2 hours. so we go to bed expecting to find a dead horse in the morning, but I hope not she seems to be so week that she can not raise herself. good night. . . .

Sat. 29. this morning we sat at the table telling what we dreamed. Henry & I dreamed just the same thing that Foxy was in the stall standing up. Pa dreamed that he saw a black dot (which is a good sign) & ma could not remember what she did dream, when Pa went with the milk this morn we went down where Foxy was & was standing by her she raised clear up on her side, ma just braced with all her strength and held her until H & I got some straw & put it under her & she stayed that way until after pa came & we fed & watered her, this was before we done up the dishes & we stood there by her she tried to get up & pa helped her & sir! she got up but [pa] had to steady her or else she would fall as it was she had to lean against the stack. . . & finally pa kindly held her & rubbed her legs & shoulders & she got up in the stable with Betsy. We all said, Good! & So you see our dream came to pass, after! all! Uncle John was here to dinner pa & him went to town this afternoon he (Pa) told Kinney (horse doctor) he would give himself $10 if he would cure Fox. help ma. I am tired. . . .

April 1879. Wed. 2. help ma, get lesson, Aunt Hattie was over stayed 3 1/2 hours had a good time. I got a letter from Mary Tyler Sat she said that she got a good necklace & a writing desk. wish I had some I think I might have too. Cold. A little snow. Cold. . . .

Fri. 11. gave ma her shawl pin. she is 41 yrs old to day. I spanked her. 42 times stay out doors all-day   ma & I build hen & turkey nests & trim up evergreens. Very warm. . . .

June 1879. Fri. 27. go to school. I got sopping more than wet this morning the rain ran off in a stream on my face for all the parasols. But it cleared off by night some so teacher came home with us to stay all night & till morning. When we went past Mr Chapmans Fred Charlie & their hired men (2) were all snickering & talking about me. I hope they saw all they wanted to. Rain. Warm. . . .

July 1879. Thu. 3. go to school. tis the last day Speak pieces etc. The teacher gave prizes. she gave Henry in the A Spelling & Grace Ferry in the B spell for leaving off head most times each a Chrome all framed. they were real nice. & those who did not miss a day were Ida Beal & me we each got an Autograph Album mine was Green & hers Red. then she gave nice Cards all around. Pa & Ma & Mr B. Beal, were up to school. Rain. . . .

Sat. 5. I feel kindeeye s-i-c-k—t-o—t-h-e—s-t-o-m-a-c-h to day. I am tired, help ma some. Warm. . . .

Mon. 7. Well! I am 14 yrs. old to day, pretty near sick, finish Braiding that Chemise tho. Warm.
   Almost sick, in the fournoon But I help ma Fry cakes in the afternoon I got very warm & do did ma. Very Warm. . . .

Thu. 10. Henry & I waded in the slough we had a good time. help ma she made & cut out for me a new pair of Drawers & skirt & made me a new part of a chemise for me & sewed on my white Dress. they are very very nice. Cool. . . .

Sun. 13. I went to S. School Congregationalist & wore my new suit of clothes. Pa went with me as far as the hill & then watched me the rest of the way on acct of tramps. Pooh! what do I care for Tramps, Cousin Sarah went with me & stopped at Aunt Hatties & got my dinner ma said I must not stop there much. I wont Aunt Hattie has enough work to do without me there I walked there & Back I am very tired & warm. . . .

Thu. 31. Piece on quilt. I intend to take it to the fair if I get it done I think it will be nice. Warm.

August 1879. Wed. 6. Help ma all day   In the afternoon I made another Apron for myself. Mr Farlinger Here My Ears are very sore. Ma opened one next to my ear but not where it was pierced & squoze an awful lot out. Cool evening. Warm. . . .

September 1879. Thu. 4. Henry is 16 yrs old to day Aunt Hattie Susie & all the children, except Ada & Baker were here. Uncle here to supper I went with Betsy all alone & took Aunt Hattie & the children home. ma & I took milk to the creamery. Freddie fell off of the porch & knocked his tooth all loose. he walked off the Porch a purpose & then he would cry. Aunt Harriet was awful Fidgety all the time. I never saw the ~~Beat~~ she was afraid that Betsy would run off the Bridge when there was no more danger than a shrimp running off of the ground. ma killed a turkey that got hung in the fence last night. . . .

Sun. 21. Got into trouble all day H nearly broke my Back & hit my head with a walnut & I won't know what I done to him I know I hit him & ma said I always hurt him worse than he did me, but I know Better than that I feel like flying some times & wish I could. . . .

Sun. 28. ma & Henry & I go up to Uncles after some butter. Uncle gave me a puppy that is nearly a year old his name is Jack his mother is pure blood shepherd & came from Scotland. Oh! he is a nice fellow some movers stayed here last night 2 men & 2 horse, there were some Emigrators went past here to day with 5 Jacks & Jennies just as high as the wagon box some were very nearly black & some a very light drab & there was one little young one not any higher than the table & about as big as a good sized dog but his Ears & tail was all of him about he looked funny enough & they asked $100 for him. Real Windy. . . .

55

October 1879. Thu. 2. did not go to school on acc't of rain. Henry wanted the Umbarella & all I said was that if Henry did not want it I did & he would not take it on that acct, when I told ma he could take it if he wanted to, she did not believe me, & she dont believe what I say but if Henry says any thing she believes him. do some examples Chas Chapman goes to the Academy. I wish I could. 3 loads of movers here to stay all night. one of them played on an accordian it is real muddy H got wet through. Rain. . . .

Fri. 10. Go to school. The Boys act like very bad boys. Henry was sitting astride the fence & (the boys have been making fun of H & I ever so long) Will Vanalstyne & Fred Chapman come up 1 on 1 side & the other on the other side & caught hold of his legs. H did not like that so he hit Fred on the head & that made him let go & Will still hung on so Henry went after him & told Wm that if he did not want to get into trouble to leave him alone & then Will pitched onto him & I told the teacher & she started out there but they ran & H went to the steps & sat down. we stood where we were a few minutes, & then we (teacher & we girls) started back to the schoolhouse & then those boys went back where Henry was the teacher said it would not be well for them to touch Henry, & every time the teacher would start to go out there & call to them they would Run. But after awhile teacher & we went in the schoolhouse, & the boys (after awhile) came too, & Fred C put Dees hat down in the Privy & made "[Dee] cry, & the teacher" [made] Will & Mat & Fred take their seat's & sent Dee after whips down to the Willows. when he got back it was time for school to call, so teacher gave the boys a little speech & then she called them out one at a time & whipped them over the head & legs & she whipped little Charlie Vanalstyne in his seat. O but the boys were mad. ma came to school she was so disgusted with those boys that she wouldn't make any remarks. . . .

November 1879. Sat. 1 go to school last day Miss Thompson gave me one prize of box of stationery .50 cts. she also gave Susie Stewart the same in B spelling & Dora Millet got a nice knife. very pretty in C spell. Besides giving cards all around & very very nice ones too. Hurrah for the first snow storm. Hurrah for the 1st Snow Storm. . . .

Thu. 6. help ma! help ma!! help ma!!! all day Pleasant

Fri. 7. ma & I & H & pa go to town, ma & H & I go over to the Academy to see about going Mon. ma got some New Appletons 5th Readers for us. ma took her premium money to send us & I was awful sorry, too. Mr Kissell asked us to read from them new Readers & I faltered more

than I ever did before I had Rather Read before 500 than just him alone.
help ma. Rain. . . .

Mon. 10. commence to go to the "Academy" to school. we study
"Appletons 5th Reader" "Robinsons Progressive Arith" "Read & Kel-
log" "Gran and Sumtoms Spelling & that all. like it very well, but seems
a little different from our school up here. Rain. . . .

December 1879. Mon. 1 go to school. last night there was some great
mischief done the pedulums to the clocks were both hidden, & the one
the clock upstairs we dont know anything about, & then the chairs were
all inverted & the organ meddled with so they could not play on it & a
light of glass was broken also. at 2.30 P.M. Mr Kissell called the school to
order & gave out these questions No 1 "was you in this Academy building anytime between 5 o'clock P.M. & 7 o'clock A.M. between the 1st &
2nd of December. No. 2. do <u>you know</u> of anyones being in this Academy
Building between the above time mentioned." and everyone answered
no Sir to both questions except Mr Kusay Clark & Avery Amsden & then
Mr Kissell told them to take the C room down stairs & then he followed
them. Foggy. . . .

Thursday 25. Christmas. Santa Claus was a very decent kind of a gentleman this time he-she brought me an Acc't Book or journal. 4 handkerchieves one silk & linen finish with a very nice wreath of flowers around
it. & 2 white ones & H & I traded a white one for a red one. so I have 4
& then the <u>best of all</u> was a set of cuffpins they are very nice they are a
plain body with 2 tinted leaves on it colored & then I got a journal. 240
pages in it. we went down to Aunt Harriets Ma. Henry & myself to
spend <u>Christmas</u>. Mr & Mrs McGee were there. Frankie got a drum &
Sarah got a trunk & Fred got a 2 wheeled bell & Mr & Mrs Farlinger
were there also. Henry got a shirt, set of studs 4 handkerchieves & journal. I had my first sleighride With Mr McGee home. I am totally bank-
rupt. -24 below Zero at sunrise this morning. Oh! pa got a check of
$3.37 for Ducks from Ma for <u>his</u> Christmas present. 24 below Zero at
sunrise. Cold. . . .

Wed. 31. 1879 last day of 1879 very Pleasant. help ma some   ride
on sled same as Monday.
    "Good Cheer   Good Cheer   For the happy New Year   Is smil-
ing gladly before you.
    And merry Bells ring   And Happy Hearts sing   Good Cheer, Good
Cheer   To the Chorous.

The Diary of Mary Griffith, 1880

When she began keeping this diary during her fifteenth year, Mary Griffith was living with her parents, Mr. and Mrs. Ben Griffith, and her siblings—Alma, Kate, Ben Jr. ("Thebie"), Paul, Platti, and Abraham—in the western Iowa town of Harlan. During the 1870s and 1880s many white settlers were traveling from eastern to western Iowa and, from there, on the Overland Trail to the West. Entries in Mary Griffith's diary describe such migrations as well as her schoolwork, her activities with family and friends, daily work in the home, tornadoes and wind storms, and virulent outbreaks of scarlet fever and diphtheria. The original diary, measuring two and a half by three and three-quarters inches, is clothbound with a tattered cover. Inside the cover is printed a calendar for 1880. The diary entries typically run fifteen to twenty lines each. They begin on January 3, 1880, and continue throughout the year. Mary Griffith died when she was seventeen, not long after she completed this diary. After she died, her diary went to her older sister, Alma R. Griffith, who married the ethnologist John Wesley Powell. The young couple traveled west to California. Many years later the diary, along with other Powell family papers, was donated to the California Historical Society, which in turn donated the diary to the State Historical Society of Iowa in Iowa City, where it remains today.

January 20, 1880. We ironed this morning. Thebie <u>actually</u> came before <u>twelve</u> for his dinner. The social was to have been at Mrs. Hunts this evening, but was put off on account of Pinafore till Thursday evening. I went with Aunt to the M.E. Church this evening. Mr. Franklin preached a very good sermon on <u>Faith</u>. There was one man got happy & <u>shouted</u>. I run home from Aunts, alone. Nothing caught me.

January 26, 1880. This being rather a bad morning we did not wash. Jennie Kemp & Mr. Sabin called this afternoon. Went up to the store and to Mrs. Potters this afternoon. Louie Benedict was there popping corn. He leaves Harlan tomorrow. I helped him eat the corn and talked to him a long time. He told me to "tell Kate good bye for him." Been working on a coffee sack most of my spare time today. Went over to Aunts a little bit this evening. . . .

February 18, 1880. Ironed this morning Did not even go to see Grandma to-day. Went to prayer meeting Mother said I could not have any excuse if I could go to Mr. Harveys last night, I could go to Prayer Meeting, this evening. These were not many there. This would have been a better night for the social than last. Saw "A.B." back in the store in his shirt sleeves taking it easy. He had no one to remind him that it was his duty to go to prayer meeting. . . .

February 28, 1880. Snow on the ground this morning. Very cold and windy—Went over to see Grandma. She was up at Mrs. Frosts yesterday. Walked home—Aunt don't want any more Friday visiting. Had a regular blizzard after diner—The wind and snow blow at a fearful rate—Wilber was here & spend the afternoon. The children had a good time—Father and "Thebie" come late to dinner—About eleven o'clock, Mother came in & told me to get up & see the "Moon Dogs." It was a pretty sight. . . .

March 17, 1880. Teacher & I went over and done up the work for Aunt. She is real sick—Hiram left in the evening train for Oregan—He called and bid us "good bye". . . .

March 27, 1880. It blowed a perfect streak last night. Our bed felt like waltzing—Fish for breakfast . . . Wind & dust, dust and wind, has been the order of the day—It has not ceased a moment and is still raging as if it expected to keep it up all night. How it moans. It puts me in mind of high water times at home. Only it sounds worse. . . .

April 3, 1880. A damp, foggy morning. Smart Girl—Got my morning work done before the train come in. A flock of wild geese went over this afternoon. Kate & I started out to make some calls. Met Frank on her way to the "P.O." She went with us. We called at Will Bowlins, the Riley's and Bucks. Came back to our house stayed a little while then went up to the Library. Called on Mrs. Gibbs, then we went home with Frank. Mr. H. L. Bridgman is dead.

April 17, 1880. Very windy. Kate & I have been busy sewing and work-ing. We went down to see Mary this afternoon and over to see Grandma. We are both about half sick. Kate is a little more than half. So much dust in the house, it is impossible to get it all out. Seems like we don't have any thing but wind. Grandma wants to go home in May. We will miss her when she does go. . . .

April 28, 1880. Raining this morning. "Gentle breeze" after breakfast. Mother brought Grandma over a while ago. I run up to Sabins a minute to see if I left a heel tap there. They were eating breakfast. Went in to see Mrs. Stephenson and make it all right about me not going to the social last evening. Another child of Mr. Davis's died with scarlet fever and two more not expected to live till noon. It rained nearly all day. School closed this evening on account of scarlet fever. I took G___ over to Aunts this evening. Mr. Fisher come for Mother. The little girl is very ill. . . .

May 4, 1880. A beautiful morning. Went to the P.O. Stopped to see Grandma, Mr. Elser and talked to Mrs. Burgin over the fence. Very windy this afternoon. Mrs. Jack called. Will & I went fishing this evening. By the time we got "Fred" out of the buggy, got our poles and were ready to fish, it commenced raining & we had to leave. The place was brightly perfumed with a couple of dead cows. One fish was all we caught. We got home before the rain. Oh! But it is raining nice. Such a nice easy rain. Mother brought Grandma over this evening. Two or three more cases of Scarlet fever reported. . . .

May 19, 1880. Wednesday. Cool & cloudy. Got up at 7:30. When I got over to Aunts they were eating breakfast. Grandma looked as "peart" as you please. Was the first one up. Could hardly wait till the buss come. It was a splendid morning for them to start. We all went to the depot to see them off. Father went to Avoca with them. Rec'd letters from Velmer and mollie. "Pollie" sent the news. "Nancy" sent her photo. It looked very much like a storm this evening. It actually sprinkled a little. It looks queer not to see Grandma. Did not go to prayer meeting. . . .

June 6, 1880. Oh! But the wind blew after I went to bed last night. About eleven Mother came in & said she thought the roof would go off. Expected we would all have to go to the cellar. Wanted the lamp put out down stairs & a candle put in its place. I took the candle down. How pale they looked by candle light. Sure now. Kate & I went to bed after 12:00. Decided we would not be like a horse. Took our shoes off any-how. Clear & bright this morning, but terribly windy. Where's the bit storm? Part of the new Hotel was blown down. Houses moved, trees twisted &c. Mr. Copeland was "providentially" here & preached this morning—Presbyterian sermon (so they say), Not much. . . .

July 27, 1880. Tossed from side to side, turned my pillow &c. Last night, but nothing had any effect. It was impossible to go to sleep. What was I thinking about? Fire? No indeed Aunt locked Wilber out "accidentally on purpose". Then she "raked" him about 2 hour. About 11:30 I heard some one scream fire I rushed in & called Aunt. It was Jimmy Longs Stable. Could not save it, burned four horses. Made a big blaze. After Will came home we had a wake. Kate looks as though she caught a severe "cold" last evening—We walked up to see the ruins. "Caswells" sister came very near pushing Kate off the side-walk.

July 28, 1880. Windy, dusty & hot. Didn't have any ideas I was such a big coward till last evening after I went over to Aunts . . . They were telling such big tales I was afraid to go to bed "pretty nearly." This has been a "big day" Barnums Show was in town. Half of Harlan turned out to see the show. Uncle Will & Dr. Bayer came home this morning. I wont need to be cremated to night. Kate & went to P.M. There was none. We went in to Aunts. Will came home with us. . . .

August 3, 1880. Splendid day. So nice & cool. Ironed, swept &c. Kate got her trunk moved down stairs. Oh! Yes we are busy. Went over to Aunts this afternoon. No one at home. Went up to see Frank. They <u>are very busy serving</u>. The mail arrived this evening. Quite an interesting dialogue was carried on under my window, about the time <u>little girls </u>should be in bed (Little boys too). It took place all the same. Of course I was busy, or should have retired before now. . . .

August 21, 1880. Sew, sew, sew—We have the silk pretty well on the way. I would not want to assist for more than one "Affair" in hot weather. Don't think I could stand it. Kates buttons gave her away to-day. Platti is getting pretty sharp. "Desperate fancy child." Frank came down to go to choir practice. I went up street with her. The court house was locked. We went to Porters. Then took a walk around the square. It is decided that Frank will start for Grinnell the 3rd of September. I will miss Frankie. . . .

August 30, 1880. Damp, cloudy and a mist of rain this morning. Cleared off and was nice this afternoon. Two years to-day since we arrived in Harlan. Kate and I sewed on my dress. Mother baked a fruit cake. Made plumb butter jelly &c. Frank came down this evening. Kate & I took her home. "A gentleman cow" took after us. "Indian warhoops," we had to come back & go up the other street. We stopped to see aunt on our way home. . . .

September 1, 1880. A lovely morning. Rain came down in torrents about noon. Busy all day getting ready for the wedding. Went up and told H. to come down a little bit this afternoon. We wanted to show her Kate's dress &c. I never saw any one so surprised in my life. She was coming to the wedding whether she was invited or not. Couldn't she? Will and Kate were married at 8:30 P.M. The ceremony was performed by Rev. Sabin. It was a very quiet "Affair." Frank got here sure. Ben couldn't find the ice that's on sills. Platti took a <u>bawl</u>. Will & Ben took Katie's trunk over. Hated to see them go, but it cant be helped. I suppose Platti will <u>bunk</u> with me. . . .

September 19, 1880. Heard wind storm about seven o'clock A.M. Not much rain. Cloudy, rain & very windy, till towards evening. Went to church. The bride and groom, Mr. & Mrs. Bert Whales, made their appearance. Did not stay for S.S. Ben took dinner at the Bowlins (Frank's), Platti was nine years old to-day. She was very much surprised by a new doll from father—Will & Kate were over a little bit this evening. The Court house was full this evening & (Wonderful) "Louisa" was late. They had to sing the first hymn without the organ. Lots of funny things happened. Lovely moonlight night. . . .

September 27, 1880. Monday. Splendid washday. Mother and Kate did the most of the washing. Went over to Aunts about 3:30 P.M. for K. to go up street. We went to Nathans to see Lena. Took a walk. We went home with Kate. Waited till Will came for supper. "Be-come." Lena came down this evening. Ah yes the skirt was a good fit for Kate. Talk about <u>scare crows</u>. We went up street to the store &c. Saw them escort the Garfield speaker to the Court house in good style. Torches band &c. Will bought a sack of plums down. No I didn't measure my length on the board walk. . . .

October 2, 1880. Poor Ben was very sick during the night & all morning. Some better this afternoon & evening. "Come here calfie It's your <u>mamie</u>" &c. It's enough to make any one "<u>smoil</u>" to hear him talk. By but I've had a stiff neck to-day. Sore throat &c. It rained all afternoon. Kate came over both morning & afternoon. Will & Kate came down a little while this evening. I was not "presentable." Have to get the oil off my neck before I make my appearance before <u>strangers</u>. "I think so."

October 3, 1880. A lovely day. Ben is better. Sat up visit all day. I did not go any places to-day. It don't seem like Sunday to me. Will and Kate came over towards evening. They want to see Wheelers (in the house). I wrote to Frank this evening. Will says the next time he comes over he wants me to have this "rag" off my neck. The <u>idea</u> of calling a 5 cent <u>kerchief</u> "a rag". My neck is about well, I don't need to wear it much longer. . . .

October 9, 1880. "Fury Git out." Wind & dust, dust & wind. Kate & I went up street this morning—went in every store in the City. Could not get what we wanted. Got eyes, ears, nose and mouth filled with dust off "Charlie" had called last night, he would have seen my "Get white dress" sure. I stepped out in my "white wrapper" to tell Ben to lock the door. It was Will & Kate I left suddenly. Kate did nothing but "snicker" and giggle while she stayed. It was awful funny for her. Aunt Lyde arrived before two. . . .

October 16, 1880. A dreadful stormy night. The ground was covered with snow this morning. The storm raged all day and is still at it. A regular blizzard—I've often heard of them, but never saw any till I come to Iowa. My how the wind roars. Kate was over both morning & afternoon. When the fringe arrives, her dress will be "finished"—Started to make a cloak out of my old ones. "It's as good as new" Only its nearly worn out. . . .

October 18, 1880. "Young Winter." I agree with Mr. Coverman. It seems like it is "Old Winter" more than a young one. Snow storm this afternoon. Kate was over a good part of the day. Will has the sore throat. I never knew him to go to "Long Branch," but what he was sick after the trip. Rec'd a letter from Core. Hurrah for Garfield. Torch light processions, speeches, illuminations. We illuminated the houses this evening. . . .

October 24, 1880. Was too sick to know much about any thing. It is not any fun to have the diptheria. Aunt came to see me. Said Will had the sore throat too. Mother went to see him in the afternoon. Kate came over after dinner to see me. Father said there was church in the morning and very few in the evening—The choir where was the choir? All gone. All there in the morning. All gone in the evening. . . .

November 20, 1880. A lovely morning. Turned whispering cold about noon. Two blizzards in the afternoon. Mother is not much better. No one come to temperance meeting. Worked real hard all day. Finished Ben's coat. Head to go up street—Stopped to see Aunt—Next up to Wheelers a little bit. Kate came home with me. Mother & I finished Pants Shirts. . . .

December 5, 1880. Bitter cold—Every thing frozen stiff in the kitchen last night. Went to church & S.S. Mr. Mc____, Somebody that looked very much like Fred Linsley, preached this morning and evening. He was a H. P. Preached a very good sermon. Rather lengthy. Will & Kate were down this evening.

December 6, 1880. Clear and bright, but bitter cold. We washed—Such fun hanging up the clothes. The clothes were as stiff as boards that we brought in—We left the most of them out—If any one wants them bad enough to tear them off the line, they ought to have them. . . .

December 9, 1880. Nice day—Kate came down this morning—We went up street. Kate went to get her "picture took" this afternoon. I took my work and went up and stayed with Lena. Got a splendid <u>Christmas present</u> this eve. Ben brought me a <u>very nice set of mink furs</u>. He is the best boy I ever saw. I hated to take them. It seems too much. . . .

December 25, 1880. Merry Christmas. Ground covered with snow, Sleigh bells jingle, &c. My presents are all splendid—Furs, shoes, picture-frame, painted shells, looking-glass, hand-kerchief &c. A great many more than I expected. Platti has "come down with the mumps"—Took very sick in the night. Took Frank her Christmas present this morning. She was down towards evening. Kate was down to see her presents, they are splendid. We went to the store to see Will.

December 30, 1880. A gloomy day—Took dinner with Will & Kate, at the store. Two supper's last night, two dinners to day. I will get fat if I keep up. Started to go up to Sabins, had not gone far till Kate followed me. Prof. Kimball was there. So we had the pleasure of hearing his play afterall. Thoes boots were killing. Went on over with Kate to see Lena. Waited till after dark, thought Will would come. He did not come Lena & I started. We met him. Some people wont give an inch of the side-walk.

December 31, 1880. The last day of the Old Year. Good Bye 1880. A lovely day. Lena & Kate were down a few minutes. Frank and I made a good many calls this afternoon. The all absorbing topic appeared to be the Gentlemen that expect to make New Years call. The question of the day was Are you going to receive your callers tomorrow? The fun of it is we cant help our selves. We cant tell them not to come. I feel as little like the Old Year, about Gone—To Sleep—Farewell.

The Diary of Etta Luella Call, 1881–1882

Etta Luella Call was born on January 21, 1866, to Ambrose and Nancy (Henderson) Call, two of the first white settlers in Algona (Kossuth County), Iowa. Etta's father was a government mail contractor who later became president of the First National Bank. She was the third of seven siblings: Florence, Edith, Etta, Bertha, Chester, Roscoe, and Myrtle. In 1888 Etta married William K.

Etta Luella Call. Courtesy Lucille Hutchinson.

Ferguson, and their son, Arthur, was born in 1890. She died on December 26, 1907, at thirty-nine.

Because her family was relatively well-to-do, Etta Call was better educated than most white girls growing up in north-central Iowa in the 1880s. She began keeping her diary two months after she arrived at St. Mary's Academy in South Bend, Indiana, a private school for girls that was associated with Notre Dame. St. Mary's, originally located in Bertrand, Michigan, was moved to a site across the road from Notre Dame in 1855 and became one of the earliest Catholic colleges for women in the United States. Mother Angela Gillespie served as director of the academy from 1853 to 1870; by the time Etta Call began attending classes there, Mother Annunciata ran the school. Among the Sisters of the Holy Cross on the teaching staff were Lucretia, Ursula, Bethlehem, Fidelis, Claudine, and Eugenie.

Etta's diary, kept during her fifteenth and sixteenth years, is a cloth-bound journal that measures approximately six by eight inches. Inside the front cover is the diarist's signature, along with the words *Home, Home, sweet Home.* On the title page is this inscription: "Etta Luella Call, St. Mary's Academy, Notre Dame, Ind." The diary contains 108 numbered, lined pages, almost all of which have been filled. As the introduction to her diary reveals, Etta had a mischievous side as well as a serious side. Several diary entries show that she was consciously creating a record of adolescence that not only would describe her experiences but that also might be reread and enjoyed in years to come.

Introduction: I have been going to commence a diary ever since I arrived at St. Mary's, but before today I have not had a good chance to commence. I expect to keep it up during my stay at boarding school and perhaps longer.

I am in the Third Senior class and study Rhetoric, Philosophy, Ancient History, Botany, Reading and French. My teachers are Sister Lenore, Sister Eugenie and Sister Twin.

I like school very much, but was terribly homesick during the first months of my life here.

In this dear diary, I shall put down all my experiences and trials, sorrows and fun, so that, in after years I can read this book and recall to my mind all that happened during my school days, and who knows how much pleasure it may afford me.   —E. L. C. Etta Luella Call

November 24, 1881, Thursday. To day, Thanksgiving, November 24, 1881, finds me at St. Mary's Academy, Notre Dame, Ind., where I, accompanied by Eda, Mary Em and Emma Chrischilles, arrived Sept. 3th, 1881. This is the first Thanksgiving I ever spent away from home, and it is not a very happy one. Hal[lie] Davenport and myself spent most of our time in promenading the halls. It was too cold to be out-doors and we did not have much fun. Took <u>two walks</u> on forbidden ground. Am lonesome and wish I was at home. Rec'd letter from Charlie S. saying would call, but did not. Juniors had an entertainment in the evening.

November 25, 1881, Friday. Oh! what terrible things will happen! to day when nearly noon, Mother Lucretia came into the study hall and said that Mamie Greble had been expelled. What a silence fell upon the school! Mamie, the favorite of all the scholars, gone! She was expelled for corresponding with a boy whom she had never seen. Mother was as white as a sheet and could scarcely keep from crying while talking to us. At French we did not recite, and Sister Eugenie told us about Mamie. At 15 minutes of 11 Mother called her and she went dancing into Mother's room and said, "Want me, Mother?" Mother told her to put on her hat and cloak and she said, "Why, where am I going?" and when Mother told her, she did not speak a word but turned as white as a sheet and nearly tore her lip off. She said "I am guilty" when the letters were shown her but did not tell on any other girls. Sister Eugenie feel terribly. The school seems as dull as can be and we are all as solemn as if a funeral had taken place. This ought to be an example to the other girls and teach them not to put such confidence in boys, for the boy whom Mamie wrote to showed the sisters the letters himself. Mary was led on by Maude Wiley, most probably, and everyone thinks that she ought to go before Mamie.

This is the most miserable day that I ever passed and I will pray for Mamie to night. Thanksgiving she was as happy as a bird and she knew nothing of her having been betrayed until 5 min. before she was in the bus.

November 26, 1881, Saturday. Eda received letter from Flora. A lovely day. Feel a little better than yesterday. Sisters say Mamie went home. Was afraid she would not. Emma is sick. Had my lessons, am provoked, because Sister Lenore put Junnie Barlow 1" in all the competitions, when I was as good as she, partiality; Prof. Lewis, dancing master, gave first lesson in dancing. So conceited. Didn't learn much. Am writing in study time. Poor Mamie. Can't help but think about her; would like to pound that boy. He ought to be put in prison. Was not Mamie's fault, poor girl! She is an orphan and her sisters and guardian care scarcely anything for her. . . .

December 6, 1881, Tuesday. Cold. Arose at 15 min. past 6. Catholics had black coffee and 1/2 slice bread for breakfast. Thankful I am not one. Took long walk after breakfast. Got back at 10 A.M. Very tired. Temperance lectures and auctions given by the girls. Lots of fun. . . .

December 13, 1881, Tuesday. Cold, gloomy day. Wind howls, and makes my thoughts wander back to several years ago, when a little girl seven or eight years old, I kept a diary for Papa. Little did I think, then, that in a few years, I would be going to a Catholic school, so far from home. I cannot study, for I think how soon it will be when I shall see Papa: I think of home, the babies, Mama and all the folks. In seven months I will be with them and then—Oh! how happy we will all be. This morning S. Fedalis changed J. Bulls bed, and put C. Pease in her place. I am so angry. I shall not stand it, if she smells as bad as she used to. Hope Julia will not be good where she is, but cut up all the more. S. Claudine, is so queer. She used to have a mania for fresh air and as soon as she entered the study hall she opened all the doors and windows and nearly froze us. M. Lucretia told her not to do that and now she goes around gathering up all the pens and pencils when the girls are at class, puts them in her desk, and then the girls wonder where they have gone to, and S. Fedalis how so many got on her desk. She gives us "private lectures," comes and pats us on the head as if we were puppy dogs, smiles such sickish smiles, that we are all disgusted with her. S. Bethlehem is a thousand times nicer, and I am so glad when it is her turn to preside in the study hall. Had good deal of fun French class. Knew my lessons. Walked with Eda, M. Fishburn and Mary Price after supper. . . .

January, 5, 1882, Thursday. Well, dear diary, you have had a long rest. I must confess that I forgot you when I went to Elkhart. Papa came Friday and when I saw him all the tears that had been stored away in my eyes for him flowed most rapidly. Went to Aunt Nina's at 11 A.M. No one can imagine how happy I was to be with the folks altho' I had never seen them all. Had a grand time. Oh! how I dreaded to come back. Got to crying the eve. before I came back, and Eddie teased me most to death. Like him quite well . . . Cora came to South Bend and we stayed there all forenoon and came here at one. Kind of glad to get back. S. Eugenie glad to see me.

Commenced lessons today. Not a very good beginning. Eat at S. Leonore's table. Can not get the courage to eat much. Doesn't taste half as good as it did before we went away. Rec'd. splendid letter from Bert yesterday. S. Claudine bad as ever. Will not leave that clock alone. Mary Em went home with Uncle Asa Dec. 21. Have not heard from her. Cannot imagine why she does not write. S. Eugenie rec'd news of her father's death last eve. She heard class but looks badly. Feel so sorry for her. Eda nearly sick and gone to the infirmary. Alice Mowry and I got a match and tried to smoke a cigarette, but it would not burn. Cora Belle Reynolds, Jennie Kern, Emma, Eda and myself had our pictures taken. Lots of fun.

January 6, 1882, Friday. Little weeks. Alice Mowry, Emma and I had a little fun, but it made me homesick. I felt as if I would give anything to be at home. 170 days from to day and I will not be here, but at "home". Never before did I know what home was, but now I feel every bone in my body the old hymn, "Home Sweet Home." Ah! how few are those who appreciate their home before they have left it. How few know the value of a mother & father, sisters & brothers, before they are separated from them. Truly, we must all make sacrifices, and we must all be educated, but it seems hard sometimes. Put pie on our chairs at dinner, and at four went in after it. Emma's gone, but mine there. . . .

January 8, 1882, Sunday. Once more Sunday has crept around. Once more we don our white veils, and, with a sister at each end, march to the little chapel at St. Mary's, beautifully decorated with evergreens & flowers. Once more the hymns are sung, and prayers repeated. And, while I sit by Mable, my eyes become and my thoughts wander to other parts of the world. To a home where all is cheerful. Fires burning brightly, little children playing around and a warm breakfast being eaten. Wrote to Flora and rec'd one from her. Pie for collation. Lots of fun at 4, eating bread and strawberries and ground cherries. Estelle Todd back. Alice Mowry left. Some fun at Vespers. Mary Em and Eda have decided to go home in Feb. That will leave Emma & I here to quarrel between our selves. . . .

January 17, 1882, Tuesday. Had a "picnic" with Sr. Eugenie. None of us knew our lessons and she scolded the whole class in general and then told us to study. In a few minutes she heard us recite and I could not take all that and I said, "I do study and I am not lazy" and a lot more that I cannot remember, and of course, I had to cry like a big baby, and I was so angry that I got up and left the room. She sent Sarah Walsh out to console me and get me to come back, but I informed her it was of no use and finally the bell rang and then I went up to the dormitory, washed, combed my hair and then felt like myself again. As I reached the door to go down, who should I meet but S. Eugenie. I turned, went back to my bed and she followed me. Then I commenced to squall again and was as stubborn as a mule. She finally persuaded me to go downstairs and then she said she was so sorry for I always had my lessons and she told the girls afterwards that she ought not to have said that to me, but she did not think it when she said it.

She put her arms around me and hugged and kissed me and said, "Etta, didn't you know it was not for you? Haven't I praised you all session? And don't you think some of the girls are lazy? Never mind that page. There are plenty of others in the lesson for ex. If you can't learn it, go right on and it will be all right." and a lot more of such talk, while I, like the big goose that I am, stood there crying as if my last friend had died. Finally I stopped and half made up with her and started to go downstairs when we met M. Lucretia. She asked me what was the matter and put her arms around me and talked to me, said I was nervous and she was afraid I studied too hard, what good marks I had, how pleased my father would be, etc., and so on. Then I went in with S.E. to hear her first class recite and was all right. After supper the girls read a paper which was quite good. Went to bed as usual, and slept soundly.

January 21, 1882, Saturday. My birthday. 16 yrs. old. None of the girls thought of it and I did not mention it. Had French instead of reading. Got along very well with my lessons. Did not do a thing but scribble and talk, in composition class. Had dancing lessons but I did not dance. Hal Davenport and self walked on porch and in halls. Went to Benediction after supper. . . .

January 26, 1882, Thursday. Well, thank ___ one examination is over. Fathers General & Walsh, Mothers Superior, Ursula & Lucretia and several sisters were there. We were ex. orally and each sent to the board to write a dictation. I almost forgot to say it was a French Ex. Sister called on me when F. General was there, & as a natural consequence I was frightened half to death. I got through all right, & F. General made the remark that he guessed I know the whole book. All well pleased. None failed. Eda examined in French and German, and Emma in German. All did well. Stayed up to Infirmary nearly an hour with Mary Em. After dark, E. Wright, M. Beal, H. Davenport and self, walked on the bricks & around the house. Wind blew terribly. . . .

February 4, 1882, Saturday. The Indian girls came last night. There are five—two seniors and three juniors. Sr. Fidelis brought them in the Rec. room at ten . . . They speak quite good English, are rather bashful. Came from the Indian Ter. Sent by the Gov. Mother Lucretia gave us permission to go on a walk. I started with Kate Donnelly and Jennie Barlow, but we saw they were going up the R.R. and we came back. The Indians all took a bath, & when they came down we took them & talked with them. They all eat at the same table & are so queer. Prof. Lewis came, gave dancing lessons. I did not dance. Commenced a composition on "Ambition." After supper the Cath. all went up stairs and the rest of us talked with the Indians. Their names are Edith Abner, Eliza Charlie, Lizzie Finley, Elmer Abner & Luxy Wadsworth. Lizzie's Indian name is Peochta. Two waltzed for us. They talked and laughed a good deal. We went to Benediction as usual.

February 9, 1882, Thursday. After breakfast we were all ordered to go outdoors, and get some fresh air. Emma and I concluded to go, and putting our rhetorics under our arms, and shawls on our heads, we started. At noon we rec'd a letter saying Pa would be here to see us today and would take Eda home with him, as Mary Em said she was not well. What was our surprise? I couldn't study altho' I knew none of them. Went to Philosophy Class, and just as it was my turn to recite, Emma said Eda wanted me.

I asked to be excused and my face was nearly burning up, when I went on a skip, hop and jump to the parlor. I stood at the door a minute, then rushed into see him. There sorrow was mingled with joy; sorrow at thinking of Eda's going home and joy at seeing Pa. Well, it was all settled, Eda must go. So we packed up her things and got her ready, thinking all the time that this was surely a happy birthday for her. Her eighteenth birthday.

Well, they went, and while I am sitting here writing this, they are in Chicago. I did not feel very lonesome at first, and E. and I contented ourselves with eating bread and butter (which we got today) and jelly and some candy and nuts Pa brought us. Well, five o'clock soon came, and I went to the study hall, and Emma to music, where she had her cry.

The next thing on the program was supper. I couldn't eat a bite, and pretty soon it commenced to rain, and my kerchief went to my eyes, and there I was. Sr. Eugenie got up and told me to come with her. As soon as we were out of the Refectory she put her arms around me and said, "Poor little Pet" about a thousand times and took me into the Mimms Rec. Room. We sat down, and she talked quite a while, and then told me to stay there 'til the girls came back, and she went back to her supper.

The minute she was gone, I went into our own Rec. Room, and sat down and played all the old tunes I could think of. The lights were turned down, and as I sat there all alone, with the hall doors open, all the ghost stories I have ever read came to my mind, and I imagined that there was an Indian in every corner. I soon gave way to tears again, and laid my head on the piano, and cried for all that's out. The girls came back, and E. gave me a cookie, and then Hal. Davenport, Martha Beal and I, went out on the pavement and walked, and gazed at the beautiful sky. . . .

February 14, 1882, Tuesday. Well, 'tis St. Valentines day. I didn't expect to be here a year ago today. I wonder where I will be one year

71

from now. No one can tell. At four E. and I walked on the bank. Sophie
Papira found a mole, and chased the girls all over the yard with it. Most
of the girls went walking. We did not go, but went up in the dormitory
and stayed 'til after five, and then came down in study hall. I wrote in
Emma's diary for her, and we talked and laughed in general. M. Lucretia
gave us a lecture just before retiring. Rats were in the dormitory, and as a
natural consequence we had lots of fun.

February 16, 1882, Thursday. Rather cool, knew my lessons. Rec'd a
lovely long letter from Eda and one from Jessie. It makes me feel so
funny to think that Eda is home. Oh! dear! how I want to see the babies
and Chester. but why do I give way to feelings of homesickness? Is it not
as much of a sacrifice for my parents to send me here as it is for me to
remain? Do I not have to go to school somewhere, and, in fact—is this
not as good a school as any in the United States?

February 21, 1882, Tuesday. Well, this is winter. It snowed last night,
and so the ground is all white and the trees covered with frost, and as the
winds howl I think of home, and last winter, so different from this. Annie
Glenmore had some canned peaches in the collation closet, and she and I
went in there, found a can opener, and opened one can, and I went to
the refectory and got two spoons. We stayed in the closet some time eating them, and when we came out—Lo! not a girl was to be seen. We did
not know where they had gone, and so sat down in one corner and ate.
We nearly died laughing for at every other mouthful (only one peach at a
time) we would spill it all over our dresses. Soon we heard someone coming, and what should we do! We crammed peaches, sugar and spoons in a
drawer which happened to be near, and commenced reading a book very
diligently—it proved to be our Prefect; and she told us to go and find the
other girls. Went to benediction. Was never so sick in my life. The
peaches were too much for me. . . .

February 28, 1882, Tuesday. Oh dear! I am homesick this morn. I
don't know what makes me, but I am. This is the last day of February. At
four o'clock I was very happily surprised, by receiving a letter from Nellie
Boryan and another from Eda. She is coming back next week. Hurrah!
Harry Call is a great deal better, and think he will recover. I stole 4 pieces
of cheese for Emma from the table, but after all it was not good. We went
to benediction after supper. Sr. Sophia has gone away for a few days.
How sorry I am. Annie Leyden came to my bed in the night and wanted
me to holler, but I was afraid to and would not. She made so much noise
that just one minute after she got in bed, who should come but Sister

Fedelis. Mable snored so loud that I could not sleep, so I threw a lot of water on her. She squirmed and scolded, but snored no more.

March 3, 1882, Friday. Today has been a great deal more pleasant than yesterday, if that could be possible. The grass & flowers are actually beginning to grow, and we all wear sun downs when we go out doors. Emma and I commenced "The Art of Conversation" by Carleton. 'Tis very interesting. We walked on the bank and E. read out loud. I have had all my lessons to day. Sr. Floreine praises me so every time she gives me a music lesson that it makes me sick. Sr. Henrietta died last night of consumption. She has been sick 20 years, and felt a great deal better yesterday, so went out riding, but it seems it was too much for her, and so she departed from this life in the night. We went over to the convent at four to see the corpse. It was in the parlor, on a white bier, strewn with flowers and leaves. At her head were two lighted candles and a crucifix, and in her hands her beads, and vows, which vows she had not seen since she rec'd them, according to the customs of these nuns. I never, never can forget that face, so ghastly and sunken, nothing, nothing but skin and bones, one eye partly open, and that thin long body, about 6 inches high, those white clasped hands. Oh! 'twas perfectly terrible! I hate to look at dead people. It impresses me so that it is a long time before I can get over it. I did not go to French Conversation in the eve., but stayed in the small rec. room and listened to Emma read. I have not recovered from the effects of that walk yet. Am so lame that I can scarcely walk.

March 5, 1882, Sunday. This morning the bell rang for prayer before we were half dressed. Ever so many of the girls were not ready when the bell rang and at breakfast M. Lucretia informed them that they would be put in penance, and so after Mass they had to learn the first eleven verses of the eighteenth chapter of St. John and recite it to her. Emma was among the number. We had a grand sermon from Father Hudson at Mass. I almost fell in love with him. He spoke of Christ's Crucifixion, and altho' I tried to read my bible as hard as possible. I had to stop and listen to him. How I wish they would have him all the time instead of F. Shortis . . . Went to Vespers in the afternoon. Was so provoked. I took "Art of Con." in the chapel to read, and then Sr. Eugenie made me sit next to Sr. Joseph, and I couldn't read a word. I might have known something would happen. I stayed in the house and read nearly all the time after Vespers. I was 99 in lessons. J. Barlow 98 & N. Keenan 99. Jennie is furious. I think I got as much as I deserved. In the dormitory I went over to Annie Lyden's bed and was talking to her, when I saw Sr.

Fedelis coming down the aisle. I wasn't going back, as long as she had seen me, and so she came down, put one arm around me, said "Ettie you mustn't go to other peoples' beds, but just stay in your <u>own little cell</u>," and led me to my own bed. I do not believe I was ever so disgusted in my life. It made me sick all night. Horrors! . . . .

March 17, 1882, Friday. Oh, dear! Old diary, I am getting sick of you. It is harder work than I ever knew to keep a diary. Something ails me lately. I have lost all the patience I ever had.

Oh, dear! Cannot compose or write a letter to save me. in my diary I can write nothing but the basic facts. I am so nervous. can not bear to do one thing more than two minutes at a time, and I feel so funny, and have such a longing for something, I know not what. I have a perfect mania for letters from home. I do not feel as I ever did before.

Later. Oh! how much better I feel than I did this morning. Have had lots of fun. After dinner I worked on some fancy work in the rec. room, when suddenly "Boys, Boys" was heard on every side, rushing to the windows, we saw only the "minims" out for a walk, and returned to our seats. In about half an hour the cry of "The band, band" rang from every room in the house, and we all went "pell-mell" outdoors, and soon there appeared among the trees towards the gate, the green flag of "Old Ireland," and by its side the flag of the United States. One moment longer and music reaches our ears, and we perceive the college band. Oh! what feelings of glee and sorrow mixed, fill my frame. how natural that music sounds! We are soon ushered into the study hall, the windows are thrown open, and we all cram into them and stick our heads out to see the boys. They stay in front of the porch and serenade us for about half an hour, and are then invited in for refreshments. We turned around, and lo! locked in the study hall, we found ourselves. In about 1/2 hr. the boys came out and after playing 3 or 4 pieces, went to the Convent and then home. I stayed in the rec. room from then 'til supper. I took a terrible cold watching the boys. . . .

March 19, 1882, Sunday. Well, here you are again, old Sunday, and I will have to go through all the trials of Mass, Vespers, and Points. We had a French sermon this morn. I could understand but a very little. Had vespers at five. I nearly died I got so tired. J. Barlow and I commenced reading the history of France and England. We take turns reading out loud. I like it ever so much. I was 98 in lessons. Lily Lancaster recited the "Golden Rose." Every year the Pope gives to the best women in the Catholic world, a golden rose. It generally falls to some princess or queen. In imitation of this, F.G. gives to the best girl in the school a rose, made of paper. I am glad Lillie got it. I think she deserved it, for she had been here four yrs. And has not been off of the tablet once. As it is St. Joseph's Feast, we had no French or German exercises today. . . .

March 23, 1882, Thursday. We had a competition in Rhetoric this morning. Most of us did very well. Sr. Sophia is sending everybody to penance lately. The nuns turned the piano to the wall so that we could not have music to dance by, as some waltz. In the eve., we got combs and played on them and sang tunes for the girls to dance by, and the Sisters had to give up, for they knew not what to do.

March 26, 1882, Sunday. Another Sun. Well! It does not seem long since the last time I wrote that word. 90 more days and I will be home. They say that Longfellow died yesterday morning. Poor man! I always wanted to see him but now all my hopes are blasted. He will long live in my memory. I love him and his works. I got "Bracebridge Hall" by W. Irving from the library, but have not read much of it as yet, for every time I get settled down someone comes and we get to talking and cannot stop. . . .

April 1, 1882, Saturday. This wonderful day has come at last. When I arose this morn my dress was missing, and then I went hunting all over the dormitory. I found the skirt over on the other side, but the waist— where was it? I accused every girl in the dorm of hiding it, and looked everywhere but in the right place. Finally Sister found it—tucked snugly down in the corner of Ed's bed.

Had Composition and Sr. Eleanor was so cross that J. Barlow and I determined we would play some joke on her before night. After dinner I got Jennie and we went upstairs and found her classroom locked. After while Sr. Hortense came along, and she lent us her keys and said to bring them down in the reception room when we were through. We got in, took some string and tied her chair fast to her desk so that when she went to sit down the chair would remain stationery and she could not sit. Next we took all her plants and hid them, some in the desks, others in a box, and others behind the chair. Not satisfied with this, we took down Father General's picture, and carefully wrapt it in a piece of clean white cloth and laid it in a desk. Then we got some black fur, put pins in it for eyes, and put it on the dictionary behind her desk, and then we closed every blind in the classroom, which made it pitch dark, and left in a great hurry for fear she might come and catch us. When we went to lock the door, the key stuck and Jennie broke the chain pulling it. We had a terrible time, but finally extracted the key from the door, mended the chain and went downstairs.

When we went up to History everything was just as it should be, with the exception of F.G.'s picture which she had not found and two plants. Sr. was very kind and good-natured all during class, and when she took out the dictionary, did it as coolly as you please, in spite of the mouse in her desk. J. and I nearly died for we wanted to laugh so bad, but luckily she commenced with us to recite, and so we grew calmer, but I never passed such a long two hours. How I kept my face straight so well is a mystery to me, but the time was finally passed and she said not a word to anyone about it. Jen and I felt rather taken back at not having the pleasure of seeing her surprise, for we did not think that she went to her room before class time. At four, the two "Seniors" told us that they were in the next room and heard her when she went in. She slammed back the blinds and made a terrible noise, scolding about "Those girls, whoever they are." She came out and was inquiring for M. Lucretia, and they saw her talking to Sr. Fedelis about it. She was furious they said, but she probably thought that the best way to turn the joke on us was not to say anything about it. I expect they will find out who did it but I don't care. After supper the girls hid the bell in the Rec. room.

April 18, 1882, Tuesday. Beautiful day. I had my lessons pretty well. Nellie Galen taught our French class, as "Ma Soeur Eugenie" was out to the farm. The air was so pure and fresh at four that it seemed impossible for us to go into Literary at five, so we coaxed a walk from Mother and started. We went down to the ravine, crossed it on a log, climbed the bluffs on the other side, and followed the river.

When we were over on the prairie, Lena, Mag., Martha, Lida and I stopped and gazed back at the academy. The scenery was beautiful, and it seemed as though I could not drink in enough of the beauties of nature. We stayed there some time, and were then obliged to go on, as the others were far ahead of us and waiting. After climbing several fences, scratching our hands all up, and getting our shoes full of sand, we reached them and returned home on the R.R. All had a lovely time, and I enjoyed it very much. It reminded me of my rambles with Stella and Julia last summer. I rec'd. a nice long letter from Bert. After supper I was very tired and bed-time was welcomed with great joy. My foot is so sore that I don't know what to do with it. . . .

April 22, 1882, Saturday. Rather cold and rainy. One poor little wasp created a deal of excitement in the History class. It was on the flowers and I saw and spoke about it. After while, just as I began to recite, it crawled out from under my chair. I, of course, gave a little jump, and we all commenced to laugh. Sr. Eleanor took a book and threw it right down on it. This made me so sick I didn't know what to do, so just turned around. We all got to laughing, and I laughed until the tears came, and then I lost all control of myself.

I would recite three or four words and then laugh. After while Sr. E. told someone else to recite as I was nervous. I was all quieted down by the time class was over, but when they all began to say "Etta's crying for the wasp." "I didn't know she was so sympathetic," and etc. I laughed again, and got up and went downstairs. Went to Bene. after supper. Grace Taylor, the sweetest girl that ever lived is back here to remain several days. Stayed in the Rec. room and talked at four and after supper.

April 23, 1882, Sunday. Went to Mass & Vespers. Had French Ex., study and Points. I was a 99 in lessons last week . . . Lovely day. Lida and I were walking on the bank and we both forgot and went beyond our limits. When coming back, S. spoke of it. We saw some nuns pointing their fingers at us, and hurried back. Then we sat down on the steps leading to the river, and someone clapped their hands at us. L. got up, but I did not, for a little while, and then we both went in so we would meet whoever it was motioning to us. It proved to be Sr. Eleanor & "Detective Rosa." The latter said, "Are you Etta or Eda?" I said, "I am <u>Etta</u>," with a good deal of emphasis. She said, "Well, you're the one who I told to go downstairs the other day and who didn't do it. Lida got up when I told her to, and you tried to pull her down." I said, "Excuse me, but I did not try to pull her down." Then she said, "Well, remember that the third time is the charm," and took out her pencil, meaning, I presume, that she would mark me the next time. I said nothing to her, but I treated her very coolly and walked on. She made me furious. Why didn't she say something to Lida and not address it all to me? Sr. Eleanor didn't say anything. . . .

April 30, 1882, Sunday. Hail. Most welcome day! With what joy do I write "April 30." I will now have to bid this month good bye, and with it you, dear old diary. Many, many a time have I found enjoyment by writing in you when I could do nothing else. I did not expect I would keep it up so regular when I began last Thanksgiving. But yes, not a day have I missed with the exception of the Holidays. Yes, dear Diary, you have laid in my desk unmolested for a long time, and I will now be obliged to deposit you in my trunk, and buy a new book, but it will simply be a continuation of your self. I would not take a good deal for you, my old Friend, and how much more will I appreciate you in future years. Perhaps I will be able to keep you 'til ~~I am~~ my hair is white as snow, when I am surrounded by grand children and (Oh! horrors! the idea of me, a little school girl, writing such nonsense as this). 'Tis a beautiful day, but I spent all the forenoon in the house. After Mass (during which I read ten chap. St. Luke) I went to the Library and got "Lives of Novelists & Dramatists" by Walter Scott. I read the life of Goldsmith but it put me in

such a dreary mood that I could read no more, and so I sat there and
built air castles 'til dinner time. I should love to be a writer. I wish that I
could write even the simplest little rhymes or tales. After dinner, I walked
a while on the bank with Lida and Maggie, and then came to the study
hall, and have written these lines. . . .

The Diary of Polly Caroline Bullard, 1897

Polly Caroline Bullard, the daughter of Will and Clara (Failing)
Bullard, was born in Elgin, Illinois, on May 2, 1881. She and her
younger sister, Marjorie, kept diaries during the same years while
they were living in St. Paul, Minnesota. Polly was fifteen when she
began writing on April 15, 1897. She used her diary to record and
comment on daily events, her school work, and her relationships
with family and friends. Sometimes Polly would write one long
diary entry that recounted the activities of a week or more or that
included family reminiscences as well as personal recollections.
When she was grown, she became a teacher; one of her teaching
assignments was in Eveleth, Minnesota, from 1908 to 1910.
Today her diary is housed in the Minnesota Historical Society's
manuscript collection in St. Paul, as are reminiscences of her and
her family's life. Her diary also contains a good deal of information
about her family's history.

Many years later, when Marjorie Bullard Kohlsaat was preparing their diaries for donation to the Minnesota History Center, she
wrote a reminiscence of Polly, musing, "One wishes that my sister
had begun earlier in life to write and paint, and that she had not so
modestly concealed her abilities." Polly kept her diary in a blank
composition book, the type used by students of St. Paul's Central
High School, from which Polly and Marjorie were graduated. The
excerpts from Polly's diary that follow present a detailed portrait
of one adolescent girl's life at the turn of the last century.

Thursday, April 15th, 1897. It is so long since I have written in here
that I have a great deal to say.

Several weeks ago I went to see Nancy Wood, to return her visit.
Beside myself there were Winifred Brill, Margaret Routh, Edith Dabney,
Mary smith, Katharine Abbott, Rita Armstrong and Constance McDay.
The girls played a rather mean trick on Margaret Routh. She and Rob

Wood cherish quite a fondness for each other. Rob was down at the gymnasium for most of the afternoon and Margaret came in rather late. So the girls before she came fixed a button-pin with ribbons in the High School colors, red and black, in an envelope. When Margaret came, after she had been there a while, Katharine handed her the envelope, saying that Rob had left it for her before he went. M. took it, looked at it rather curiously, and then with a rather embarrassed laugh, tossed it aside, without opening it. But after some time we noticed that the pin was fastened to the rever of her coat, which she had not taken off. After a while Rob unexpectedly came home, much to the chagrin of the girls who had conspired against Margaret, so Nancy tackled him in the hall and told him about it, so that he would not give them away. He did not seem to mind it very much, and M. has not yet found out how basely she was deceived. The other day she remarked to one of the girls, "That pin is quite an addition to my room." (Evidently she had placed it somewhere about the room with her other mementos) Strange to say a rather strained expression appeared on their faces, and Rita laughed immoderately. Week before last we had our Spring vacation. Monday several of us went over to Rita's. I went to make my party call. Beside myself there were Allison McKibbin, Nancy Wood, Mary Smith, Sadie Ames, Margaret Routh, Edith Dabney and Winifred Brill. We did nothing but sit around and talk gossip and eat apples, a very silly way to spend an afternoon. I didn't have a very good time. Tuesday I stayed home all day and enjoyed myself. The children were out all day playing sandstore with Amelia and Theodore Olmsted. Wednesday I went to a lunch at Winifred Brill's. It was her birthday and she invited, beside myself, Clara Smith, Julia MacMasters, Katharine Abbott, Allison McKibbin, Edith Dabney, Harriet Armstrong, Margaret Routh and Nancy Wood. We had place-cards, each with a sentiment, supposed to be appropriate. mine was, "Those who love music are gentle and honest in their tempers." Rita's was "There is little of melancholy in her nature," which was a most appropriate sentiment. We had plenty of good things to eat. First came bouillon, and crackers, then veal chops, green peas, and Saratoga or French fried potatoes, I could not distinguish, any way we ate them with our fingers, then lettuce and cucumber salad, then ice-cream, and cake, candy and chocolate. The ice cream was very very good, and so was the cake. The girls used all their ingenuity to tease Margaret Routh about Rob, but she will not be teased. They made numerous references to the bobbing parties of last winter etc. I thought most of their remarks rather silly. After lunch we went into the parlor and managed to amuse ourselves with very little trouble until five o'clock. Winnie brought out some of the Elsie books and read us some very edifying extracts. How she would not play a piece for the company on Sunday although her father commanded her to do so, because it was not a hymn. "O Papa," said she with tears in her eyes, "I cannot break the Sabbath," and finally, having been compelled by her father to remain upon the piano stool until she was willing to obey him, at the end of two hours she fell upon the floor in a deep swoon. In her more cheerful moments a tear only trickled down her cheeks, while at times her form was shaken with sobs etc. etc. etc., a very tearful book, I sometimes wonder that she didn't turn into a fountain like Niobe of old.

Thursday Mrs. Martin came to spend the day. She told us all the news from the Park. One of her confidences to Mama was about Ned Parker. Mama told me afterward. Mrs. Todd told her that Ned was in the habit of swearing sometimes, and this troubled them both. Mrs. Todd didn't like to speak to Mrs. Parker about it, because her own boys are very far from reproach. Mrs. Martin thought about it, and worried for some time and finally she wrote a note to Mrs. T. asking if she might speak to Mrs. Parker about it for she thought she ought to know. Mrs. T. answered that she must do as she thought best. So finally she told Mrs. P. about it. Well, one night she Mrs. P. was in the kitchen alone, when Ned walked in. Her mind was so full of it that she could not keep still any longer. "Ned," said she, "are you ever profane?" She needed no answer, for she saw in his face that the accusation was true. "Yes," said he. And then she talked to him for over an hour. how he was her oldest son, and how, now that his father was dead he was the head of the family and what a responsibility rested upon his shoulders, so he quite melted down and became very penitent. After she went to bed, quite late in the night Ned came into her room; "Mother," said her, "you may be very sure I will never do so again."

Friday I was sick with tonsilitis, and continued so 'til Wed. Thurs. started in school again. Today I have such a bad cold that Mama has kept me in all day, so I could not go to school nor to Miss Mott's. I forgot to say that Saturday Morning Miss M. had one of her musicales, at ten o'clock. She intends to continue to have them on Saturday morning, until July, when she leaves for her summer vacation. Her room is on the sunny side of the building, and in the afternoon it would be unbearably hot as soon as the warm weather comes, which will be soon. We are having almost May weather now—have had hardly any rains this month. Only occasional blusters.

April 19, 1897, Monday Yesterday was Easter Sunday, and we all took dinner at Grandma's. In the morning Marjorie and I went to church and Sunday School. The church was beautifully decorated with lilies and palms about the pulpit, and it was very well filled. The music was good, too, although one number was very disappointing. Miss Coghlan started a Solo with the words "I know that my Redeemer liveth," and Marjorie and I thought she was about to sing that grand one of Handel's, from the Messiah, but it turned out to be a different, and very inferior one. At Sunday-school our large central room was crowded, holding beside the usual classes, the primary and infant classes and a large number of visitors. The infant class graduated, and came marching in, each with a large lily or rose, holding only the flower. As they passed by the platform each one handed the flower to a teacher standing there, who thrust them into a large cross of evergreen, which stood in the centre of the platform. When they had finished marching the cross was covered with great white Easter lilies, and I thought it a very pretty little scene.   The wind was frightfully high yesterday morning, amounting to almost a gale. As I was coming home it blew my skirt up almost over my head; Mama was certain we were having the "left-over" from a grand cyclone, but we have heard of none yet.

When all of our Bullard family get together at dinner we make just a proper table full—eleven, counting the baby. After dinner Auntie took some pictures of us with the camera that Uncle Charlie brought her. She finished the plates almost immediately after she took them, and showed Marjorie and me how it was done. We went into Uncle's Closet and shut the door. A few weeks ago, when I was there at dinner she took some photographs of us which turned out to be rather ridiculous. In this one I sat somewhat in front of Uncle, and it gave me the appearance of a giantess. In the first one I was leaning back in the chair, which put my head and shoulders in a different focus, and makes a rather bad appearance.

Yesterday Papa was talking to Grandma about Grandpa's old papers that were left, and she brought down three old wallets full of bills and papers. He made them of leather, in the old carriage shop. Grandma gave one to Papa, one to Uncle John, and one to Auntie.

Some time ago Grandma gave to me some facts about her father and my father's Grandfather and Grandmother Bullard.

Great-Grandpa Bullard came from Barre up to Swanton [Vermont], when he was quite a young man. He started with all his belongings tied up in a handkerchief, on a stick. At Bennington he stopped and laid a stone wall, for although of no especial trade, he could turn his hand to almost anything. Having finished that he went on to Swanton, and started in business by making kitchen chairs, and spinning wheels.

Grandma had two wheels made by him, and she says that they are back in the old wood house chamber on the farm, but Mama and Papa could not find any when they were there. After remaining a while in Swanton until he had earned a little money, and was started in the town, he went back to Barre, and married my great grandmother Achsah Hammond. She worked out for a woman by the name of Smith, until she was eighteen, and that, I think, was until she was married. Her mistress, when she left, gave her a dollar and a half, and she saved it carefully, not telling Grandpa anything about it. After they had been married some time she took her gift money and bought a short gown—it was during the time of the "petticoat and short gown"—but Grandpa was quite put out at such extravagance. He said the money would have helped to buy a cow. They lived in a little frame house, with no glass in the windows, but instead, she pasted up greased paper. When anything was going by which roused her curiosity to any great pitch and she was very anxious to look out, she would poke her finger through the paper, and peep through it.

Grandpa, beside being able to lay a stone wall, was also a kind of turner, and made chairs, tables, and other articles of farm-house furniture. They were very poor, and the furniture he made for the house, he was always ready to sell, for he could easily make more. Grandma says they some times had not a chair in the house. His mother, Sarah (Barbour) Bullard came to live with them after her husband died. Grandma can remember her as a little dried up old woman, over ninety, with black snapping eyes.

Grandma has often told me of great grandfather's wedding garments. His hair, which he wore in a queue, was tied with a great length of black satin ribbon; his coat was of green velvet, with brass buttons; black velvet breeches with silver buckles, and silk stockings—she says he was a very handsome man. I wonder where he got the money to spend on all this finery, when he was so poor. Great grandmother wore a white muslin dress, all embroidered with nun's work. Aunt Lucy has, or had, some remnants of her father's and mother's wedding finery. Great-grandfather used to say that his wife was the handsomest woman in town when she was young. Now about Grandpa. He and his brother George went into the business of carriage making together, when he was a young man. They remained in partner-ship for four or five years, and then Grandpa bought out his brother's share of the business, and carried it on alone from that time until he died. He had his shop on the farm, and carried on the two things at once. He was a very good financier and a very successful business man. Sent his children away to school, and always had a good comfortable home, getting most of their food from the farm. All the education he had was obtained at the village school, but he wrote a beautiful hand, and had an inclination toward good things; he was one of the most respected men of Swanton; I think he must have been something like the traditional village Squire. He was a very good singer and led the church choir for thirty years. After he was married and had children, they joined him. Aunt Mary, and Papa, I think, sang with him, and Grandma. He was very active in church affairs,—one of the leading members. He was clerk for twenty five or thirty years. He and Grandma joined the Congregational church at the same time. They had been married about three years. A year before he died he built a house in Swanton village, which was, and is yet, the finest house there. It is now occupied by Mr. Jewett. Grandma has a picture of it, and one of the old farm house, which his father built when Grandpa was a young man, before he was married. He and his father built it together, and my father and his brother and all of his sisters were born there. they moved into the village on August 1st, and a year after, on exactly the same day, he died. Grandpa Pratt, my grandmother Bullard's father, was born in Chesterfield, New Hampshire. His family came to Swanton Vt. when he was seven years old. He was one of ten children:—Polly, Susy, Cynthy, Betsy, John, Ezekiel, Serena, Allen, Maria, Sophia. They came from Chesterfield in an oxcart. From St. Albans to Swanton there were no roads, only marked trees. His father took up a small claim, and they lived as economically as possible which was very frugally in those days. Their fare was mostly bean porridge. On Sunday mornings they had shortcake. The children were never allowed to come to the table; they had their tin porringers, and brown bread.

After he grew to be a young man he worked with his father, but I don't know what he did. When he was twenty-four or five he married Rhoda Robinson. He bought a farm of forty acres, and lived in a little log house that was on the land when he bought it. they had a child born there that grew to be six weeks old and then died. Grandma was also born there. He soon built a new house, and his wife sewed and made bonnets, earning ten dollars, with which they bought shingles for their house. Grandma was two and a half years old when they moved into it. great grandfather Pratt was a good farmer, and a "good likely man as ever was," as Grandma says. His word was always as good as his deed. Her mother, his first wife, lived to be forty-four, and then died leaving Grandma a girl of eighteen, with a little baby sister to care for. He married as his second wife Milla Hoxsie, who was not such a peaceable woman, but I know very little about her. He died at the age of eighty three or four.

Saturday, April 24th, 1897 Monday and Tuesday of this week I stayed at home in the afternoon, sewing, studying and practicing. Wed. afternoon I went down to the Historical Library and stayed most of the afternoon. Thursday afternoon I went up to see Maud Steward, and from there I went on to Grandma's, to see if they had any of Joaquin Miller's poems. I found them deep in the midst of housecleaning, so only staid a few minutes. Grandma gave me a bundle of pieces for Betty, who is contemplating the project of making a patchwork quilt. Friday afternoon I staid to a meeting of the "Literary Academy," down at school. This is a very new society, organized only about a month ago, and composed of twenty pupils of the four classes at the High School. The names are proposed for membership by the faculty, and chosen from among those whom they consider to be the brightest members of the school. These names are voted on by the "seven charter members" who started the idea, and persons which are chosen, are invited into the Society. We meet every two weeks on Friday. Yesterday the subject for the afternoon was Joaquin Miller. . . .

Saturday, May 1, 1897 Yesterday was Arbor Day, and we always celebrate it with appropriate exercises at School. The Seniors each year present to the school a growing shrub or a young tree, and accompany it usually with speeches and recitations. But this year they turned aside from the established course, and presented a one-act farce, which they had written themselves.

Sunday, May 9, 1897 Last Saturday I was interrupted in my writing and did not have a chance to finish my record. Saturday morning just as I was putting the pillows into their clean cases, while I still had on my old working dress, Miss Cooper and Helen Plant came. Helen came, of course, to see Betty, and Miss Cooper ostensibly to bring her but she seemed to enjoy her visit. We had not been expecting any company to lunch, and Hilda was very indignant. However Mama managed to make out a very good lunch of tomato soup, and strawberries and cream.

Sunday was my birthday, and we had the whole family down to dinner for the first time since we have been in town. It was the first time that the baby has ever been inside of our house. I played on the piano for him and he seemed immensely pleased. Then I took him in my lap and he pounded with his little finger on the piano-keys. Every time I stopped he would take hold of my hand and pull it up to the key board. He is very cunning now. In a week or two he will be a year old, but he is very backward physically. He has never crept at all, nor tried to stand up. But he has a very strong little mind, and his brother Jack will soon find the palmy days of his sovereignty over when Dana is old enough to have his say. I had a very lovely birthday, and a very happy one, accompanied, of course, with many appropriate remarks about "sweet sixteen." Grandma and Papa compared notes about Grandma's visit to Elgin when I was five months old—about squaling and kicking, and how Grandma cried when she left after a long long visit never expecting to see me again, much less to sit down at my sixteenth birthday dinner-party.

Grandma and Uncle together gave me a very pretty rocking chair for my room, Mama gave me a very handsome brown leather belt, Marjorie a black satin hair ribbon, and Elizabeth a very fine pencil, with a compartment at one end for a lead pencil, and one at the other for a pen and an eraser. Best of all Papa gave Marjorie and me tickets to the Carreño Concert for Monday evening.

Monday afternoon Mama and I went down town to get our spring hats. Mine is the brown straw that I wore last summer trimmed over with brown ribbon and yellow dandelions. Marjories is her green straw trimmed with rosettes of green chiffon and pink and white clover blossoms. In the evening we went to the Concert which was, of course, magnificent. Madame Teresa Carreño, is without exception, the finest woman pianiste in the world, and some say the finest of either sex. The second number on her programme was Beethoven's Moonlight Sonata, which Miss Mott plays, and of which I have attempted to play the first two movements.

Miss M. says her teacher in Germany, Oscar Raif, used to say that he had never heard any musician who had a fine enough technique to play the third movement. But I am sure he would have been satisfied with Carreño's rendering of it. She played it so tremendously fast that one had hardly time to appreciate its full beauty, and it fairly made my hands ache to listen to her. Then she played five numbers of Chopin, which so enraptured Marjorie that she completely changed her opinion of his music. She and Mama have had a most unpleasant dislike to it, which they have heard mostly under my playing, which is indeed a very poor sample, for them to judge by. The little Etude in G Flat so delighted the audience that she was obliged to play it over again. Papa came up after us, and reached the place before the performance was over, so he walked up stairs into the upper hall and upstairs to the balcony door, and seeing that the hall was not nearly full he slipped in and heard the last three numbers, including the grand La Campanella, by Paganini-Lizt. In that number she gave the most wonderful tremolo, keeping it up for several moments so fast that we could see nothing but a whirr of fingers. . . .

Marjorie and Elizabeth have gone upstairs into a room in the third storey, and I have my room to myself, now, of which I am very glad.   this week has been so warm that we now have on all our summer clothes. The leaves are all coming out and everything is beautifully green. I forgot to mention that a week ago Friday Marg—and I went to a musicale at Miss May Strong's, given by her pupils. It was very interesting indeed. We were invited by Amelia Olmsted, and beside us, there were in our party Mrs. Olmsted, Theodore O. and Addie Faivelle, who is visiting Amelia. One of Mrs. Olmsted's friends seeing me with her two children asked if I was not her daughter because Theodore, who is ten, and I look so much alike, she said! I must not by any means forget to say that Uncle presented Marjorie with a bicycle week before last. It is a last years "Waverly". . . .

Saturday, May 23rd, 1897 To-day Marjorie and Betty intended to go out to the Park with the Olmsted's before Addie Faivelle goes away, to get wild flowers, and take their lunch. But last night and this morning were so rainy and wet that they had to give up their plan, and instead, they are to have supper at the Olmsted's. This morning Marj- and I washed the breakfast dishes and swept our rooms etc. We each have a room to take care of now. We are having our kitchen floor painted so we have to work down in the laundry, which is most inconvenient. A few minutes ago Amelia came over to have the children put on their rubbers and go over to the croquet grounds, as the sun has come out. So they have gone for the afternoon. Yesterday (Friday) was our High School Field-Day. Of course we girls all went, and had a most exciting time. When I got out to the Fair Grounds, where the exercises were to be held, they had already begun, and the other girls were all there. Laura, Mary Cutler, Louise Cochran, Helen Mairs, her cousin Clover Gardner, with Sam Mairs, & Mun Cochran, took dinner at the Davies's, and Helen Davis (!) chaperoned them. She spent the afternoon sitting on the fence around the race track . . . Mun Cochran entered the lists for the one mile bicycle race, and won. He had only been on the bike twice, and only practiced fast riding twice. He entered for the two mile race, too, and that was most exciting. They started out bravely, Mun soon getting ahead, and went around the first time and half way round the second mile safely, Mun keeping at the head. We kept blowing our horns and shouting every few minutes, to Louise, "He's ahead, he's ahead, Louise! He surely will win!" But she was too excited to appreciate our enthusiasm. She kept waving her hands at us and shouting frantically, "Let him alone, let him alone, O do let him alone!" Half way around the second mile there was a grand smash-up. One boy ran into another and those behind tumbled over them. But Mun was ahead and kept on, coming in first. This was declared a "foul," whatever that is, on account of the accident, and they tried it over again. This time, alas, Mun came in only second, and poor Louise was broken hearted. She was so disappointed that she could not keep the tears back.

Another very exciting event was the pole-vault. Fred Owens and Bob Wood were the only competitors, for the other two boys backed out. Fred and Bob had been practicing together every day, for some time, expecting to compete together against the other two. But when we found that they were against each other, we were very much interested. Mrs. Abbott took Katherine A. and Rita Armstrong out in the trap [carriage], and we could see Katharine standing up on the back seat, most deeply interested. Fred fell finally, and hurt his ankle, so Rob beat, going 7 ft 7 in. Then there was a grand hubbub among our crowd. Every one was shaking hands with Jane and Nancy, and with Margaret Routh, and when she came up she had a knot of the school colors to pin on his coat . . . Last Wed. I went up to Winifred's to make my dinner call. She was making "fudge" when I reached there, so she put me into the library with the last number of Life, and her Memory-Book. It is a blank-book, originally, and you paste in the menu-cards, and favors (if they are pasteable) clippings from the newspapers, anything you wish, to remind you of your good time. Nancy soon came in, then Margaret Routh, Edith Dabney, and Allison. We had a very nice gossipy time. Win brought in some lemonade and ginger cookies, which with our fudge, made most agreeable refreshments.

Sunday, May 30th, 1897 Today I have not stirred out of the house, for the weather is bleak, chilly, with a raw wind whistling around the corners and rattling the windows. This morning I wrote out a list of the family names in my Record Book, from which I intend to make an index. This afternoon Papa is asleep on the sofa down stairs, with Mama's old red shawl over him, while she and the children have gone up to see Grandma and Dana. So I have had the house to myself, and enjoyed it, too. Have been reading Elia's essays on "Valentine's Day," "My Relations," "Mrs. Battle's Opinions on Whist" etc. I bought essays of Elia and De Quincy's "Confessions of an Opium-Eater," last Monday, coming home from my music lesson. Wednesday afternoon we held a meeting of our C.A.R. [Children of the Revolution] Society, at Caroline Saunder's home . . . Allison read to us a sketch of the old Carpenter Hall, in Philadelphia, and Katherine played a piano piece for us. Then we had ice cream and cake, and adjourned to the side porch where we discussed current events until it was time to go. We talked about the Junior-Senior reception which is to come off next Friday evening. Caroline will go, of course, being a senior, and Franklyn Smith, a Junior, but the rest of us are barred out from the enchanted event. Harry Robbins, altho' a member of the Junior Class, starts for Europe, that same evening, June 4th. Mrs. Burbank is to chaperone his two sisters, Emily and Grace, and himself, on a European tour for this summer. Grace is away at Vassar, but they will meet her at New York.

Thursday we had a meeting of our Boards and my humble self was elected Lady High Manipulator of the Gavel. We had to adjourn (after) the election, on account of our Literary Academy which was to meet at half past one, and the members have to be there on time or they are punished by being called upon to make an extempore speech, which is dreadful. The topic for the afternoon was Lew Wallace [Civil War hero and writer] . . .Friday afternoon I spent at the Historical Library, and yesterday, for the most part, I cleaned my room, and then cut off my gray skirt to make it the right length for bicycle-riding, which brings it just to my boot-tops. 5:30 p.m.

Friday, June 4th, 1897 Thursday was a red-letter day in the annals of our Boadicean society. The '99 Boads gave a big spread to the '97 Boads, who graduate this year. We have been planning it for some time, for several reasons. In the first place, when we were in our Freshman year they gave us a big spread and initiated us into the Society. Then we thought we ought to do something for them before they leave us, because they have helped us in various ways, while we were still not quite acclimated to school ways. And now I feel quite assured that we have canceled all our debts. . . .

Sunday, June 13th, 1897 Today is the hottest day we have had this summer. There is scarcely a breath of air stirring, and there is a sultry feeling in it. About half an hour ago Uncle came down on his wheel and he and Papa went out together toward White Bear Lake, on the cycle path. Yesterday was very warm, and people came out in full summer attire. Last evening I went over to the Ramsey's and Laura and I did our Latin together. On our way Mr. Langford stopped us and took us up onto the porch. He gave part of one of Cicero's orations against Cataline, which he had learned when he was a boy, and of which he had not thought for nearly fifty years, until last night, he said. Then he showed us some of his puzzles, of which he is so very fond. . .

While we were getting our Latin, which was the 14th chap. of the 3rd book of Caesar's Gallia Bella, and rather difficult to translate, the Governor came in and sitting down near Laura asked her to open his boots, which evidently is her nightly task.

"You haven't any old grandfather about your house to have you open his boots," said he. "But you're not so very old Grandpa," said Laura. "Oh, Methusalem was older," he answered with a gruff old chuckle. "Mrs. Knox's mother is older than you," said she. "Mrs. Knox's mother forgot herself, or she would not have been so old," said he, and stalked off to bed. After a while Nita and Mrs. Furness came home, bringing Martha Gilfillian with them. We had some root beer and then I went home.

Friday we had our last meeting of the Literary Academy. The first thing on the program was a spread. The boys furnished the eatables, while each girl brought two saucers and two spoons, and Miss Pollock contributed her chafing dish. We had a Welsh rare-bit, which Miss Pollock made, crackers, bread and butter, pickles, radishes, and ice-cream and cake. The boys were rather inexperienced marketers, so we had about a pound of cheese, nearly half a pound of butter, and several crackers, cakes, and so forth, which all went to Pat, the janitor. The next thing on the program was the literary entertainment which was of a very light sort, for amusement rather than intellectual profit. . . .

Friday, June 18th, 1897 This morning I went down to school to get my report card and say good bye to school and teachers for the summer. Miss

88

Beach said that perhaps we should have her for a neighbor next year, as she is thinking of living with the Pollocks in the Sloane house, here on Sherman St. Last night Uncle and I went to the H.S. Commencement exercises at the People's Church. They were very interesting to me but I am afraid he was slightly bored. The essay which I liked the best was by Mabel Stoughton, entitled "The Art of Arts." It was about the Drama, and from the tone in which it was written, I half suspect that she intends to do something in that line herself. She is quite dramatic, and has a most bewitching voice and delivery, which would do wonders for her on the stage. She is one of the sweetest girls in the whole class of '97, and I hope she will make a name for herself. Her essay was the success of the evening. The applause was great, and she was called back again to bow. . . .

The Diary of Marjorie L. Bullard, 1897–1898

This is the second of two diaries kept by adolescent sisters living in St. Paul, Minnesota, just before the turn of the century. Marjorie Bullard, her older sister, Polly, and their younger sister, Betty, were the daughters of Will and Clara (Failing) Bullard. When she began her diary, which she kept from January 1897 until April 1898, Marjorie explained that she had decided to keep a diary because Polly was also keeping one.

Marjorie's diary entries describe family activities, school work, and visits with relatives and friends. Her diary also records a sad event in her family's history: the death of Grandmother Polly Pratt Bullard in March 1898. The final entry in this diary describes Marjorie's response to the beginning of the Spanish-American War that same spring. Examined alongside one another, the diaries of Polly and Marjorie Bullard provide fascinating glimpses into similarities and differences in the ways sisters kept diaries during the same period.

Jan. 1, 1897. As Polly is writing a diary I thought I would like to, so I am going to see if I can keep one this year. I have just been reading the "Schonberg-Cotta Family" and noticed that they called them Chronicles.

This morning we got up at about 9 o'clock which is rather late for us but as it was New Years we thought we might indulge a little.

After breakfast I sat down and read a little in "William Henry's Letters". This is the second time I have read it, and it is a good book to have in the family to read when ever you feel like it.

As Papa had a bad cold and Mama thought he had better not go out, he wanted Polly and me to go down to the store and get his bills to get ready to send away. But we all three went as Betty wished to go, and enjoyed our walk very much.

When we got back Mamma and Papa directed the envelopes and I pasted them by means of a cloth and a glass of water. Uncle John came while we were doing that and then we stopped.

At dinner we had a new kind of salad I can't remember the name of it. After reading a while when dinner was over I went out and took a walk with Betty. When we got back it soon got too dark to read so I helped Papa some more with the envelopes.

Mamma got the supper and Polly and I cleared the table. I have just now been helping Betty hunt for Mercy's present.

I suppose some superstitious people will think Friday a bad day to begin the year on.

Satur. Jan. 2 [1897]. Polly and I stayed in bed till Papa had gone to the store. While we were in bed we could hear Betty hurrying around to go with Papa down to the store. From there Fred Bowen was going to take her to Mercy's. We swept up our room and had a general cleaning. While we were putting on the pillow-cases I happened to run down to the mail-box and found a letter from Blanche. She said in the letter that she wanted us to come to lunch to-day. We asked what we should do and she said we could. Polly had wanted to go to the Historical Library and I to the Public Library. But we got ready and took the eleven o'clock car. Mrs. Bruce and Ellen were on the car when we got on. When we got to Blanche's we went up to her room and talked until dinner-time. After dinner we went for a walk. We went down to the grocery-store and I bought a bag of Mamma's favorite candy (old fashioned peppermint) for her. When we went back the boys were skating on a pond out in the Park. Just as we were going out of the grocery-door we met Eloise and she wanted me to come and see her very much but as I had not time I could not.

We took the quarter-after-four car and reached home a little after five. Mamma had been to the library and brought back a book for me called "Polly; a New-fashioned Girl." I read it about half through in that one night.

I forgot to say that just before we started for the Park, Betty came home, for as Fred had a bad throat he could not come after her.

I am rather sorry that to-morrow is our last holiday.

Thurs. Jan. 7 [1897]. We went to school this morning at the usual time. We have to keep a report of our disorders, and I had two. I also had two in the afternoon.

Yesterday afternoon Mr. Bond came and gave us a writing lesson. He put a verse on the board from Whittier.

Yesterday morning there were about five or six pupils tardy, and these same ones had been tardy many times before. Miss Witt told them that they should not go home until she told them to. So they stayed all the noon, until Miss Witt came again.

When I got home from school this afternoon I had some bread and honey and read the "Youths Companion".

Mon. Jan. 25 [1897]. It has been very cold to-day the temperature, being when Papa went down town about 28 below zero.

This morning we had an examination in arithmetic. Amelia Olmsted and I got through a little sooner than the rest so we get home earlier.

This afternoon Virginia Russell was absent so Mr. Baker had Amelia play, and I kept time for her. This was at exercise time. When she had stopped playing Mr. Baker let us go down and visit the kindergarten for a short time. Mr. Baker asked me to learn to play a march, which I shall begin to do soon. After coming home from School I didn't do much but read which I always do. . . .

April 1 [1897]. This is April's Fool Day. Hilda fooled me as soon as I got down stairs. she called me to the window and then said "April Fool"! As Mrs. Martin was coming out we had to clean our room very nicely. After Mamma had fried the croquetts Polly and I dusted the parlor and dining-room. Polly had a sore throat so I had to go down town to get the Lady-fingers.

We started a sand-store yesterday in our back yard. By "we" I mean Amelia, Theodore, Betty and me. A little boy named Orley Reynolds gave us all his sand.

When I got home from town I found we had made thirty pins already. Mrs. Martin came soon. After dinner she sat and talked all about the people there, and I wish now that I had staid [sic] in all the afternoon and listened to her. I just love Mrs. Martin and I wish she could come here every Saturday.

May 3 [1897]. This evening we went to hear Madame Teresa Carreno play on the piano at the Peoples Church on Pleasant Avenue. She played perfectly beautifully . . . I believe I liked the Etude best. It was short but sweet. She played it twice as she was encored. One that I liked best was the one by Beethoven. There is something so pathetic about him. . . .

June 21 [1897]. I have had a perfectly fine time to-day. A meeting of the C.A.R. (Children of the Revolution) was held at Mrs. T. T. Smith's out in the country, & Mrs. Smith invited me. We took the Mississippi & West St., Paul car and rode to the end of the line. There Mr Smith had provided horses & carriages to take us out.

We followed the road on which the car-line was, until we came to a little road that runs right through the woods. Clara Smith had stuck flags on a tree at the beginning of this road, so that the ones who rode on bicycles could tell where to turn. This road winds in and out, and along the edges are evergreen trees which Mr. Smith himself planted. We followed this road and it leads up in front of the Smith's house. When we got there, several had arrived before us.

The meeting was held out on the lawn. After the meeting we had our supper out there too. When supper was over several of the girls & boys played some games, but as I did not know many, I did not.

Lucia took me up to the barn, which is 100 ft. x 50 ft. Just before going home many of the girls that have memory books, went around hunting for things to put in them. I decided that I would get a memory book so I brought an oak-leaf, ~~and a little piece~~ a wisp of hay, a bit of asparagus and a little piece of an evergreen. Clara Lucia drove us down to the car. When we were almost there the [street]car started, so we rode around the Bluff Road.

Franklin was also driving some people down, too so we followed him. The horse was quite anxious to get home, & acted quite bad. Before we started home Mr. Smith gave each girl a beautiful rose. We did not get home 'til about 8:30.

Dec. 24, [18]97. This morning we did up our presents and got things all ready for to-morrow.

To-night we Polly, Betty and I went down to the church to an entertainment we were going to have. When we had got to Seventh St. Dr. Egbert came along behind us and he took my hand and held it nearly all the way down. When we our class, were at his house one evening he asked us why Michael Angelo's "Moses" had horns. I found it out in one of Mamma's art Books and told him. It is this: Michael Angelo had an edition of the bible called the "Vulgate". In it, when Moses came down from the mountain, it said "And Moses knew not that his face was horned," while in our Bible it says "And Moses knew not that the skin of his face shone."

We went right down to our Sunday-school room, and the girls had brought our present to Mrs. Sanford in a box. When she came, she of course opened it and found a bust of Beethoven. She was very much delighted with it and invited us to her house Friday afternoon and she wants each one to tell something about Beethoven.

By-and-by when the children were all in the Sunday-school room

Mr. Dyer called the name of each class and they passed up in to the church one by one.

we sat near the back of the room and Mr. Bigelow's class was behind us. The carols were sung and when it came the time to take up the contributions all of our class went up. We had to sing something so went right into the choir-loft. Pretty soon Lilias Joy got up and spoke her piece. At the end of each verse the rest of the class sang "Glory to God in the highest, on earth peace, goodwill to man." We were supposed to sound like the angels which the shepherd boy heard. After that we went down and pretty soon Mother Goose came running down one of the aisles. She was Louise Jewett all dressed up. She said some funny things and the children were almost crazy. Before she left us she gave each one of the primary department a cradle to the girls, and a shed of candy to the boys. And the rest were given a box of candy.

It was over soon and we went home. We hung up our stockings filled them with presents and soon went to bed very sleepy.

Dec. 25 [1897]. "Christmas Day." Early this morning Betty called out to me, "Merry Christmas." I suppose she thought she had waked me up but she was mistaken. We dressed very quickly and I went down to Polly's and Betty's room. They had to get several things out of Emma's room that were too large to take down the night before. At last when all was ready we went down what should we see but three chairs which looked like those of Papa, Mamma, and Baby Bear's. There was one which we all gave to Papa, one that Uncle gave to Papa and Mamma and one from Mamma to me. It is a lovely red chair and just right fore me, and Papa likes it better than his own. Under my stocking was a big book filled with 19 of Mozart's Sonatas from Papa, "The Last Days of Pompei" from Polly and a picture with a large frame from Kate. Also there was some blue flannel for a dressing-jacket from Mamma, and in my stocking was a little glove buttoner from Betty. Mamma thought the irons which I gave her were fine, and she says she shall want to use them right away. The bag that Polly and I gave Betty she likes very much and goes around carrying it on her arm all the time.

When we were having breakfast Amelia and Theodore came over and to bring me a little knife. They had to carry a lot of things around to people living on the "hill". When we had washed the dishes we admired our presents and ate candy. About twelve o'clock Betty and I walked up to Grandma's. When we were near to the house we peeked in at the window but did not much of the tree which was in the parlor. Dana is getting just as cunning now, and he can walk quite well. When we were all up there dinner was ready. The food was very good except that there was no gravy. The plum-pudding came on and we had great fun about Uncle. Before he had said that his stomach was full but afterwards he said that it was all right.

We had the tree right after dinner and it was lovely. We all had lovely presents and especially Grandma. Her lap was full and she kept saying, "I have so many more presents than the rest of you. Not very long after we went home and it seemed as it always does very lonesome to get home with the house all dark.

It has been altogether a very happy Christmas day.

March 16, [18]98. It has been more than two months since I last wrote in here and to-day I have something much sadder to write about than last time.

Last Friday night Mamma was going to one of Dr. Burton's lectures, and instead of going right to the lecture went to Grandma's for a while. Polly was to follow after with Mrs. Olmsted. When she got up there Grandma was very sick with a sore throat. She was so sick that Mamma thought she had better stay all night but they (Auntie & Uncle Charlie) said not. Mamma could not find anyone to go with so rode way around on the cars.

Saturday Grandma seemed to be a little easier but the doctor was very much afraid she was going to have pneumonia. Sunday morning Mamma went up to find her worse. A trained nurse was sent for and arrived in the afternoon. Mamma staid nearly all day and Papa went up in the afternoon. Grandma grew worse and worse until at one o'clock she died. Papa came home then and told us. It seemed as if I did not go to sleep that night for about an hour.

The next day Mamma was up there nearly all day and Polly & I stayed home. I could not help thinking of Uncle down in Mexico. He has been gone about six weeks and as he is traveling around all the time and writes very few letters of course we could not sent a telegram to him. Think how he will feel when he gets home!

Yesterday soon after dinner a carriage came after us to take us to the funeral. It was the first one that any of us children had been to. We went up the back way to avoid people at Grandma's. Of course all the family was to stay upstairs so we went into Auntie's room. Auntie wanted us all to see the flowers on the coffin so we went down. They surely looked beautiful and were sent by a great many friends. When the minister Mr Sinclair came we were upstairs stood out in hall and could hear as well as those down-stairs. It was a very short service, and soon the coffin was carried out and we went on our way to the cemetery. There were only five carriages and all of our family rode in one. The cemetery was near Como and very beautiful. There is a beautiful little chapel there filled with flowers. The coffin was put in there. We all stood around while the minister said a short prayer. Then we rode home. It was so much nicer to put the coffin in the chapel than to see it put into the vault as they did afterwards for when Uncle comes home it will be carried to Swanton and be buried next to Grandpa.

It seemed as if Grandma had an almost an ideal way of dying for until she was given morphine she had full control of all her senses and was remarkably healthy for her age. She was 81 almost 82.

How lonesome it will be for Auntie having lived with Grandma all these years!

April 24 [1898]. Everything now is war, war, war. The newspapers are full of it, and they can not always be relied upon. Ever since the Maine disaster we have thought that something was going to happen. The Senate has had a terrible time deciding what to do and at last on Tuesday April 19, Congress declared war. It is queer that the Revolutionary War began on the same month and day.

The night before April 19, the newspaper said that he soldiers from Ft. Snelling were going to march through the city and go by railroad to Mobile as they wanted to have troops all along the southern coast so that if the Spainiards attacked it they would be ready. Papa said we might be excused from school and go down to his store to see them march. The next morning Mamma wrote Polly and me each an excuse. But when we got down to the High School we found that the soldiers were not going to march through the city but take the train at Ft. Snelling. I went to school earlier than Polly so when I heard that I thought of course we could not see them. But after school had begun Polly came into the room and told me that we were going out to the fort and to get my things on. This I did leaving my books on a shelf in Miss Hookers room expecting of course to be back before school was out. Polly had to get the excuses signed by Mr. Smith so I waited down in the hall. When she came back she said that Mr. Smith told her that she need not have brought them because they would be all right tomorrow. Just before we went we saw Catherine Abbott coming into school. We called her, told her all about it, and she went with us. Polly had before told Halstead Moody so he joined the party. Outside we met Mun Cochran and he went with us. We all went down to take the Ft. Snelling car and found it full of High School boys yelling all the yells they could think of, and waving flags. They had all skipped of course. It took us I should say about half an hour to get there. When we started we heard that they were going at nine, but on reaching the fort every-body said at 11:15. So we walked up and down the streets waiting. Meanwhile the boys had been parading around in front of the officer's houses yelling and singing. At last they

went into the barracks and found a great many old things that the soldiers had left such as, old hats, coats, pants, bullets, cartridges and so
forth. They dressed up in these acting like wild Indians. When it was time
we went down to the train only to find that it was not coming till 1:30.
Well, to make a long story short we waited till the train did come. Then
the soldiers began to march down a road leading from the fort. They
looked very well and when they were all in the train moved along and we
hurried for the electric car. On reaching home at 2:00 we found Mamma
had been worrying and that it was so late we could not go after our
books, so I went over to Amelia's and got nearly all of mine.

The Diary of Elspeth Close, 1918

Elspeth Close was a fourteen-year-old living in Iowa City, Iowa,
when she began keeping her one-year diary on January 1, 1918.
She wrote daily entries throughout the year while completing her
freshman year and beginning her second year at Iowa City High
School. She lived with her parents, S. L. and Elena (MacFarland)
Close, and her younger brother, Chalmer.

Elspeth's diary, a National Diary with a maroon cloth cover,
measures approximately four by seven inches, with twenty-two
lines per page. On the lefthand inside cover page is a "Counting-
House Calendar for 1918" with several dates circled. These dates,
which correspond to references to visits from "grandma" or "St.
Nicholas" in Elspeth's diary, may have been her way of encoding
menstrual periods. Her desire to keep her diary private is reflected
in a handwritten request at the top of one of its pages: "Whoever
finds this book please return it to the address below without reading the contents." The entries describe not only activities with
family and friends but also school work, friendships, and adolescent crushes. Several diary entries during November 1918 describe
events, such as the signing of the armistice and the return home of
troops, that marked the end of World War I.

In 1984 Eleanor R. and J. Merle Trummel of Iowa City
donated Elspeth Close's diary to the State Historical Society of
Iowa. In response to my letter asking how they had acquired the
diary, Eleanor Trummel explained: "Several years ago my husband
and I attended an estate auction here in Iowa City, where we purchased a box of books which happened to include the diary. We

knew nothing of the family and had no personal interest in the diary, except to read it to learn what we could of the time period it covered. We thought it would be a shame to just toss it in the trash, so, after having it around for several years, in October 1984 we donated it to the State Historical Society Library with no strings attached."

Tuesday, Jan. 1, 1918. Snowy and cold. We had a late dinner and had one of our own hens. At about four o'clock Chal & I went over to Margaret Lucas's to slide. M. and I went to Pattersons to get Loretta Miller and then I went home at six. After reading "The Deerslayer" we had prayer meeting. . . .

Saturday, Jan. 5, 1918. My teeth hurt terribly and my gland is swollen. I wonder if I am getting mumps. I played paper dolls and read all day. I'm afraid I'll never see Flossie, my kitten again because Daddy put her out doors in the snow. We have called her to no avail. Mother has promised us another one if she doesn't reappear.

Sunday, Jan. 6, 1918. The kitten came back this morning. I read and played paper dolls today. My toothache is better and I think I can go to school tomorrow. It snowed all day today and drifted a great deal. Twelfth night tonight and we burned our Christmas greens. Mother read Riley to us. . . .

Tuesday, Jan. 8, 1918. I went to school today and saw Zip twice and Florence three times. Florence has been acting awfully queer lately. I took my lunch today but came home and found nobody home and had to eat on the porch. I almost froze. Janet got mad at me today—I should worry! Chalmer sprained his ankle and I read to him. Winona and I had a heart to heart talk. I believe someone knows about our dippiness. We are in the intricacies of mystery! . . .

Tuesday, Jan. 15, 1918. I saw Zip twice in school today. He was simply adorable and he kept looking at me! Janet is just about as bad as usual. Winona came over after school and we had loads of fun. She stayed for supper and we had suet pudding. Um-yum. . . .

Thursday, Jan. 17, 1918. There was a coal shortage at school today and we only had ten minute periods in the morning. I am exempt from all tests and I have chosen Latin as I think that will be easiest. Chalmer read this book today and told Mother some of the things in it. I keep it locked up now. We have vacation next week. Glory! I saw "It" today. My St. Nicholas came today. . . .

Tuesday, Jan. 22, 1918. Took my Latin exam this afternoon and got thru fairly well. Went with the boys to see Doug Fairbanks in "The Modern Musketeer." It was awfully good! He impersonates a Modern D'artagnan and played with Margery Daw. I love them both—as Movie stars I mean. I walked home with Bob Larimer afterwards. We are going to have a Bob party I think in Walter Trumpp's Bob. . . .

Friday, Feb. 1, 1918. This is the first of a new month and I have written faithfully every day all the last month. I was very cold today and I staid in except to go to Smith's Grocery. I started pasting in my scrap book this afternoon. W. Hurley and Fred Sutz were buried here today. Tomorrow I will learn whether there will be school next week or not. Daddy came home today and brot me the darlingest underwaists.

Saturday, Feb. 2, 1918. Oh! Such a wonderful day! Mother was sick from too much work. In the afternoon at 4:30 I got the car for Dotty's taking my Macaroni. I came in on the 7:15 car and with Trudy I went to the game with O.R. I met Chalmer and Margaret H. there and we witnessed the most wonderful game that I ever expect to see. Zip had grippe and stuck it out till the latter part of the last quarter but then had to go out. Of course we beat, 26 to 10. . . .

Tuesday, Feb. 19, 1918. School today. It has turned very cold and at this moment I am hugging the fire in my room. I named it today "The Blue Paradise." Winona doesn't like Margaret and I am getting to like her less and less. She is so snippy and sarcastic. I wish Toots was here, or Wini W. I got a book today . . . "Two Little Women on a Holiday" by Caroline Wells. It is very good as far as I have gone in it. I will read it in bed I expect.

Wednesday, Feb. 20, 1918. I finished that book last night and enjoyed it very much. It is so cold. My room is freezing. I saw Zip today and I imagined some <u>nutty</u> things. Winona and I have had some <u>very</u> personal talks lately. I think she is a lovely friend. Gym tomorrow! I do wish I could make baskets. I am afraid that I'll never be much of anything and I do <u>so</u> much want to be. . . .

Saturday, Feb. 23, 1918. This afternoon Margaret Howell came over and we had <u>loads</u> of fun. We made a fairy palace on the rockery and used my little doll as a Princess. We made a lake for her to swim in and it looks lovely. It has been a <u>wonderful</u> day and there is a lovely moon tonight. I wish I could take a walk with "somebody". . . .

Friday, Mar. 1, 1918. Oh! Bliss! I went to my first mixer tonight. It was perfectly <u>great</u>! 'Nona telephoned after supper and asked me to stay all night with her. She didn't go to the game but I went with Alma Payne and we sat down stairs. One time Zip—oh beloved—fell against the people just below me and I know if I had been there I would have "Obeyed that Impulse" and disgraced myself for life. I danced with lots of girls and had a <u>wonderful</u> time! Oh adored one! . . .

Sunday, Mar. 3, 1918. I saw M. Howell at S.S. today and she told me that she had seen Zip and Pat M. and Cy Hotz on the street down town yesterday and they were all smoking—cigarettes! I cried about it in church all the time. We all went up to Strain's for dinner then at 3:00 Marge and I went to Edwin's to take care of him. Margery had to go at 5:00 but I staid to super. Mrs. Strain is here tonight. There was a new boy in the choir who is <u>spivvy</u> looking! He looked at me all the time!

Monday, Mar. 4, 1918. I saw the object of my devotions in school today. 'Nona and I went down town today and looked up Lineage at the Library but didn't find anything. I cut my finger tonight so it is rather hard to write. Gwendolyn P. and Lyle B. are engaged! They are <u>so</u> young. I hope it proves satisfactory and that they are happy. My sign is MZE

Tuesday, Mar. 5, 1918. I wrote a letter to Hope to day and sent it. We ate our lunch out of doors today as it was so lovely. Alpha [Club] today! It was very good. I think it was the best. Edith Buck super-intended it. I started "Barbara Worth" by H. Bell Wright. Miss Golden telephoned today and said that I might be in the Advanced English Class! I am so glad altho I don't see how I am going to manage it! . . .

Wednesday, Mar. 13, 1918. Zip bumped into me today in the hall! In the Chicago Tribune it said that he was the most noted boy in the state of Iowa! And the best all-around athletic. Also he is on the all-state basketball team! My hero! We had assembly today. Mr. Rubsell talked first, and then it was turned over to a mass meeting. Mr. Brigham made a speech and Barny Dondore. After school I went down town with 'Nona and then when I got home I studied. My St. Nick came today.

Thursday, Mar. 14, 1918. We are going to win the Championship I <u>know</u>! I saw Zip today and he was so near. I guess Janet is all right again.

Poor <u>simp</u>. If she thinks I'll ever be her friend again she's <u>very</u> much mistaken! We got our Red & White today. I studied all afternoon and evening. . . .

Monday, Mar. 18 [1918]. My <u>new</u> sign MZEK I saw Zip this morning in school. Gee! But he's plucky! All the boys were red eyed—Slimek seemed to take it the hardest. After school M. Frances & I went to Houstons to practise our play. Afterwards we went downtown. We were by Racines Cigar Store when we met Zip, Pat and Bob Leinbough! The two former were smoking! They grinned when they saw us and then they turned around and followed us clear up to Bennison's! I just know Zip knows me! I hope so! Mrs. Gregory is here taking care of us.

Friday, Mar. 22, 1918. I went downtown this noon and had the picture taken of we Y.W.C.A. girls. I hope its good. Marie McGwire spoke to me this afternoon and Lyle B. smiled! I wonder if they know? Edith and her friend Maude Price are here now and is going to stay all night. Some <u>spivvy</u> times! Helen is just dippy! Maude has gone to the Junior Prom with "Bob"—She looked darling! . . .

Thursday, Apr. 4, 1918. Zip had his <u>wonderful</u> sweater on today. Oh! I think he must be so proud to have one with 3 stripes and a <u>star</u>! Oh! Just think how much it will mean to him later! I went up to 'Nona's after school and played a while. Bruce was here to supper again tonight and after supper I tried to learn to throw. Chalmer hit me in the head with a clod and knocked me unconscious. It was a wonder I didn't let out more than I did!

Friday, Apr. 5 [1918]. After school today I got my B.B. picture. It is simply wonderful of all the boys, especially Zip. When I showed the picture to Mother she said about Shim "he's sweet! But such a young boy!" and about Shorty, "I like him!" and about Hay, "He looks like a bear" and about "My own" "His ears!" I don't care he wouldn't look a bit like himself without them! He is perfect! (To me) "Distance lends enchantment" I wonder if I'll ever know anything to make me love him less?! No! Never! I found Zip's signature today in a lot of paper torn up on the desk in Miss Golden's room. There's a lot more but can't figure out.

Saturday, Apr. 6, 1918. Helped Mother in the morning. At one o'clock went to see Dr. Morrow. He looks fine in his soldier suit. He took my wires [braces] off never to be put on again! After that I went to the Library and met 'Nona and we went together to see Dustin Farnum in "The Spy." It was dreadful! He was tortured by being stretched! Oh! I never saw anything so terrible! Pete saw right behind us and they played the hymn America. I stood up and most of those lazy nutts wouldn't. I said to him "stand up, you big nut" and he did. You ought to have seen his face in the awful part! . . .

Friday, Apr. 12, 1918. Zip spoke to me in School today—smiled and spoke! I smiled but didn't speak. I know he knows me now. Had my floor painted today and am going to move in tomorrow maybe. Bruce came over in the afternoon and my St. Nicholas came—I am so happy! . . .

Wednesday, Apr. 17, 1918. I was just behind Zip in school today and turning dizzy I stepped on his heel. I said, "Oh, pardon me" and he turned around & said, "Oh, hello" and I said, "hello"—I don't suppose I should have. This noon 'Nona & I were going to school and Adams came along in his car full of fellows. They all looked at us and laughed! I wonder why? Went to the dentist after school. After supper went over and visited with Mrs. Horn. In the press in telling about assembly yesterday it spells Zip's name, "George Close" ! . . .

Monday, Apr. 22, 1918. Saw him in school today but was afraid to look at him. I don't know why? 'Nona came over after school today to stay all night. We got all "bunged" up playing football and we yelled so that anyone a mile off could have heard us. I don't like to feel myself getting old and prim—I'd like to have a kid romp every once in a while. We played and sang a lot. 'Nona can play wonderfully! I wish I could! Got E in an English test. . . .

Friday, May 10 [1918]. Zip bumped into me—or at least his elbow did—in the hall today. He said, "Pardon me" and I said, "Sure." Some doings. This afternoon we went on a picnic. Mary H., Ruth, 'Nona, Peggy, Pearl P., Mildred C., Margaret G., Lucile R., Alma P., Miss McRaith, etc. There were 13 in all. I took cookies and we went to the park. Played base-ball most of the time. While we were out there a whole gang of W. Liberty kids came out and we yelled all our school yells while all they could do was stick out their tongues! When I got home at 8:00 I cried & cried. I don't know why but oh! How I cried! I love him so—it isn't fair that I shouldn't know him— . . .

Monday, May 20, 1918. Today is my birthday. Zip skipped school and 'Nona saw him riding around in Adams' car. 'Nona gave me the sweetest I.C.H.S. pin; Grandmother $1.00; Daddy $3.00; Mother a hat. Which will have to be exchanged as it is too small; Aunt Mildred, a hairribbon; Chalmer hairribbon and Kingsley a box of stationary. Mother bought me some music too but left them somewhere. 'Nona has a dreadful cold and I hope it isn't bad tomorrow. Had angel food cake and ice cream with chicken, strawberries, etc. for supper. Mrs. Gregory is here now as the folks are away. . . .

Thursday, June 6, 1918. I am writing this by candle light as the power is off. Washed my hair and went to commencement. Saw Zip! He looked so nice but he was awful naughty. He sat next to Marg Bennison and they were so "fussy"—It made me tired. The George O'Brien cup was presented to "no other than George Kloosbetter" known as "Zip"—Oh, I was so glad! He stood up and bowed his thanks but was very bashful. They clapped more for him than for any one when he got his diploma. Saw him afterwards—smoking!

Friday, June 7, 1918. Went for my report card with 'Nona. Got an average of 3 Es and 2 Gs. Went down to see the river which is flooded way up to within 2 inches of the top of the park bridge and they are expecting it to wash out any minute now. Butler's bridge has gone and the Coralville dam is 1/4 gone. Walked around and saw no one in particular. Came home and went back almost immediately to meet Mother and see Forbes Robertson in "Masks and Faces." It was an all-star cast and just wonderful! Doris found her watch today!!!!

Saturday, June 8, 1918. Several interesting incidents today. In the first place there was an 85% eclipse of the sun from 5:22 to 7:23. In the second place the water washed the ice houses away including all our summer supply of ice! Got a thrift stamp today and brot Frances & Aunt France home with me to stay from 6 to 9. Got some new books at the library called "The Spirit of the School" and "Cange Signals" both by R.H. Barbour. Took care of Billy for an hour and a half. . . .

Tuesday, June 18, 1918. Helped Mother in the morning. Finished the soldier scrapbook and made my memory book this afternoon—I put all the things I've been hordeing up ever since I started in school in and made quite a book. Mailed those letters and went to Horn's after supper where Helen D & Aleitha asked me to stay all night. So I am going to sleep with Helen tonight. It was very cool today and is tonight. I want him <u>so</u> badly— . . .

Thursday, July 4, 1918. A glorious Fourth! Found a 4 leaf clover. We woke up at 6:00 this morning and got up and shot off just piles of firecrackers and salutes and torpedoes, snakes, sun of a guns, etc. Frances &

I took a walk at about 3:00 and came back about 5:00. Mrs. & Mr. Schafer with Charles, Mrs. Grain with Bruce and Margery and Aunt Franc came later and we had a picnic supper in the yard. Just as we were finishing it began to rain and we had our night fireworks nevertheless with the addition of Wilma & Robert E. The folks had just gone at 11:00 and Margery is here for night. . . .

Thursday, July 18, 1918. Drew and helped Mother all morning. Went down town at noon and with Frances went to see Cousin George. Went to Margery's from there and staid all afternoon. Came home with Frances who staid all evening. We drew. The Allies have started a great offensive and the Yankees have had wonderful victories. . . .

Wednesday, July 31, 1918. Frances came over at ten and weeded in the garden until after lunch when we went up in the barn. Mother & Chalmer & Kingsley went to a movie and staid to supper at Aunt Franc's. Frances & I fixed up a studio in the barn and we scrubbed the floor & everything. Frances & I got supper for ourselves at 8:30 after taking a bath to remove the lice borrowed from the chickens! Went to bed before anything exciting happened. . . .

Friday, Sept. 6, 1918. Frances and Aunt Franc are going to live at Horn's all winter! I went to Schedule this morning and it seemed to wonderful to be back in school again. Oh, <u>football</u>! I can hardly wait. Mother has said she thot I might go to the mixer. Oh, I'll try to be good so I may. Made a darling fairy palace out in the yard this afternoon. Cleaned my room today and it looks lovely! Oh, <u>Zip</u>!!! . . .

Monday, Sept. 9, 1918. Went to school this morning with Frances. Had 10 minutes for each period and 2 assemblies. In the first one Mr. Beck explained things to the new kids and in the 2nd Mr. Voight gave a speech about athletics. He said he had great hopes for a great team in football! He said just the opposite a year ago. ~~Played~~ Frances and I went down town to get our books and some ice cream when school was over. We went thru the hospital yard and saw Florence—I spoke to her and she ditto—and then went past Racines and saw Zip!!! . . .

Tuesday, Sept. 24, 1918. I took my physical examination today and weigh 99 lbs and am 5 feet 2 inches tall. I can grip 62 with my left hand and 63 with my right. Got supper and did all the dishes for Mother today. Mailed a long letter to Mac and received one from Isabel. Am going to write a letter to Grace now. . . .

Monday, Sept. 30, 1918. After supper went to see Douglas Fairbanks in "Say, Young Fellows" with the family and Aunt Franc and Frances. I sat with Frances and the place was so crowded—Two soldiers sat beside me. Of course I was greatly excited (?). Frances and I walked home together.

Tuesday, Oct. 1, 1918. University began today. After school I went up to Mrs. Strains. Margery and I watched the Mechanics drilling but I didn't see Zip. Frances H. and I went to a church supper—Mother and her mother were there—and had lots of fun! We two walked home alone thru town at about 8:00 o'clock. We went past Racine's twice and he was in there!! He looked <u>so darling</u>!! Oh, I am so silly? If I weren't I might be much more popular. . . .

Monday, Oct. 7, 1918. Frances was sick this morning. They don't know whether its influenza or not. I read and drew all day—had a fire in my room. Grandmother came over after supper and spoke of the influenza being invented and spread by Germany. Mother seemed quite surprised but I have thot so all along. Thats why I don't want to get it. I don't want to be given any inconvenience by their d—m propaganda!

Tuesday, Oct. 8, 1918. Frances is a little better this morning. Cut out and set up a stage by for the play "The Wild Swans" which I sent to Frances this afternoon. Mrs. Burnett came for supper tonight. She is a little German lady but just as sweet as she can be. She has a brother in the German army, but she has a very strong feeling against the Kaiser as any right minded person should have! She brot her zither and played for us. . . .

Sunday, Oct. 13,1918. Stayed in bed all day tho I'm not sick. Finished "The House of the Seven Gables" by Hawthorne which I began Friday. Read, played in my doll-house and made a stage. The news at the war is that the Kaiser has accepted Pres. Wilson's peace terms!!!!!!! It may not be true, but oh, I <u>hope</u> so!

Monday, Oct. 14, 1918. Got up this morning because I didn't have any more sore throat. My St. Nicholas came today. Played in my doll-house, lounged luxuriously and rode my bicycle. It was a perfect day today. I only hope there are many such. . . .

Monday, Oct. 21, 1918. Frances & I walked down town this afternoon for our bikes. After riding around in the North end of town for a while we went down past the armory and across the Iowa Avenue bridge. A couple of boys met us and tried to stop us but we paid no attention. We got into trouble with the guards going back and found that we weren't supposed to go in there without a pass! Met Wilder and shook hands with him. He looks so nice in his sailor suit! Went to see 'Nona.

Tuesday, Oct. 22, 1918. It wasn't a very nice day today. I didn't do much but play in my doll house and draw all day. I was just thinking how silly I've been and I'm going to try to turn over a new leaf. . . .

Sunday, Oct. 27, 1918. We all went to Grand Mother's for dinner today. Afer doing the dishes Helen, Alice and I went for a walk. We went across the river and back across the Iowa Av. Bridge. As we walked past the armory there were about a thousand boys who yelled, whistled and did everything to attract ~~the~~ our attention. We paid nothing to them and after difficulties with guards we managed to get thru. It is much colder today and rained all last night. Robert Larimer has been very sick with influenza. He has been taking 60 gr. of asperine every day for 7 days! . . .

Wednesday, Nov. 6, 1918. We had a peach of an assembly this morning. First Miss Buckner gave a talk on "Victory Girls and Boys." Then "Bunny" Wassam gave a talk on the same. Then the rest was about football. Dick Horrabin, our leader, called Cy Hotz "another Zip Kloos," and asked him for a speech! I didn't know Cy was on the team! He plays right half-back!!! Shim came to school this afternoon. He's a military police in the S.A.T.C.

Thursday, Nov. 7, 1918. The war is over! Hip! Hip! Hooray! Germany has signed an armistice to an unconditional surrender!!!!!! I can't realize it. I'm putting the article in the paper in my memory book. I am appointed sergeant of the Junior Loyalty League. It rained today but shows signs of clearing up tonight. The big game is tomorrow afternoon. We start school at 8:30 tomorrow morning and have all periods in the morning! <u>I'm so excited</u>!!!!!!!! My grandma's here again. . . .

Monday, Nov. 11, 1918. This morning at 3:00 the whistles all blew and we heard that Germany had agreed to all the terms!!!!!! <u>Think</u> what that means! Went to school and all we ~~we~~ had was a fifteen minute assembly in which we sang, "Over There," "If he can fight like he can love," "Oh, How I hate to get up in the morning," "Mr. Zip," and others including, of course, "America" and "The Star Spangled Banner." And yell—oh how we <u>did yell</u>!!!! "If you're up, you're up—If you're down, you're down—and if you're up against the U.S.A. you're <u>upside</u> down"!! The "locomotive" was a <u>regular roar</u>!! & more "peppy" assembly I <u>never</u> witnessed and I don't imagine many people have. After the assembly 'None,

105

Gladys, Frances and myself went down town—Oh, the great times! We each bought a flag and walked, ran and skipped thru the streets until 10:00 when we decided to home. At one o'clock we again met at the school house carrying our flags. (Frances could not go with us but rode up later with Mrs. Horn). All the school children formed in line and joined the parade down-town. After an hour and a half of romping thru the town streets in company with about a mile and 2 parade, Gladys and I adjourned! After hunting every place for 'None whom we had lost in the crow we went to a movie. On our way to Englerts we saw Zip just behind us. (Gladys doesn't know) He went into the theatre wile we were deciding what to do and that settled it as far as I was concerned. We went in but met him coming out!! We went on in but on finding it was 40 cents we gave it up, also! What are things coming to, anyway? One might think that since the war is over prices might lower! Quite the opposite, it seems, however. We then went to the Garden and saw John Barrymore in "Raffles." It was <u>fine</u>! On coming from there it was 4:00 o'clock and luck was with us, for we met Janet and 'None 5 minutes later. We then went to Reichards's, which was <u>very</u> crowded and got a sundae each. After seeing retreat, the lowering of the flag at 5:30, we went home.

I saw so many seniors today, among whom were Kappler in a sailor suit, DeBrie in a soldier suit, Pat Moore, Wilder—and Bob Leinbaugh has a beautiful new Velie! I'm <u>so happy</u>!!! . . .

Tuesday, Nov. 19, 1918. Saw Bob this afternoon but he wasn't at school this morning. Got our report cards today. I got E in English Composition and Latin; G in Botany and Eng. Literature, and M in Mathematics. Bob was just behind us when we went for our cards to the gym and just ahead of us coming out. I nearly cried last night on account of my slipping away from my old love Zip. Still, I do love him so! Bob (we heard him say) got 3 Gs and an E! It's much better than Zip got, no doubt! Robert means "bright in fame" and George means "husband man"! . . .

Thursday, Nov. 21, 1918. Saw Bob lots of times in school today! After school 'Nona and I staid to make up our botany. Afterwards we watched the fellows practice. We had a lot of fun doing it! After supper Frances, 'Nona and I went to Helen McChesney's for a Y.W.C.A. party. We went into Whetstone's on our way and saw Ky Hotz. I spoke & he did too! We danced at Helen's most of the evening. But toward the last 'Nona and I got a chance at the "Ouija" board. We asked it whom I was going to marry and it said—"Bob Leinbaugh." I am to be married when I'm 20! Frances is to marry R.S.

106

Thursday, Dec. 5, 1918. Miss Foley was here today. At noon she told me that Dr. Horn had said he had never seen a girl run the way I did. That I was like a "professional"! Read and finished "The After House" by Mary R. Rinehart. It was <u>wonderful</u>! Our basketball schedule has been semi-arranged. We are to play Davenport, Cedar Rapids, W. Waterloo, Oskaloosa, Newton, Marshalltown. I'm <u>so</u> glad! . . .

Tuesday, Dec. 24, 1918. Helped Mother & wrapped Xmas presents all day. There was a <u>regular</u> blizzard all day today. It was simply <u>beautiful</u>!! This is Xmas eve and I don't feel a bit Xmasey! It's dreadful. Frances and her Mother are here for all night.

Wednesday, Dec. 25, 1918. Xmas day. Frances woke me up this morning with Merry Christmas!" I looked on the mantle and there, O! Joy! Was my dear picture of the 1917 "State Champs." It was from Frances— and <u>pleased</u>? Well I guess! On the foot of the bed lay a <u>beautiful</u> eider down flannel bathrobe from Mother. All red and white!!! After we were all dressed we went down stairs and had the beautiful Xmas tree and the rest of the presents, the list of which I will put in my memory book. Then after breakfast, Frances and I took my new sled and hopped "bobs" to bring presents to Edwin and Ida Stewart and to dear 'Nona. She gave me her picture . . . and a book of appointments. . . .

Monday, Dec. 30, 1918. Margery came over this afternoon and we made Xmas cards. I guess we surely believe in preparedness! At four we went coasting with Frances and Billy and some other girls. We came in at about 5:00 and Daddy made Tante let Margery stay all night. Mr. Paul is here, also for all night and they are now playing cards. Mother has gone coasting with Shafers and "when the cat's away the mice <u>will</u> play"!

Tuesday, Dec. 31, 1918. Margery went home at 1:30 this P.M. Slid and drew all day, the former with Frances & Billy and the latter with Margery, in the morning and alone in the afternoon.

And here ends this silly, silly folly of a year in my girlhood. There are many things in it that I should like <u>so</u> much to erase, but I will not, knowing that some day, perhaps, this now seemingly valueless history, will be of some value to me & mine. So this is all except to say that I remain ever faithful to <u>dear</u> Bob and Zip!

The Diary of Kimberly Bunkers, 1992–1993

Kimberly Bunkers was born on June 20, 1983, to Barbara
(Ahrens) and Dennis Bunkers (my brother) of Altoona, Iowa. Her
younger sister, Kelly, was born three years later. Kim attended
Delaware County Elementary School and Willowbrook Elementary School, both in Altoona. She continued her education at
Southeast Polk High School until her family moved to Spokane,
Washington, in August 1998. Kim Bunkers is now a senior at
Mead High School in Spokane, where she is on the soccer and golf
teams, plays the French horn in band, and is maintaining a 4.00
grade-point average. Recently, Kim has started skiing and especially likes to cross-country ski, with her family and friends.

On January 1, 1992, when she was eight-and-a-half years old
and a third-grade student, Kim began keeping a diary in which she
made entries until the end of May 1993. Individual diary entries,
which describe family and school activities, reflect the phonetic
spelling system that she developed. During 1998 Kim prepared a
typescript of the entries in the diary, maintaining her original sentence structure and orthography. Then she e-mailed the entries to
me, and I selected the excerpts that appear here.

1-1-92. Dear Diary, Wow! What an exciting day! I woke up this morning
and ate a family bretfest. We took down all the CHRISTMAS deorroins. It
was fun taking down my CHRISTMAS tree. I even got caught in the
lights. Around noon we went to Kenteky Fried Chicken. Then we went to
South Rige Mall. Dad was talking to some of his friends so was Mom. Kelly
was even talking to Mary-Helen a girl her age. I lost intest so I looked at a
Make-up store near by. Dad said I could look at the front of the store. I
found a 10 dollor bill. Mom and dad said I could keep it. Wow!

1-2-92. Dear Diary, I woke up at 5:45 as I usually do. I went to the
bathroom. All of a sudden I yelled and told mom to get a bucket. Mom
went and got a bucket while Dad cmfeted me. I pucked in the bucket.
Mom had dieoreaoa. So Mom, Kelly, and I stayed home. All we did was
watch T.V. Today is Wesday.

1-3-92. Dear Diary, Today I got in trouble. When we got out of the
K.W (that stands for kids world) van I called someone a name. I went
and saw Beaty and the Beast. My fative part is when the Beast turns back
into a Human.

Kimberly Bunkers, 1999

1-4-92. Dear Diary, Today we are cleaning the house. I am doing the dusting. Mom and Dad are rearaining Kelly's room. . . .

1-7-92. I am so exiced to write about X-mas. Fist I went to Grandma A. I got Laura Ingalls Wilder books. I also got a chalk bourd on a tub . . . By the way I got it from my coisons. Then I came home and got lots of cool stuff!! I even got a game name Carron. I'm look foward to playing with. Then I went to my other grandma's and I'm wearing the sweater I got there!! Today is Monday. Love, Kim

1-8-92. Five more min. till we get out of school! We have a sub. Tonight I'll go to baketball pratice. I will sell girl scout cookies in one week. . . .

1-11-92. Wow what a prefect day to play outside. The sun is out and not a cloud in the sky. I am going to ride my bike today. I will go to a church and party. The party is for renew. . . .

1-13-92. I am wearing my hair down. I have on a shirt with flowers on it and some pant with stipes to match my shirt. Today is Monday. . . .

1-17-92. I can sell girl scout cookies today. So far I have sold 55. Girl scouts is fun! I am trying to sell 185 boxes. I did not have to go to school today because S.E.P. is giving a day off. The reason why is that we should be in the second semester. . . .

1-19-92. I am going to go to chuch. At chuch I will sell some girl scout cookies. I have 159 sold.

1-20-92. Today Iowa test of Basic Skills starts. I am looking forward to it. We are judged in percentig. Last year I got a 99%. Thats the highest you can get. . . .

1-24-92. We had a musisin come today. My fatvite trick is when he makes a rabbit come alive. From out of a pot.

1-25-92. I just was in a hot tub. Guess What? I had a super time! I asked a lady how to turn up the hot tub. I was walking and I stoped. A little boy was peing. YUCK!

1-26-92. We are coming back from the motel. LOOK! A truck from Alaka. NEAT!. . . .

1-29-92. We have music today. I sing a Deoet with Shanon DeJoode for the program.

1-30-92. We have P.E. today! WE shot baskets. I made one from the freetwou line. The ball usallee bonces off the backboard. I have basketball practice.

2-1-92. I played with the dog today. My dog is cute!!! Woof! Woof! Here she comes now! Bye!!

2-5-92. Darn! The weekends done and were back it shcool. Here is a poam; Shcool is cool   But sometimes not   Like when friends Show off   And act lik snots!. . . .

6-13-92. Well I haven't wrote in here for a while. I think "A job worth doing is worth doing right." Well today we will go to the pool. My aunt is down here and because my mom's and dad's aniversery is tomorow. . . .

6-14-92. Dear Diary, Today is my mom's and dad's aniversery. At 3:00 They went on a date. They watched movie then ate divver at Percons. Today is there 13th year of marige.   Love, Kim

p.s. Kelly and I played in my pool p.p.s. Kelly is learning to ride a bike.

6-15-92. Dear Diary, Today I played with a boy. A very cute boy to be eggzact. His name is Brandon Bettin. He'll be in my class next year. He go got a hamster. He named his hamster Chub afer the hamster in Runaway Ralgh by Beverly Clerey. I think I might have a crush on him. . . .

11-3-92. Wow! Have I not written for a long time! Tonight is the night we pick the preadent.
    8:01 Clinton   Bush   Perot 238 33   0   I am for Clinton Yea! Today we had a big day. We voted at school hear are those results.
    Clinton   121   Bush 74   Perot 74
    If Clinton wins since 1955 all schools have been right. Mabe this year all exspet Willowbrook!

11-4-92. This is the headline of the paper, CLINTON WINS BIG! yes! I knew he would win. The bad thing is our school voted wrong. Oh well! At least I get a change for 4 years. . . .

12-25-92. Dear Diary,   Merry Christmas! Fourth grade is great. I think
I have a crush on Brandon. Boys want to sit near me. I think to copy me
because they know I'm smart. Now back to Christmas. I got a Troll Tot,
3 button-down sweaters, Fantastic Flowers, Colorblaster, Resure Ranger
hand-held game, 2 strech pants. These were off the top of my head. We
are going to get new carpit and a grandfather clock next week. Did I forget to say Mrs. Cressey is my forth grade teacher? Well you know now.
Gots Go!. . .

12-28-92. We are getting new Carpit today. Guess what? You can see
the carpiters butt! You can see the crack. After the carpits in we have to
take off our shoes when we come in. I'm playing with my Brain Quest.
Kim. . . .

12-31-92. We went to Rockwell City today. The radio store fixer's win-
dow had been shot out the night before. New Years night I spent with
Kara, my best friend. We went to The Scince Center & The Art Center.
We watched Stars & Comites at the Scince Center. The art in the Art
Center didn't make sence. HAPPY NEW YEAR!. . . .

1-4-93. I keep writing 92 on my papers. Justin Good triped Kara today
on the way home from school and she's telling tomorrow. Mrs. Kemp is
our helping teacher for awhile. I wore a button down sweater, a turtle
neck and strech pants today. Kelly just barged into my room. Sorry I shut
my pin in the diary. Today was a fine day. . . .

1-5-93. If I was any colder I'd be an ice cube walking to school. I wore
my new pants with flowers and poka dots on them and my matching op.
Today was O.K. I found out Amie Streeter had surgery and has a cast.
Kara let me borrow a scarf to stay warm. I'm doing well on Life Trek For
Kids.   Kim

1-6-93. Today was great. Every Wenesday we will do an unit of birds.
We will spend 12 hours on film, papers, and class decution on birds. I like
the road runner. Even though its not brightly colored. Brandon when we
were doing pattern patchs wrote Christy's name in.

1-7-93. I went to swimming lesson today. I am fine. I just need to learn
how to get bounce on my dive. I wore my pink button down sweater
black strech pants and a black turtle neck. Today kara likes my sweater.
The Altoona Librayan was helpful to find info. to do my report with me.
Kim

1-8-93. Today was OK. We talked more about the Solar System. We watched to films. My New Years Resolitions have lasted 8 days. I read to books. Dad has been watching this work show for 1 1/2 hours. I hope I don't hafe to when I'm older. Our meal at the Ground Round was $21.00.   Kim

1-10-93. I am still doing well on Life Trek for Kids. Kelly is babying the dog saying "Smookums my baby," Go back to school tomorrow. Mom and I spent 2 1/2 hours working on making Orion the Hunter to apper on the ceiling with a flashlight in an oatmeal box. I am still writing in you diary.   Love, Kim

1-11-93. I shared Orion today. People thought I was a genis. (All though I admit I am). Kim. . . .

1-17-93. I have sold 205 girl scout cookies. I think I am the top seller in my troop. I wrote a letter to Granma Bunkers who is in Arizona. I finished my 12 page long log of my trip across the US. I am fine. We can't deceide to go to Orlando or North Carolina for vacation.

1-30-93. I got hit on the head with a broad in the basement today. It felt like a brick. I felt dizzy at first and I had to sit down. Mom thinks I still am, but I don't. I was at the badge lab on Friday night. We played house on Saturday. Kim.

5-29-93. Sorry I haven't written for so long quite a few things have happened. Mom has gone to Floriday/Georgia and got me a Mickey Mouse pen and pencil. (I'm writing with the pen. It's a little wobblely.) Some hotel shampoos and condintion and some postcards. Floridia the Sunshine State and a Stone Mountain t-shrit. While she was in Floriday a bug that was about 1 1/2 inches long got in her shoe and she stepped into it. She cried. I got new glasses. Now I have blue and pink glasses. This summer I'm going to make my room aporperite for a 5th grader. I'm taking down things such as my Carebear Counsins bulltin board.

The Diary of Kelly Lynn Bunkers, 1996–1997

Kelly Lynn Bunkers was born on August 4, 1986, in Altoona, Iowa, to Barbara (Ahrens) and Dennis Bunkers (my brother) of Altoona. She has one older sister, Kimberly. Kelly attended Willowbrook Elementary School in Altoona until her family moved to Spokane, Washington, in August 1998. She is now an eighth grade student at Farwell Elementary School in Spokane. Kelly's favorite school subjects are math and social studies. Kelly also enjoys reading, soccer, basketball, softball, and talking on the phone. She recently enjoyed writing her family's history.

Kelly Bunkers was ten when she started keeping her diary, which she received for Christmas in 1996. Initially, she wrote daily entries about family and school activities, visits with friends, and the family's 1997 move to a new house in Altoona. Her diary entries became more episodic rather than daily as 1997 continued. Individual entries reflect the straightforward sentence structure, along with fluidity in spelling and punctuation patterns, common to writers of her age. Kelly Bunkers transcribed her diary and sent it to me via e-mail; I chose excerpts for inclusion in this book.

12-25-96. Today is Christmas. Grandpa and Grandma [Ahrens] came. We opened all of our gifts. I got lots of stuff. I got this journal, tights, Arizona jean jacket, country CD, AOL, shoes and stuffed animals. I love all my gifts. I also got a snowman tea set. That was one of my favorites. I love Christmas, I had a wonderful Christmas this year. We have a wall full of Christmas cards. We have cards and pictures all over the place. We have a real Christmas tree this year, just like last year. We have Christmas light on the house. We have trees in our bedrooms with lights and bulbs. . . .

1-1-97. Today is New Year's Day. Kim babysat until 2:45. She babysat for six hours and only made $15.00. She slept in until 11:00. She is grumpy today, but I understand.

1-6-97. I am working on a book about the family in Omega. I interviewed my great-Aunt June for the book. There are a lot of pictures in it. . . .

1-31-97. I've been having a wonderful month. Next week is my half birthday. On the second, Lindsey Gillon and I are frosting cookies. I have recently wrote a book on my family. I binded it today. . . .

2-14-97. Valentine's Day was a blast. I got a lot of cards. Missy Hansen had her 10th birthday. Mrs Goepel (4th grade) is the #1 teacher next to my kindergarten teacher Miss Peterson. . . .

Kelly Lynn Bunkers, 1999

115

3-23-97. We went to the Embassey Club for lunch to celebrate Mom and Dad's and Grandma Ahrens' birthday. They had great food. The Embassey Club is at the top of a building called 801 Grand, the building is 40 storys high. The restaurant is at the top. . .

4-4-97. It is raining a lot. The old saying April showers bring May flowers might come true again this year. I am getting good grades in school still. . . .

6-14-97. Today is the day we moved. We bought my parents balloons for their 17th anniversary. Kim's birthday is coming up on the 20th. . . .

7-25-97. Today Lindsey Gillon celebrated her 10th and myself the 11th birthday. This year we played games at Gillons house and spent the night in the new house here. It was fun, we had pancakes the next morning for breakfast. . . .

8-4-97. We are in Branson, MO celebrating my actual 11th birthday. I got a CD player and a cute Minnie Mouse cake. We rented a trailer to sleep in in Kansas City on our way down here. . . .

9-1-97. I found out I will have a male teacher, Mr Wignall for 6th grade. I can't wait to have a male teacher for homeroom for the first time. . . .

10-31-97. Tonight Megan Miranda came over and spent the night. This year we hardly went trick or treating, but we still got a lot of candy. . . .

11-27-97. Tonight we opened gifts with Grandma Bunkers. I got overalls from Grandma Bunkers and books from Suzy and Rachel. . . .

12-22-97. I can't wait for Christmas. It has been a year since my great-grandfather, Stanley Ahrens and great grandmother Frances Keling have died. I am sad, but just finished classes for it. We had a special class on death and dying at school. We have a two week vacation from school.

12-23-97. Today we are going to the Embassey Club for my grandparents Anniversary. Afterwards Kim and I are going to downtown stores like JC Penney's and Younkers to go shopping. I am waiting for grandma to pick us up. I am watching channel 23 on TV. I finished decorating my room with Christmas lights. It looks great lit up. Mom said she'd teach me how to use the sewing machine so I can make a huge piece of cloth called a quilt. I want LeAnn Rimes new CD for Christmas. It has the song "How will I live without you" on it. I got a white shelf the other day. I am done decorating it. It looks great. Christmas lights fell again on me last night. I have a red spot from them on my neck.

This year I got an art set from Kristina and ear rings from AJ. Lizard earrings from Sara. Ryann gave me a Mickey Mouse Christmas decoration and a WWJD bracelet. WWJD stands for What Would Jesus Do, Walk With Jesus Daily and Why Would Jesus Die. We got a fake tree this year because we put it up at Thanksgiving and decided then not to get a real one. I like the fact that my mom trusts me enough to let me go shopping with just Kim. I am now friends with Eddie and Nathan. Today I did get me the LeAnn Rimes CD "You Light up My Life" and an off white hair tie. Molly and I have also become close friends.

12-24-97. Today my mom is taking the day off. We are going to make Christmas cookies tonight and then I will serve at 11:00 mass. I hope we can all stay up that late. Tonight I was a big help in the church service. I was what we say number one server. The special things I did was I helped with the incense and after mass I passed out candy. It took two Cherry Mini Starbursts. We got back from church at midnight.

12-25-97. Two minutes ago I said it was 12:00 am. We are already joking about opening gifts early. I hope I get the things I really want like CD's, hair rollers and books (maybe Lurlene McDaniel) Well, I better go to sleep now.

The Diary of Megan Kennedy, 1994–1999

Megan Marie Kennedy was born on December 20, 1985, in Owatonna, Minnesota, to Linda (Bunkers, my sister) and Daniel D. Kennedy. Soon after Megan's birth, her family moved to Mason City, Iowa, where they have lived for more than a decade. Megan is the middle child in her family; she has an older brother, Matt, and a younger brother, Ryan, both of whom are, as Megan points out, taller than she is. Megan now attends Newman Catholic School in Mason City, Iowa, where her favorite classes are reading and math. Her favorite extracurricular activities include volleyball and softball. She has been an active member of her Girl Scout Troop for several years and recently traveled to Savannah, Georgia, along with other members of her troop and their chaperones.

Like her mother, Megan received her first diary as a Christmas gift. She began writing in it shortly before her ninth birthday in

Megan Kennedy, 1999

December 1994. Addressing her text as "Dear Diary," Megan continued writing sporadically in it during a five-year period. At one point she was forced to take a break because she had lost her diary; fortunately, she found it again. Like several other young diarists whose writings are included in this collection, Megan Kennedy's diary entries reflect her own distinctive sentence structure, spelling, and mechanics. All of her diary entries from 1994 to 1999 are included here. The original diary remains in the diarist's possession.

12/17/94. Dear Diary, Hi my name is Megan and I'm seven years old. I'm will be eight on Sunday and I'm going to have a party. We are going skating at Roller City.

12/20/94. Dear Diary, It is me again. Today was my party and someone got hurt, she cracked her chin open. Besides that I had fun. Good Bye for now. . . .

1/7/95. Dear Diary, Sorry I haven't wrote in so long. Will I have be haveing fun. We are starting times and dividing but I'm not every good at it. Oh will maybe I will get better at it.

1/18/95. Dear Diary, It has been so wierd around here and my dance is going will. Bye. . . .

2/14/95. Dear Diary, It is Valentine's day and I so happy it is so cool. I got a lot of candy.

2/18/95. Dear Diary, Lately I have been takeing care of some things and have not got around to write. . . .

12/20/95. Dear Diary, I lost the diary that is why I haven't wrote for so long. I'm nine year's old that is so cool and I'm in 3nd grade. My teacher is Mrs. Branger and she is so nice. Well I have to go. Bye. . . .

5/9/97. Dear Diary, Matt turned fourteen and is going to get a permit. Oh no every body needs to get off the road as so as they can. Help us Matt is going to be driveing. Jokeing Matt will be a good drive. Oh well he can only drive with my parents for now, but I'm sure he will be a very good driver. I have to go take Roxy my dog for a walk. Bye for now, Megan. . . .

2/3/99. Dear Diary, I went to school which I don't like. I'm getting ready to watch Law and Order with I dad. I gets did my homework and I missed the first part of Law and Order, but it was still really good I had never seen this one be for. Some times they play one I have seen but I watch them any way. Will I have to go to bed now good night.

2/7/99. Dear Diary, I was saleing cookies this weekend and I have to turn it in tomorrow I don't think that is right I gets got it almost oh will that is the way it goes. See ya Megan.

2/8/99. Dear Diary, I had dance tonight it was all right. it is not that I don't like it I'm really tried so I'm going to bed early. Wate I have to test tomorrow a Math and Vocab. test.

2/9/99. Dear Diary, I home sick it really stinks. It is around 1:15 or so and I'm really really bored my mom got tickets to go see river dance or some thing like that. I can't wate to go. It is almost Valentine's Day and I'm not done shoping, I still have my brother Matt and my dad.

2/10/99. I'm so bored.

2/11/99. We got out of school early today that was cool, but I'm got bored. I don't think we will have school tomorrow but we might. I hope we do because I don't want to make it up at the end of the year. I don't what to stay In school any longer then I have to. See you later, Megan

The Diary of Megan Kesselring, 1998–1999

Megan Elizabeth Kesselring was born in Mankato, Minnesota, on February 15, 1986, to Bonnie (Gardner) and Keith Kesselring. A lifelong resident of Mankato, Megan recently completed the eighth grade at Dakota Meadows Middle School in North Mankato. Megan, an Aquarius who lives her life by her horoscope, would like to be a writer, perhaps a songwriter, when she grows up. Megan says that her dog, Toto, has been her "pride and joy" for nearly ten years.

Megan, whose nickname is "KK," began keeping a journal when she was four. Her first entry was "Today we went and I got my ears pierced, and my earrings were purple." When she started keeping her current diary at the age of twelve, she planned to write

Megan Kesselring, 1999

only about daily events, but she soon began writing about her feelings. She also began writing poetry in her diary, which is kept in a eight-by-eleven-inch spiral notebook, and which remains in the possession of the diarist. Megan allowed me to read all her diary entries and select some for this collection. The original diary remains in the diarist's possession.

Hello! This is my "Journal." I'm not really big on calling it a Journal, cuz I wont write super personal thoughts in it. But i cant call it a Diary, cuz I got one of those already.

This is kinds like Harriet the spy. But not really.

It is cuz I'm gonna write what I think of people.

Ya know, kids in my class, kids in my school, Mom, Dad, Hanson, Robyn, Spice Girls, whoever or/and whatever I feel like writing.

So . . . Go ahead . . . TURN THE PAGE!

June 28, 1998. <u>Deep Thoughts</u>

Okay, it's June 28, 1998, and so far, my summer is seeming to be really weird.

I don't know if I'm depressed, or what. Lately, I've been taking my eskolyth so I'm pretty sure that I shouldn't be feeling like this.

I feel, well, I don't really know. I think that I like have a hole in my soul, or something. I don't have any friends. Well not really any way. Just Rachel, Mackenzie, Karly, and Casie. I mean, like last summer, for example, I had a lot of friends. Ya know; I was friend with like . . . all those kinda people. Ya know what I mean.

Does this mean that
I've already live
"The best years
of my life"?
I hope not, cuz I sure did
take advantage of them.
Well, I'll probably
write -chya 2 morrow,
Bye
LoVe aLwAyS,
Megan KK

July 1, 1998. Okay, well, ya know how on the very first page, I said this isn't really a Diary or Journal. Well I think that Im kinda' wrong.

Ya know what . . . On Monday June 29, I snail-mailed Kevin asking him out. Then yesterday he called me and said no. But he told me that he really liked me.

OMIGOD! Im so sorry. I am having a really hard time writing tonight. I can barely read my own writing.

Im so depressed. Every day Isaac is in my thoughts. I can't stop thinking of him. I Love him so much, you wouldn't believe it.

If I had 3 wishes, they would be . . .

1. Have my Grandma be alive and healthy, and would want her to live until she's at least 80.

2. I would wish I could turn back time, back to March 19, 1998, so that I would never have dumped Kevin. Then I could live my life "the right way." Ya know so that when I got reunited with Isaac then maybe I wouldn't of messed up so bad.

3. And third, I would wish to meet And become a friend or maybe a girlfriend of one of the Hanson brothers.

I don't really have much 2 say. I think I'll write a song on the next page.

Bye 4 now.

KK

"Dreamer"
So I
Bet you think you're on top of the world
When
You start making some friends
And
Bet you never knew
that makin money
would be so hard
Well don't chya know yet just a dreamer
Dreamin up those scary nightmares
You better wake up, and face the real world
cause the Real World's Gunna wake you up
You better turn on the light
Before the ghosts and goblins come
and
Eat chew up
GET TO WORK OR YOU'RE GUNNA GET FIRED!
Hurry up
Yer gunna be late (PAY YOUR BILLS)
Chorus:
Don't sweat the petty things
And pet the sweaty things

But think of it like this   its better to be
Pissed off
Than to
Be Pissed on

July 3, 1998. Well, happy fourth of July eve! So far my day has been really uppy-downy, so to speak. OK it's time for a "pros and cons" list . . .

Pros	Cons
I didn't have to work 2 day	I woke up at 7:30 AM for no reason at all
I found out that Suzanne has Hanson concert tickets for Rachel and 2 friends. I'm one of the two.	I don't think Suzanne will pay for it. I and/or My mom would have to pay her back.
I finally got my hair cut!	I Hate how it looks on me. I look like I'm from Either the 60's or the 70's, one of those Tacky Decades. Now I'm sooooooo UGLY!

Well, that's all for my "Pros-Cons" list . . . I'm sooooo sad! About my hair that is. I hate it so much. Tonight, when we got home, I just came right to my room, and started crying.

Right now I'm Really Really Tired. So Goodnight. KK

July 14, 1998 A cry for Help!

Help me!

Tonight I was watching The Late Show with Jay Leno, because HANSON was on it. And whenever Taylor would sing, I broke out into tears. I can't figure out why though. And then, when they were just talking to Jay, Zac was sooooo Hot! I just wanted to jump into the TV, and kiss him to death, oh, yeah, and when they were singing (River), Isaac looked soooo Hot and laid back and sexy. It was like Ike really was my "new fav" . . . but only for about 3 minutes.

Omigod! I'm so tied. It's 12:30 AM. There's a really big/bad thunder storm, and my radio just wen out. I'm going to go turn on my CD player. BRB

Ok, I'm back. Guess what I'm listening to . . . Nope, you're wrong. I'm listening to Lisa Loeb. I got her new CD yesterday. Its called Firecracker. It's on the first song right now. Its called "I DO." Sorry, I don't have much else to write about.

Know what? I'm glad that I'll die knowing that I went to a hanson concert!

I'm really depressed. I don't normally admit that sort of thing, but 2 nite is an exception.

Well, I better go to bed now.

Its 12:37 AM, and I have to get up before 10:00 AM because I have a meeting with Laura, so . . .

Goodnight. Love Always,   KK

PS I love my mommy!

Hi! Long time, no write, wouldn't you say?! Know what? I'm going to make a tape and send it in to FANATIC @MTV. I would have it be about Hanson but they already were met. So I'm going to make it for Jay Leno. Because He's the nicest talk show host in the whole world.

OK, well, enough about that. I have 20 minutes to kill. Because itz 10:40 and Jay Leno starts at 11:00. Then at 11:30, I watch Sifil & Olly. That show's cool! Although I suppose I could be watching The Golden Girls, right now. But I'm kind sick of that show. I mean. God. I watch it 6 times a day. Wouldn't you be?!

Wanna know my normal late night TV schedule? OK.

9:30	Real World
10:00	FANATIC
10:30	Golden Girls
11:00	Jay Leno
11:30	The Sifil & Olly Show
12:00	Lay Leno
12:30	Connan O'Brien
	Go to sleep by then

Well good night. Love always, Megan KK

Sept. 1, 1998. 12:30 AM "Mom" I guess I just expect my mother to be superhuman or something. But then when I stop and think, you are only human. And you do your best to keep me alive, and happy. Plus, I have to stop and think about the fact that this is the first time you've ever been a mom to someone, let alone to a 12 year old girl.

I'm sure I'm not the daughter you've always wanted. In fact, I know I'm not. I bet you wanted a girl that had long brown (her natural color) hair that she let you curl, braid, and style any way you wanted to. And the girl you wanted got good grades, and never got in trouble, and hung out with good people (Republicans). The girl you wanted probably had lots of talent, and patience. She probably was pretty, skinny, has perfectly straight teeth, perfect eye sight, and beautiful blue eyes.

I'm sorry Im not the daughter you've always wanted. I'm sure if you had a choice, you would trade me in for Drew Barrymore anyday. But for now you're stuck with <u>me</u> for another six years. And I'm stuck with you.

Remember, Mom, we're in this together. We're both new at this

"Mother daughter" thing. I love you, and I wouldn't trade you for anyone. Not even for Dianna and Walker Hanson!
All my love,
Megan Kesselring

Dec. 2, 1998. Hi, School started a long time ago. I was just writing because I feel like writing in my "Journal." It's 10:16 PM, AND I have school tomorrow. I'm listening to the radio, the song "Runaway Train" is on. This song makes me think.

Okay, there is this guy in the 8th grade, Tom, and I'm like in love w/him. So I'm starting a little thing, for future info. It will start on the next page. Maybe I will write again 2morrow. I dunno.
Goodnight. Love, KK
PS Life is pretty Good Right Now!

"Tom Encounters"

Dec. 1, 1998—I called Tom. I was very calm and cool about it. We talked for about 10-15 min. I think he knows I like him.

Dec. 2, 1998—Me & Rachel were walking home from youth group, and Tom was skateboarding. This is how it went.

Me	Hi Tom!
Tom	Hi!
Me	Whatz UP?!
Tom	Nothin, Where you goin'?
Me	Home
Tom	Oh, did you just come from confermation?
Me	Youth Group. Yeah, pretty much. You're a skateboarder?
Tom	Yep.
Me	Cool.
Tom	Well, see ya later.
Me	Yeah. Bye.

IM IN LOVE!
Megan + Tom = Nothing <u>YET</u>!

December 3, 1998—I did not make much contact w/Tom today. When I was going to lunch, I smiled at him, and he sorta smiled back. I think he just looked at me. Maybe he has a "natural" smile built into his face!!

December 4, 1998—Today Tom saw me staring at him at lunch (outside). I ran inside. I was so embarrassed.

December 5, 1998—No Tom encounters today.

December 18/19, 1998—I will not continue Tom encounters. I do not like him anymore, and he is going out with Avery Smith.

December 18, 1998
Dear Journal,
I have much to say, but Im very tired, so I might be sloppy or unclear about what Im trying to say. I will list them.
1. Today President Clinton had an empeachment hearing. Tomorrow they will vote yes or no to impeach him. I hope they do not impeach him.
2. Yesterday, The U.S. dropped a bomb on Iraq. Sadam hoosane (?) is not dead, which means they will probably drop a bomb on us. Therefore, we might have another war, which really sucks!
3. Tonight we had a dance. It wasn't anything special. It was sorta fun. I don't dance much. Im not very good.
Rachel said, "Kevin came up to me and was like, 'Where's Megan?' " and Rachel's like, "over there," so Maybe Kevin will ask me out. It's not too likely though. Chances are slim to none!!
4. If me and Kevin were still going out, it would be 1 year, and 2 days. I even told him that, and he's like "Oh, wow!" sarcastically though. He didn't mean it.
Um . . . I don't know what else to write. I'm soooooooo tired.
Good night,
KK

The Diary of Alena Johnson, 1999

Alena Johnson was born on August 1, 1986, in Mankato, Minnesota, to April (Moen) and Clark Johnson. The younger of two children, she has an older sister, Ida. The Johnson family lived in Mankato until Alena was two, then moved across the Minnesota River to North Mankato. When they spent a year living in Mexico, Alena attended a local school and learned Spanish.

Alena recently completed the eighth grade at Dakota Meadows Middle School in North Mankato. One of her favorite pastimes is playing tennis; she collects candy, gum wrappers, and plastic shopping bags. Alena's idol is Mulan, a Chinese girl who lived

Alena Johnson, 1999

many centuries ago and whose story became widely known when
Disney turned it into an animated movie. Mulan dressed as a man
and went to war, fighting the Huns.

Alena was twelve when she began keeping a diary in January
1999, which is when she wrote an entry in the form of a letter,
along with a poem. Both entries, which are detailed and introspective, offer insights into the life of a contemporary American adolescent. More recently, Alena wrote another diary entry in which
she described her feelings about becoming a teenager. She allowed
me to read the original diary and include these entries in this collection. The original diary remains in the diarist's possession.

Dear Chris,

I did a lot of thinking last night. I don't know if what you said about
you and Katie was true. I like you a lot and it hurt me when you said it. I
real reason I am writing this is because I don't think you like me that way
and never did. I think you were just playing with me. If that is true why
did you go out with me in the first place? I like you a lot but not enough
to let myself get hurt bad. The only thing that is on my mind is Mexico. I
can't think of anything else. Maybe that is the reason I liked you in the
first place. Some days I wake up and think life is not worth living but I
put on a smile and plug on. I don't know maybe some day I won't have
the smile and the confodence to move on. What I concrate most is waking up in the morning and breathing in and out everyday. Nothing more.
I just live. So if you don't want me around just say the words I'm very
strong. All I wanted was someone who cared. I was wrong about you. I
imagined things in you that weren't there. I made you up like a character.
You don't know me and I don't know you. You are not the first to do
this to me. Others have. I thought you might be able to bring a smile to
this face that was real happiness. Stop playing around. I am scared of
tomorrow. I need the good memories to move on and think positive. You
probably never knew this.

Yours   Alena

I did a lot of thinking
about what went on
All I know is that it hurt me
I hurt my heart all night long
I don't know the real reason that I cared
maybe just because I thought of
the many things we shaired
I loved you enough to cry over you

maybe someday I will
but now all I really want is you
just to love me still
love me for my personality
love me for who I am
don't play with my head
like your Hope, Jenny, or Pam
for you I really care
and not just for your looks
for you personality
remember boys before books
you made me want to smile
to be happy all the time
your breath was like a song
your words were said in ryme
I wanted you to hold me
and tell me that you cared
remember these are the things
I thought that we had shaired

July 15, 1999. I am 12 not even a teen-ager. If you saw me you would think I was 13. I'll be 13 in about a month but the whole year of 7th grade I already felt 13, but now I don't really want to be 13. For the past year I have done things that remind me of my childhood. I watch Sesame Street in the mornings and listen to tapes at night to fall asleep to. I love the Carebears and find myself drifting to the children's section in the movie store to rent cartoons from the early 90's. I love watching those shows but I feel that I should grow up because I'm going to be a "teen-ager". It is almost like Peter Pan with Wendy I don't want to grow up yet. When I think of growing up I think in steps; high school, collage, marriage, kids, then growing old. I know a lot of people who want to grow up. They try smoking, become pregnant early, do drugs, wed at an early age and so on. I am just going to take my time and grow up, as I should. Childhood is great and no one should waste it by wanting to grow up all the time. I like to live the day and suck in every moment. I don't like pictures, I like to remember things, to picture it in my mind. When I do grow up I want to have kids because I'll need a childhood relief. I hope reading this you wish me not a happy birthday, on the first of August, but a year to grow up a little but still in some ways stay a small child year and year on. To grow up but even when I'm 85 still in some ways stay a child.

The Diary of Mary Madigan, 1999

Mary Madigan was born on January 3, 1986, in Mankato, Minnesota, to Marsha (Hanson) and Scott Madigan. The second of three children, Mary has an older brother, Mike, and a younger sister, Marisa. Mary recently completed the eighth grade at Dakota Meadows Middle School. Her favorite subject was public achievement, which she enjoyed because she likes to do community work. Mary enjoys playing tennis and softball in her free time.

Shortly after her thirteenth birthday in January 1999, she began keeping her diary in the format of a response journal; at the time she was a student in Judy Stow's seventh-grade English class at Dakota Meadows Middle School. In her diary/journal, Mary wrote poetry as well as lengthy, introspective prose entries that state opinions and beliefs as well as reflect on memories important to her. She allowed me to read all her entries and select these.

Jan. 7, 1999. "Rights" I think that the teachers in DMMS should let us were our coats if we want. And let [us] do a lot of other stuff. I mean if they were cold they would were there coats. "Not fair." When you come in to class and your chewing gum that's OK with some teacher. If one teacher dose not like it you will get in trouble. I think we need more rights just because were kids doesn't mean we should not have choses. We are the future Americans.

Jan. 11, 1999. When I started school I remember I had the nicest teacher. We always sat on the circle that was the ABC's. It was fun to go to school we never had homework. The thing I remember most was I was afraid of the bathrooms. When ever it was my day to do the envolobe, I would stop and use the little people bathroom.

It was even worse to go in the up stairs bathroom, that's were all the big kids went. After a bit I was fine. One of my fave parts of my day was free time. We would go play in the kitchen set and some times get to paint. We had a wooden kitchen set with pots and pans we would play house and all that fun stuff. Later in the year we did a play called Peter Rabbit. I got to be the cat. And was a good cat oh yes.

We also did a Norway play that was a fun time and we sang and all this stuff.

It was Almost the end of the year and I still did not know how to tie my shoe. And there was this girl name Alena Johnson who showed me how. I was so happy when I could tie me shoe it was a miracle.

Mary Madigan, 1999

A little before that time we got some baby chicks in the room. They were so cute. But we had to keep them under warming lite. It was the last few weeks of school and I still had not lost a tooth. And our tooth poster was so important to be on. But I never lost a tooth but that's OK. I think if I could go back in time I would want to be in Kindergarten. . . .

Jan. 20, 1999. Starting driving at 18. I think it's so dum that there moving the driving age up. The only thing that will happen is more dead 18 year olds. We didn't do anything. I think a chance. If they had some time, like they have to be at home by 10:00 till there 18. Just maybe that would help. Because I can't wait till I can drive and I don't want to wait 2 extra years. I think if they just trust us it will be fine. . . .

Feb. 2, 1999. I think that we should have less school. We go 7 hours and forty-five minutes every day. So there for when we get home some of us have 2 hours more of school. We have so much homework to much. I don't understand why teachers don't understand that we have a life. Like people with sports after school and some go till five. Then if they go out of town the don't get home till 9:00 or 10:00. Some people just want to have fun. I know thats what summers for but we are only young once. If we had to come to school later we would also do better in school. If they take off one hour of school homework would be fine. This journal is also bad because there 2 much to do out of class. Some people also don't have study hall anymore.

Feb. 4, 1999. Today we are still moving our house is the size of like 2 of our old houses. I think we will like living there and will not miss are old house. Today we are going to start moving bigger stuff on Sat. we are going to rent a moving truck. Also tonight Alena is going to come and spent the night. I think moving is hard because people keep asking if you fell sad about moving. I think it makes it a lot harder when people do that. Now its begining to fell a little more like home. But it sad because I spent 13 years of my life there. Some people it comes easier because they move so much but they don't understand. I remember getting ready to leave for my sister to be born it all happen there. That where I had heard my grandma die in. There for it makes it harder and harder but I hope my life will go on happy.

Feb. 11, 1999

> Looking far beneth
> the ski here I
> lie ready to cry

The stars so bright
there shine light
makes me fell chiper
You may ask
why or why the
sky but I will tell
you each day and time
we climb to get
to the stars and I
can not say why oh
why but thats how we get our flies.

Feb. 20, 1999 Long time no see
Dear Journal,
Well now we live in a huge house. We moved Feb. 1, 99. Hard to say
what I fell but I know it caused us to have money trouble. Now I don't
know if it was a good move. My moms work is treating her like shit at I
fell sorry for her. OK on to the trip hey I went on a trip with Rach. It was
fun because I got to get to know Rach a little better. Then we went to
her Uncle Franks house that was OK. But all together I had a good time.

Anna wants to go to Mexico next year and I think it would be fun to
go.

Boys

I want go out with someone But who? Sam He is sooooo sexy but
he would never go out with me.
God help Me
Signed Poor Girl

The Diary of Rachel Bunkers-Harmes, 1999

Rachel Bunkers-Harmes was born on October 17, 1985, in
Mankato, Minnesota, to Randolph Harmes and me. She has
always lived in Mankato and recently completed the eighth grade
at Dakota Meadows Middle School. Her favorite sport is volleyball. She also plays the clarinet and collects miniature Volkswagens.
During the summer she likes to travel and has spent time in Mexico, Canada, England, Luxembourg, France, and Belgium. Rachel
enjoys taking care of her five pet cats and, as she puts it, "hanging
out" with her friends at the one of the local malls.

In January 1999, when she was thirteen, Rachel began
keeping a diary in the form of a response journal while taking a

Rachel Bunkers-Harmes, 1999

seventh-grade English class from Judy Stow. Like the diary of Mary Madigan, Rachel's diary includes poetry as well as intro- spective memory pieces and imaginative prose. Rachel allowed me to read all the entries in her journal, which she kept in a lined, eight-by-eleven-inch spiral notebook. I chose the excerpts reprinted here. The original response journal remains in the diarist's possession.

January 7, 1999. "Our Trip Home." Our early morning began at 5:30 a.m. on January 1. It was New Year's day and we were in Ajijic, Mexico. The night before, we went to a big New Year's eve bash that left us com- pletely exhausted. So when my alarm went off that morning I slowly got up to begin my day.

After showing and getting dressed I quickly packed and was ready to go. Our friend, Steve, picked us up and drove for half an hour to get us to the Guadalajara airport. When we got there we unloaded our bags and said our good byes, then walked to our check-in counter.

Soon we were on our plane ready for departure. As we took off we looked out the window and saw the heavy smog all around. But quickly the smog turned to clouds, then to pure blue as we settled back our seats for the flight.

When we arrived in Dallas, we found our bags and had no problem going through customs. Then we hopped on the airport train to take us to our next check-in. At our check-in we were told that our flight was canceled and that we could take the next one in three hours. So we had some late lunch and found a seat at our gate.

"Flight 208 to Minneapolis/St. Paul has been delayed," we hard on the loudspeaker. "It will now depart at 4:15."

"Okay, it's only another hour. I'll read my book," I thought.

"Due to mechanical difficulties, flight 208 will now depart at 4:45," said the voice.

Soon enough we heard, "Flight 208 to Minneapolis/St. Paul has been canceled. Please report to your gate to be rescheduled on another flight."

Now my mom was getting frustrated. She marched up to the gate and impatiently stood in the long line. Finally we were rescheduled on a flight that was about to leave, so we rushed to that gate, but could only hope that our bags would catch the same flight.

Luckily when we finally reached Minneapolis, we were relieved to find our bags. With them in hand, we found our shuttle to the hotel, where we checked in and went to sleep!

January 11, 1999. "Describe creature from science" (Parrot & cat)

Yesterday, my mom took me down to the pet shop so I could get a new animal. The pet shop was very busy when we arrived, everyone was crowded in the back corner. I rushed to see what all the commotion was about. Finally I pushed my way to the front and looked around. I soon saw an animal sitting before me, a sign on its cage read "Paracat." This paracat was brightly colored, just bursting with red, green, blue, and purple. It looked very much like a cat that had rolled around on a paint pallot. Then I noticed two bulges, one on each side of its stomach. "What are those?" I asked myself, but before I could answer the bulges began to lift up. The bulges spread out bigger and bigger until two graceful, feathered wings were before me. "What an amazing creature!" I said out loud. "And you haven't even heard it talk yet," said a voice.

I rushed back to my mom and whispered, "Mom, can we get the paracat?"

Then the pet shop owner said, I'm sorry, this animal lives in the rain forests of Brazil. He's only here for a day before he goes home. He couldn't survive here because we can't provide the forest plants, which is what he eats. But we do have some very cute puppies for sale.

So yesterday I took home Earnie, my new puppy. He's my best friend.

Jan. 12, 1999. "Kindergarten memory." It was about one week before kindergarten was to begin and I was sitting in the doctors office with my mom. My mom told me that I was there for a "check-up." The nurse had just taken my temperature, my weight and was just finishing taking my height.

"Boy! You're the best patient we've had all day!" she told me cheerfully. "I'll be right back. I need to get something."

Moments later she casually walked in, hand behind her back. She was hiding something. "Why don't you have a seat right here?" she said as she patted the exam table. I hopped up and waited for the surprise from behind her back.

Then she turned around to face me and revealed the hidden object. I screamed! It was a shot, a big shot! The needle must have been at least 5 inches long!

As the nurse began to walk toward me I jumped up, and ran across the rom. "Please come sit down," said the nurse. "I promise it won't hurt."

"No!" I screamed as I ran away from her again.

"Rachel, please come sit down," said my mom.

Finally she got me seated and stuck me with that horrible thing. Then it was covered with a band-aid.

I looked up at the nurse with my tear stained face as she said, "Boy, you're one of the worst patients I've had all day."

Jan. 19, 1999. Ten, nine, eight, seven, six, five, four . . . my time machine is counting down. I'm about to blast myself 100 years into the future. I think it'll be an exciting journey.

I've been preparing for my mission for at least a year, and now it's finally time. It all started when my T.V. broke; actually looking back I'm sure glad it did. I spent way too much time watching that box. Anyway, since my T.V. was broken I found other things to do, including thinking. Thinking is a wonderful thing, you can see people and go places all in your mind, and that's what I did. I began to spend much of my time just daydreaming about the future. What would it be like? Who would be there? How [would] they act? That's when I had the most wonderful idea. A time machine!

I began at once, finding old scrapes of metal, plastic, and colorful light bulbs. Piece by piece I created my masterpiece. When it was finished it looked marvolus. It was a sphere shape, made mostly of plastic scrapes welded to gether. The door was made of a large piece of sheet metal I'd found in the garage. It had a window in the front that you could only see through from the inside, from the outside you couldn't even tell it was there. When you stepped inside your eyes were immediately drawn to the control panel. It was an array of lights in all colors. It had about 30 switches and a few plugs to put on head phones. The rest of the inside consisted of two seats from our old mini van and a try for pop and snacks. I was amazed at what I could create.

Well that pretty much brings you back to now. I'm ready to take off so see ya later!

Three, two, one, blast off!

Jan. 20, 1999

> Red, orange, yellow
> Green and blue
> Purple and pink
> Black and white are too.
>
> We are all so different
> And yet we're all the same
> We all have different faces
> And go by different names.
>
> But put us all together
> And you will surely see
> That we are all one people
> Him, her, they, you, me.

Colors are just colors
But they make us all unique
The inside's what you judge by
So that's what you should seek.

Jan. 21, 1999. "Three Wishes." Not too long ago, as I was walking home from school I spotted a four leaf clover sticking out from a crack in the side walk. I bent over and snatched it from the ground.

"Ouch!" I heard.

"What was that?" I murmured to myself.

"Me, who'd you think it was?" the clover snapped back. And just then it began to transform. Before I knew it the clover had become a leprechaun.

"Okay, you saw the clover, you picked the clover, it turned into me. I'm a leprechaun, a leprechaun who'd like to get back to sleep, so with no further ado could you please make your wishes?"

"Wishes?" I questioned.

"Yeah, you know, Leprechauns . . . wishes, fairy tales. That sort of thing."

"Oh, and how many wishes do I get?"

"Gee, where have you been? Are you telling me you've never heard about leprechauns granting wishes?"

"I guess."

"Fine, here's the deal. I grant you three wishes. They can be anything you want with the exceptions of death, birth, and more wishes."

"Wow! That's awesome."

"Yeah, it's super-cool, now can we get on with it?"

"Um . . . my first wish is for world peace."

"You get three wishes and you waste one on everybody else," he shook his head. "Okay, next."

"Next, I wish that I could fly like Peter Pan."

"Done, last?"

"Last, I'd like for me and my friends to meet Hanson."

"Okay, I'll give you your wishes with the understanding that you'll never pick another four leaf clover again, because if you do, boy will you be in trouble."

"Okay," I told him, "I promise."

And with that he granted my wishes and disappeared as quickly as he'd come.

Feb. 5, 1999

Dear Rachel,

I'm eleven years old and am under much stress. Last week my best friend commited suiside. I haven't been able to walk, speak, or even think since. We met in the first grade and have spent almost everyday together. We have gone through good times and bad, but we promised we'd always be there for each other, but who's here for me now? —Miserable in Milwaukee

Dear Miserable,

Suiside is a horrible thing that no one should have to deal with, especially not at eleven. The best thing I can say is to get back going. Go to school and talk to your friend, you guys are the best listeners. Remember the good things about your friend and always keep them with you. Soon you'll move on, but your friend will always be with you. —Rachel

Feb. 9, 1999. "Keep your eyes on the stars and your feet on the ground."

I think that "Keep your eyes on the stars and your feet on the ground" means that you should have hopes and dreams, but to also stay realistic. I think "Keep your eyes on the stars" means to always have goals to achieve and to always keep them in mind. It means reach for the stars and keep going. "And your feet on the ground" means to realise where you are and what you've got. It means to live life one day at a time and stay focused on what your doing now. When you put "Keep your eyes on the stars" with "and your feet on the ground" together it means to strive for your goal but at the same time realize the present.

Feb. 10, 1999. "Teletubbies." This morning my mom announced that Jerry Falwell had written an article about the teletubbies. Being a fan of the cuties I asked what it said. My mom then answered that Jerry believed Tinki-Winki was gay. "What?!" I shot back. Apparently Falwell had claimed that Tinki Winki was gay on the basis of his hand bag, his color (purple), and his teletubbie symbol (a triangle). He said that the bag was femenine as was the color. He also said that his triangle symbolized gay pride. I think that it was rude and prejidus, even if he was gay it shouldn't matter. I hope that eventually this only results in positive publicity for the teletubbies. I also hope that someone responds and teaches him what's really important.

Coming of Age

2

This chapter focuses on the diaries of nine young midwestern women and follows their passage from late adolescence into young adulthood. In some cases these passages are literal passages from one place to another. In other cases these passages are rites of passage—emotional and/or psychological journeys that have their genesis in events, relationships, and feelings that come to be associated with turning points in a diarist's life.

I present each diary in the context of historical events, race relations, changing cultural mores, and/or evolutions in spiritual growth. The diaries describe coming of age in several historical periods: immediately before and during the Civil War, at the end of the nineteenth century, during the early twentieth century, and in the post–World War II era just before the beginning of the civil rights movement.

Each diary reflects its writer's search for identity. At one point Ada James looks back on her recent past and makes this resolution for the future: "The past few weeks have been a very trying period, but I have made one deep resolution to be honest, frank through it all, & not to do one act that I will regret in years to come" (1895, 176). Writing of the role her diary plays in her life, Gertrude Cairns reflects, "But this is but a miniature, a dim reflection of the real Life Book I am writing every day, every hour, whether I would or not. There are no gaps in that. Every page is written on. Some I would gladly blot out if I could. Some of it I cannot read now but I shall read it some day and know truly how I have builded, whether for good or ill" (1896, 189). Although their culture offers few, if any, formal rites of passage, these young women's diaries reveal that the maturation process is fraught with joys and anxieties as their writers discover what it means to come of age.

The Diary of Sarah Jane Kimball, 1854–1862

Sarah Jane Kimball was born in Cabatsville (now Chicopee Falls), Massachusetts, on October 10, 1838, to Abner and Sarah (Spinney) Kimball. When she was five, Sarah's parents moved their growing family to Mukwanago, Wisconsin. From there the Kimball family went west to Jones County, Iowa, in 1856 and settled on a farm in Madison Township, a few miles southwest of the town of Wyoming. Sarah Jane was the oldest of six children; her younger siblings were her brothers, Merrill, Murray, and Marshall, and her sisters, Ann and Ellen. As a young woman, Sarah Jane began teaching, continuing her work in rural Iowa schools from 1860 to 1869; she later cared for her aging parents at home.

She began keeping a diary in 1854 when she was sixteen. She titled her work "Some Sketches of My Life, 1854." At first, she wrote sporadically, commenting on life on the farm, family activities, visits from friends and relatives, and her work as a student. Soon she began writing more regularly in her diary, often penning lengthy introspective entries that reflected values and beliefs important to her as she moved from adolescence to adulthood.

Her life on the family farm was a busy one: she raised chickens and marketed their eggs, she kept a large vegetable and flower garden, and she raised birds, specializing in canaries and doves. In the winter she worked indoors, cooking, cleaning, and creating decorations for the family's home. She continued keeping her diary until 1912, when she was in her early seventies. On January 10, 1924, Sarah Jane Kimball died on the family farm near Wyoming, Iowa. She was eighty-four.

Sarah Jane Kimball. By permission of the State Historical Society of Iowa, Iowa City.

A poem hand-copied into the pages of her diary offers some clues that the diarist viewed her diary as a work of life writing and as an artifact by which she might be remembered many years after she died:

> 'Tis sweet to be remembered
> In the turmoils of this life,
> While toiling up its pathway,
> while mingling in its strife;
> While wandering o'er earth's borders
> Or sailing o'er the sea,
> 'Tis sweet to be remembered
> Wherever we may be.
> When those we love are absent
> From our hearthstone and our side,
> 'Tis joy to learn that pleasure
> And peace with them abide;
> And that although we're absent
> We are thought of day by day—
> 'Tis sweet to be remembered
> By those who are far away.

Some sketches of my Life

May 26, 1854. This morning we children were all excited in thinking about that great eclipse which was to be in the afternoon. At noon mother said after I had got my work done up I needn't do any more until after the eclipse had passed by. So when the afternoon came we smoked some glass and watched. It was some cloudy but we could see it some of the time. It was only a partial eclipse of the sun so that it sh'd not get quite dark. We children enjoyed watching it for it was the first eclipse of the sun that we had ever seen. . . .

May 31, 1857. Today is Sunday and it has been raining nearly all day which makes it quite unpleasant. every day last week but one it rained. Father went to Anamosa and we expected him back Wednesday but it rained nearly all day and he sh'd not come. But he came Thursday and Aunt Lavina came with him. We were glad to see her but would have been more glad if we had had a good house and plenty of provisions. But as it is our house is small for our own family eight of us in all. I hope we shall have a new one sometime.

After it had stopped raining a little this afternoon I went out to look

144

at my flowers just coming up and I had just time to see how nice they were when there came up another shower which drove me into the house. After the shower was over I went to look at my doves down to the hen house. They were not all there but soon came. Quinmi my darling little blue dove came first to see me. He's little cannot fly very well and he will not have them long at a time. He drove his speckled mate Fanny away and is going to take a white bird for a mate which I shall call Julia. She is handsome and I think they will raise pretty birds.

It has stopped raining and the sun shines. I hope tomorrow it will be pleasant for I think it has rained enough at present.

July 4, 1857. Independence day and bright and beautiful. As I arose this morning I heard them firing the anvils. We stayed at home all day and worked hard. At night it being Saturday night I told mother I should not go and stay with Caroline Reed unless for special invitation. She came in here a little while after but what for I didn't know. She then left and went to Mr. Newell's but soon returned. I went after some water and in coming back I met her. She said she expected to be alone and asked me to go with her. I told her I could not very well and she left me. After she had gone I began to feel sorry for her for I know she was afraid to stay along, so in about an hour I went over there. Mary Ellen Newell was there and stayed too. We talked awhile and I read a story in the Eureka and then Mary Ellen and Caroline sung, I suppose for my edification. We then looked at the clock and it was 20 minutes past 10 o'clock. We then went up stairs to go to bed. I sat down by the window and looked out on the beautiful landscape and kept all the while thinking about our old home in Wisconsin. While I was doing so Mary E. got into bed and Caroline got in with Loretta Arnold. I then got up and went to bed with Mary Ellen. We lay and talked quite a while and then heard the boys coming from Wyoming. Merrill went home but the others stayed. After that we went to sleep. . . .

May 17, 1858. Did not get to school until after the bell rung. I took my seat but found it uncomfortably cold so far from the stove. Went nearer and commenced studying. Soon got warm and went back to my seat. 'Twas now time to recite our grammar lesson. Philena Scroggs asked to leave her seat, went and set by Cally Graham and whispered so loud that teacher asked her if she was setting a good example before the little ones. said she didn't know as she was and went to studying. School noisy all the time. Grammar lesson over we took our seats. Could not do an example and called teacher to do it. Then heard some little girls read and spell. I brought my dinner as it was too muddy to go home for it.

All the girls went home but Helen Skinner, Cally and I. The girls

145

and boys are going to try and get up a paper and teacher asked me to join. I told him I did not want to. I don't think I could write anything good enough for it. School was out but a little while before it called again. Girls all busy with pen, ink and paper. Philena came to borrow my pen. Hester Ann Porter came this afternoon, has not been at school for a week. School out and girls so busy with their paper they can not stop and ask the teacher if he is waiting for them to go and he says he don't care if they stay until midnight. Cousin Mary went to the P.O. and got back just in time to come home with Philena and Samantha Scroggs. . . .

May 24, 1858. This morning I rode to school with cousin Merrill. I saw the girls coming and waited till they got there. Samantha and Helen went by without speaking but Cally, Philena, Charlotte did not. The day is warm and pleasant but it rained last night and is very muddy. This morning I asked Mr. Luther to do an example for me. He tried it and got it the same as I did. On comparing it with another book it was found to be wrong in my book. May Fisher did not come this morning but at noon when they had all gone but me, May F. and Alice Crane came in. They did not stay long when May proposed that they should take a walk. They went and soon after Samantha came in and asked me to go with her down town. We went down to W. R. Miller's store where we found all the other girls and Orrin Miller and Watson Henber. We stayed a little while, then Cally and Samantha went to school. I did not want to stay so I came away along and went into school. The others did not come in till a great while and Mr. Luther said he should not begin until three o'clock tomorrow as he saw the scholars were not disposed to be at schooltime. Mr. Phinney did not come in until we were reciting our grammar lesson and when we were parsing he came and set down by me and looked over in my book.

Just before school was out, Lib. Shaffer came to tell the teacher that Mr. Show's little girl was lost and they wanted the large boys to go and help find it. Mr. Luther told them and then dismissed school. I started to home when the bell was rung for people around to come and look for it. I told the folks at home about it then started off to join the rest. There were about a hundred persons collected and all started off in different directions. I went with Lib S. and Maria Ford and we looked all over in among the bushes and everywhere but could not find her. At length we came to an open place and were hesitating which way to go when all at once the cry of "found" broke upon our ears. We hastened to the spot and there was the lost little Jenny Snow. A man had found her a mile from where we were, sitting in the road crying. She was carried home to her parents who were overjoyed to see her. I then came home and as I

146

had to pass Scroggs house Philena came out to ask me all about it. Today is Samantha Scroggs 16th birthday. . . .

Jan. 2, 1861. Wednesday—Oliver Brownel, William Tozier, and Thomas Groat came for us this evening to go over to Madison to a spelling school. Merrill was not at home but Murray and I went. The night was pleasant and the sleighing was good. We called at Dr. Tozier's and got Lucilia and then went on. The schoolhouse was full and nearly all of them spelled. John Niles was a brag speller and the boys said they wanted me to spell him down. I didn't expect to do so but as luck would have it I did. I spelled him down both times. Our crowd cheered for me and I felt pretty well. Coming back we stopped at Toziers and the old folks being gone we stayed until they came back. We played and sang songs and had a good time generally. It was eleven o'clock when we got home.

August 10, 1861. Saturday—What in the name of anything did you have that Jerry Groat come over with you for, I said as Lucilia Tozier first came in. For more than two weeks before we had been calculating to go to Brown's schoolhouse to see the soldiers train; but had not thought of any one going only William and Celia besides us except Oliver Brownel a distant relative of theirs. Wilbur was to take their team and my brother ours, so we should go with a four horse team. That Jerry is a big headed fellow and not very smart and I did not like the idea of his going with us. "Why," said Celia in answer to my question, "he wanted to go and as pa has gone off with one of our horses, we could not go with a four horse team unless we took him with his horse along." O well said I we want to four horse team anyhow.

The boys were down [at] the stable busily engaged in getting the team ready and soon they drove round by the gate and we went out to get in. It was just about one oclock and the sun shining bright with only once in a while a cloud moving across its shining face. It was quite warm. Oliver with that easy graceful politeness which is natural to him, helped us in the wagon and we started off. Jerry Groat being our driver and a good driver he proved to be too. Besides Wilbur and Jerry and my three brothers Merrill Murray and Marshall, was Isaac Bender, and of girls there were three of us. My sister Ann, Lucilia and I.

Just as we started Hiram and Rily Arnold dashed by on horseback and we knew that they were going there too.

The place was about 4 1/2 miles distant and when about half way there we saw a fellow a little way ahead of us sitting on the grass while a stick and a bundle lay down by his side, it was evidently a traveler resting before he proceeded further. But what was our surprise on nearing him to recognize Thomas Groat, Jerry's brother, though very much unlike in personal appearance. The boys insisted that he should get in and go back with us which he did. He had been at work there at Onion Grove a place 9 miles from here and was returning home when we met him.

When we arrived at the parade ground which was in front of the schoolhouse we saw collected there about two hundred persons. The sun being hot, Celia, Ann and I went in the schoolhouse where were collected quite a number of women and little children but not many of which we knew. The military companies had not yet all arrived but some fellows got hold of a drum and drummed there under the window in the back of the house. We waited awhile then we heard some one say, "they're coming" and looking from the west windows we saw them coming, marching down the hill led by their captain Don A. Carpenter. They halted before the schoolhouse and obeying their Captain's order formed into ranks.

A fine appearance they presented. There were three companies united and Carpenter was their captain. He was a pleasant and smart looking man and walked with a proud firm step. The boys all seemed to like him well. 'Twas not known by us what they intended to do and we watched them with interest. But we soon found out that they were getting up a company to enlist to go to the war. Mr. Niles made a speech to encourage the boys to fight for their country. The martial music was enough to excite any one, and I was almost afraid that Merrill would be tempted to enlist. Captain ordered all the volunteers to form into a line by themselves. I was glad for then we could see who were going. I saw but three fellows that I know and they were Oliver Brownel, Elisha Madison and John Niles. I didn't care so much for the others but I disliked to have Oliver go. I knew it was the excitement of the moment that made them enlist and I was glad that Merrill was not tempted. I believe there is enough to fight for their country without him. We had a good time there and just before sunset we started for home. Celia and I scolded Oliver for putting his name down but our talk did not swerve him from his purpose for he only laughed a little and said he never felt better pleased with anything he had ever done for he was going to Washington. We told him he felt better now than he would after he got there. Then we all asked him to sing a song for us as it was the last time we should have a chance to hear him. He sang and Tom and Jerry joined him. We overtook the Arnold boys for they had started ahead of us and Hiram to show how he could ride ran his horse as fast as he could go.

We came home pretty fast for it was cooler than when we went. The boys all stopped here for supper. Tom said he didn't know but he should enlist yet. Oliver was as full of fun as ever until after supper. When he bid us all goodbye, his voice trembled and I knew he was thinking of home and friends although he wanted to go, and I said Oliver be true to your country if you go. In a moment he disappeared from our sight. Shall we ever see him again? We can't tell. Lucilia will stay with us tonight and I am glad. . . .

September 28, 1861. This morning Ann thought she would be well enough to walk to Wyoming to get the mail. She went but when she got back her throat was a great deal worse. We were sorry she went. Father and the boys are getting out the cane juice and boiling it to molasses. This afternoon after I had gathered all of my flower seed I went out to see them work. Mother had been out sometime. when I was going I saw Mrs. Tozier there too. I went, looked at the molasses, tasted a little, then we came to the house. She rode as far as here with Dr. Tozier and then he went on to the Holmes. when he came back we were eating supper and after supper he looked at Ann's throat and told us to put turpentine on it and tomorrow he will send over some linament which he knows will cure it. But as we had no turpentine in the house I went home with them on horseback to get it. Lucilia seemed glad to see me, but I could not stay there long as I was in a hurry to get back. It was quite dark but I was guided by the light from the arch where they were boiling molasses. I soon got home. Ann was crying and we put on the turpentine but it does not do her much good as yet. I'm glad mother is almost well and hope Ann will be tomorrow. Last night we had our first frost of the season. . . .

October 26, 1861. Saturday—Today Mr Groat's little boy came to tell us that a yearling heifer was lying dead up by their house on the prairie and they thought it was ours. After dinner was over Father and the boys went to see and sure enough it was our Maggie. The boys skinned her and Groat took the tallow for she was very fat. She died yesterday, the disease being the blackleg. Tonight just as it was growing dark mother and I went out to give the yearlings some salt. They were out behind Leamons field. Fido went with us. Mother and I have been baking this afternoon and tonight we are tired. . . .

December 15, 1861. Some time has elapsed since I have written in my journal. Partly because I hadn't time and partly because I have been negligent. One week ago last Thursday evening we went to Wyoming to the Teacher's Association. The air was warm and as the ground was thawing it was somewhat muddy. We went around by Mr. Fisher's and had Laura Horton go down with us. As we were going past Mr. Brainerds he came out to ask if August and Miss McFarland couldn't ride with us. Merrill said they might and he went into the house and soon came back with them and carrying a lantern to light the way as it had by that time become quite dark. We started on and soon arrived there.

We entered the meeting house where the Association was to be held. We had quite a pleasant time and returned home at 10 oclock.

Next morning was rainy and Ann and I couldn't go but the boys went. The Association continued until Saturday afternoon but as it was rainy all of the time I could no go again.

Sunday the clouds cleared away and it became very warm. Monday morning we arose early as father was going to Anamosa to attend court. Mother and Merrill went with him. It looked some like going to rain in the morning but before noon it cleared away and the sun shown the rest of the day. I was busy all day baking pies and at night Mr. Bingham was here and ate supper with us. We did not expect them home that night so we went to bed at half past eight but were awakened at half past ten by some one in the house whom we found to be Mother and Merrill. They had started after sunset to come home and the road being so muddy they could not come sooner.

Tuesday Mother and I sewed all day and at night Merrill, Murray, Ann and I went to a party over to Mr. Lockart's and had a good time. There were about 60 young people there and we danced until 4 oclock in the morning having had two fiddlers and two sets dancing all the time, one in each room. It was between 5 and 6 oclock when we got home and were somewhat chilled by our ride so we built a good fire, warmed up and laid down to wait for daylight, which was not long in coming.

Mother and I did a big washing that day and did not get through till near night. After washing I mopped the floor and had got nearly through when I was surprised at seeing Lucilia Tozier open the door. She had come to stay all night and I was glad to have her. I went out to milk my cows and Mother and Ann got supper ready. After supper was over and the things cleared away we sat down to rest.

January 10, 1862. Friday. Here we are Merrill and I sitting by the table, he siphering and I have just finished fixing Ellen's doll. the table with a bright lighted candle on it is drawn up near the stove, in which roars a blazing fire. 'Tis a cold winter night and the wind which has been blowing and the north, all day has subsided leaving the air still cold and biting out of doors, and the moon is shining very bright on the clear frosty snow making night seem almost like day.

They have all gone off to bed but us and we must go soon. There I've left the table and gone and sat by the stove. But hark! who is that we hear running along the path then on the piazza. Rap rap rap in quick succession then a trial to open the door, but it is fastened and I hasten to open it. Why good evening Mr. Aldrich. Why are you out so late this cold winter night so far from home?

"Late," he says, "no, nor cold. Where's all the folks? Gone to bed? It's not late yet."

And so he goes on talking so fast and soon Mother and father emerge from the bedroom.

"Why what is up that you are off to bed so early?" he says. "Going to have a regular old fashioned downeast Connecticut quilting and want you Mrs. Kimball to come—have been up north to Smith's, Cohoon's, Gilbert's, O, and lots of others have got about 26 on the list—want to get 40,—must come by zounds. Going to have a husking too, yes sir," turning to father, "cause you see want to get my corn out,—cattle in it every day—have been out since 1 oclock, am going from here over to Curtis Blakely's, Fay's"—and so he goes on rattling off one word after another in his fast way.

We partly promise to go and in half an hour he leaves. He is a curious fellow. We don't wait long after he is gone before we are snugly packed between the sheets each in our respective beds defying Jack Frost to enter. . . .

January 23, 1862. Thursday—A painful scene was presented to us today. Mr. Simmons came here just before dinner and said that last night as he went over to where Groat lived to get some straw he saw a nest of four puppies living and one dead. As he came near them they set up a pitious howl and those that were able crawled out of the nest to come to him. They have had nothing to eat for more than a week. He had half a mind to kill them then and relieve them of their misery but did not know as Mr. Groat would like it. He came in to tell us about it and see what best to do as it was too awful to leave the four little helpless creatures there to perish in that wicked manner. We urged him by all that was merciful to hasten over there and Merrill would go with him and kill them. Dinner was just ready and after eating, they hurried off. When Merrill came back he said that there were but two alive and Simmons killed them. How cruel is Groat to leave them so. He was up here a week ago today and said that he was coming again Saturday but has not come yet. It makes no difference whether he wants them or not. If he had he might have taken them away as he has had plenty of chances to do so and if he had not wanted them before they knew how to suffer. How cruel and unfeeling some folks can be to dumb animals. . . .

March 1, 1862. Spring has come to us in a very rough way. A cold raw wind is blowing from the east while it is snowing and the wind blowing it in heaps as fast as it falls. It has snowed all day and I think it will continue all night.

151

Tonight as we were sitting around the stove listening to Merrill as he was reading a story in the "Dollar Newspaper" called the "Belles of the Revolution" the sky was lighted up with a flash of lightning which was soon after succeeded by another. It caused some surprise among us to see it as it is so cold and has been lately, perhaps it is a harbinger of warm weather. . . .

March 29, 1862. Saturday—It is very warm for the season today, and this morning the sun rose clear and beautiful. The atmosphere was a little smoky which gave a mellow soft light to the sunshine like many days we see in Indian summer. As I went out early to enjoy Nature's loveliest part of the day everything seemed to be alive with music. The prairie chickens at a distance were booing their loudest while the little meadow larks near the house were whistling their loudest songs. Our hens singing and cackling, the doves cooing, the cattle lowing, the horses every now and then neighing for their breakfast, while the dogs barking at every imaginable noise, all conspired to create emotions which can only be felt in the morning. I am a great lover of Nature and I enjoyed this morning exceedingly. I commenced breakfast and then went down to the yard to feed my cow, Jennet.

I listened awhile to Nature's music then came to the house and went up stairs to see if Celia was up yet. I found her nearly dressed and told her she was losing the best part of the day. Then I told her the Creek was very high but I thought our folks would take her home after breakfast. They did so and I rode over with them. It seems lonesome now that she is gone. . . .

March 30, 1862. Sunday—Today is very windy and not very warm. Merrill went to Wyoming and got a letter from Uncle Alvah Kimball. He writes that Grandmother Kimball is very sick and not expected to live. this is sad news. I hope for the better but fear the worse. She is very old nearly 80. It will be hard for Grandfather, they have lived together so long.

April 6, 1862. Sunday—Another Sunday has come around and I now seat myself to record the events of the past week. Monday was warm and pleasant and we did the washing. Tuesday was All fools day and a rainy day it was. Father killed Old Shep and the boys skinned her. Wednesday morning father killed Belle. O how sorry I felt to lose her, from little thing. I thought so much of her. She was so pretty and good. But we couldn't keep her and as she had to be killed she might be first as last, for the longer she lived the more I hated to lose her. The boys and father tanned the dog's skins as it rained so they could not work out of doors. It

152

cleared off in the afternoon and the wind blew very hard. Thursday was very warm and pleasant without any wind. We started for Wyoming at noon as we were going to the teacher's examinations.

We got there in time just as the last bell was ringing. 'Twas held in the schoolhouse. There were 17 teachers including myself. Messrs. Niles Briggs and Paul were the examiners. Mr. Thurman the C. Superintendent having been detained on account of the bad roads. They kept us there until nearly sunset. We got home just as it was growing dark. Today is quite cold again and it is snowing some. I have just written a specimen of my writing to be given to the board of examiners at the earliest opportunity.

April 8, 1862. Tuesday—This morning was cold stormy and icy. Everything was covered with ice even the smallest blade of grass. Everywhere we looked we saw everything crystallized. Toward ten oclock it grew warmer and the wind blowing shook each tree and bush, sending numberless crystals to the ground. Ann Mother & Marshall went out to gather some but found them as false as summer friends breaking in pieces almost at the slightest touch. They gathered a few however and brought them in. Merrill went to Wyoming and returned at about 2 oclock. He brought several papers and besides a letter from Uncle Freeman announcing Grandmother's death. She died Friday March 28th. It seems hard to lose her but she has lived to a good old age, and though we regret her death, yet we must feel resined for God in his mercy has spared her to us many long years. . . .

April 14, 1862. Monday. Today is very warm and sunshiny. Father went over to Mr. Lockard's this morning and returned at noon. He says I can have the school by teaching three months for twenty dollars. I think I shall do so. It is a good place to go to. . . .

April 25, 1862. Friday—Have sown my flower seeds today. While I was standing in the garden late this afternoon I was surprised by being accosted by an Indian who was going along the road. He was mounted on a small Indian pony which was walking as fast as it could and the Indian keeping time to his gait by humming a monotonous tune. 'Tis the first one I have seen since we have been in the place.

April 26, 1862. Saturday—About 11 oclock this forenoon I saw three Indians going by and stopped out on the porch to see them. They stopped at the gate and I went there. They wanted some meat and flour. They were going to Wyoming and would take it when they went back. They went to Arnolds and traded one of their ponies for Rily's colt. They have gone back this afternoon. Their camp is on the Wapsipinicon river. . . .

May 6, 1862. Tuesday—Went to my school early this morning. Found a number of children there awaiting the arrival of the new school ma'am. I gave them a pleasant good morning and soon called them to order.

There were 17 in all. I went through the common way of hearing them read and spell and finished just before noon. At noon I walked to Mr. Lockard's for my dinner.

Afternoon the same as forenoon at school, and just as I finished Arnella Fay came in to see me. I haven't any watch and I asked her what time it was. She said 20 minutes after three. I was surprised. This must not be so again. We both went up to her Uncle Horace Fay's. Sophronia Blakely was there and was ironing. I was glad to see Amanda but she has changed very much since I saw her last. Her baby does not grow pretty. It looks very much like its father Albert Fay. I loved to sit there by the door and look out on the green lawn, it seems so much like home to be there, and home to me is the most delightful spot on earth. We did not stay long however. We both came back to the schoolhouse and stayed a few minutes then she went home and I came here to Mr. Lockard's. Ellen Ward went off and stayed until after dark leaving me with the children. . . .

October 31, 1862. Friday. 'Tis the last day of October and what a beautiful day it has been. One of those days of Indian Summer calm warm and just smoky enough to let the sun shine with a soft mellow light making every thing around appear so delightful. Father Merrill and Marshall went off early this morning up to help thresh grain. Ann went up to Holmes visiting and Mother and I have been busy writing letters most all day . . . At night mother and I had to milk the cows then feed the cattle with cornstalks. While we were busy at it the sun went down looking like a great ball of fire. Ann came home just at dark while we were feeding the horses. As night closed in the moon which was past the first quarter shed its silver beams o'er the hill and valley making night not less beautiful than the day had been. The men did not return home until quite late and all have gone to bed but me. I am by the table drawing pictures with a lead pencil for my own amusement. O how I enjoy such days as this has been and such evenings as this is when all is calm and still. I am tired of writing and will now seek sweet repose. . . .

December 11, 1862. Thursday night—December first was a very cold day. Marshall and Ellen were sick with the measles. Tuesday Marshall was better but Ellen worse. she lay on the lounge by the stove with the southwest window darkened by a curtain, she was very sick and her face was broke out bad. Wednesday morning she was a little better. . . .

December 25, 1862. Thursday night and Christmas night . . . I have a cold in my head and at night I was not feeling very well went to bed first of all. This morning was warm but cloudy. 'Twas Christmas it has been the warmest Christmas I ever saw. no snow on the ground and so warm it does not freeze. . . .

The Diary of Addie Tripp, 1864

Adelaide (Addie) Tripp was born on April 18, 1843, in Fowler, Ohio, to Mary (Ellsworth) Hawley and Holder Alder Tripp. Addie was the oldest of four children; her younger siblings were George, Amelia, and Sarah. The family came west to Wisconsin when the children were young, and the Tripps were living in the La Crosse area when Addie began keeping her diary on January 1, 1864, when she was nearly twenty-one. She kept her diary throughout the year, writing brief daily entries about her work, her family's activities, the travelers who boarded in their home, and her budding relationship with John W. Johnson, whom she often called "Johny" in her diary.

As is the case with many nineteenth-century diaries, sentence structure, spelling, and punctuation are fluid in Addie Tripp's diary. Her entries rarely show emotion, nor does the diarist discuss her feelings, yet 1864 would prove to be a momentous year in her life, as her final diary entry reveals. Early in 1865 she married John W. Johnson, who was born in 1833 and who lived in Campbell, Wisconsin. The couple farmed the Johnson family's homestead, taking over the operation from Addie's in-laws. Addie and John W. Johnson became the parents of Ellsworth, Grace, and Agnes Pearl Johnson. In 1901 John W. Johnson and Ellsworth Johnson, along with J. P. and M. L. Gedney, purchased the Onalaska Brewery and began the Gedney Pickle (later the Onalaska Pickle and Canning) Co. The family continued to live in the La Crosse area throughout their lives. On September 26, 1905, Addie Tripp Johnson died at the age of sixty-two. She and her husband are buried in the Onalaska Cemetery.

Her original diary eventually was passed down to her granddaughter, Adelaide Mahlum, who described the diary in this way: "The diary was given to Adelaide by Hiram Lovejoy, Sr., who apparently was an admirer. Adelaide's diary is a black leather-bound volume about three and one-half by five inches. The cover is an expanding envelope with three pockets. The envelope flap has a tab, which closes by fitting into a leather loop. The black cover, now with a worn, bluish appearance, has leather loops to hold a small pencil, lost long ago" (Heider 1981, 88).

Friday, Jan. 1. We were all at home til noon. Then we went to attend a dinner party [at] Mr. Veir's Mr. Barlow and Mrs. Drake were with us. Mr. Downey and Rona did not go. Helen stayed to make a visit.

Sat. Jan. 2. At home all day, nothing at all transpired. . . .

Wed. Jan. 6. Mr. Dunham is here and we are fixing for a leap year sleigh ride. Mr. D. carries me down to Mrs. Johnsons and I invite Mr. J.W.J. to go with me on the ride. . . .

Sun. Jan. 10. At home all day and have a good sleep. In the evening Mr. Lovejoy calls for me to go out riding. Their is preaching at the school-house but I do not attend. . . .

Wed. Jan. 13. At home and at work on my valencia dress. . . .

Mon. Jan.18. At home do not wash but sew most all day. . . .

Friday Jan. 22. At home all day and do not feel well. Rona has a spelling school. I do not feel well. I do not feel able to attend. Mr. Barlow is here to stay all night.

Sat. Jan. 23. Father and George are halling hay off the marsh. Capt. D is feeling better and goes with them. After one load I do not feel at all well. Mr. Lovejoy and Vanwaters call. . . .

Thurs. Jan. 28. At home all day—no one call's. In the evening John and Ella comes. Father, Mother, Sarah go to Salem to a Donation Party. John and I take a ride to Salem and I come home with them. . . .

Tues. Feb. 2. I am here at Mr. Johnsons this afternoon. Mrs. Johnson has gone over to Matte's John comes home from town this evening much to my joy. Oh how I enjoy his company and how pleasant it is. I only hope it may always last. . . .

Tues. Feb. 9. This afternoon Mr. Johnson calls for me to go out riding this evening. I go & we ride out to his fathers. I also had an invite to go to a Masquerade but I do not attend. . . .

Thurs. Feb.11. This afternoon Mr. Johnson calls to know if I will go with him we go & get up to his house in time for supper than we go into Salem & meet all our folks we go home and stay all night. . . .

Sat. Feb. 13. Mrs. Barlow & I go down town   I get a callico grey dress. . . .

Fri. Feb. 19. Father and Mother are here I receive a valentine one that was taken out of the office at Salem. I go down town with Mother. In the evening I go down to the Singers hall with Mr. Johnson. . . .

Mon. Feb. 22. Washingtons birthday. In the evening I attend a dance at the Singers hall with Mr. Johnson. The buss cals for us at 9 o'clock. The colored lady comes this morning.

Tues. Feb. 23. At home but feel hard from last nights exercise

Wed. Mar. 2. I am at home all day, no one calls.

Thurs. Mar. 3. This afternoon I go down town shopping. I get one of my photographs, like it very well. Mr. Johnson calls to see me this evening. . . .

Sun. Mar. 6. Today Ella & I are quite sleepy. George comes down this morning from home and stays till after supper. Mr. Johnson make me a short call this afternoon   in the evening Mr. Ulsaver calls. . . .

Mon. Mar. 15. At home in the evening Mr. Johnson calls. The first boat of the season goes out today. John supplies it. Now I know that he thinks more of me than a passing friend.

Wed. Mar. 16. At home till afternoon then I go down town & make a few purtshes.

Thurs. Mar. 17. At home in the evening Mr. Johnson calls and I am assured of his love to me, happy evening. . . .

Sat. Mar. 19. I go downtown & take my magazines down to have them bound. & get a bill of grocers for Mrs. B in the afternoon I go to photog taken but do not have a good one. Mr. Johnson is here this evening.

Sun. Mar. 20. This morning I am geting ready to go home. At 2 o'clock Mr. Johnson is here & we start for home. We stop at his house & take supper We get home before dark [and] he stays & spends the evening. . . .

Fri. Apr. 1. To day we go to town Mother father Helen & I. Mr. Barlow goes with us. We get there & find Mrs. Williams there She comes home with us & Helen stays I meet John on the street. Mother gets a carpet. . . .

Sun. Apr. 3. Helen expected to get home today but has not come yet Charley Gardner come from town this morning & stays till after dinner then he takes Samira up to Salem I have been expecting John but he does not come yet. . . .

Thurs. Apr. 7. Uncle Donel's folks and are at the depot George goes up after them. This morning father buys two packages of cloth of the men that staid all night it come to a $100.60. . . .

Tues. Apr. 12. Sarah irons. I am sewing on my apron. . . .

Thurs. Apr. 14. Today father lets us have the colts & we go to town Sarah Helen & I we stop to Mr. Johnsons & Matta goes with us. . . .

Sun. Apr. 17. There is preaching up to the school howse we all attend. This evening Mr. Johnson is here to spend the evening with me.

Mon. Apr. 18. This is my birthday. Sarah & I wash

Fri. Apr. 22. Father goes with the beaf cattle to Bangor to have them weighed & take the money in the afternoon Mr. Johnson & Mr. Black come to buy the cattle but they were sold. I receive a letter from Mr. J. E. N. . . .

Sun. Apr.24. I am in town today   this evening Mr. Johnson calls to see me. . . .

Wed. Apr. 27. Mother & father & the 2 little girls go to town. This evening we are very much frightened we find out that we have been exposed to the small pox Maria stays in town Augusta comes home

Thurs. Apr. 28 vaccinated to day   we are all
    We still expect the Aunt has the Small Pox . Father goes over & gets Mrs. McClintock to come & stay through the day with Aunt she pro-

nounces it the Small Pox. Father goes to town after maria & takes
Augusta back she has not been exposed

Fri. Apr. 29. Aunt is still quite sick but is not broke out quite so much.
To day is Mr Johnsons birthday. I wish to see him very much but can not
his business is such that he cannot leave

Sat. Apr. 30. To day Mrs. McClintock is in to see Aunt she is better her
breaking out is most all gone & says it is not the Small Pox we are
thankful if it proves not to be. It is Marie's birthday she is eleven years
old. . . .

Tues. May 3. I am doing general housework I do not get time to do
much else I worked out in the yard a little while this morning

Wed. May 4. I iron to day & after that help father clean out the Sistern
after supper I go with George after sand up the river.

Thurs. May 5. This afternoon it rains very hard for the first time in all
most a year. . . .

Sun. May 8. I receive a present of a splendid Album   I present a paire
of Slippers to the donner of the Album They have not got home yet this
morning. This afternoon Mr. Johnson comes to see me with splendid
horses & carriage we go out for a ride & leave Sarah to get supper when
we get back Mother is not home. . . .

Wed. May 11. This morning I take up the carpet in the sitting room &
Mother commences painting. . . .

Sat. May 14. To day we finish painting the first coat Augusta and I clean
down suller Sarah is sewing I trim two Shakers this week one to day I
black the stove & pipe that goes in the sitting.

Sun. May 15. This afternoon we all go up to the School house expecting
to hear preaching but the preacher does not come. This evening John
comes   I did not expect him to night I make a promise that will make
me happy or miserable for life. . . .

Sun. May 22. It is a beautiful morning   George takes us out riding over
to the farm This evening Mr. Cooledg calls & stays all night   David is
here to stay with George. It rains quite hard this evening. I write a letter
to Mr. Downey.

Mon. May 23. We wash to day I send my letter to the office to day. . . .

Sat. May 28. We all go to town to day & we meet John coming out home I get me a new hat $5.00. I stay all night & see John in the evening   Helen comes home with our folks   Johney take me home tomorrow.

Sun. May 29. I am in town it is a beautiful day. This afternoon John brings me out home we stop to his house & stay to tea. . . .

Mon. May 30. We wash to day although I do not feel much like it. . . .

Mon. June 6. We wash to day Jo is here this afternoon   I go to sewing my dress. There is a man stops with a lame horse to stop till it gets better. . . .

Sat. June 11. They are busy doing their Saturday work. I make a jell cake the first on I ever made. . . .

Thurs. June 16. To day they pick the first peas of the season six bushel for the first time. Johny does not go in town till most noon. . . .

Sat. June 18. I come home this evening   Lucy & Eugene bring me home   Mrs Johnson gives me a canary bird   Johny come home about eleven o'clock and staid till after three   Ella & Matta are to start up

Fri. June 24. Johny comes out after me with splendid horses & carrage to go in town to a Masonic festival we have a pleasant ride in town   I enjoy it very much   I stay to Mr. Barlows all night after the festival. . . .

Mon. June 27. Helen & I wash nothing of importance happens   David comes after supper horse back with Dabs saddle on I get on & have a short ride the first time fore more than a year. . . .

Wed. June 29. Father bought 88 sheep this morning at $2.50 per head there is no a single man here for dinner   a wonder

Thurs. June 30. Father and Mother go to Salem this afternoon   Mother gets me a calico dress 35 cts per yd   gets cotton cloth at 60 & 70 cents Rona calls here this evening. . . .

Sat. July 2. I am baking for the forth   Mr & Mrs Veits come before dinner. . . .

160

Mon. July 4. This is the forth we are all up early and are started for town by seven o'clock Ella goes with us Mr. Johnsons folks are all at Barlow to dinner Johny with the rest in the evening we go to the Menagerie. . . .

Sat. July 9. This morning we do our work up early and go over back of Mr Robes field after rasberries Helen Sarah Augusta & I while there there comes up a thunder storm we all of us get thoroughly wet through.

Sun. July 10. I do not attend church this morning but Helen & Sarah do & David comes home with them & stays till afternoon. Then we all go up to church & here an excellent sermon Johney comes this evening. . . .

Tues. July 12. To day Mrs Johnson Saney and Martha come before dinner I go up in the field to drive reper this forenoon   in the afternoon I do not go I hive a swarm of bees Just before tea Mrs. Barlow & Stella come.

Wed. July 13. I commence to help Helen iron but have to drive the reper   drive till noon then go up at 3 o'clock. . . .

Sun. July 17. We staid to an old house this side of the Caterack This morning drive on 5 miles in an other directions and get all the berries we have to bring home we start at 2 o'clock get home at twelve o' cl all very tired and not much pleased with out bluberry excursion. . . .

Thurs. July 28. To day I am ironing & baking Mr. French & the old lady comes for Mother to over to see their little child. . . .

Sat. July 30. Mother and Sarah are making jell & wine Sirna Sharpless is here to supper   Sarah goes up to Salem this after som shugger gets $5.00. . . .

Thurs. Aug 4. We go on board the green egle Jo is washing I go down town and get some graseres Mrs Roba comes & stays till after dinner I go down town with Lucy this afternoon This evening Johny calls a short time & for the first time since I come down. . . .

Sat. Aug. 6. Johny was in this mrny & wanted to know if Lucy & I wanted to go to the circus Johny & Jessa come to go with us but we conclude not to go in the evening they come and we go & get ice cream Johny spends the evening. . . .

Sun. Aug 14. This morning Sarah & Nathan come. Johny comes a few minets but has to go suply a boat. George goes up to the depot with him George comes in to bring Mr. Barlow home Johny is here this evening

Mon. Aug. 15. Today I am washing Mrs B has a sewing girl come today. . . .

Wed. Aug. 17. This is the first night of the Theater in town Johny comes for me to go & like it very much. The Marble heart is the play. . . .

Sun. Aug. 21. Johny takes me out home to day we stop at his house & take supper Miss Willet is there we go on up home from there I eat the first ripe plums. we meet George & Augusta going home.

Mon. Aug. 22. I do not feel like washing I make some pies to day. . . .

Mon. Aug 29. This morning they call Dr. Chamberlain for Stella I go down town on an errand for Mrs. B and meet Deb McClintock on the street Frank has enlisted to day & see Johny a short time this evening I am unwell tonight. . . .

Wed. Aug. 31. Stella is better Mrs Loomis & Miss Smith call this afternoon. . . .

Mon. Sept. 5. This morning George & Mother came down Mother is sick with a fellon on her hand she has to have it lanced I come home & she stays I go down town & get me a pair of gloves George a shirt bosom Johny comes to say good bye. . . .

Fri. Sept. 16. This morning they are here for breakfast. We have 22 in the family while the Thrashers are here.

Sat. Sept. 17. They finish threshing to night. This evening after supper I am taken with a vilent pain in my right side it makes me quite sick.

Sun. Sept. 18. I am not at all well to day. Johnny comes & is here to supper I go down home with him it is a beautiful moonlite night. We have first frost of the season. . . .

Sun. Oct. 2. It is very unpleasant to day. I had expected Johny but there is no prospect of its being pleasant This evening much to my surprise & disappointment he comes but stays only a short time. . . .

Sun. Oct. 16. Johny comes this evening mutch to my hapnys. . . .

Sun. Nov. 6. I take Ella home this evening Johny comes this evening Georges horses get a way & he does not get home till morning. . . .

Wed. Nov. 16. Yesterday Mother was in town and got me a pair of shoes I put them on to war to day.

Thurs. Nov. 17. The School ends to day we go up to exhibition this evening. I receive a letter from Y. M. Downey. . . .

Wed. Nov. 23. They all go to town I go as far as Mr. Johnsons and stop there. They are preparing for a Thanksgiving supper. I did not think of staying all night but they insisted upon it. . . .

Sun. Nov. 27. Johny goes home to day after supper. . . .

Tues. Dec. 6. The children fore of them start for school. . . .

Sat. Dec. 10. Johny come up this evening and stays all night.

Sun. Dec.11. Johny asks fathers consent to our marriage this evening father is very short. . . .

Sun. Dec. 25. Johny comes today John Card comes this afternoon Johny goes after the preacher I go with him one week from today we are to be married. . . .

Wed. Dec. 28. Johny comes this evening and stays all night & takes me in town in the morning to have my black silk fitted & get my cloak We stoped at his fathers when we went down & come back.

Thurs. Dec. 29. This morning we start for town we stop at his fathers going back & coming back Father gives me $10. Johny gives me 15 youse 10 & give 5 back. . . .

Sat. Dec. 31. Black Sarah is here to day George gets back this afternoon Mr Sharpless comes with them. Tomorrow I am to be Married.

The Diary of Margaret Vedder Holdredge, 1865

Margaret Vedder was born on February 26, 1840, in West Milton, New York, to Abigail (Hartwell) and Abram Vedder. Margaret was the youngest of eight children; her older siblings were Chauncey, Eva Eliza, Dewitt, Laura, Mary, Sarah, and Elizabeth. The Vedder family came west to Wisconsin when Margaret was very young and settled on a farm west of Berlin. On September 9, 1863, Margaret married Burton Holdredge. Their first child, Charles, was born on November 19, 1866. He died less than two years later on May 22, 1868. Margaret and Burton Holdredge had six more children (Laura, Birdie, Burton, Eva, Vernon, and Mary). Only their daughters Eva and Mary lived to adulthood. Burton Holdredge died on March 8, 1907; Margaret died on May 18, 1920, and is buried alongside him in Oakwood Cemetery in Berlin.

Margaret Vedder Holdredge's diary, which she began keeping a year and a half after her marriage, was started on January 1, 1865, while she and her husband were in New York visiting her husband's family. When Burton went off to help with the Union war effort, Margaret returned to Berlin, where her family owned a book and stationery store as well as a meat market. In her short daily entries Margaret wrote about family activities; her longing for her husband, who was absent for several months; the assassination of President Abraham Lincoln; and the closing days of the Civil War. In 1983 David R. Lucas, a great-grandson of Margaret Vedder Holdredge's, donated a typescript of her 1865 diary to the Berlin Historical Society, where it remains today.

Tuesday, January 10, 1865. It was so late when we went to bed last night that we overslept this morning. I made fried cakes this forenoon the first I have made since I have been married. This afternoon I did my ironing. It has been very unpleasant most all of the forenoon and turned into rain this afternoon. It froze as fast as it came down which makes a crust on top of the snow. Emma and Kinney spent this evening with me. Have gone to bed. It is after nine and Burton hasn't come yet. I wonder what keeps him. . . .

Saturday, January 14, 1865. Snowed all day. Wasn't very cold this forenoon but grew dreadful cold towards night. didn't have much to do. Knit on Burton's sock most all day. Emma is knitting the mate to it. Burton is going off so soon. I shall have to work very steady if I get all done for him I want to. I hardly know what I shall do when he is gone. It will be so lonely without him. Oh if only I could go with him but I cannot so must try and make myself contented without. His mother thinks I don't feel as bad as she does about it but I don't believe in showing my feelings if I can help it. . . .

Friday, January 20, 1865. It hasn't been quite as cold today. I baked bread today; had pretty good luck. Emma, Elizabeth and I went up to the daguerrotype office this afternoon. Lib and I had our photographs taken. I had to sit twice before I could get a good one. I attended the festival and had a real nice time. Burton danced with me twice; didn't dance with anyone else. . . .

Sunday, January 29, 1865. It has been cloudy all day but hasn't snowed much. I didn't go to church today. It was so late when we got up. I received a letter from Mother and Eliza last night and answered them today. Burton's engine started yesterday and I expect he will follow it some time next week. Oh how I do dread to have him go. Burton has been at home with me all day but has gone to the mill to see Mr. Davis this evening. I told him to be sure to come home at eight but it is most nine and he is not here. . . .

Monday, February 6, 1865. Has been pleasant but cold all day. I didn't wash as I had so much else to do. Didn't have time. The dress maker was here this afternoon and fitted my dress. It fits nicely. I think I shall like it very much when I get it done. Lib has been with me all of the afternoon and is going to stay all night with me. Jerome has gone to Utica. Burton started this morning. Oh how I did hate to have him go. It is so lonely without him. . . .

Monday, February 13, 1865. It has been quite pleasant but cold. I left Boonville [New York] for Chicago this morning at eight. There was so much snow on the track that we didn't arrive in Utica until after two in the afternoon. The Western was to start at half past three but didn't get in until after five. We then started for Buffalo. I am afraid we will not get into Chicago until late tomorrow night.

Tuesday, February 14, 1865. Is quite pleasant. I arrived at Buffalo this morning. Changed cars at Syracuse in the night. Before we changed we had each a seat by our selves but after only had one between us. I am dreadful tired. It seems as though I can't stand it until I get to Chicago. We are now in Cleveland where we expect to change again. A young married lady got on the cars this afternoon at Erie and is going to Chicago to get her sister's baby. She took a seat with me. Thinks she will take a sleeping car. I wish she was not. . . .

Thursday, February 16, 1865. It isn't very pleasant today but snows quite hard. We arrived in Toledo at midnight last night as we expected. Mr. Hurlbert didn't feel very well and was very tired when we got there. He said as I wouldn't have to make any more changes after I left here, He thought he would stop here and rest some. So I came the rest of the way alone. I arrived at Chicago at about one this afternoon and took them all by surprise. They were expecting Lib but instead I came. . . .

Saturday, February 18, 1865. It has been very pleasant overhead but dreadful under foot. Mary and I attended the theatre and went through the museum this afternoon. Enjoyed it very much. Went with Mrs. Swain and her sister. Finished trimming our dresses. Baker has not gotten home yet. I am real tired tonight and will retire before long. I haven't heard from Burton yet. Oh how I wish I could see him. . . .

Saturday, February 25, 1865. It has rained all day and is raining still. It makes me feel almost homesick. I received a telegram from Burton tonight, or rather Baker didnt. He wanted to know where I was. Said he had not heard from me since I had left Boonville. It seems he is back there. I wonder what brought him back so soon. Oh if only I could get a letter from him. I wish I had not come away so soon for I want to see him so bad. . . .

Wednesday, March 1, 1865. Has been quite pleasant all day. Laura and I went down town this afternoon and went to the store and then to the dentist. Laura had a tooth filled and when he got through with her I had him examine mine. He said three of my front teeth ought to be filled right away. He charges six dollars for gold. I thought that too much so I did not have them filled.

Thursday, March 2, 1865. I thought when I first got up this morning it was going to be unpleasant but it soon cleared away and has been very pleasant. I went down town when Baker did this morning and carried my circular cloak to the dyers to be died. I will have to pay one dollar fifty for it. While down there I received a letter from Burton, the first I have received since I left Boonville. Oh I feel so much more contented since he said he didn't know but he would come here and go in business. . . .

Sunday, March 5, 1865. Weather continues pleasant. Laura, Lizzie and Baker went to church this forenoon to the First Methodist. Mary and I attended the Catholic this afternoon. It didn't amount to much. . . .

Friday, March 10, 1865. Has been pleasant but cold all day. Lizzie, Mary and I went down to get Anna's picture taken this afternoon but couldn't get a good one. Just about the time we got home, it began to snow and was so cold I thought I should freeze my feet before we got here. The baby doesn't feel as well today.

Saturday, March 11, 1865. Has been pleasant all day. Lizzie and I washed in the forenoon. I sent by Raker for my cloak but he forgot to bring it, but brought me a letter from Burton which I was surprised and delighted to receive. I will answer it tomorrow if nothing happens to prevent. . . .

Tuesday, March 14, 1865. Weather continues unpleasant and rainy. It has rained most of the time all day. Lizzie took the cars to go back to her husband this evening. Laura and I went to the depot with her. She took a sleeping car—she was the only lady in it. We hated to leave her and she hated to leave us. Anna cried to come back with us. Little Burton has been a little better today.

Wednesday, March 15, 1865. Continues to rain as hard as ever. I wonder when it will stop. It is real lonely now. Lizzie is gone. I have missed her very much all day. Dear little Anna, I miss her so much. She is such a little jabberer. I wrote a letter home last night and sent it by Baker this morning. I wrote I should start for there next Tuesday. Baby is a little better. . . .

Tuesday, March 21, 1865. I left Chicago this morning for Berlin and arrived there safe. Found Father, Mother and Elizabeth and Mrs. Hibbard at the depot waiting for me. Baker went to the depot with me at Chicago. It commenced raining before we got there. It continued to rain most all day. I was afraid it would rain when I got to Berlin but did not. . . .

Thursday, March 23, 1865. It continues to be pleasant although it is colder than it was yesterday. I went downtown with Father and Sarah this morning. Got some ribbon for my hair and I think it is quite pretty. Sarah Hibbard came up to call on me. I like her very much. Before the evening was half spent, Willie Cook came after her to go home as a young man was there. . . .

Sunday, March 26, 1865. It has been very pleasant. I did not go to church for my face is covered with cold sores which makes me look splendid. I had a letter from Burton today.

Monday, March 27, 1865. The weather was very pleasant. It rained some through the night but cleared off before morning. I thought some of washing this morning but my people persuaded me to wait until Saturday when they are going to do theirs. I feel a little lonesome and began to want to get another letter from Burton but I would a little rather see him. . . .

Sunday, April 2, 1865. Another pleasant day has passed. Mother, Eliza, Chauncey, George and I went to church today and stayed until after Sabbath school. I went into the bible class with Eliza. They have a very interesting school. I received an answer to the letter from Burton today! Oh how happy I am to hear from him. How I would like to see him. Hope it will not be long before I hear from him again. . . .

Wednesday, April 5, 1865. It has rained all of the forenoon and part of this afternoon. But the rest of the day has been quite warm and pleasant. Sarah moved down town today. When Father came down with a load tonight I came with him and am going to stay until Friday. Mr. Hill came on the cars this evening. Is going to install a window in Sarah's front room. I received a letter from Burton tonight. He is in Boonville yet. . . .

Monday, April 10, 1865. This has been a beautiful day. I helped Eliza trim her shaker this forenoon. Made a couple of little flags, one for Eliza and one for myself; we wore them down to Mrs. Hibbards this evening. George was here a little while this afternoon and went down town with Father and Mother. I thought perhaps I should get a letter from Burton, but was disappointed.

Tuesday, April 11, 1865. It is very unpleasant. Has been so all day. Commenced raining towards night and I think we are going to have a wet spell. We have been having good news from the Army for a week past. A week ago yesterday, the third of this month, Richmond and Petersburg were taken and since [then], Lee and all of his Army have surrendered. They had great rejoicing over it in Berlin last night. Oh I hope we will not have any more fighting. . . .

Saturday, April 15, 1865. It looked so unpleasant and rainy this morning Eliza and I almost gave up going to Mr. Bakers, but as it cleared away some, we went. We didn't enjoy our visit very much on account of the dreadful news of the assassination of Lincoln. Mr. and Mrs. Bartlett papered Sarah's front room this morning. Lincoln was shot in the head last evening and died this morning. Seward was also killed. I wonder what our country will do now. Oh it is dreadful to think of. Eliza and I walked home.

Sunday, April 30, 1865. Has been very unpleasant all day. Snowed some this forenoon. I finished a letter to Burton this morning. Father had some letters to mail and went down to Berlin to carry them so I sent mine. None of us went to church. Father brought a letter to Lizzie but I didn't get any. . . .

Sunday, May 7, 1865. It was quite cold this morning but has been uncomfortably warm this afternoon. We didn't any of us go to church. This evening Father, George and I went down to Sarah's. She is looking very pleasant in her new home and seems to enjoy it very much. She had a letter from Laura last evening. Said. she and Mary went to see Lincolns remains when they passed through Chicago. Lizzie got a letter from Wallace last night but I didn't get any from Burton. . . .

Wednesday, May 17, 1865. It was very warm this morning but soon began to grow cooler. It commenced raining this afternoon and is quite cloudy now. Looks as though we might have more tonight. Lizzie and Mother spent the afternoon at Mr. Hibbards. Father went down and took tea with them. News came in, the night before last, that Jefferson Davis was taken dressed in his wife's clothes. Eliza and I thought of going down town this afternoon but it was so unpleasant we didn't go. . . .

Friday, May 26, 1865. Has been quite warm and pleasant but rather warm. We need rain very much. We had cranberry beans for dinner. They were very nice. The rest of the family was so busy this afternoon that I got supper —made pancakes. Mrs. Hibbard and Mr. Starks called here tonight and stayed a short time. George went down town this afternoon and got a letter for me from Burton. Lib came down this evening and we played two games of backgammon. . . .

Thursday, June 1, 1865. It has been uncomfortably warm all day. Oh how I wish we could have rain. Eliza, Lizzie and I went down town this afternoon to do a little trading. We stayed and got the mail. While Eliza and I were in the post office, a man touched Eliza on the shoulder. She looked around and stared at him as much as a minute before she knew who it was. It was Uncle Morris Hartwell. Mother says he has changed very much. Lizzie got a letter from Wallace and I from Burton. Oh how I wish I could be with him now. . . .

Wednesday, June 7, 1865. We didn't get any rain last night but it thundered and lightninged and looked a great deal like rain. It is a great deal cooler than it has been. I went down and got the mail this morning before breakfast. I received a letter from Burton and Emma in one envelope. And one from Mary. She sent me some samples but didn't like any of them. All of the family came down and spent the day with Sarah. We had a nice time. Lizzie and I are going to stay here through tomorrow night. I wrote a letter to Mary this evening. . . .

Wednesday, June 28, 1865. When I awoke early this morning I found it was raining very hard. It stopped before~it was time to get up but still looked very much as though it is going to rain more. It was nearly ten o'clock when Mr. Hill came over to get the horse ready. After he had gone after the wagon, who should come but Eliza, Chauncey and Lizzie after me. They brought me three letters, two from Burton and one from Laura. Oh I was so glad to get then for it is now almost two weeks since I have heard from them. . . .

Friday, June 30, 1865. Another pleasant day has drawn to its close. I helped Mother get dinner and this afternoon devoted my time to reading the Confession of Faith. Tomorrow I hope to go forward and present myself to become a member of the Presbyterian church. . . .

Saturday, July 1, 1865. This has been a very pleasant day and doubly so to me for I feel I have done right in confessing Christ. Oh I should be so happy if Eliza and Mary had joined with me and my dear husband, if he was only a Christian. Irene Marion was the only one that came forward with me. I hope and pray I shall never forget my duty before God. . . .

Monday, July 3, 1865. It has been very pleasant but rather warm. We got up pretty early this morning and got our washing all out by ten and since, I have written a letter to Burton and told him what I have done. I think he will not be displeased for I don't feel as though I have done anything wrong but all that is right. Mrs. Groves was here today and said she heard DeWitt was in Chicago and would be home soon. I hope it is so for I want to see him very much. . . .

Thursday, July 6, 1865. No showers last night. It has been very pleasant all day today. I went out after breakfast and picked blackberries until after two this afternoon. We are going whortleberrying tomorrow. I made a raspberry pie to carry. I picked about fifteen quarts of berries and put them up today. Mother and DeWitt went down town after tea. Mother got back but he did not come with her. Brought me a letter from Burton. He doesn't know wheather he will come up after me next month or not. . . .

Friday, July 14, 1865. It has been pleasant although rather cloudy most of the day and rained some towards night. I went down the lane a little ways this morning and when I came back Kary Hitchcock was going to school. I walked down with her. Just as we got to the gate DeWitt and another soldier came along. DeWitt brought me a letter from Burton in which he said he had sent me money express. Doesn't think he can come up after me until September. Oh how can I wait until then before I see him. . . .

Sunday, July 16, 1865. Another pleasant Sabbath has passed into eternity and we are all one day nearer the grave. We know not how much nearer. Perhaps we have many years more to live and yet it may only be a few short days. How little we think of this, lie still live on as though we were to have many more happy years here on this beautiful earth. Eliza, Mother, Chauncey, Dewitt and I attended the Congregational church this morning. There wasn't any preaching in the Presbyterian church. Next Sabbath, Mr. Starkes will be back. Didn't have as interesting a Sabbath school today as usual. . . .

Friday, August 4, 1865. This has been a very pleasant day. Eliza and I got up and commenced sewing at five o'clock. I didn't get as much done on my dress as I would have liked to. I finished running the hem and put in three tucks. Father and Mother went to F'rs. Bartletts this morning to spend the day. Haven't got back yet. Dewitt came home after I got to bed. He had a letter for me. Laura brought it up to me. It was from Burton. Oh he is coming after me soon. I am so glad for I want to see him so much. . . .

Wednesday, August 16, 1865. It continues to be beautiful weather. I finished sponging my cloth this forenoon; I cut it out this afternoon. Eliza, Laura and I went down to Sarah's. I meant to stitch up all of the seams on the machine but Sarah had some work to finish up for Laura. She is going back home Friday. When the cars came in, I went to the depot to see if Burton had come. I saw someone who looked like him but wasn't sure so went back to Sarah's. When we got back home we found him there. Oh how hopeful I feel now.

The Diary of Ada L. James, 1895–1902

A lifelong resident of Richland Center, Wisconsin, Ada L. James was born on March 23, 1876, to Laura (Briggs) and David G. James. Ada James's ancestors had come to Wisconsin from New Hampshire in the 1840s. She had an older half-brother, Oscar (whom she called OB), and two younger sisters, Beulah Louise and Vida Laura. Ada's mother was an advocate for women's suffrage; her father was a Civil War veteran who became a well-known Wisconsin legislator and sponsored the legislation that led to Wisconsin's ratification of the Nineteenth Amendment in 1919. Ada went to high school in Richland Center and battled with increasing deafness, for which she received treatment in early adulthood. She was especially close to her cousin, Ada Briggs, who visited regularly from Milwaukee. The two girls wrote periodically in one another's diaries, and those entries suggest that they read one another's diaries as well. This sharing of diaries was common among close friends at that time; the diary of Ada James suggests the central role of the diary in maintaining and strengthening such relationships.

Her diary also reveals a personal struggle that helped to define the diarist's sense of self. As a young woman, Ada developed a romantic interest in a young man named Charles Bingham Cornwall (often referred to in Ada's diary as CC or CBC), and they were supposed to marry in 1897. Cornwall's clandestine attempt to court Ada Briggs and Ada James at the same time proved unsuccessful when it was discovered by both cousins. This discovery sparked opposition, delays, and finally cancellation of any marriage plans. Ada's diary records the circumstances surrounding this difficult period of her life. Just after the turn of the century, she eagerly anticipated the wedding of her younger sister Beulah to Robert DeLap in May 1901, but the marriage was cut short by her sister's death from Bright's Disease a month after the wedding.

After Beulah died, lengthy introspective entries in Ada's diary reflect her attempts to come to terms with grief. Following the death of her mother, Laura Briggs James, in 1905, Ada worked with her father on behalf of women's suffrage. Ada James became a central figure in the movement for women's suffrage in Wisconsin, served as president of the Political Equality League of Wisconsin,

(From left to right) Vida, Ada L., and Beulah James. Courtesy of the State Historical Society of Wisconsin Whi (X3) 52043.

and was a member of the War Resisters' League. A lifelong diarist whose entries span more than fifty years, Ada James remained in Richland Center. During her later years she shared her family home with her close friend Mary J. Ahlhorn. Ada James died in her home on September 29, 1952, at the age of seventy-six. These selections from her diary begin when she was eighteen.

January 1st, [1895]. Am undecided whether it is an inspiration to make many resolutions or not. To know you are free from all assigned work is not a feeling of freedom by any means. For now I have no excuse if I am not principled in religion, familiar with the different political questions, and above all awake to the many opportunities which must occur for the exertions of charity and benevolence. I mean the charity of time and attention. I would so love to make others love the lessons and laws of Christ; but I am very far from setting them an example. But the surest way of coming into communion with mankind is through our own household. I feel that if I am all that I can be, and do all I can do at home, I have accomplished something. . . .

Jan. 19 [1895]. To-day has been one of the most miserable of my life. I can not bear to put it where I shall have to remember it. It is easy to say "Thy Will Be Done" when "Thy Will" is My Will but Oh! How hard it is when Thy Will is not "my Will". . . .

Jan. 21 [1895]. Helped invoice. I wonder why some people are always happy & others are not—I think our conditions have but little play—I was thinking to-night I am really happy but so little. I am afraid I can't be either I feel that either pa or I will have to suffer a great disappointment inside of the next year. . . .

Feb. 2 [1895]. I am feeling very sorry for my self to day. There is a gambling establishment here & it is claimed our best young men are attending. OB says dreadful things about CBC it broke me all up & not only that but Beulah happened to find it out & of course it is a bit a news that she can tell OB about as decidedly a good joke, it is dreadfully hard to have one's deepest feelings paraded—I am not going to obtain any information from members of the family. Friendship means a good deal or it means nothing—the next time I see CC I am going to have an explanation from him if it is so then I shall withdraw from the card party & never go with a young man again & I shall <u>never</u> dance or go with another young man. . . .

Feb. 22 [1895]. My mothers birthday and she not at home; in the evening Elsie, Miss W. & myself went to the Church Supper. I forgot and ate meat for supper. I had made a vow never to eat anything that had to have its life taken, that my appetite ~~had~~ might be satisfied. It is hard for I am so accustomed to eating it.

Feb. 23 [1895]. I am trying to learn to keep house while ma is away they all tell me I succeed but I imagine they will all be as glad as I to see ma in her old place. I thought surely C.B.C. would call in the evening. Had to satisfy myself with "G M & D." We must, of course, be able to do without whatever is denied us; but when the heart is hungry for any honest thing, we may surely use all honest endeavor to obtain that thing, contented myself as usual by combing pa's hair. . . .

Mar. 4 [1895]. I am from now on going to read an hour every night and be alone, for awhile before going to bed. I know that is a medicine that will cure me of my irritableness of thought & action.

Mar. 13 [1895]. Mama went to Madison to attend Suffrage Hearing—There is a man that lives across the road that starves his horses. I went and had a talk with him about it this afternoon, "his old woman" was wrathy, had all I could do to keep from laughing at her then & there. I was as calm as could be acted as though it was an every day occurance. . . .

March 22 [1895]. This is the last day of my eighteen[th] year. I hope the 19th will be an improvement. To-day Abbie and ma gave me such nice little keepsakes, Ma gave me Lilian Whitings "The World Made Beautiful" & I know it will be a great help to make the World more Beautiful to me.

March 23 [1895]. Nineteen years have I lived (& can't spell 19 yet) and how little I know of what my future will be like; Oh! How I wish I had more force of character "like the vine how I envy the oak." Nevertheless I am going to have for my principle, to fill my assigned place in life, do the duty that lies nearest & be happy." L.W. "Happiness, like health, is the normal state, & when this is not felt, the causes should be scrutinized & removed." In the evening Ada Mc Ada B Elsie & Miss Wright spent the evening with me. . . .

Friday, Apr. 5 [1895]. I rec'd a letter from Mabel; she will be married in June, her letter made me feel better for I do feel lonesome when I think of the girls getting married, not because I am not glad that they are going to make their lives more complete, but I will miss them much more than they do me—Miss W. don't seem to think I will ever be a success as a woman she doesn't say it in so many words but that is her idea. . . .

April 9 [1895]. I went to Shakespeare Ada was there I am very much afraid that we girls are permitting an indescribable feeling to spring up between us, sometimes it is hard to choke the tears back—but—I don't know what I can do to help it; I am only afraid of making matters worse. . . .

April 16th [1895]. I am very tired. Ada staid all night with me, we had a long visit before we went to bed. I kept thinking she was trying to get up courage to ask me something. I didn't know what—until she did ask me if I cared for anyone in a serious way. The past few weeks have been a very trying period, but I have made one deep resolution to be honest, frank through it all, & not to do one act that I will regret in years to come x x x x x So I told her all I felt that I ought.

Wed. Apr. 17 [1895]. Ada wrote to C.C. and asked him to call at Pease's for me & after we went Ada told me she had had a dreadful letter from him, it almost spoilt my whole evening, he didn't notice Ada all the evening, I don't think either one of them felt half as bad as I did. I wanted to ask him for an explanation when we came home, but as Ada asked me not to refer to it I did not.

Sat. Apr. 20 [1895]. I am very tired—Ada, Marie, and Jen staid to tea with me. Ada had another note from C.C., he loves her & I don't blame him. Why not fill one's usual place in life? I have all the material comforts and privileges of life it is not necessary that I be rich in happiness or hope. I care a great deal for them both, and shall do all I can to make them care for each other and be happy my happiness may come in the quiet of sacrifice. "The happiest life is the life of the largest mission, the disinterested life, the more abundant life which comes from following Christ". . . .

Wed. [April] 24 [1895]. We spent the evening at Aunt Maggie's. I was looking over my diary and Oh! How sorry I feel for the poor girl that wrote those almost desperate words,—that period was the saddest of my life, the world looks so different to me now & why?. . . .

Friday [April] 26 [1895]. Ada & I are reading Daniel Deronda [George Eliot's last novel] aloud. I think it wonderfully & beautifully written. The subtly varied drama between man & woman is often such as can hardly be put together except as dominoes, according to their fixed marks. The word of all work Love will no more express the myriad modes of attraction than the word Thought can inform you what is passing through your neighbor's mind. Poor Gwendolen, she was a girl of conscience, but her will power was so much stronger than that of her friends that she had no resources outside of her own. I don't quite understand Grandcourt's infatuation for her, it certainly was not <u>Love</u>, for I believe he loved Lydia, & would have married her had he not known that he could live with her any way, she certainly was charming—a noble woman even if she had erred, it was through love. . . .

May 6 [1895]. Ada is completely under the will of Jen; she Jen tells horrid little tales & has us understand they are town talk; I feel all that I can do is to bear it bravely but it is almost unbearable, & when I am trying so hard to forget the way she has treated me, she attempts for the second time to pass it all over by sending me flowers;—Oh! How dreadful it did make me feel, for she isn't sorry it only means "I should like to use you for my purpose a little longer Can I <u>ever</u> forget & <u>forgive</u>." When she cares so little for those I care so much for.

Oh, Ada we can never be the same no matter what the future brings forth, our love can never be quite the same in <u>this</u> world. Our relation to each other, has been a complete change but now we have broken a link; I tried so hard not to—I even hoped you would go home—before <u>some-body</u> succeeded in spoiling all—but it is too late—Oh! Ada some day may we understand <u>each other</u> better—"We shall know as we are known". . . .

May 19 [1895]. I resolved not to write another word until I could without any unkind thought or a bitter word, it has been so very hard, but I hope now I am ready to begin to live where I left off. I will try to learn of Gwendolyn and Ester & say "I will not grieve anymore." It is better—it shall be better—with me because I have known you.

Since I last wrote there has been a frost which has not only blighted vegetation but my hopes & as the weather always affected my morale & spiritual welfare, I am in hope that when the sun chooses to shine, my ambition will grow too. (My sweet peas are nearly 6 inches high.). . . .

July 1 [1895]. I went down to Lone Rock with C.B.C. he had business I had a very pleasant day, coming home we came to an understanding concerning the trouble in the Spring. I feel paid for going through all the little annoyances I did without saying anything about it. Mr. Cornwall is a friend I like and care for in the sense of companionship, who can never come too often or stay too long. . . .

july 9 [1895]. I have one of the schools here this fall, am very glad. It will be such a satisfaction to be able to at least <u>prove</u> my self a failure. But I am so anxious to teach that I don't feel as though I could do anything else than succeed. . . .

[The following entry was made by Ada Briggs in her cousin Ada James's diary.]

July 22 [1895]. Monday Evening. To-day, after a week of impatient waiting, I met at the St. P. depot my Ada and Bula, and Ada and I are just preparing to sleep side by side, where two cots have been placed together. How I do enjoy every minute with her. And haven't we improved the time since one o'clock this P.M.?

Dear Ada, let us endeavor to be together next year at this time, July 22, 1896. And let us remember our conversation and confidences exchanged in my little room in our home at 1545 10th St., Milwaukee.

Prophecy:—A fair young teacher, after a year of most successful work in the schoolroom, steps out into the world once more, followed by loving thoughts and dearest wishes of the little flock who will long for the return of Sept. because it may bring with it the bright presence of the girl who loved everyone of them. The girl who never tired of studying them, while she taught. Will she return to the school-room in Sept. 1896? Yes, I think she will, but her determination to make teaching a life work—or rather to confine her efforts principally to giving instruction in our public schools—is not quite so strong as it was when she told her coz. That she meant to become a fixture in the schoolroom. What has modified her determination? Well, ask that tall, athletic young gentleman who so cleverly sends the balls across the net to his fair opponent, for, methinks, he it is who should received the blame for what our schools have lost. No, it is quite true, that "Miss Ada's" face and actions will give us little information in this direction, but I have seen. It is July '96, and she is going to spend the 22nd day with her coz, Ada. I will let her tell you what her cousin confides to her upon this occasion, for I'm sure she means to tell Ada B. all about the tall young man with a slight foreign accent, and I've no doubt, will receive in exchange something less interesting, but—

[Ada James resumed writing in her diary with the following response.]

Sunday [Sept.] 8 [1895] . . . In the evening Charlie came up. Pa makes me feel very uncomfortable he aught to have made his objections a year

ago—am sorry but it is too late now. Nevertheless I don't intend to let it
worry me. I think a great deal of them both & they of me. I don't think
either will ever do anything to make me unhappy. . . .

Sunday Night Oct. 27 [1895]. Charlie was up this evening and we
went over to Irene's I don't think I realize how much I really care for
him—since my prayer has been answered so fully it has made me not only
selfish but ungrateful. I do love him enough and I know it for this
evening passed so quickly and I don't like to think it will probably be a
week before I will see him again. I realize now that I am not qualified to
go through the world alone. I want somebody in whom I have perfect
confidence to sympathize with me—I love my home and it is hard for me
to think of making a new one, at the same time I can be near all those I
think so much of, it isn't as though I was going away; it really means such
a slight change in my life. How mistaken Annie Hines was when she
thought I didn't care for him. If I can only be all I hope to be as a
woman. It is ten I just go to bed, that I may be fresh for the children tomorrow. I can't let my future dreams, effect the reality of their lives. I am
far from tired my forty-little folks. I am so <u>very very</u> happy all the time
now. Is "anticipation greater than Realization"—I can only hope not.

Sunday, Nov. 3 [1895] . . . Elsie and I have had a nice visit to-day—and
she has given me a splendid talk to-night she makes me sure I love CC
very dearly and if only pa & ma were willing I would be ready to marry
him anytime. I begin to believe that the sooner we are married the better
it will be for both of us. I wrote to Ada B. about it to-day. Oh! What
would I give to know exactly how she feels on the subject. . . .

Nov. 15 [1895]. Charlie's Birthday. I painted a porcelain placque for
him—the Eliot Club met here to-night. I like Romola very much especially after Son of Hagar—it is such a comfortable story. Last night I went
over to Irene's. I wonder if she is really happy or is only acting a part.
Perhaps it is only my imagination but it seems to me her spirit is broken.
I can't talk with her lately or look at her without feeling a sort of sadness.
I believe a girls first love is her deepest; the emotions are so new & doubt
of any kind isn't to exist. I don't believe any girl can say to a man unless
she loves him dearly ("Take my life & let it be as you will it") with out a
most dreadful sacrifice. . . .

Dec. 25 [1895]. Christmas. I have had a very pleasant day Elsie came up
to spend the day with me. CC called in the morning brought me Farm
Legends. I faired very well. Two handkerchiefs—doiley—basket, 5 books
& bookmarks. Handkerchief case & hair pin case. Aunt Lizzie's people

were here to dinner. In the afternoon Elsie & I went down to Miss W's. We had a very pleasant time. Miss W. goes to Milwaukee to-morrow . She wore my ring she is going to show it to Ada.

Jennie B. came last Friday she knew nothing of my engagement or did she ever suspect it. She seems to think Ada is in love with him, but I am inclined to believe Jennie is a little romantic & thinks it would add to the story to have two such friends & cousins in love with same man, but I think those things are horrid!. . . .

Jan. 14 [1896]. I have just finished my letter to C.C. he has misunderstood me. I told him no person ever lived or ever would live to whom I could give every bit of my love I have many friends who have choice locations in my heart. I know he doesn't want my whole heart & he couldn't have it if he did. I don't ask for his knowing it wouldn't do me any good. . . .

[Ada Briggs wrote the following entry in her cousin Ada James's diary.]

July 22, 1896. 1226 Prairie Street, Milwaukee, Wis.

To-night my Ada and I sit, as we did just one year ago, at 1545 10th Street, writing and talking, not by mere coincidence, but by appointment, and each has begged the other to open the diary of "the other Ada" with a prophecy for the coming year. These two pledging themselves to meet on the evening of July 22nd '97 for the same purpose.

My prophecy made for Ada has been nearly fulfilled—indeed, my success in this forecast has made me not a little conceited, since I commence this one with all confidence in its fulfillment.

Yes, my girl is to be married, is to leave the school and its children whom she loves and who love her so fondly, and is happy. Thus far, my prophecy has been correct, and Ada would allow the fact of my having described the one who was to rob the children of their teacher, as being directly opposite to the real "culprit," detract from her cousin's power as a prophet! In my opinion, such an unimportant point should not be considered. However, I shall prove myself the true prophet by giving a brief description of Ada's life between July 22, 1896 and July 22, 97.

She will be married, while it is yet summer, to a noble man—her ardent lover and her cousin's dear friend. Her house will be a very pretty nest, its decorations and many of its comforts being the work of her own skilled and loving hands.

I close my eyes and see these two enjoying each other, love, friendship, prosperity. How happy they look! The two perpendicular "grooves" which have so often haunted and marred my girl's forehead, forget to come, and if there is occasionally an anxious expression on her loving face, its cause will always be firm and how loving she is with the little one entrusted to her guidance! For her efforts and care she is repaid in the unbounded love and confidence of the child and those to whom Lora is most dear.

Ada is not selfish in her love, but love's mission is fulfilled in her lie, which is a constant effort to secure greater happiness and goodness for those who enter it.

I could write much more, but it is growing late, so I will close by writing of Ada as I see her on the evening of July 22, 97.

In looks, she has grown younger, and as I speak of the past year (perhaps with a sigh as I compose, contentedly, such lines), she falls into a reverie, and then tells me that the year has meant so much to her—laughs at the little failures, (which, by the way, have been confined to beef-steak, bread-making, laundrying of white shirts, and the like) and admits that she has not "lost the hold" of which she spoke regretfully a year ago, and that she is perfectly happy. So am I——

Conceitedly yours, <u>Sibyl</u>

[Ada James resumed writing in her diary with the following entry.]

Aug. 2 [1896]. Charlie was up last night, and I had such a nice visit. I feel as though could I only see him as often as I want to, I might be happy. I don't think he has any idea how much I love him—and can't anyone know how much it hurts when they tell me "he" doesn't love me—but then it is more wrong for me to listen to anyone (who knows so little of him) than it is for them to tell me. No one need try to make me think I can care for anyone else as I do for him—because if I should ever find he didn't love me <u>no one</u> else will I <u>ever</u> sacrifice my love and confidence for. I prayed for his love and my prayer was answered and if it wasn't best I should have it, my prayer never would have been drafted. Now I only ask that I may be a help and inspiration to him forever. Some times I think he doesn't care for me as much as he did—then I try to study him carefully and I come to the conclusion that something that doesn't directly concern me is worrying him—he has spells of being so absent-minded. . . .

Sept. 11 [1896]. It has been a rainy but a very enjoyable day—this morning I read Aurora Leigh aloud—we all enjoy it so much—I am reading Middlemarch to myself. I like to be reading two or three books at the same time, it is like visiting with just as many different people.

181

This afternoon Irene came over and we played cards, made candy, etc. I don't accomplish as much work as I mean to—it seems to be so hard for me to concentrate my thoughts or any degree of purpose. I am trying to the best of my ability not to let myself become despondent, or unsatisfied with my present aimless, neutral position in life, but I do hope it won't last long. I want to practice all the time. I can hardly keep away from the piano. I went to play at Goodwin's yesterday. I dearly love music—wish it didn't take a lifetime to become proficient in it.

Yesterday I was wondering why it was so hard for me to write in my diary this year. Sometimes I think it is because I don't write nearly as well as I used to. I must study more and write more.

I am just the age of Aurora where her story begins, perhaps this is just the beginning of the story of my life. I know it is an impossibility for me to live such a life as I would like but to have it within my power to do a great deal—and I must not worry others, or allow myself to think too much of my physical condition, Oh! If I only felt sure of my hearing but sometimes lately I have almost felt it slipping away. But I haven't the courage to consult a doctor or even to admit the fact. I must bring myself to do in the future as I have done in the past—namely—reassure myself that no matter what happens it is all for the best. I only wish I might know in time to make necessary plans for my future. It would be so much harder for me to have to be deaf now than it was three years ago. . . .

Sat. Oct. 3 [1896]. I can't help wondering sometimes if CC does love me as I do him. I wish he would come up oftener. I will be glad when every thing is settled. I am impatient to be occupied with something. For some reason I worry so much about Charlie—I realize now as never before that it would be very hard to go on living without him, it would nearly kill me to have to be separated always.

Nov. 1st [1896]. Last week Friday I felt as though there was nothing left to live for. It is a lovely Sunday morning and now I begin to feel as though I might live on and wear a cheerful face, even if the worst comes. I have felt since Oct. 20th as though I never could stand it, but to-day I feel full of new resolutions. I won't let myself hate and grieve any more I only hope Mr. B. won't come to Sunday School. Aurora Leigh would say this is my "heart's large seasons, when it hopes and fears, joys grieves and loves". . . .

[Ada James' diary entries became more sporadic during the months that followed. By the summer of 1897, however, she began to write more regularly in her diary.]

July 8th [1897]. I spent the 4th at Hub City with Can, Elsie, George, Irene & C.B.C. & Etta. About noon Winnie & Harry C. came over—all in all we had a very nice time.

I am surprised to find how much stronger I am both mentally and physically. I think I owe some of [it] to a science Dr. who has been treating me lately. I have read three books lately. 1st. A Woman Who Dares,—I liked better than I expected to—it was a description of a woman's married life, and it proves just what I have always believed, that her life will be just as pure as she makes it. I have just been greatly surprised at the insight of one or two of my friends married life that had a great deal to do with my not being a wife by this time, but her influence has all left me now. I know all kinds of Life are just what we make it. I hope no one will ever tell me of their personal experience again though she loved me dearly and told me just what she thought I ought to know.

I next read a Knight Errant—and enjoyed most of it very much. I only wish Edna Lyle wouldn't feel called upon to make her heroes & heroines so much more miserable than there is any need of.

This afternoon I finished Ideala if it had been my own life, it couldn't have been more real—she was probably a woman on a grander scale than I shall ever be, but never the less I know our values are very much alike. One quotation in it I particularly admired "All are but parts of one stupendous whole Whose body Nature is & God the Soul." That was given to prove that although possibly individually it may have been right for her to have married Lorrimer, the crime would have been from her influence. We, all of us owe a great deal to society, and we should feel ourselves under the most rigid observance of her laws. How often or unconsciously we depend on society to protect us, then let us if necessary sacrifice ourselves to defend that great system of which we are a part.

[Ada Briggs wrote the following entry in her cousin Ada James's diary.]

July 31 1897. A.L.J.'s Room. Prophecy No. 3
Another year has passed without the complete fulfillment of my last prophecy for my girl. Warning of Electricity! Just five minutes more of light in which to make my forecast for my girl's next year!

Only this I have to say—that my prophecy for '97 will be fulfilled in '98, that she is happy in the pure and unselfish love of a husband who could have been blamed only as he had been misunderstood. That he is happy in the love of a noble wife—   Ever lovingly, Sibyl

March 10th '98. Since I last wrote in my diary how very much has happened. This year has been sad, so sad,—Beulah is in Boston and my other sister, Annie, in Heaven, Oh! To think O.B. a father and a widower, I have wondered & thought so much about Annie and baby to-day. Oh! Annie's life was so sad, but I think I should much rather have lived her life than that of either of her sisters,—

"Life at present does look so sad, but my religion, is to try to be happy, at least to seem so and try to make others happy xxx I am happy because I am busy and that is everything but how deeply I do feel at times when I am not on my guard.

I have thought of this poem often lately and find it so hard this "standing alone."

I shall soon be twenty two, I dead my birthday.. I am so weary of "standing alone". . . .

Oct. 26 [1898]. Went to Milwaukee and staid two weeks, I had a very nice time. We girls all went to see Julia Marlow, she is a beautiful woman. C.B.C. was up twice while I was there. If we had both of us only been different from the first "It might have been." I sometimes regret that we weren't married three years ago. . . .

May 16th [1899]. Was a very hard day in spite of Uncle B's & Aunt J's care, we went up to St. Paul in the morning & the Dr gave me my first treatment [for deafness], we couldn't fiind a boarding place so I had to go home with Cousin Henry—it was hard Oh! So hard for me to say good bye to Uncle B & Aunt J each day has made them so much dearer to me. x x I spent the eve by myself reading Marcella, the other went to a social—their home is very large & perhaps grand but not cosey or homey. I like Helen very much & stay in Newport until Sat. but it is too hard on me to go back & forth.

Fri. night [May] 19th [1899]. I went with Helen for a long walk it was a beautiful walk, from the top of one bluff we could see where the St. Croix emptied into the Mississippi & on one direction & St. Paul is on the other while the Miss. flowed just below us. . . .

June 4 [1899]. Arrived home. . . .

June 23rd [1899]. Had the best Alumni we have ever had much better than would have been possible had I remained president. Met C.B.C. several times.

C.B.C. married June 25th. . . .

March 23rd [1900]. Am twenty-four—Mama gave me a set of Shakespeare's, "Hannah Thurston," a book of quotations and a Browning birthday book, Beulah gave me a fancy corset cover & Elsie a spoon.

Beulah went to Madison where she will spend a couple of days, with Maude and Vera before going to Milwaukee. Bertha Ott died this morning at four. Mama & I called. She was the most beautiful corpse I ever saw. Oh! If we only knew more concerning death. . . .

April 2nd & 3rd [1900]. Taught for Belle over to the kindergarten—I should love the work if my hearing was only acute enough—I should be tempted to take up Kindergarten work—They were all cunning but little Amanda Crocker comes as near perfection in both looks & character of any child I know. I hope Crockers will always stay in the neighborhood so that I can't at least see her once in a while—. . . .

March 3d [1901]. The girls are here to lunch. B[eulah] got white organdie for her wedding dress it is going to be ever so pretty. . . .

Wed. April 24 [1901]. Beulah is sick but I am doing what I can to help her get ready. I am determined nothing shall happen to darken her plans. These days are rather sorry reminders for me—but I have no one to blame but myself—therefore I mustn't make other people unhappy—I have times of feeling awfully hard toward anyone who said anything against my marrying when I wanted to so I have been careful to keep anything against Rob from the family. He is ever so much like C.B.C. they would neither be financial successes—but would make up for that loss in their sunny dispositions. Well I have lost <u>all</u> of the best life has to give but I still have the second best & Oh! God might I pray my Father help me to hang on to that—never again let the <u>worst</u> in life tempt me. . . .

Thurs. May 2d [1901]. Elsie & Irene came early & we worked fast getting everything fixed before twelve. B & R were married at twelve sharp by Mrs. Loomis—Mabel played the march—Bernard [Pease] & I stood up with them it wasn't half as hard as I thought it was going to be. Just as Mabel struck the first cords Bernard kissed Beulah good-bye. The ceremony was ever so pretty & immediately afterward the Ewing family played Mendelsohn's "Spring Song" they played all during dinner too. Elsie got the ring.

I had made my preparations to give Beulah a great send off—and when dinner was over, Mabel, Bess & some of the other young people went down after their rice shoes etc. B went over to Aunt C's to say good-bye & as she went bareheaded I never suspected a thing until nearly train time when they told me she had been on her way to La Farge for nearly an hour—Papa got up at four and took the double carriage

185

with her hat & grip down to Terry's barn—& she stopped off down there bareheaded,—Terry & Maud took them up there—Well I went down to the train anyway & it was lots of fun to see the others get left, Mabel insisted on sending her rice by Morris Carrol—to throw on them if they got on at the crossing . . . In the evening we girls went over to see how grandma stood the day—but she seemed to be feeling real well . . . The wedding presents were scrumptious & we were so surprised at some for sending anything & Dr. & Mrs. DeLap gave them a handsome dining room set, besides Mrs. H. gave Rob hemstitched sheets, pillow cases, blankets, comfort, sprad, etc. for a bed . . . They had a reception for them at La Farge—the band was out and they had a little banquet. . . .

June 10 1901. I am sitting by the side of Beulah—I have such a terrible feelings about giving her up now, physically, of course. I won't have to any other way—my hand is in her hair, I combed it just as she did when she was married—Oh! Beulah it is going to be so lonely—but I shall try to grieve for you as little as possible for you dear unselfish sister that is what you would have us do I'm sure—Tell me if you can sometime why it wasn't me for a can't see how you could be spared—if you can communicate with us in any way you must answer all the questions I want so much to ask. Try to let us know what you would have us do. . . .

Jan. 1/02 [1902]. The day was dreadfully lonely. I have thought for some time that I knew what it was to be sad but I didn't suppose one could suffer quite so much to feel so badly you can't cry but ache all over. Just a year ago last night Beulah, Vera and I went over to Lottie's to watch the old year out—had I known what the new year was to deprive us of I never could have met it. This is the first time I have written in a diary since Beulah died,—Oh! You dear beautiful sister do know how I love even worship you? A year ago last night you won your solitaire over to Lottie's and how they all teased you.

The Diary of Gertrude Cairns, 1896–1898

Gertrude Cairns was born on December 9, 1872, to Abbie (Leavitt) and George W. Cairns of River Falls, Wisconsin. He was a native of New York State who had immigrated to Middleton, Wisconsin, in 1849. From there he moved to River Falls, where in 1866 he married Abbie S. Leavitt, a native of Maine who came to Pierce County in 1857 and taught school. Their four children

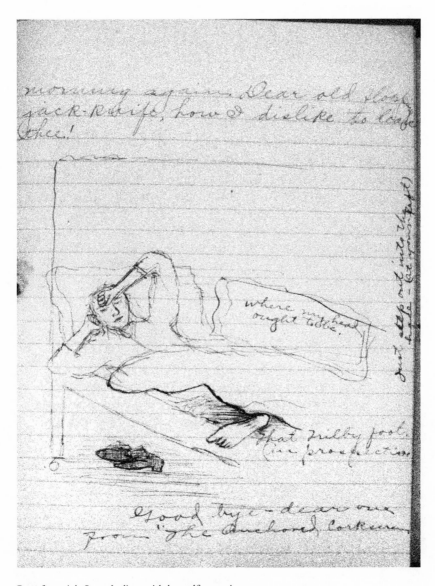

Page from Ada James's diary with her self-portrait

187

were William, who became a professor at the University of Wisconsin (and for whom the Cairns Collection of American Women Writers is named); Rolla, who became a medical doctor and practiced in River Falls; Gertrude M., who went on to graduate from the University of Wisconsin in Madison and taught school at Durand, Superior, and Ellsworth, Wisconsin; and George Wilfred, who died at age five.

Gertrude kept diaries for most of her life. Her early diaries are tiny bound books, the first of which, "The Ladies' Note-book and Calendar," was published by the World's Dispensary Medical Association in Buffalo, New York. She began writing in it on December 30, 1883, when she was eleven. Her third diary, comprised of loose-leaf pages, covers the years from 1896 to 1898 and contains lengthy introspective entries written while she was attending the University of Wisconsin in Madison. No diary entries from 1899 until 1903 are extent; in 1903 Gertrude began creating a sustained life record, which continued until 1936, all on loose-leaf eight-by-eleven-inch pages. She wrote two hundred to three hundred pages per year until December 31, 1936.

Gertrude often referred to her diary as her "Life Book," and numerous diary entries reveal that she wrote with the intention of her diary's serving as her version of the story of her life. During this period she sometimes made notes during the week and then wrote a lengthy and detailed diary entry at the end of the week, recounting the week's activities and reflecting on their significance. Sometimes she wrote retrospectively, simultaneously creating diary and memoir.

Gertrude M. Cairns died on October 12, 1959, and is buried in Maple Grove Cemetery in Ellsworth, Wisconsin. The volume of her diary from which the following excerpts are taken was written during an extremely difficult period in her mid-twenties, a period that truly marked her coming of age.

Ellsworth, Wis., May 3, 1896. It is nearly two years since I last wrote in my Life Book,—I do not know what name to call it by,—and there are a number of things that I should like to have recorded. Not that my life during the past two years has been so eventful. On the contrary I should call it very uneventful, yet there have been a few things which have influenced my life sufficiently to make me wish that they had been written down. Some of them I may record yet though I had much rather they had been written at the time. I had almost thought that this was folly, until I read over some of the records of two years ago. It is not simply the pleasure that it gives me to read over the story of those other days and the opportunity to laugh at what I laughed at then and to recall the forgotten pleasures of those days but it is a record of growth and through it all I can trace the development of my character, weak and faulty as it is. When I compare my thoughts of that time with those of to-day I can measure myself and see whether I am growing better or worse. So I mean to make it as before a true record. There will be things in this as there are in that, that I will wish to blot out! But this is but a miniature, a dim reflection of the real Life Book I am writing every day, every hour, whether I would or not. There are no gaps in that. Every page is written on. Some I would gladly blot out if I could. Some of it I cannot read now but I shall read it some day and know truly how I have builded whether for good or ill.

I think I better begin back and take up the thread of my life where I dropped it and bring it down to the present time as but I can, writing of course from the standpoint of to-day, but touching on the most important events that have occurred in the past two years, and filling up a little the gap that seems to yawn between my present self and that I left in my former record. Then when any thing worth while does occur I shall feel ready to record it here. Meanwhile I shall keep in mind the object and aim as expressed in the opening of my new book, February 1, 1894,—"It is to be filled with 'freales and fragments,'—anything which comes into my head which I have a fancy to write down."

The last entry I made bears date of June 6, 1894, but this is merely the production of the Rhetoric class entitled "The Catbird." The last real record was written June 2. The next day I went out to Will's to find a rather unexpected arrival in the shape of a six pound boy. Dora was planning to celebrate Will's birthday the next day but was forced rather unceremoniously to change her plans to accomodate the newcomer. I went out every day during the rest of my stay there to see how Dora and the baby were getting along.

Tuesday afternoon I went out and got supper and looked after things so Will could meet with the Literature Seminary. Mrs. Bateman came. There was a Silhouette Social that evening that I wanted very much to go to but was too tired and besides I had my lessons to get. I found myself too exhausted to accomplish anything.

Next day the crash came though I did not realize it for several days. My eyes failed me entirely so I could not use them at all. The next day Rollo took me down to see Dr. Everett. He gave me a long and rather painful examination,—opthalmic I suppose he called it,—and concluded by fitting me with glasses and telling me I must wear them for a while and give my eyes complete rest during the summer and they would be all right. He also gave me a lot of tonics. I knew better than he said for I felt that the trouble was more serious than that. When I got the glasses I found they did no good. I might use my eyes a little longer with them, but the pain was the more severe afterwards. That was a horrible time. I shall always remember it. Everyone was busy preparing for examinations, so I could not inflict myself on my friends. Any use of my eyes was out of the question as far as close work was concerned, so reading, writing or sewing which would have occupied my time was denied me, and for once I had more time than I knew what to do with. Thinking was ~~out of the question~~ torture for I could think only along one line and the knowledge of what the news would mean to mother drove me almost wild. I think I kept up a little hope until I tried the glasses Everett gave me Saturday and found I could not use them. Then I was almost in despair. It seemed as though all the hopes I ever had, all my plans for the future were suddenly without foundation and I was left alone I knew not where.

Sunday I reached about the depth. I went to the services as usual with the exception of evening church service. Someone from away was to speak and the light hurt my eyes so I thought best to come home. Mr. Cowles asked me to go into church but I answered him almost rudely and told him to go along, that I was going home. He came with me of course. I was worked up to a fever heat and I talked bitterly, unreasonable, wickedly, I felt almost desperate when we reached the Hall and he did what he never did before insisted on my walking farther. It was a lovely night and he talked to me and tried to reason with me until when he left me I was quieter and more reasonable than before. During the week that followed I passed through a trial that seemed all I could bear. It <u>was more</u> than <u>I</u> could bear alone but through God's help and the kindness of friends it was borne. Prof. Freeman, Dr. Turner, and Prof. Van Cleef gave me oral examinations. I wrote a little for Prof. Frankenburger then gave up. He worked me well though. Latin was the worst. I knew my class work had been poor, I had no chance to review and was too afraid to try to take an oral examination so I tried to write. I worked about twenty minutes but my eyes pained me so I almost fainted and I hurried from the room without thinking of leaving my examination book. I might have passed on what I had already written but I never thought of that.

One of the brightest things during this dark week was Lucile Schreiber's kindness. She came up and spent all Wednesday afternoon reading Greek to me. Of course she could have done twice as much work alone, but she was so good she sacrificed all that to help me.

Thursday of this week June 14th, I went on a "Dove Basket Picnic," given by the Henwood girls. About sixteen of us went. I do not recall all now but can name a few,—Mrs. Henwood and her two daughters, Mrs.

Snyder and her two daughters, Marie Woll, Rilla Post, Lucile Schreiber, Mary Walbridge. There were sixteen in all. Rilla Post's little brother was the only boy along. We took the car out to Elmside and explored then walked back to Schuetzen Park where we had our supper. We wanted to go in swimming but some men came with the same object in view and we finally surrendered to them. The electric car was in the dark part way home but the moon was bright and we had a lovely time all around.

The Sunday following, Baccalaureate Sunday, it rained hard all day. We took the car to church in the morning. Dr. Updike preached a splendid sermon on the "Relation of the churches of the State to the University." The University Y.M. & Y.W.C.A. have since had it published and distributed copies through the state.

That night T. C. Richmond delivered an address to the C.E. [Christian Evangelical] Society. I tried to lay aside my prejudice and value it for what it was worth. I think I learned something from my experience in speaking of him. Mr. Cowles came home with me though I urged him not to for he had been sick for several days.

May 7, 1896. This is a perfect day, too warm some might say but surely one ought not to complain with such a delightful breeze blowing. As I sit here by the window in my room listening to the clear notes of an oriole I can rise my eyes and look from the window at the apple trees in full bloom and all the time I am writing I breathe the sweetness of their perfume. Altogether the world seems so sweet I almost dread turning to those dark days but I am determined to finish my record so will take up the thread where I dropped it last Sunday. The last I wrote of was Baccalaureate Sunday, June 17, 1894. Monday night I went to the Senior Class Pageant at Library Hall with Mr. Cowles. The Pageant was arranged from Midsummer Night's Dream with the introduction of interludes appropriate to the time, as the Senior Thesis, Synoptical Lectures,—Paleontology and Geology,—and the Psychology Class. I enjoyed the evening very much. Mr. Cowles was not feeling much better and I made up my mind to scold him for working so hard, so when he came the next evening to take me to the Science Hall Reception as it was quite early I in part suggest[ed] walking up the hill. I attempted to carry out my purpose on the way but he only laughed at my scolding and I got mad and quit. I enjoyed the Science Hall Reception though I was unable to use my eyes much. Mr. Cowles was continually surprising me by the account of information he had picked up from sources which most people would have overlooked. . . .

Mr. Cowles and I said Good bye that night. Our parting was much like our acquaintance. There was nothing sentimental about it. Certainly not on his part. When he said he hoped to see me back in the fall I told him "No" our parting was for good and all. It would probably be some time if I ever returned to the University and he would be gone before I got back.

That was the last I saw of him that year. The next night I came home. The journey was hard and disagreeable and I dreaded what was coming. Will had in part broken the news to mother but it was hard enough as it was. And oh! That summer. Cousin Alice was here dying of consumption. The heat was terrific and it was so dry and dusty. Mother was without help and as sure as I tried to help her I was clear down I can only shudder as I look back at it. I could not read, I could not sew. The only occupation I had was a little knitting and tearing a few carpet rags. All the writing I could do was with a tight bandage over my eyes. The folks tried to read to me a little but that was not like reading as I had been used to, and much of the time I was alone with my thoughts and at times thinking was almost madness.

It was not until cooler weather in the fall that I saw any improvement in my eyes and then it was but slight. About the beginning of the New Year I began to use my eyes a little by daylight on bright days. I was glad of that but it was so little to one with the ambitions I once had. The doctors told me I would recover but there seemed little hope. Of course I knew the truth. The difficulty was not with my eyes. It was a general break down and I had that most trying of diseases, Nervous Prostration. Most trying, because few that have not suffered from it can ever realize anything about it. It seemed so hard to know that people said nothing ailed me. It was all imagination. If I would only go to work I would be all right. Had they known what it meant to me to leave the University they never could have said so. The last year with the exception of those last few weeks of misery when I knew I was breaking down, was I believe I can truly say the happiest of my life. If I had only given up that Latin as soon as I felt the strain—but I am done with regrets. Well, it is over with now. I dare not hope that my eyes will ever be quite the same but I am growing stronger I believe right along and the Doctor says I may go back in the fall if I take two years instead of one. I don't mind that now for my class is gone and it won't be the same. I think I have lost some of my ambitions and dreams but I have been through a fiery furnace and I hope I have come out purified.

Of one thing I am thankful. Through the darkest days of all, at first when I felt as though a door were suddenly closed in my face and I could see no farther or during that dreadful summer and fall,—through it all I never for a moment lost sight of God or my faith in Him. I couldn't understand it and I rebelled like a wilful child but all the time I felt He knew best and some day in some way he would make it right. He has. A little over a week ago I found myself saying "I am glad that my eyes failed me." Yes, I am glad of all that these two years have brought. Glad of it all for I am nearer God than I was two years ago. I thought when I left Madison with its glorious Church privileges, its opportunities for Bible Study and the Christian Endeavor and Christian Associations that I was leaving all that would help me grow, but the material for growth is ready here and I have grown nearer God and I can say now more truthfully than two years ago. "Thy Will not mine be done."

May 8, 1896. This must of necessity be in fragments. I will add a little to-day though I do not feel very much like writing.

There was little occurred during that first year of my house stay that is worthy of recording. Saturday June 30, the Excelsiors went to the Rush River Club House to camp for a week. I went down with the crowd but was there only part of the week. My stay there was very pleasant, though nothing particular occurred. We spent the time eating and sleep-ing,—though I didn't succeed very well at the latter,—lying in the ham-mock, playing bean bags, or fishing. I succeeded in catching one trout and a number of "shiners" ~~and~~ as the boys called the smaller fish . . . One thing impressed me quite forcibly, and that was the contrast between this crowd and the one I had just left at Madison, and more I was especially privileged in having the friendship of such boys as I knew there. Our Excelsior crowd included the cream of the Ellsworth boys, and yet I could not help feeling that something was lacking. I should not care to trust them as I would have trusted the boys in our Madison crowd. . . .

May 10, 1896. There was little happened during the rest of that year. I was much worse in the fall but began to improve slightly in the winter though the severe cold was rather hard. Alice died in February. When her mother's letter came it found Mother coming down with a very serious illness. She had inflammation of the bowels and grip and for over a week was in danger but thanks to Dr. Hancock's excellent care she recovered though slowly. All through March she scarcely sat up and it was well into April before she was about again. Of course everything fell on my shoul-ders and it was rather hard for me but I was very thankful to be here to help care for her. When she began to improve Dr. Hancock commenced treating me. He gave me enough medicine but laid all the stress on rest and general toning up. I believe he did as well as anyone could and now I hope to go back in the fall. . . .

May 14, 1896. This is as disagreeable a sort of a day as one could wish for. In fact it has rained almost steadily since night before last with only occasional breaks to give one hopes of cleaning off to be as quickly disap-pointed. Every thing is drenched and as I sit here listening to the monot-

onous beat of the rain upon the roof I feel too stupid to write or do anything else . . . The event of interest that occurred Friday was the arrival of
John and Will Dixon from Maiden Rock. They rowed up in the morning.
Of course we all knew that it was Alice's birthday and after the first greetings surrendered John to her. Will was around chatting with all of us
until dinner-time. Afterwards he sat down near me and we were soon
chatting on various subjects. Some water lilies excited his interest and he
suggested going in search of some, provided I wasn't afraid to risk myself
with him as he never rowed before that day. The lake was still and I told
him I wasn't afraid, besides I could row myself. So we were soon across
the lake. I didn't know just where the lilies were. We went clear to the
main channel, interviewed some fisherman and went back as far as the
lotus lily had only to learn that the water lilies had been all gathered to
take to the circus at Red Wing. Then we started back but took it very
slowly . . . The time passed swiftly enough and we were in the midst of
our discussions when we reached shore. Other things occupied our time
until supper when he sat beside me and when we finished suggested
another boat-ride. The lake was finer than ever and I was ready but others had secured the boats so at his next suggestions we were soon comfortably seated in a hammock at the top of the bank where we could
watch the lake. Here our discussion was continued and we talked of a
great many things. I enjoyed talking with him for he had thought and
spoke for himself. When the first boats returned we were again too late to
secure them and he declared that he was going to have a boat-ride if he
had to wait until midnight to get it. About ten o'clock one of the boats
came in and he was ready to go. I objected because of the late hour but
he urged that John and Alice were still out and we might as well go out a
little way. I wanted to tell him our relations were slightly different from
those of John and Alice, but finally yielded.

That was my first mistake. It was too late and I knew it, but it was a
perfect night and I knew it was my last night in camp and it would be a
long time before I should have another boat-ride. He had so far proved
very agreeable company and I knew no reason why I should not expect
him to continue so. The temptation was too great. If I had only resisted
it there might have been nothing unpleasant to remember, but I will not
forestall my story.

We were soon out on the lake. The moon shone full and clear, so
bright the stars scarce showed in the blue above; the surface of the lake
was scarcely rippled and the air was so warm and soft that though I took
a shawl, I needed no wrap and sat luxuriating in the beauty of the night.
Mr. D. paddled slowly or drifted about, sometimes talking sometime in
silence. We saw a boat far in the distance and a few moments later heard

John's deep, mellow voice singing the air of his favorite ditty. Then all was silence save the lap of the waves against the side of the boat. I felt perfectly contented, and yet through it all I think there was a feeling of foreboding. My uneasiness was greatly increased when after making some inquiries about my comfort he wanted to know if that seat was not large enough for two. It was large enough for three or four but I didn't care to share it just then, still when he said he guessed he would move over there and try it as he didn't find his seat without a back very comfortable, I hardly knew how to object; and moving to one side I gave him plenty of room. He was scarcely seated before he became more solicitous than ever about my comfort, urging me to lean back but I insisted that I was all right. Then he expressed a fear that I was getting cold and in spite of my denials wrapped the shawl about me, and as might be expected forgot to take his arm away. I leaned forward turning towards him so as to leave it around me as little as possible and continued talking, while I was busy with an under current of thought trying to decide what was best to do. I was beginning to get angry but was not quite sure as to what course was best to take when after several unsuccessful attempts to get me nearer he invited me as coolly as though he had merely been offering me his arm to lay my head upon his shoulder. I was too surprised and angry to make much of a reply but managed to say "No, Thank you," in a tone that I think conveyed my meaning more fully than words. I had suggested going in several times before but he had objected but when I did so again he said "all right" in a tone of icy politeness, took the oars and in a very few moments we were on shore. I was so angry when I went to the tent that I could scarcely think but my anger was directed chiefly against myself and I called myself a "fool" many times for allowing him the opportunity and then not telling him what I thought of it. As far as the last goes I have ceased to regret it. If I had said anything I should undoubtedly have said too much and I feel sure he understood my mean-ing as it was. I have naturally thought quite a bit about it, and though I don't know what kind of society he has moved in to make such things so much a matter of course, I do not think he intended it for an insult, and though I do not in the least approve of it I know how some people regard it and am willing to overlook it for the most part.

The mosquitos routed out the party the next morning and by four o'clock the boys were off for Maiden Rock and I have not seen him to speak with him since. I did meet him on the street one evening last sum-mer and he did not speak but I thought perhaps he did not recognize me. He called to see Mother once since and she said seemed very friendly, but I was gone. Well, it was only an episode and I hope it will grow less unpleasant as time passes by. . . .

Ellsworth, Wis., May 31, 1896. Sunday. I have been so busy lately I have found no time to write and to-day my head aches so I cannot think much. I have been trying to get mother ready to send to Madison on a visit. I have done a little sewing and as I am slow at that I do not progress very rapidly. This record will have to wait for its completion a little longer. Meanwhile I will try to keep up all that is worth recording, but before I go farther I will add a fancy that occurred to me last evening when thinking of the other members of the class of '91, R.F.H.S.

> "I too have lived!
> Not such a life as yours that bears rich fruit,
> Which all men, looking, may behold,—
> Yet have I lived! And as the sculptor
> With careful touches, scarce perceived,
> Works out his thought and molds it into form
> That all the world admiring sees;
> So in these seemingly idle years
> My life has framed itself and wrought
> Such changes as though not seen on earth
> May yet be visible in heaven."

July 12, 1896. It has been a long time since I last wrote and so many things have occurred that I don't see how I shall ever catch up with my writing. I don't know whether my life has suddenly become more eventful, or whether I take more note of events since I have been recording them. Certainly there are some things which I want very much to have written here, so much so in fact that I shall not attempt to follow chronological order but write those first and then record the others if I have time later. Just a month ago Mother started for Madison on a visit and was gone until June 30 when Rolla and she returned. During much of that time father was gone surveying. I spent two nights alone with the dog but most of the time Etta Rounce stayed with me. Wednesday June 17 was the first night we ever slept together in spite of our long acquaintance. We didn't sleep except the last part of the night though for we did considerable talking. We discussed a good many different people but some way Will Dixon came in for rather more than his share of interest. We became confidential and Etta told me of an experience which she had had with him, which though entirely different from mine yet showed one side of the peculiarities of the man. I had kind of partially pledged myself to confession in view of hers, but hardly had courage to proceed when I found the line along which hers followed. However I did tell of the little occurrence on the lake. She expressed her surprise. Said she had heard before that he was soft but never imagined he went to that extreme. I

196

asked her the same question I have asked myself many times. In that case "why didn't he show it before?" There was plenty of opportunity when we were alone there in the hammock and a hammock is generally supposed to afford the most excellent opportunities for such things. Yet he kept very considerately to his end of the hammock and in fact threw me completely off my guard. She was no better able to answer the question than I. The only explanation I can give is that he is so intensely original that he can't even be "soft" except in an original way. As to what his real intention was I am no nearer a decision than ever. Sometimes I really believe it was an intentional insult and at others I feel it was wholly due to ignorance. As to which is true or whether either is I am wholly undecided. Well, this isn't the worst of it all. I think the reason for our discussion of him in the first place was the fact that he was attempting to get a Summer School here. I had caught a glimpse of him on the street but did not really meet him until the following Sunday at church. I went into church just behind Mrs. Canbacker and her mother and just as I went into the door Mrs. Brown was shaking hands with some one and looking up I saw it was Mr. Dixon. His hand was still extended and I could hardly help doing the same but I barely spoke and passed on. Etta gave a sly wink but I tried to keep my face expressionless though I felt sure it was flushing. I took a seat beside her and a few moments later I was conscious without looking around that Mr. Dixon took a seat behind us. I saw nothing more of him however for he passed out as quickly as the service closed. I saw nothing more of him and heard nothing of the Summer School until last Monday. . . .

Dec. 9, 1896 THE VIEW FROM MY WINDOW

Oh! That I had the poet's tongue
To sing thy praises now,
Where rosy cloudbanks low are hung
Along yon hilltop's brow,
Where Learning's mighty halls arise,
Tall tower and stately dome,
Dark outlined 'gainst the sunset skies,
Our Alma Mater's home.
Fair scene that greetst me as I gaze,
Soon fad'st thou from my sight,
And o'er thy beauties now there lays
All black the pall of night.
So soon the pall of years must come.
May I as peaceful wait their doom!

No. 631, Langdon St., Madison, Wis. December 19, 1896. Here is a long gap. I did not think when I left this it would be so long before I took it up again but I have kept so busy at other things I have found no time to gratify my taste in this line.

I don't know as I have much to write to-night. Enough has happened in the interval but I am not in the mood to write it. The fact is I have been having a genuine attack of the blues though I am ashamed to own it. The reasons for it are various. In the first place there is a bit of homesickness. I have never spent a Christmas away from home and I don't want to this one, but it will cost so much for Rolla and I to go home that we don't feel as though we could afford it. I felt almost desperate I wanted to go so much but to-night I feel more at peace. Another thing that troubles me is about my room. Unless I get a room mate, I must make some change and the question is what for there is little prospect of a room mate that I can learn of. This with some extra work and a cold have combined to make me feel the most like a fit of the blues that I have this year but I have tried desperately hard to fight it off, though with doubtful success. However I feel somewhat better now. I should be abed but Esther Gordon has come up to study so I am writing for her.

Tuesday, December 22, 1896. I am in no mood for studying to-night. In fact I don't feel like doing anything. This will be the first Christmas I ever spent away from home and though some of the other clouds have cleared away and I had even thought I could see the sun through that it still is there. I have got most of my Christmas presents in order and to-morrow will send them off. I have done far less than usual this year but have tried to remember some of the most intimate of my friends. As for myself I don't know yet what I should do. Dora has asked me to take dinner there in case we are to remain in the city, and we have about con-cluded to do so.

The room question is settled by my deciding to take the little room and I suppose I shall move in soon. Well, I shall be glad to be settled. As for the other troubles, I believe I shall be glad when this Christmas Vaca-tion is over. I wonder if I am wicked. I am afraid I am. After all there are many things far worse than the disappointments I bear. It is selfishness that ails me and I mean to put it aside and make these last days of 1896 happy ones. This is enough for the present and the future. Now for a ret-rospect. So many things have occurred in the last few months that I scarcely know where to begin, and yet none of them have been of impor-tance as far as I can see. . . .

How does it feel to take up the thread of life here again? Very good in many ways, and yet I cannot help feeling that it is not the same strand that I dropped. Others have outgrown me. The world has moved on in these two years that I have been doing nothing. Those who were below me then are above me now. I must be content to have it so. Our old crowd is pretty well scattered. A few however remain. . .

New Year's Eve, 1897. Here I sit listening to the driving of the rain,—for it is raining outside this last night of the old year,—weeping for the departure of 1896. I wonder of what the tears are symbols. Will not 1897 bring as much of joy? Will it hold greater sorrows in store for me as well as others? God alone knows, and I thank Him that I have learned to trust all things in His hands. What blessed lessons this old year has brought me! Some of them were hard to learn, but well worth the learning. How much of happiness and yet how much of pain! That blessed glimpse of the other world, caught through the loss of that one who had come to be a dear friend,—Would I part with that? Even to bring him back again? For myself, no. But how my heart aches at the thought of those others far dearer to him, for whom the gates did not open wide enough for them to see through the blinding tears.

Then the happiness of return to work once more,—how it thrilled me, and all the blessings that Christian Endeavor has brought me,—sure this year has been rich. Friends,—there is one thought there. I have true, dear friends among the girls, those who love and trust me I believe. I have acquaintances among the boys, those whom I should dare call upon for assistance if necessary, though I do not expect to need them as long as I have Rolla with me, but yet in the deeper sense I scarcely feel that I have any masculine friends. I wonder why. Is it my sharp tongue? They seem to like that, and they know I do not mean the unkind things I may say. They are considerate enough to take them in the spirit in which they are spoken, and yet after all I wonder if they do not lead them to think that I have no heart no feeling for the deeper things. Surely they cannot, and yet I am not the one any of them choose when they need help. I do want to help somebody. Perhaps my forte is not with the young men, but yet I don't want <u>even</u> them to think me without feeling. I wonder why I inserted that "even." After all I believe I am in a wondering mood to-night. Perhaps I better chance to a resolve. Resolutions are in order, or will be to morrow. How is this? "Resolved that I will guard my tongue more closely this coming year." That certainly is a wise resolution. May God help me to keep it.

I must stop this. It is growing late and I shall catch cold sitting here to say nothing of being too sleepy to get up in the morning. I had fancies though that seemed determined to get on paper, and here they are, or at least such of them as stayed in my heart long enough. . . . .

199

Madison, Wis., June 21, 1898. Tuesday. The mood is on me & I must write to-night. I scarcely know what though. I may be interrupted any moment & then the spell will be broken but now I wish to write. I am just closing a book of my life, closing it forever. I have begun on the last chapter. To-day I attended the Class Day Exercises of the Class of the U.W. '98. Two days more and I shall have my diploma and be a full-fledged graduate & what then? Ah, what then! But I am not very sad to-night and I do not mean to allow myself to be. It is time there is a vein of sadness, a vein I cannot free myself from, at the thought of leaving here forever. I have won friends here, who are very dear & whom I may never meet again. I have found associations which must be broken. I have enjoyed my work here better than anything else I ever did and I love Madison and the dear, old University and I must leave all this and I real-ize it. It is not strange that I should feel somewhat sad, but I am far from hopeless. I realize that my future lies in the same hands as my past. I look forward to it without shrinking, simply trusting it in the hands of the dear Father, who has cared so tenderly for me in the past. In his hands I know it will be sage. I leave a bright, a glorious, a happy life here, but with God's help the future shall be brighter & happier. I have ceased liv-ing in the past. I mean to live in the future. Not that I shall forget the past. Far from it. It will be a precious memory to me, but I shall remem-ber that there are opportunities for happiness in the future as well if I will but seek them. When I closed the door on my High School life, I felt that I was closing the door on any happiness, yet I have been far happier than I ever was there. So as I close the door on the happiness of Univer-sity life I trust that I shall open it to the richer fuller life beyond. What does it hold for me? Sometimes I long to know, but often I am glad I do now know. It must hold sorrow and disappointment. It could not be oth-erwise, but those I would have hidden from me and the happiness I can picture and dream of, and I am too fond of dreaming, so I had rather live each day as it comes & not know the future, but if I use the lessons I have here learned the future must grow brighter, and so each year of my life shall be happier than the last throughout this life and, I believe, throughout eternity. Such is the message of this time to me.

The Diary of Dorothea Barland, 1903

Margaret Dorothea ("Thea") Barland, born in 1888, was one of six children of Dora (Schlegelmilch) and John C. Barland of Eau Claire, Wisconsin. The Barland family, which was not well-to-do, lived on a dairy farm near Eau Claire, and Dora often went to stay

with her "Grossmama," Augusta Krueger Schlegelmilch—the
mother of Dorothea and Agnes's mother, Dora Schlegelmilch Barland. Dorothea and Agnes (excerpts from whose diary appear in
chapter 3) had four brothers: Thomas Gordon (mentioned in
diary as Gordon, aged fourteen), John Howard and George
Clarence (the babies mentioned in the diary), and Charles Herman
(mentioned in the diary as Herman, aged nine). At times Thea
cared for her younger siblings while her mother, who had periodic
bouts of ill health, was staying at Grossmama Schlegelmilch's.

Thea's family valued education, and she received her under-
graduate degree at Oberlin College in June 1912. After that she
taught history, German, arithmetic, and bookkeeping in the
Mellen, Wisconsin, public schools in 1913–1914. By 1915 she was
living in Madison, Wisconsin, then taught in Waseca, Minnesota,
later that year. She later received her master's degree at the University of Wisconsin–Madison. By 1919 she had returned to the
Eau Claire area and was living in the Schlegelmilch home along
with her brother Charles Herman and her aunt Louise
Schlegelmilch. Dorothea Barland suffered a heart attack and died
at fifty-eight on July 7, 1946; she was buried in Forest Hill Cemetery in Eau Claire.

The 1903 diary, which she began at fourteen, is a "Daily
Reminder." It is small (four inches by five inches) and red covered,
with a calendar for 1903 inside its front cover as well as memoranda pages, address pages, populations of the U.S. states and
cities, rates of postage, and a calendar for 1904 at the back of the
diary. The diary is housed in the Barland-Schlegelmilch Family
Papers at the State Historical Society of Wisconsin Area Research
Center in Eau Claire.

Never give in. Never say die.
Always be punctual.
Always do what you say you will.
Be a girl that can be trusted.
Be concientious about work.

January 1, 1903. The first day in 1903 has passed and it has been very
full. On two days notice papa arranged to have us entertain the Elkertons
and Aunt Isse's family. The Elkertons came over and helped to clean up
for themselves. We did not get up till after 8 o'clock and things looked as

Dorothea Barland. Courtesy of the State Historical Society of Wisconsin Whi (X3) 52044.

though they would fizzle out. But everybody worked with a will and things soon began to clear up. Mama baked 5 pies. But papa did not arrive with the oysters (on which we were counting) and aunt Isse until after ~~three~~ two. We did not eat dinner until nearly three and then at five papa took us all down and gave us a sleigh ride all over town and took Aunt Isse home. There we went to prayer meeting and are now home. Ed who is working for us drinks and swears and I doubt that he is a Christian. I wish that he could be saved for he is worth it. He is a good steady worker and would make a good citizen. Papa tried it tonight but he has no tact and I am afraid he did more harm than good. . . .

January 3, 1903 Saturday. I want to start in this year and be a regular Christian in deeds, but am not succeeding at all, in fact I am as cranky and horrid as can be and no one likes me a bit. I got so far as to wonder last night how papa could talk of God as though he really existed. To-day I ment to study and get my story written so that I could go to night to that party at Mrs. Smith's. But this morning mama went away and did not return till tonight and left me to do the work The boys are awful bothers and made me lots of work this morning, and I haven't done a thing all day in study. Isabel Lyon came this ~~morning~~ afternoon and kept me from study then but I had lots of fun though but I can't go to the party because my studying isn't done.

January 4, 1903 Sunday. I have been at Grossmamma's this week and did not have this diary here. Nothing particular has happened though. My name was proposed in Christian Endeavor last week tonight and will be voted on next Sunday. I tried to get Gordon to have his name proposed too but he would not. But I'll try my best to get him in for all that. He has started to be a Christian. He says that he stood up in one of Mr. Biederwolf's meetings and it seems to me that Christian Endeavor would keep him at it. He is just in the awkward age.

January 7, 1903 Wednesday. This is the first night that I have had the book this week to write in. I went home to get my skirt for the banquet this evening and brought this with me. I went to the Banquet and had a fine time, but I might as well face the fact that the girls don't like me, and that I can't talk anything if I do get a chance to speak to them. I am getting so gloomy lately. I can't laugh at a funny thing much. I just have an inward feeling of fun and that's the end of it But I guess it is mostly selfishness that causes it, for if I can even for a moment lose my self consciousness I have a fine time. But somehow the more I determine that I will not be always conscious of my self the worse I get. I sat in a corner and looked on the whole evening while the other young people of my age walked around and had a good time.

[The diary contains no entries from January 8 until March 4, 1903.]

March 4, 1903 Wednesday. For various reasons I have not been writing so far, but I will begin now. This pen and ink are wretchedly poor. Mr. Rattery was married today to Mrs. Widland. We thought that he would all along, but he denied it so emphatically. I have had a horrid old time today. I hope I won't get a spell of the blues again. I want to outline my faults and good points so far as I know them.

Faults	Virtues
Indolence	None
Slovenliness	
Disorderliness	
Fickleness—no persistency	**Tools**
Jealousy	Fairly good brain power
Gloominess—no cheerfulness	Usual amount of will power
	Power to see my faults and a great wish
	To overcome them.

With these tools I wish to make myself over, to turn my faults and there are many more of them that I can't remember, into their opposite virtues. I will make them out of deeds.

March 6, 1903 Friday. I can't write very much. The Chippewa teachers visited our school today. One was in our German class and looked so glum and cross the whole time. I am glad I don't have her for a teacher. Because I helped Mama last night I had to be excused today in Latin I couldn't make it up. I wonder if I am not on the wrong track in trying to change myself. Everything seems topsy-turvy to me and the world all wrong. It is making me so self conscious and I see so little accomplished. I wish I could find <u>one</u> woman I wholly admired and thought was <u>fine</u>. I have seen <u>one man</u> and have read of lots more that I thought were splendid but I have never even read of a woman let alone seeing one I admired. . . .

March 21, 1903 Saturday. I have taken a bath to night—the first one in 4 or 5 weeks. Have worked today as usual. About ¼ of the raking in the front [yard] is done, one whole big strip. We want a pretty lawn this summer and a pretty house too for that matter. Am getting along pretty well in my self improvement. But somehow with it the world seems upside down & all wrong. In a sermon Mrs. Grant said that the way to serve God was to serve your fellow men. It was the sermon on choosing which God you would serve. I am afraid I am serving Mammon but how I can serve God & go on in my self improvement I can't see. But with my self improvement I am getting very self conscious & that will be at the bottom of my troubles in life.

[No further diary entries appear until April 18, 1903. After that date, a number of entries, although not daily ones, were made in the diary.]

April 18, 1903 Saturday. I am terrible in keeping this. Nearly a month has passed now. At times I have been on the hights of cheerfulness &

then again in the lowest depths of gloom. I have meant to start this before but there was never a pencil around. Today Mrs. Day came up. Fortunately I had cleaned up the front room today which has laid dirty & unswept for weeks. Aunt Agnes & Alex came in the evening & things did not look as bad as they might otherwise have done had we not worked as hard as we did. Papa decided not to go west with Alex who will start Monday. . . .

April 27, 1903 Monday. I did not get up & get breakfast as usual this morning & put on for the first time my spring jacket. I thought I would be late & walked hard but was quite early. On the Park I met Blair McGrath. I knew I looked horrible & I hated to go past him but there was no other way. We had a quiz in geometry today. I am making out my lit. note book. I ought to have started that long ago but Gordon is horrid. He pokes his hand in my face when he knows I am reading slaps me & is horrible in every way. He is beginning to despise me. I had an eye opener the other morning as to it.

April 28, 1903 Tuesday. I stayed home today and did not go to school. Early this morning I came up here, made a fire & started to study but I just fooled around at it & it took me nearly all day to get half a page of Latin. I tore up a lot of rags for a rug to day, and I made out my list of roses. It will go to-morrow and I will very likely get them about the end of next week. 19 little chickens came off today & some more are ready to come off. One old hen who is setting fought with the mother of the chickens for them so that her own eggs were chilled as bad by we don't know whether they will hatch or not. They were duck's eggs. The 19 chickens came from 2 hens or 26 eggs.

May 8, 1903 Friday. When I wrote that last I did not think what was going to happen. Saturday after I wrote that grosspapa was taken with a very bad spell. Mama was sent for and Monday he died. To day he was buried. I have stayed out all this week except Monday. The funeral was what might have been expected. It was from the house. Mr. Augustine preached. He eulogized grosspapa very much though ~~nearly~~ everything he said was true. But it was just like torture to the mourners. Aunt Louise who had not broken down before broke down & cried after the sermon & at the grave though she did not keep wiping her eyes as the rest did.

May 9, 1903 Saturday. Mama had rheumatism this morning & Agnes & I had to get up & get Breakfast. Lately since mama has stayed down there I have been going to bed so late & getting up so early that this morning brought the culmination. I have been tired all day. It passed as usual with Agnes doing more than her share of work. She is going to be a fine woman no doubt. But the Saturday work in general was not done. Mama was in bed a good deal today. She will take a cource in the Lanphear Institute next week. Tom & Mollie & baby drove up today this evening. The house looked horrible. I did not invite them in. I did not go out to them. They talked to Baby & H. only. Mama sick & Papa working. . . .

May 13, 1903 Wednesday. We had a hard quiz in Lit. today & as I was coming home late I was surprised suddenly to hear some one say—Well I have not been seeing you very much lately how are you. I had been looking at the water all the time & was so utterly astonished I did not know what to do. For I saw it was a well dressed woman whom I had glanced at, coming up in front of me. It was Miss Lothrop the teacher I like & admire most in H.S. Stammered out How . . . do you do Mrs or Miss Lothrop. She said did you not recognize me. I said no I did not. I must be more self controlled & not let my thoughts wander. . . .

May 20, 1903 Wednesday. Mama came up today at about 6 oclock & helped us bake up things to last us. To-day, as I expected, I went to grossmamas for Aunts Ruth & Navy were there & to say hello. I went in the back door & Aunt E. came out to the kitchen for me. I did not smooth my hair or anything and she took me in the dining room where they were. I had to go up to them both & kiss them & after that they all discussed me for about 10 minutes. If mama did not exaggerate what Aunt Naevie said Edda wouldn't mind if I wrote to her.

May 21, 1903 Thursday. We have had lots of fun today but have not done much. Agnes, Herman & I played in the front yard, & I have but half of my latin done. Am writing in the dark as Herman has taken the lantern to his room. . . .

May 26, 1903 Tuesday. Gordon has been especially horrid today & to night I told papa about it as I expected papa told him not to do it anymore. I got Herman to bed at 9 (we go to bed at half past 9 & 10) but I had lots of trouble to do it. We are going to have a quiz in Latin tomorrow & after that I won't have hardly any more studying to do. But I have not prepared for my quiz as I ought to have for we had only the warning this morning. It seems so queer that I am such a sober girl. Gordon is jolly & I feel sure that he will make a success of life just as I have a presentiment that I will be a failure. That is what adds spice to my dislike of Gordon with his actions as a cause.

June 4, 1903 Thursday   X all week. Papa has given me the contract for the strawberries. I am to hand over ⅓ of the money that comes from them. The other ⅔ I can keep after the pickers have been paid & other expenses met. I am trying to weed them now. Gordon has by many ways gotton together 3 times as much money as I have. I want to get $50 this summer if possible. I am working hard now but the rest of my tired muscles pays for the work done.

June 7, 1903 Sunday. I am in one of my cheerful moods when it seems as though I never could be gloomy blue morose & depressed again. To night I took Bertha to Christian E. meeting. It was not one of our best meetings & I am afraid she won't come again. We are going to begin to pick berries to morrow. I hoped will make a good deal of money from them. I finally decided to night that I would take the summer's earnings and give it to Christian work.

[Dorothea made no further entries in her diary until September of 1903.]

September 11, 1903 Friday. Since I wrote that last a great deal has happened. Aunt Maggie & Uncle Dr. were here stayed 4 days at our house. I went to Uncle Hermans cottage & then all but Gordon & papa went to the Elk Mound Training school & finally today I have found peace & looking to Christ for salvation I shall begin anew on the Christian life & try to stick to it. I cleared $19.50 from the strawberries so $2 goes for God. I think that I will give it to missions but I don't know. I have determined this year to be the best one in my classes & to get my studying in 2 hrs out side of school.

September 12, 1903 Saturday. Tonight we learned that Hubbard Robbins is dead & we are all going to the funeral tomorrow. We are painting the dining room over a cream color & have the wood work about 2 finished. Mr. Robbins' death has put papa into a sober & almost melancholy mood & he is reading poetry & commenting on Life & other abstract themes on that line now. I havent studied a particle today. I havent a solitary friend in the world & I seem to be one of the queer odd people who are always alone. I lay it mainly on my serious self assertive nature.

September 13, 1903 Sunday. Papa insisted that we should be early at the funeral & so I didn't go to Sunday school. We got there among the earliest when Mr. Hatch preached a great many cried from time to time.

When it was over we went in & looked at the body & in coming out we passed through the mourners room. It was dark but we could hear people sobbing & crying. Laura particular sobbed & cried a great deal. Why they have great long sermons reminiscent of the man telling his good qualities, etc., etc. I don't see. It is just like torture to the mourners who feel bad enough as it is. It seems to me that prayer reading from the Bible & singing are enough. Tonight we were afraid that Gordon was drowned in the flood on the creek, but he was all right.

September 14, 1903 Monday. I was 40 min. late at school this morning & I got there wet through & through. Mama drove me down. When I got home this afternoon I played with George quite a while & had lots of fun. I would like to know Laura & have more to do with her again. She seemed to feel so <u>very</u> bad at the funeral. The creek is very high but is beginning to go down. They are afraid of a flood at Eau Claire if this rain keeps on. Our house is overrun with mice since we took away our cats.

September 15, 1903 Tuesday. Today I was 1 min. late but I did not like go to in so I didn't. When I came home I came up stairs & read Rev. [Revelations] nearly all through. It used to frighten me so much but tonight I read it through with no feeling of fear awe or anything that I would observe. I am getting so apathetic in my christian life I grope & grope Believing in the Divinity of Christ & accepting Christ as my Saviour for I know that I can not save myself & I am a lost soul if I don't) is that all. I feel as though there was something lacking the being born again part of it. There is no small voice within urging me on as last year only a great fear of becoming.

The Diary of Pauline C. Petersen, 1907–1908

Pauline C. Petersen was born on November 8, 1884, at Elkhorn, Iowa, to Amelia (Stendrup) and Peter Iver Petersen, both first-generation immigrants from Denmark who had arrived in the United States in the early 1870s and married on April 12, 1874, in Davenport, Iowa. The Petersens and their family settled in Harlan, in western Iowa, and Peter Petersen served for many years as surveyor of Shelby County. They had ten children: Peter, Anthony, Magnus, Hannah Johanne (who died at twenty-five), Garfield Christian, Pauline, George, Otto, Roy, and Edna.

Pauline C. Petersen, ca. 1906. Courtesy Pauline Dallner.

Pauline, the sixth child and oldest surviving daughter, began keeping a diary in November 1907, when she was twenty-three and teaching in Harlan. She kept her diary for the next three years, often writing lengthy introspective entries, many of which explore her spiritual beliefs as well as analyze the belief systems of those around her. She married N. P. J. Nielsen, who was a Lutheran pastor, on October 18, 1911, in Harlan. The couple, who had no children, lived in California, Wisconsin, and Iowa. Her husband died in 1950, but Pauline Petersen Nielsen remained in good health into her nineties, and in the early 1980s she entered the Lutheran Home in Cedar Falls, Iowa. She died in Cedar Falls at the age of 103 on September 19, 1988.

In the early 1980s her diary was discovered by her niece, Pauline A. Levendahl Dallner, who was cleaning out the Nielsen home when her aunt Pauline entered the nursing home in Cedar Falls. A typescript of the diary was made and distributed to relatives, friends, and county historical society archives. The excerpts that appear here come from the first volume of Pauline Petersen's four-volume diary.

Nov. 10, 1907 Sunday. I have always wanted to keep a diary but somehow have never done so but I am really now going to try it. I hope I will get much good from it in more than one way.

Today is Sunday and our first snow this season. It is so cold and sharp. Friday and Saturday when Edna and I were at Oakland, it was so summery and nice. Today it is so extremely the opposite.

The change is too sudden for me. I notice the cold so. But we did so enjoy our trip to Oakland. Friday was my twenty-third birthday. Am I really that much? The reverend went away that Friday morning.

Went to visit his folks before going to Philadelphia. Rev. Harrison was at our house today. He seems to be a very nice man. I guess I broke him in that he is to talk English to me. but he does talk beautiful Danish. I should think he would be an American minister. . . .

Wednesday Nov. 13, 1907. Mother in bed all day today. Has tonsillitis and grippe. Real sick too. This having mother in bed makes everything go all wrong. I wonder why it does? Wish I knew more about doing for sick folks. I'm simply at a loss what to do.

Another thing I simply cant assume this responsibility and above all the work and management of household affairs with such a family of boys. I really ought not to be home just now so the boys could get a good taste of a woman's work. I'm sure to its not all fun. And yet I haven't did anything extra these days.

Thursday Nov. 14, 1907. My! So many years of housekeeping as mother has had. How in the wide world has she ever managed it all. I don't believe I'll ever undertake such a responsibility. Was uptown this afternoon, got me some stuff angora yarn for a hood also some school supplies. It doesn't take long for a fine dollar bill to vanish.

Friday Nov 15, 1907. Mother is up now. Goodness me, just having her up and around makes everything go better. Did all the sweeping today. I do enjoy sweeping and straightening things up if they would only stay for a while. Nevertheless there is so little satisfaction in cleaning and sweeping.

Sat. Nov 16. 1907. Made bread today and had fine luck with it but oh dear it wont last anytime. I think it would be pleasure to keep house if only a little, little family where everything goes like clock work, and not so much work that it makes you cross and ill-tempered. Was up town this afternoon, payed for all I had gotten, feel alright when I'm square with everybody. And that is the only way to be.

Sunday Nov. 17, 1907. Sunday Morning! Such a glorious day too! Now the reverend has been at his destination for sometime. Know he must enjoy his prospects for the coming winter. Hope he will come back a broader and nobler man. Also be more proefficient in his English with a stronger love for it.

Did not go to church this morning but had a good Endeavor lesson also a fine sermon this evening. Dr B___ from Grinnel College preached both morning and evening. His subject this evening was "Ye cannot live by bread alone" etc. But oh how contrary to this we all lived. Of course we must not neglect our work but what of the most wonderful part of us "the Soul". Neglect of the soul! The world says live for what you can get to eat, to wear and what you can get out of this life. World says live for "material wealth." We are all too busy with our work and all petty things and do not take time to care for the "Soul." We are constantly "thinking what shall we eat, what shall we be clothed in" These do not count so much when it comes to the end. Change of environment does not necessarily change the man. The scoundrel may be found in the finest dress and house while the prince and man is clothed in the common cloth and under the thatched roof. What we need now days is "soul culture." We need to "live rightly then we will live righteously." When we do this all we be added unto us in good measure.

211

Monday Nov 18, 1907. Monday morning! and my winter's term begins. I'm really glad after all. Glad to be working at what I like. Such a beautiful morning it is too. Hope I may be able to do a good deal for these children. Want to do my very best in every way.

Started to board at Frederickson's today. Think I shall like it real well, just so the winter doesn't become too severe.

Hope I may grow in grace this winter and learn to control myself a little better. Oftentimes I do let my temper run away with me and especially when I am at home. It don't seem to when I'm boarding. I guess its because we don't want other people to see all our sides but hold in check the bad. I'm going to try to hold the bad checked all the time. . . .

Friday Nov 22, 1907. Friday morning! Almost a whole week of school passed. I hope the time has been well used, that I have been a pretty good influence for these little ones. Friday morning! And such a bright clear frosty morning at that. Somehow I haven't minded my walks these days at all. Hope I may so continue all winter. I'm going to walk home this evening. Hope the road will be real good. I wonder if mother has been well this week. Somehow I don't know what in the world I should do without her. But presume that time may come sometime, but I guess I'll not worry about it.

Monday Nov. 25, 1907. Monday Morning! Such a bright beautiful day too at that! Several new people entered today so I'm kept still more busy. Yet I enjoy it all. They are all good nice children.

Saturday was indeed a busy day for us. And Sunday! Yes it was a beautiful Sabbath. Heard Rev. Hawson preach . . . gave a fine sermon but I could not understand a great deal of it. I cannot get the details. Sunday we heard the Thanksgiving Song Service at the Congregational Church. It was fine in every way. Also the little talk by Rev. Beardsly on Thankfulness and Thanksgiving. He is small but oh my! He can say such wonderful things. Has such beautiful ways of presenting his subjects.

In my secret heart I so often wonder if I can love any other church with real true love, or can I learn to do so?? Is it prejudice?? I cannot believe it.

I was down at Miss Johnson's Saturday evening and we talked over the book Silas Mariner by George Eliot. The book is indeed realistic but not idealistic. Some things put in there are too common. I hate too real things. I love things realistic but as near idealistic as possible. The characters best in the book are Silas Mariner and Eppie. But I wish Eppie hadn't married so soon. She should have been educated and made something of herself.

I don't like Godfrey Cass at all. He certainly is realistic. I don't

212

believe he ever suffered a great deal from his wrong doings. Why didn't he act the part of a man and come and claim Eppie long ago instead of coming and want to take her away from old Silas, or why didn't he offer to both take Eppie and Silas. T'wouldn't have been a bit too much. He didn't have much manhood or back bone to him. Silas believed entirely too well in people. Eppie is the strongest character in the whole book. She has a good deal of back bone to her also spunk. Wrong doing in the upper class of society can be glossed over so easily. . . .

Wednesday Nov. 27, 1907. Another glorious day before us. I think of the little lives "here hath been dawning a brighter blessed day. Think wilt thou let it slip useless away." What is time anyway? One day goes, another day comes. But let us make the most of our time. The best of it. By doing our duty as near as possible filling up the moments with what will last. The longest life, after all, is short, very short. But how well the moments ought to be used, how pure we should try to be. What is all this flitting, drifting.

Tomorrow is Thanksgiving Day and I shall go home this evening and not come back to school until Monday. . . .

Friday, Dec. 6, 1907. Friday! and oh! What a glorious December Day! Three weeks of school passed. how the days do slip by anyway. Have eighteen pupils enrolled now so am very busy. Hope I do my work well. I want to do so. Soon I shall be home. I'm always glad when it is time to leave the little school and go home but am just as glad when the morning calls me to work again. . . .

Tuesday Dec 10, 1907. The school hours for today is over. Were they used rightly? Everything is as still here as death. But blessed moments of stillness! We all need them and I love quiet and peacefulness.

I am happy, happy in my work yet there is something lacking. Something I cannot comprehend now what is it and will I always be unsatisfied and will something always seem incomplete. No I think there will always be unsatisfaction within me. Unsatisfied with myself, if not, how can I grow better. Hope I may always be unsatisfied so that I may constantly be growing, and climbing higher.

Friday Dec 13, '07. Such a day as today has been! My! I do not care for another one like it very soon! The stove smoked so we were nearly all choked. I put out the fire and we almost froze. Harry and Jesse got a long pole and poked down the chimney and oh such a smelly room as we had. but after they poked out the soot the old stove knew how to burn alright. The last part of the afternoon was spent in practicing our Xmas program.

About time for school to close, oh! I was so sick and yet I started to walk home, and I did walk too all the way, But I certainly paid for it that night. Not a wink did I sleep and oh! such pains and misery!. . . .

Wednesday Dec 18, '07. Wednesday evening! Let me see! Yes, the day was spent in scrubbing and cleaning. How we did scrub that floor. And how nice the stove is now, so black and pretty. Why don't they clean schools oftener. It is wicked to let children live in dirt so much of the time. And a sweeping simply will not do the work of soap and water. . . .

Wednesday Dec 25, 1907. Xmas Day! and passed! What a lovely green Xmas we have had anyway. It is something of a novelty to have the ground bare at this season. I have been feeling rather bad today, have had a real severe cold and seems as if I cant get over it.

We had a fine Xmas dinner today. Tony came after we were just three and ready to wash dishes. He drove home, just think of a thirty mile drive! A little long to suit me. My! But Santa has been good to me. Sent me so many nice little gifts. How I do love to prepare the little gifts to give away. It is so true "that it is more blessed to give than to receive." Mamma thinks I've been quite a smart girl to make so many of my gifts this year. I think so myself. But I believe I had a great deal of genuine pleasure out of it all. . . .

Monday Dec 30, 1907. Have served and been busy almost all day. Alma Wyland came up this evening has just gone home. She is a jolly, jolly girl. Wonder if the underneath is just as jolly or if she hides her feelings. I just discovered Edna had singed her hair all around. The foolish girl to pour kerosine down on the fire. What if it had taken all her hair off!

Tuesday Dec 31, 1907. Have been busy sewing all day, made over a waist for school, also fixed my underskirts. Made some candy this morning and sent two boxes away. Had real good luck with it. Just received Cecelia's photo. It is fine. I was so glad to get it too. Looks just like the little miss. New Years Evening! What hath the New Year in store of good or ill! We cannot tell and what matters it if we cannot. "All things work together for good," at least so we want to believe. It matters not what comes as long as we can say, "I know whom I have believed." What would we do without this one thot? It would be hard to live and not have some believe.

Hope at the end of another year I may be found more faithful, more true, more kind and thotful. Hope I may, thruout the whole year constantly "grow in grace."

214

Wednesday Jan. 1, 1908. How strange to change the seven to an eight! But presume it must be done. How fast the old year has flown! Has something really worthy been done! Have I truly lived? Lived in the best and highest sense of the word???

Have been real busy sewing almost all day, getting ready for school tomorrow. Alma just came up. Hanson was with her. She brought me an Xmas gift, a beautiful crepe-de-chine scarf, something very useful and nice. . . .

Sunday, Jan 5, 1908. Went to church this afternoon heard Rev Hanson and this evening went to Endeavor also to Church. Rev. Beardsly preached a fine sermon, subject being, "What will ye do with Jesus, who is called the Christ." In his sermon he gave a fine explanation of Jesus' trial, also Pilate's way of shifting the whole matter, as if washing his hands in water would make him clean and would take the whole responsibility from his shoulders.

He spoke of a book entitled "Letters from Hell." A picture in there shown of Pilate standing by a stream washing his hands and saying, "What! Will they never be clean!" On his face is written remorse, remorse. The hands as he holds them up appear crimson, this is conscience.

One can never forgive oneself for a wrong deed or act. God may forgive, our friends may, but we can never forgive ourselves. Conscience and remorse will not let us have peace. The speaker went on that each of us as individuals stand in Pilate's place! "What would we do with the Christ!" What are we doing with him! The picture of Pilate is a very vivid one, he was simply suffering from his own guilty conscience.

Tuesday Jan 7, 1908. Ha! Ha! Last night I had a ride home in the lumber wagon with Arthur. Got jolted up quite a little too. But I rather enjoyed it anyway.

School again, several of the pupils are absent today, suppose they must stay home and work. Dear me! How soon the time comes when work comes before everything else! It is well to work but I believe in people sending their children to school. How much can a little girl or boy do! . . . .

Wednesday Jan 15, 1908. My! how sharp the north wind is today and a light snow has been falling! Guess we're going to have winter in dead earnest now, but it is probably just as well. I'd sooner have it now than in the Spring.

It is just three years ago today since Hannah died. Twas on a beautiful Sunday morning. My! But time does pass! What has these three years brought to me!! And no one knows what time has in store for us either. Presume 'tis well we don't know of what the future is made up.

215

A little verse just come to me. "All as God wills, who wisely heeds, to give or to withhold, He knoweth more of all my needs. Than all my prayer have told." I think this is such a beautiful little verse, and so true too. I believe God knows a great deal better what is best for us also all our needs than we do. Perhaps seems as if our prayers are unanswered but hey are probably answered in a somewhat different way than we expected and undoubtedly a much better way too. . . .

Sunday Jan 19, 1908. A beautiful Sabbath day! So bright and sunny for January. I wasn't out to church in morning. Spent the afternoon in preparing my lesson for C. E. as I was to lead the subject was "How God speaks to Men" found in Psalms 19. We had a real good meeting as there was a goodly number present. "How God speaks to Men," why in countless number of ways. Everything about us speaks of God, his love and goodness. The moon, sun, the changing seasons, day and night, and the flowers. A little white lily has a wonderful tale to tell, of its love and purity and beauty. They all speak of God and His goodness and love. god speaks to us thru His Word, thru the lives and deeds of men and women, both of olden times and now. Above all He speaks to us thru His Son, Jesus. His Birth, his death and His wonderful life of love and sacrifice. As He speaks to us we must be good listeners and heed His voice.

In the evening, after Endeavour Rev Beardsly preached on "Jesus the Son of Joseph." What a wonderful sermon it was, full of appeal to live the Christlike life in every sphere and place. How wonderful he gave the whole life of the Jesus. A life, so unselfish, so pure, so holy, so divine. So full of love and goodness. Such a beautiful and noble example of love and Patience. How vividly he pictured the night of His betrayal where he went out to pray and asked the three to watch with Him. How tired they grew and when He came they were sleeping. Did he chide them? Oh no! His was all patience and feeling for others. How the second time, after returning from praying to the father, he found them asleep still. The time when He most and sorely needed comfort and sympathy. Then and there He must stand alone with not one word or look of sympathy. Did He chide them the third time on returning? No! Only said in his simple way, "the spirit indeed is willing but the flesh is weak." Sleep on now, for the Hour is at hand." The disciples didn't offer a single excuse for their going to sleep. How Jesus must have mastered himself! Had himself in such a complete control. this the time when above all others one might be given to lose entire control. What a life of love and service!! Could we but strive in a little measure to follow it. No other great person has been able to say "follow me." Jesus could and His life and example showed that he might well say it. January 19, and Hannah's

216

birthday! Three years since she passed away. She would just have been twenty eight years old. . . .

Friday Jan 24, '08. I went to church last night with Frederickson's. It was a pretty cold trip too Morris, Etta and Laura were baptized at the American Baptist Church. An Evangelist is here holding services and last week nineteen were baptized, and last night sixteen were baptized. Sunday morning another group is to be immersed. Each one to his notion is all I have to say, but let others alone then instead of constantly be tearing down all others forms and rules of worship. Others have just as well a right to their beliefs as they and just as good ground and foundation upon which to build.

Saturday, February 1, 1908. Well, I started out to walk home last night but I never could have made it. The wind was so sharp and blew the snow so dreadfully. When I came as far as Christenson's I wasn't at all sorry to see Papa coming after me. It didn't take so long to get home then.

On coming home Robina Theobald was there. She stayed over night. Her and I went to the Spelling Contest together. My! Such a crowd there was! The debate was real good too—"Resolved that there is more nutriment in the hole of a dough nut than in the scent of limburg cheese" Affirmative Ed Noble & W. L. Shep Negatives Ed White and C T Swift. Judge Lockwood decided in favor of the hole of the dough nut. It certainly was enough to cause a good laugh. And all used about the best puns I ever heard.

Today all day Robina and I have attended each in meeting. All was very good and inspiring and could not help set one to thinking. Supt. Davidson of the Oscala School certainly gave a fine address.

How careful, how honest, how sincere a teacher should be! And how well the teacher and patron should work hand in hand. How much the parents owe their children!

Robina went home this evening. She's a jolly, nice, sensible, little girl. I like her very much in every way.

Friday Feb 7, 1908. Several days have now passed since last I wrote in this journal. What a full busy week it has been too! And such nice sharp weather we have had the pleasure of enjoying. Such brisk walks I have had in the mornings. One morning twas so slippery I almost had several falls before reaching school. This week hasn't been the pleasantest for me for I have such fearful headaches and such severe pains in my back. I have also been bothered with rheumatism. But I have somehow managed to be around everyday so far. . . .

Tuesday Feb 25, '08. Elmer Sahl certainly is such a little run about. He does so like to get up and have a merry chase around the room. Shorwalk is the same little fellow, does so like to have fun. Just today I gave his history class a few questions to answer and hand in, but when it came time to answering the last two he was up the stump. There were only four questions in all, each if answered correctly making twenty-five percent. Thorwald came up to me and wanted permission to take out his book and read over his lesson again. I asked, "Why?"

"I can answer two of them and I hate to get poor." It, of course, amused me but I didn't consent to the use of the book. I have had a dreadful time these two days with my throat. I guess I'll loose my voice. I can scarcely talk whatever. . . .

Friday March 13, 1908. 'Twas the last day of my winter term today. My! How these four months have flown. Nearly all the pupils were present and a part of the afternoon was spent in playing different games.

I thot sure I would have had to walk home but, Minnie Wokersien had sent Thomas out after me. I was very glad to, as I would have been dreadfully tired if I had had to have walked clear home. . . .

Monday evening March 23, 1908. One day of my Spring term has passed now. I am glad to be at work again. It seems real natural and enjoyable.

Minnie Wokersien and I have started to drive back and forth. Hope we will be blessed with good weather and I think we will. It certainly has started out fine, such a nice bright day as today has been.

The school was so nice and bright and clean all over. It is a pleasure to be at a school where things are so bright and clean. . . .

Sunday April 19, 1908. Easter Sunday, and oh, what a glorious, blessed day it has been without, save my thot's within. They were not in harmony whatever with the glory and beauty of nature. Why do people find genuine delight and pleasure in getting up things, in making so much of really nothing? And why are there so many "mouthpieces" around? It so strengthens one's faith in humanity??? So harden's the heart and kills one's love. Sets one in a continual mental disturbance which is not at all pleasant. The Easter services were very beautiful today. All of course in harmony with the Easter season. Services in the morning and Song Service in the Evening.

I only wished I had better and different thots in my mind. . . .

Friday April 24, 1908. Today was Arbor Day and of course the afternoon was spent planting trees, rose bush, and a lilac. We also partly raked

218

the yard and picked up all the sticks and cobs. Had a real nice time working all together.

Saturday April 25, 1908. Worked at office all day but I believe all this work is too strenuous on me! I'm busy all the time. Got my new hat & slippers today. Just a little bill of $8.50. Also got my suit, another little bill, the who amounting to twenty-five dollars. Also got a pair of new gloves for $3.00. Dear me! how much a girl does need and yet I do try to be economical. . . .

Saturday May 10, 1908. Worked at office all day and was mighty tired in the evening too. Got up real early and trimmed my hat before I went down to the office. Work- Work- I guess that is what every one has to do.

Stopped in to see Miss Johnson on the way home, and my! she had just bought a new kerosine stove as Erickson's came up after theirs since they had come back from California. And the kerosene stove had smoked so that it had blackened everything in the house and Miss Johnson had to go to work and clean everything up.

While I was up at the office, in the morning Sister Mary Lawrence and Sister Acadia came up to see Magnus. Of course they were attired in their long black flowing robes and as they opened the door such a feeling as there came over me when I beheld them. Their long gold crosses hanging on their bosoms and the rosary hanging at their sides and then their robes of dead white and black.

It certainly was impressive even if at first the sight seemed rather frightening. they both were very pleasant and sociable, talked a little broken but in every way very ladylike. . . .

Special Page Monday June 3, '08. As usual Minnie and I sallied forth to school at the usual hour, when lo! when we came down to the bridges, on the other side of the road, it was all river too and impossible to cross, at least for girls to drive alone.

We got out of the buggy, tied the horse and investigated affairs. The man at the Pumping Station said he'd row us across, if we could then telephone to some of our patrons to come for us, as it was impossible for us to walk. We both hesitated and said we go home and see what the folks said. We were glad for we were not the only one's that couldn't get across. Miss Johnson, Miss Taylor, and Miss Anderson hadn't gone yet either.

On arriving up home we first went and telephoned to our directors telling them we could not have school that day.

Willie Wokersien then took the horse and said he'd go down and investigate farther. He went down and later came back, saying he had driven across and back again. So he offered to take us down, drive us across and he'd wade back, but we must promise not to scream and yell. We said we would try, so I got ready again (I had just changed my dress and was going to help wash), and away we went.

On going across the last bridge our hearts almost failed us. We were both almost determined to go but Willie said we must keep still and away we started. How Dotly did plunge! The water was flowing swiftly and was up to the buggy box. Every moment, I expected it to be higher than the box and expected to see it run in but it didn't and we at last we were across. We were both as still as we could be. On getting over Minnie said, "Pauline, are you sick, you are so pale as your waist?" (I had on a white waist and imagine I did look sick.) I told her "No," but it had been a nervous strain on me nevertheless.

Well! we both got out to school and began school about the first recess. I stayed at Sahls over night and Minnie at Juliets. It certainly was great experience for both of us. Willie didn't wade back after all, because just then a buggy came going the other way and he rode over with them.

We had quite a laugh after twas all over with, but at the time it seemed quite serious. We hated so to miss school, on account of this being the last week. . . .

Friday June 12, '08. Friday morning! and the day of our picnic! It doesn't look so very favorable as a very heavy rain came down last night, and not much sign of it clearing up.

Well, we have had our picnic and it turned out real well too. The program was given in the afternoon instead of forenoon. A good crowd was present, but several of the number for the program could not be given (two of my number had to be left) on account of the children not all being there. I felt a little provoked about it. Anna Mathiasen was there and gave her oration. Mr Taylor presented her with her diploma. I gave her a little leather book "The Deserted Village" by Oliver Goldsmith.

I drove out with Supt. H. P. Nielsen, he having to go to Jackson Township to give the address there. He seems very pleasant and nice to converse with. I only wish I had a little more confidence in myself and could talk a little more freely. I believe I'm entirely too self conscious. . . .

Friday July 3, '08. Edna, Mamma and I picked and canned currants all day I made two big glasses of jelly and we canned eight quarts of jam. We just had to hustle.

July 5 to 10 [1908]. Edna and I have kept house all week. We have gotten along beautiful, altho we have both decided house keeping is too strenuous or else we don't know how to plan our work, but it gets fearfully tiresome burring all the time. I did a little sewing also, made two under waists and a linen skirt besides made a few calls.

This churning, scrubbing, sweeping, and cooking don't somehow exactly agree with me or isn't to my liking. . . .

Friday July 17, 1908. Everything packed etc and Edna and I are on our way to Cedar Falls. It doesn't seem exactly possible and in some respects I wish I was not going, but perhaps tis alright.

Saturday July 18, 1908. Edna and I arrived at Cedar Falls about six oclock last night and oh! we were so tired of the long ride on the train and the wait in Fort Dodge. The little ride to the country was fine and we had a good night's rest so we felt somewhat better in the morning.

Saturday certainly wasn't Saturday at all here. We had a real easy time of it all day. Of course I imagined they had done the hardest work before we came. Sat out in the lawn swing most of the afternoon.

Tuesday July 28, '08. Have been on the road coming home ever since this morning and just reached our destination about eleven this evening. My but we were tired and dirty.

Marie and her father and mother took us in. My! They were so good to us all the time we were there. We certainly had a nice time. The agent from Cedar Falls was going to try to cheat me. He wanted to charge me almost thirteen dollars to go home when it should only cost about eight dollars for the two of us. But I just took a ticket as far as Fort Dodge and there bought a new one at the Great Western Depot, the agent there was very accomadating and nice. It only cost us $7.80 for the two tickets home. If I had been foolish enough to give that other agent what he asked he'd been quite a little ahead. From Cedar Falls to Fort Dodge the fare for both was $3.70 for one $1.85 Transfer for both   .50   .25 From Fort Dodge to Harlan for two 3.60 1.80 Fare for two 7.80 for one   3.90 I'll just keep an account of it so he won't try to get ahead of me again when I go.

While waiting in Fort Dodge we went up town and made a few purchases, got a few real nice things, necessary articles. If one buys a little at a time it doesn't seem as if it counts up so much.

We had quite a time lugging our suitcases home, as no one was there to meet us, as they had not received our postal, but we managed somehow. But for the next two days I was simply all done up, so tired and no energy or ambition whatever.

Mamma had had quite a hard time while we were gone, had canned so many peaches besides all the rest of the house work. . . .

Saturday Sept. 5 '08. Kept office alone today (over). This finishes my journal. I shall have to start up a new one with my tall term of school. Hope I shall have many interesting things to put in book II.

It certainly has been a pleasure to write in this one and also a pleasure to look back over the different times.

Books read this School year, beginning Sept. 1907 and ending June 1908.

1. "Scarlet Letter" by Hawthorne.
2. "Silas Mariner," by George Eliot.
3. "David Harum" by
4. "Idle Thots of Auddle Fellow" by Jerome K Jerome.
5. "Saddie" by
6. "Chronita" by
7. "Bird's Xmas Carol" by Kate Douglas Urggin.
8. "Adam Bede" by George Eliot.
9. "Sour Grapes" by
10. Phelp's to His Teachers.
11. "Being a Boy" Charles Dudley Warner.
12. "Let us Follow Him"
13. Julius Ceasar. Shakespeare.
14. "Mosses from an Old Manse" Hawthorne (not quite finished)
15. "Twice Told Tales" Part of it-Hawthorne
16. "Enoch Arden" -Tennyson.
17. "The Master Christian"-Marie Corelli

The Diary of Edythe M. Miller, 1911

In 1911, when she began keeping this diary, Edythe M. Miller was just about to turn eighteen and was living in the southeastern Iowa town of Fairfield. Although little is known to date about her life, Edythe M. Miller's diary reveals that she was born on January 28, 1893, and that she lived with her parents and her siblings, Ada and Harry Miller. In her 1911 diary, which comprised a number of volumes, Edythe wrote periodic lengthy entries rather than short daily entries. With some regularity she commented on her anxieties about her ill health, especially her frequent headaches and what she referred to as "neuralgia." This condition, called "neurasthenia" by physicians, was said to be characterized by profound physical and mental exhaustion. The most common symptoms included sick headaches, excessive nervousness, and heart palpitations. Sometimes the condition was treated medically; other times the adolescent girl was told that the problem would resolve itself once she was grown up and married. Today the issue of neurasthenia is being reexamined; some researchers view it as a condition rooted in unaddressed or denied psychosocial issues. Others view it as linked to chronic fatigue syndrome or to allergic reactions.

In the excerpts from her diary included here, Edythe M. Miller writes not only about her health concerns but also about her alarm regarding a troubling situation involving her friends Mose Tweedy and Ethyle Holmes. As she tried to make sense of the situation, Edythe used her diary as a sounding board, even copying into it a letter from Ethyle. Edythe's diary, written at a time of intense anxiety regarding her own health as well as her preoccupation with the troubling behavior of her friends, marks a turning her coming of age as a young woman.

Jan.7, 1911. Sat eve. Really life is a mystery to me. I get to pondering over it sometimes and it seems I can't understand it at all. Theres so much to ponder o'er and so many why's and where for's it seems my grain gets beaddled another volume in my journal. Papa and I went to Birmingham this afternoon. I saw "Starry Eyes." Don't know why seeing him should affect me so but when I first caught sight of him my heart went to pit a pat pit a pat. Haha. Ethel Holmes and I were together. He spoke very cool if he spoke at all and afterwards when I met him, O joy our eyes met but he gazed at me so coldly. I don't know why he should act so. If it had been Ada I'll bet he would have smiled but of course I'm different. Maybe ~~charlie~~ that little snotty toe head of a Stansberry has told him some thing. If he has I'd like to break his neck. But why so? I thot you didn't care for the boys! I don't care for the boys its just a "boy." It seems tonight that he fills my whole heart even takes the places of "Brown Eyes" and "Blue Eyes" neither of them can ever be anything to me and well "Starry Eyes" can't either. At times I almost hate him for the way he acts. I mean so cool but it is almost impossible to hate "him." Really I don't know whether I like him very well or not. If I do no one shall ever know it. Grandpa has some thing like the dropsy or else its kidney trouble. I don't know which maybe Uncle Fred will come up to see him in the morning. Do hope he will get better. Saw Dr. Morrison today told me "I looked good" ahem. well explain all about it again. I must hurry to bed it must be 10:30 at least. I've been sitting here writing poetry. One song "Would you care" and a poem "Last Love!" Its time I was in bed heard the chickens crowing but those "little leghorns" crow at all hours of the night.

Jan. 8, 1911. Sun at 11:15. well here it is Sun again Harry staid alnight at Brobster is with man [She wrote of her unhappiness at not having been invited along out with friends] . . . O well I'm nothing but "An old woman" you know. No one knows how that hurt. I wish I had thot and told Nelle they wouldn't want "an old woman" along. No one will ever know what bitter tears I have shed tonight. No one will know how I feel . . . Dear old Journal you are a comfort to me. Theres nothing else I can tell my troubles to. I thot I wouldn't have to write anything like this in this Journal but here it is the first thing. Maybe I'm making a mountain out of a mole hill but if anyone would only know how I felt tonight maybe they wouldn't wonder at me writing like this. . . .

Jan. 21, 1911. . . . Dear me this time next Sat. I'll be 18. Just think It don't seem possible. I'm not like other girls at that age. I have been thinking of "Starry Eyes" a good deal this evening. made out an order for Sears, Roebuck this evening, came to $3.22. Papa got runners to put on the buggy and it looks awful nice. . . .

Jan. 28, 1911. "Sat. Eve. My eighteenth birthday. I can scarcely believe it and yet it is true. Eighteen years old today. Dear me how old I am growing. My hair will soon be gray I'm afraid I am going to make some Birthday Resolutions.
Resolved: No. 1. That I will try and control my temper better at all times.
No. 2. That I will try and not think of B.E. in the way I shouldn't.
No. 3. That I will try and quit scolding and grumbling so much.
No. 4. That I will try and do or say something each day to make some one in this old world happier.
No. 5. That I will try and be more patient as patients and perceverance conquerth all things.
No. 6. That I will try and not quarrel so much with Harry and Ada.
No. 7. That I will try and ~~not~~ enjoy my self at all times and places even if every one acts as if they didn't care for me.
No. 8. That I will try and not be old maidish.
No. 9. That I will try and not act like an "old woman."
No. 10. That I will not be jealous if Ada happens to be treated a little better than I.
No. 11. That I will try and not do or say any thing ~~that~~ to any of the folks that I might regret in after years.
No. 12. That I will try and ~~not~~ keep all the resulutions that I have written.
No. 13. I will try not to be selfish.
No. 14. That I will not peice between meals.

224

No. 15.
No. 16.
There. One resulution for each month of the year and room for three
more if I think of any more. I got so many nice presents. Mama gave me
a book Harry cuff buttons Lela collar and pin. Papa music and Ada a stick
pin. I wonder where I will be 18 years from tonight. Roy and Cat sent
me a card and Aunt Elenor and Maria and Ada I don't seem like other
girls of my age. Harry and Ada Mose and Nelle would have gone to Liberty tonight if Mose had got back from Fairfield in time. Mama and Papa
went to Fairfield started about 11:30. Uncle George died and was buried
this afternoon. Harry went to Liberty tonight. I am pretty tired tonight.
I done a good bit today my head didn't hurt hardly any tho.

Jan. 29, 1911. Here I am on the 29th day of January sitting at an open
window ~~window~~ writing. It is certainly warm for January. I finished reading a book awhile ago, "Our Lady of the Beeches" Mama gave it to me
for my birthday. I just love it. Some way it appeals to me.

Evening. I was interrupted in my writing this afternoon. Harry Cor-
teons was here and Harry wanted Ada and I to come out in the parlor
and look at some of his postals and talk to him. It pleases him I think to
be noticed that way for his is a lonely life I fear. As it was one of my
Birthday resulutions to make people happier I felt it my duty to go.
Afterwards we talked of books and he is really an interesting talker. He
has read several we have and have some ideas the same. But it took my
mind off of "Our Lady of the Beeches" and I wanted to keep it fresh in
my memory. I dearly love it I mean to write just such a book some day.

I just finished reading "Our Lady of the Beeches" thro again. I like
it so. Perhaps I shouldn't have set up so late. Expect it is almost 12
o'clock, maybe 11:30. Guess Harry is taking the mumps. His Jaw was
sore. Frank Danielson has them wish Lela was here.

Jan. 30, 1911. Mon eve Harry has the mumps good and proper or
mump rather. Just on the left side. It hurts him very bad part of the time.
I just ~~finished~~ got thro healing him if he wanted to talk to him. Said he
would call him after while I thot is was strange. Then Mr. Tweedy called
up and asked Harry if he could go to B'ham. He told him he didn't know
said Papa was going to call and he would ask him. Said no matter how he
come just so he got there. Harry thot maybe he wanted him to take
Moses buggy down. I said maybe the boys had got into some kind of a
scrape. Then Harry said he knew what it was Mose and Billy Moore had
jangled on the train the other evening and Cruthers had took Mattox out
to Tweedy to arrest them. Harry thot maybe they had Mose in jail . . . I
do wonder the very idea Mose in jail.

225

Evening. I was wondering this morning what I would do if trouble would come to me. And it has come. I was interrupted B4 Papa come. It wasn't that that they wanted Mose for. It was something far worse. Ethyle Holmes has filed information against Mose. She is in a fix and she says Mose is the guilty one. O isn't it terrible? Just to think. But I'll never believe it never. The sherrif went around the road to meet Mose and he went across the field. Tweedy told him of course and he can't be found. Tweedy thot too that it was about Billy Moore. And I suppose Mose don't know yet what they wanted him for. I wonder where he is. And another thing that seems so terrible is that Papa and Harry think maybe it is Dr. Morrison. He went after the sherrif yesterday that was where he was, and then there are some other things that point that way. But O I can't believe that. I think it is Frank Apt. Dr. Morrison would surely know it would ruin him. I think she has went to him and told a pitiful tale (she could do almost any thing in that line) said she was not to blame and all that and wanted him to get the sherrif. O it is such a mystery. There may not be a thing the matter with her. She may just say there is so she can get Mose. She told Ada & I that Mose never said a thing out of the way to her that he always acted like a gentleman. It is terrible terrible terrible. It seems there is no rest for me. It is after ten I suppose but I don't feel like I could sleep. I got so nervous and worried tonight when I heard it. Harry phoned and said he wouldn't be home until late. I'll bet he has gone to hunt Mose to tell him all about it. I ought to write to Lela but guess I'd better go to bed.

Feb. 2, 1911. I really don't know what do to with myself. I played the organ but that didn't help any. I really don't know what to do with myself. I'm almost crazy.

Evening. I laid down on the bed and tried to cry that it would do me good. I went to sleep and slept about an hour. I feel better mentally but not much better physically. It seems I'm so tired all the time and sleepy . . . I've been reading my journal over. If any one should read it they would think I was crazy sure . . . I'm all out of sorts today. It seems I am so much of the time lately. . . .

Feb. 17, 1911. Edythe Miller you're a foolish little dunce. You said right along or that rather that you didn't care a thing for ___ Eyes and now that he's gone you find yourself feeling wretched and blue. I really thot I had more sense. But I really can't account for myself. It is still raining and has been so gloomy all day . . .

[Edythe also wrote about feeling ill and wanting to see Dr. Morrison who would measure her goiter. She mentioned that Harry had gotten medicine for her and that she had stayed home reading The Shattered Romance and Her Heart's Surrender.]

Feb. 25, 1911. Sat. P.S. Harry come home this fore noon. He went to Tweedys yesterday eve and Mose had gone to Douds. Mr. Tweedy had gone to Liberty, was going to Douds to tell Mose about it and have him go away. Harry went from Tweedys to Liberty and Mr. Tweedy wanted Harry to go in his place Mose was going to Rance Tweedys from Douds. So Harry and Irn Nicols went on the train they had to be very careful as it would be go hard with a fellow if it was found out that he was aiding anyone to escape like that. Rance Tweedys were in bed but the boys knocked. He was suspicious asked who it was Nick said it was Friends from Lick Creek got a stick of wood and called for chat. He went to the door and Harry struck a match and then he knew them. Mose come out there when Harry told him he just laughed at him and wouldn't believe it. Finally he did. But O Mose is not guilty. I knew he wasn't. He said if he had money he'd stay and fight it out Nick gave him $20.00 and he had four. He was going to leave this morning for Okla going to some of his relatives. Said to tell us folks "Goodbye" "Yes good bye Mose may not many more days pass before I look upon your face again." He told Harry he would just as leave his folks would think him guilty as was. I suppose he is speeding onward every moment takes him father away. And this is his 22nd birthday too. I wonder if he is lonely. O how I wish I might tell him I think he is not guilty. Harry saw Ethyle Holmes last night and talked to her. She gave herself away. Said she knew Mose would be awful mad when they come after him. Said Dr. Morrison filed the papers. She told something about Apt too. But Papa and Harry say its Apt and Morrison for it now. I won't believe a thing against Dr. Morrison. Of course I may be mistaken. Papa and I were going down to B'ham this afternoon. But they said he wouldn't be in his office until the first of next week. I read what I wrote last night and notice that I never mentioned a thing about pitying Ethyle. Well in a way I pity her but she knew better and then she asked Harry to do something dreadful one time. I knew she lied but didn't know that she was so dreadful. Harry and Ada are in here now and we were talking about Mose and Harry said now when he had a couple of girls in view he couldn't say "come on Tweedy lets go and see them" and he said, "Golly, I hated to leave him." "Just think Tweedys gone." He said it so sorrowful. Well it was hard for them to part as they think so much of each other.

I thot I'd just have to come in here and write. I feel so lonely and I'm so nervous. I was so worked up last night that I didn't eat only a few bites of supper and couldn't half sleep. Didn't go to bed until almost 12:00 I guess. I couldn't eat hardly any breakfast or dinner either and I'm so nervous. I can't really realize that it is true. Harry says he thinks Mose will be back B4 long. Says he may be gone 2 wks or perhaps a year. If he would come back he could clear himself. He told Harry he would like to get up in the court room and face her. Papa and Harry said I would have to be a witness if they should have it in court. Because she told me he never said a word out of the way to her and he always acted like a gentleman. I would get scared out of my wits. But would do all I could to help Mose out. I just can't think that Dr. Morrison has anything to do with it. Harry said Tom Crum told him he knew something about Morrison that was awful but didn't tell him what it was. O I do hope he hasn't anything to do with it for just think how terrible it would be. Ethyle told Harry I think it was that she told Dr. Morrison maybe Mose would not marry her and he said maybe Harry would then. She said she didn't want to marry Mose if he didn't want her. But Harry tho't maybe she just said that so Mose wouldn't think she'd marry him then and come back and they would get him. She just as much as asked him to marry her. My heart is bothering me again. I just can't keep my mind off of that it seems. It's a big wonder she didn't say it was Harry. Little did I think yesterday morning when I saw Mose leave that it would be so long e'er I would see him.

Evening. I must go to bed guess it is 11:00 o'clock. My thots are not very pleasant tonight. When I have something occupying my mind I dwell on it all most all the time it seems. I wrote to Pearl Holmes tonight and copied off three poems to send to her. She wanted me to send some. She is going to send me some music. My eyes hurt. I have used them so much . Hat and her mother got home tonight. The train was 2 hrs late. Guess Harry and Ada are going over to Tweedys tomorrow if it isn't too stormy. It rained some this evening and then it turned into snow. I wonder where Mosie is tonight. May God help him until we meet again. I must go to bed and try to get some rest. I was nervous tonight. They are all in bed but me I guess. Ada is lying on the bed. Well I hope that we'll all come right sometime.

Feb. 26, 1911. Sun. PM. Well I can't be convinced that Dr. Morrison is implicated in any way with that affair of course it may be but I just can't believe it.

Feb. 26, 1911. Sun. PM. They have been trying to convince me that Dr. Morrison is guilty but I won't be convinced. Ada says now she thinks he is. Even if he is I can't feel indignant at him for causing Mose all this trouble. Perhaps I ought but I can't. Have been writing to Lela all about it.

Evening. I have written about 11 pages written to Lela I am so sleepy guess I'll go to bed and finish in the morning.

Feb. 27, 1911. Mon. morn. Harry was at Tweedys until about 8 o'clock last night. Mrs. Tweedy is almost crazy. Mose had some pictures taken the day he was in Ottumwa and they got them Sat. thro the mail. Mrs. Tweedy nearly fainted when she opened them. Mr. Tweedy called Harry out in the kitchen to show them to him and he turned his head away and cried. He said to tell Papa to do all he could as his wife wasn't very strong and he was afraid she would go crazy. So Papa started to B'ham just as soon as he got his breakfast. Left all the work. He is going to try and see Ethyle in town and make her confess who it is. Is going to tell her that if Mrs. Tweedy goes crazy they can put her (Ethyle) thro for it. I believe papa can get it out of her alright. ~~Mose~~ I have Moses picture here on the stand. Papa said he knew how it was to have a child away from home. There was a girl in Liberty yesterday told Harry that Ethyle told her 2 months ago she was fixed. Said she would stick to it too.

11:00 o'clock. Papa went on the freight this morning not so awful long ago. Harry got to thinking that maybe Papa should need him. Ethyle could deny that she told Harry those things and what could Papa do then? So he thot he would go down on a horse. He called Ruggles to have them tell Papa to call u if they saw him. Harry wanted papa to call before he went for fear maybe he wouldn't need him and he'd have his trip for nothing. Finally he began to get ready and here Harley Graham called him up and wanted to see him at the store. Harry told him he would be down in about an hour. Harry said if Papa called to ask him if he knew he was coming for it might be a scheme to get Harry down there. They think tho that Papa has had Harley to call so people went know he's down town. Harry says he won't go to the store until he sees Papa. I do hope it isn't a scheme. O I hope it will all come right. I mean the truth come out . . . Yes Mose we will do all in our power to clear you so that you may come back among us again and everyone will think the same of you as they did B4. I just wonder where he is now. I sent a 16 page letter to Lela. Ethyle told Harry when she told Apt that she was fixed he said there was a simple remedy that would knock that allright. She told him she was 3 months gone and he said it would take $100 then mark my words its old Apt.

Carter Lawson brought the mail awhile ago. There was a letter for Harry. We thot it looked like Ethyle's writing and tho't maybe it contained something that Papa and Harry should know while they were down there and it was from her. O such a heart broken letter. I will give it Birmingham.

[What follows is Ethyle's letter, as copied by Edythe into her journal.]

Feb. 28, 1911. Mr. Harry Miller. Harry—I may never see you again. As sure as there is a God in Heaven I wish I had never seen either of you boys yet I like you both and I am about that sure that I will never see either of you boys again. I think I shall see this town for the last time soon. And please tell Mose that I am not mad at him and that while I expect never to see him again that I shall think oh so often of him and Harry tell your sister that I know I am as innocent of all crime as they are yet I can never ask them to have anything to do with me again. My own foolish and weak heart has done all. Tell them I love them dearer than I love my own life and that as I write and think I shall never see them again I truly think I wish I could die and end it all. I have been almost tempted to end it all several times. My brother will soon be here. He is coming to take me home. And only the promise that he gives me could save some people if he ever sees them. Tell Mose that if he is gone now to stay away from Ben. I hope for his sake that he is gone but I would like to have seen him once more. I do not want to bring any more disgrace on him poor boy. Tell your mother I send her my love if she will accept it. I never saw a woman I thought as much of as I do of her. When I think of the good times I have had at your house and of your mother and sister my heart seems to break. I wanted to talk with you tonight but didn't get to so wanted to write a little. Edythe said she would write me a letter and I hope she will. I would love to hear from her if but once more. Harry, I said at the beginning that I never wanted to see you again but I would like to ask you a few questions e're I leave. You said yesterday that you knew nothing of Mose and I heard tonight that you knew a good deal about him. Harry, please tell him one more thing for me. I could not bear to see him or write to him but I want him to know that I did not want this made public as it has been. Tell him I would like to have seen him just long enough to tell him Good Bye "Forever." Oh how that word haunts me. It is a word that Edythe and I had so much fun about and now it means so much to me. "Gone Forever" and "ruined Forever." Now I guess I must stop writing as it is killing me. Every word I write pierces my heart anew. Harry, I have always thought of you as a dear Friend. You told me that you didn't think less of me. I surely have trusted you a good deal and you had ought to at least think kindly of me. I shall always remember the last night we spent together and if I never see you again please as much as write me a short letter telling me I am forgiven by you and oh I wish I could see you just once more please answer at once or I will not get the letter here.
And now Harry I bid you "Farewell."

Ethyle

Mar. 1, 1911. Harry I am at home now. Ben knows all and he said that only the promise he made me before I would tell him anything could keep him from hunting this world over and finding the one that through loving so dearly I have given all to try to please them. Ben said that for my sake he wish M. would come back but I can never think of seeing again and tell him that while I am living I shall never forget him but he shall haunt me always. E.H.

There it is word for word. And O how I wish nothing had ever happened. For with all Ethyle's faults I loved her and I love her still when she was here last summer we were speaking of Mose. I think she said something about him being hers and before I tho't I said, "He will be yours forever." Ah we little knew then as we laughed and had our fun over it that it would mean so much to us one day. "Gone forever." "ruined Forever." Oh Ethyle Ethyle why did you do it. Why O why. O I can't keep from crying for she was my friend my dear friend. There was no one who understood me so well and now to think all our talks are over all all.

O I wish Pearl Holmes [Ethyle's mother] had never come here e'er such dreadful work had come from it. If she could only be a pure hearted girl again I oh <u>how</u> glad I would be. But her folks are to blame. They talked so awful to her when she processed religion and then she backslid and then this work came of it. She told me it was their fault that she backslid. O I would rather see her dead, for I would perhaps have some hopes of meeting her in the Better World but ah it is terrible. I really can't bring my self to think of it yet. On the back of the envelope she wrote, <u>credula res amos est</u>. That is latin but don't know what it means think it is something about Love. I must try and forget all as it makes me so nervous.

Harry has come back. Apt talked to him. Harry said he talked as if he was innocent. But Harry said he couldn't believe <u>him</u> it. He told him he was a wise guy. He said there was a story out on him B4 and he just folded his arms and took it but he was going to fight it this time. Tried to get Harry to tell what Ethyle said about him. But he didn't get anything out of him. The only thing that ~~made Ha~~ he said in giving himself away was that he wasn't scared but he tho't it was the best thing to drop it Said if things went the way it looked like it would that they would Morrison would go out of town on a rail. The very idea I think it had better be him. Harry said all the business men tho't Morrison was into it. Said no one pitied her. Grover said he was glad Mose got away. Someone said the Free Methodist church was going to take it up and Joe Graham was going to give money to help find Mosie. But you can't tell a person can hear everything. . . .

Papa walked out to Holmes to try and make Ethyle confess it all, we were afraid it wouldn't do any good but he phoned awhile ago and said everything was working alright. So I suppose Ethyle has confessed it all. Mama asked him if he would be home on the freight and he said he didn't know. How glad we were when Mama told us that. Harry says "we'll have old Tweedy back yet." I believe there were tears in every one of our eyes. Dr. Morrison isn't in it in anyway. Sometime I think I would just as leave have Mose to stay away as to have Dr. Morrison ruined. But still if he is guilty it ought to be known. But oh how I hope and pray he isn't. Harry said he hated to think that either him or Apt were guilty. I would rather it were Apt. I long to know it all. I don't rally think Dr. Morrison is guilty but so many things point that way some times I almost fear he is. Harry said maybe I tho't as much of him as Apt did Ethyle maybe he had said something about me being his second wife like Apt did to Ethyle but he hasn't. He always treated me alright. Just to think what a good doctor he is and how much he has helped me. But he may not be in it and I do hope he isn't. Harry said no one scarcely believed that Mose is guilty said Fenwicks tho't he was in it he guessed but of course Ethyle would make them believe it. I tell you Papa has done lots for Tweedys. I suppose he thinks what if it was his boy. Dear old Journal the truth of it can never be told on your pages but I hope that everything will come right and I can write the truth and not be so sad. . . .

The Diary of Martha Furgerson Nash, 1947

Martha Ann Furgerson was born on September 26, 1924, in Sedalia, Missouri, to Lily (Williams) and Dr. Lee Furgerson. Martha's siblings were Betty Jean, Rebecca, Lileah, and Lee. When Martha was still young, the family moved to Waterloo, Iowa, so that her father could open a medical practice there. Martha graduated from East Waterloo High School in 1943. From 1943 to 1947 she attended Talladega College, a historically black college in Alabama. Martha Furgerson received her bachelor of arts degree in history. She graduated from Talladega College with honors in the spring of 1947.

When Martha began keeping her diary on September 14, 1947, she was nearly twenty-three and had recently returned to her family's home in Waterloo after graduation. Her diary entries record her activities with family and friends, her observations on race relations in the northern and southern United States, and her

Martha Furgerson Nash, 1947. By permission of the Iowa Women's Archives, University of Iowa Libraries.

perspective as a young woman coming of age just after the end of World War II. On June 12, 1948, she married Dr. Warren Nash at St. Peter Claver's Catholic Church in Waterloo. She had met him while at Talladega. After he received his medical degree from Creighton University in Omaha, Nebraska, Nash began practicing medicine in Waterloo in August 1954. Martha and Warren Nash became the parents of seven children, five daughters and two sons.

Martha Nash, who died April 14, 2000, in Waterloo, was an activist in the Waterloo area and throughout Iowa for more than fifty years. She served on the boards of directors for the People's Community Health Clinic in Waterloo, the Iowa Health Systems Agency, the Black Hawk–Bremer League of Women Voters, the Northeast Iowa Health Planning Council, the Dubuque Archdiocesan Council of Catholic Women, and the National Council of Catholic Women, among other organizations. From 1981 to 1995 she served as the executive director of the Martin Luther King, Jr., Center for Education and Vocational Training.

The manuscript diary of Martha Furgerson Nash, housed at the Iowa Women's Archives in Iowa City, was kept by the diarist in a bound National volume (eight by eleven inches) with lined numbered pages. Diary entries appear on the first 64 pages, and the remainder of the volume's 152 pages are blank. The diary entries run from September 14 through November 18, 1947. They reflect the thoughts of an intelligent and introspective young Iowa woman coming of age at mid-century.

Sunday Waterloo September 14, 1947 It's an awful thing to have a cold—as I do—and feel as badly as I felt Friday & Saturday. A drippy nose—someday that problem will be solved.

Fall and all its beauty will soon be here. Tonite feels just like one of those crisp, cool fall evenings. Driving to Iowa City today, I thought about how pretty it will be soon. The trees will be all gold & red & brown. "October's bright blue weather" is around the corner.

We took my sister down to the University today. Watching the to-be freshmen coming in, reminded me of my freshman days. The excitement of coming to college. You dream about it a long time, you hear about it from those who've been and, all in all, it seems to be a wonderful place. But, at last, you have arrived. It's exciting, but for some of them (and you can see it on their faces) it's rather hard to see the folks go. Yes, today is the beginning of adulthood for a lot of students all over the country. Today begins four of the most wonderful years they have ever known and will probably ever know. When they leave here in 1951, those carefree days will be over forever. But, they will always look back & remember those four years. . . .

Tuesday Waterloo September 16, 1947 It is interesting to note this year's fashion. The new, long skirts. The rounded shoulder-lines—and all those other silly details as described by the fashion magazines. I have noticed the conflict in styles. Some are still wearing their skirts knee-length (haven't yet figured out whether they just haven't shortened them or whether they are members of "The Little Below the Knee" Club). Then, you will see skirts that seem almost to dust the ground. And on the short girls, these "new, long lengths" look utterly silly—cuts their height by inches. Then there are the colored stockings—greens, blues, reds, blacks, grays, etc. Can't you see someone wearing stockings that cast a sickly pallor of green on one's legs? Skirts remind one of tubes or else they seem like the hobble skirts in style during World War I. That last style was invented, I think, especially to keep women from walking—thereby making Mr. Henry Ford and his kind richer by leaps & bounds. There are so many things one could say about "Dame Fashion, 1947." But, the best way to sum it all up is—to- me—to say, "Women are so foolish." If you don't believe me—look about you on the streets & notice what they are wearing this fall.

Wednesday Waterloo   September 17, 1947 This time last year I would now be getting ready or on my way back to school at Talladega in Alabama. I probably would have packed my trunk—by throwing things in—a couple of suitcases & a few boxes. Then I'd start the long trek back. Out of Chicago, I'd catch the L & N train—traveling Pullman. Soon I'd see Illinois & Indiana flashing by. My last look at God's country for a few months. While I am asleep, Kentucky and Tennessee would go by and in the morning I'd get up in Alabama. Then I'd hurry to get dressed as Birmingham was near. Once again I'd see that old familiar station. Then the hustle & bustle of getting a taxi to the bus station. There I'd probably see a few familiar faces—going back, too. The jostle of the line waiting to get on the bus. My fervant hopes that not too many Negroes would be waiting to get on, since the back seat (reserved for Negroes) would soon get filled up & then I'd have to wait for the next bus. And then—if I was lucky—I'd be on my way. Familiar scenery would go by—Childersburg, the Coose River, the Bemis Bag Co., cotton fields, red earth, & of course, the weather would be hot. Finally, we'd round a curve & there to the left is the college. But first I'd have to go downtown. A taxi & finally the back door of the dorm—Foster Hall. Girls & some fellows, too, would be spilling out of the door to greet us. Cries of "I thought you weren't coming back" or "Why didn't you write?" or "Well, Big-time, what have you been doing?" would be heard. Then to the dining hall for lunch & more familiar faces & more greetings.

Remarks on how good it is to be back & how little the place has
changed. Then to see the Dean to get my room number & key. Finally,
the need to unpack halts all further conversation. And another school
year has begun. Gee, I wish I were going back?

Thursday Waterloo September 18, 1947 A house is being built
behind ours. While watching it go up, I have been amazed at how quickly
one can be built—even though days may pass between the times the carpenters work. Today when I left for Cedar Falls, the workmen (two of
them) had just begun laying the floors and making the frames for the side
walls. This afternoon—when I returned—the men had the frames up for
the outside walls and also the frames for the interior partitions. If they
keep on at this pace, the house will be done in a week.

Jeans and "T" shirts seem to be the height of fashionableness among
the men at T.C. [Teachers College in Cedar Falls]. It seems strange to
me, because at Talladega, the men usually did not wear jeans. In the
evenings at 'Dega, the men changed to suits and wore ties. Girls wearing
slacks on week-days was taboo at 'Dega, too. Such sights would only be
seen on Saturdays, when slacks could be worn. Restrictions and regula-
tions on types of dress are very much the norm for Negro colleges. However, there is gradually a laxening of such rules. I think those types of reg-
ulations were set up in the vain hope that ways of dressing could affect
the majority so as to accept the minority group. But, they found out that
dress has nothing to do with acceptance. Yet, those rules have certainly
helped in giving 'Dega's campus a certain air—. However, I prefer T.C.'s
way—casualness in clothes. It's more restful. . . .

Wednesday Waterloo September 24, 1947 All my brilliant thoughts &
my deep perceptions seem to have vanished tonite. My mind is a blank.
Reading shorthand has my head reeling. Let me see what I can dig (I
mean dig) from my overtaxed brain. Today standing by the entrance in
Black's I watched the people going in & out. One thing that fixed itself
in my mind was the big rush that everyone was in. They dashed in; they
ran out. Where they were going in such a rush is beyond me. Maybe they
were hurrying to get into a warm building; but, then why should they
hurry out. And that lead to musings on "Why do Americans hurry so?"
which reminded me of the story about a Chinese who wondered the
same thing & concluded by saying that they rush to save a few minutes in
which they'll have nothing to do. We here dash hither & yon, for no particular reason, usually. We take shortcuts to save time & when we reach
our destination we have time to waste. We take the fastest train or plane,
the shortest route in traveling as tho we hated to travel. If we really did,
we wouldn't go at all. And because we hurry so, we miss many good

things. The close observing of passers-by, the beautiful scenery or the ugliness of the city. We die younger (I contend) & we live at too fast a pace. My motto is "Go slow & enjoy life." And that is my bit of wisdom for tonite.

Thursday Waterloo September 25, 1947 I am taking a course in Shorthand—Gregg method. It is a very fascinating, once you get the hang of it. For one thing you have to forget about spelling, as we know it, by letters, & learn to think of spelling in terms of sound. That is sometimes rather difficult to do, & some words sound alike. Then, after you do that & learn all the brief forms (where two or three letters or sounds or something mean a word such as the signs for "s" & "m" which mean some) which make it all the more complicated, you'll find it easy to learn shorthand. But, Gregg really created something wonderful, when he worked out his system. Just think, how much easier it is to write.

Friday Waterloo September 26, 1947 Today is my birthday & I am a year older (& feel no more differently than I ever did). This leads me to the thought that people are always remarking, "You don't look that old." Which has, & still does, always make me wonder how old must one look, to look his age. How old does one or should one look at 24 or 25 or 18 or 8? Maybe I'll know the answer—someday.

Birthdays. When I was a child I waited in excited anticipation for a birthday. When you're little, you're so impatient to grow up, & when you finally reach that age you've wanted to for so long, you want to grow young. Birthdays meant parties & presents & the promise that tomorrow holds—glamorous adventure, dreams coming true. Now, I am older & with a slight veneer of maturity & supposed sophistication & so I must be dignified & not pay any attention to a mere birthday. Yet I always wonder each Sept. 26th what this year will bring. . . .

Sunday Waterloo September 28, 1947 Being the oldest child is a thankless position. I know from experience. You are the example, so you must be good & obey promptly. You must wait for the others when you go out. You have to stay at home with them and make them mind (a hard-enough job for parents).

But, that is not all. You are the experiment. All the rigid ideas your parents had about strict raising were tried out on you. You received more scoldings & probably more spankings as a child. Along with Your parents, you learned what raising a child is like—at your expense. When you grew older & wanted dates or to go out, you weren't old enough, yet, seventeen was plenty of time to begin that.

Now, you look at the younger ones & think what an easy life they

have. They all but rule the house. No spankings, not many scoldings.
Your younger sister is 15 & has dates. They go out at 14 & 15.

There is one compensation, though. You are the best-behaved
child—or so I like to think.

Monday Waterloo September 29, 1947 Music is beauty, joy, life—the
be-all and end-all. Tonite at T.C. I heard Mark Harrell, baritone, sing.
His voice has music, literally sings with ~~fullness~~ joy or tenderness, or sorrow. Mr. Harrell is a baritone, but his voice can get as tender as a
woman's. His diction is perfect. Each word, whether German, French or
Italian can be clearly understood. When he sang the spiritual, "Take My
Mother Home," the sorrow could be clearly seen. I felt tears come to my
eyes. Then, when he sang "I Got Plenty of Nothin" you could see a carefree, happy man satisfied with his life.

Mr. Harrell is not only a singer, but he's an actor. By raising an eye-
brow, or by the tilt of his head or by a twinkling in the eye or by a sad
look one could get the mood of the song. He very seldom used his
hands. Only his face & voice conveyed the meaning, and they told it
clearly. I was sorry when it ended. . . . .

Wednesday Waterloo October 6, 1947 October is here. Another
month gone by. The older I get, the quicker days, months & years fly by.
When I was little, I began looking forward to next Christmas almost as
soon as the last one was over. It (or it seemed) took so long for Christmas
to come around. ~~Days~~ Then, I used to be anxious for birthdays to come.
I waited in such excited anticipation for a birthday when I'd be one year
older.

Now the days pass by more quickly than I want them to. Twenty-
four hours in a day never seems to be enough time for me to get all my
work done. Seasons come & go, almost before I can wink an eye. New
Year's is here and gone, before I realize a year has passed.

Daddy says the time passes faster as you grow older. I wonder.

Thursday Waterloo October 2, 1947 Tonite I saw a sailor on the
street and he looked so lonesome, surrounded by civilians. I remember
the war years, when servicemen were a dime a dozen. You saw all kinds
and types—soldiers, sailors, marines, air force men, officers and buck pri-
vates. Then they dominated the scenes everywhere. They were on trains,
busses, on streetcars. You saw them in bunches or twos or one alone.
Sometimes a paratroop would pass by & you would notice his boots or
you'd see a WAC or a WAVE.

But, now, a serviceman on a street stands out. People turn to look at
him. Fellows, now out of service, feel sorry for the poor "sucker" ~~that~~

who is still in—and they are, most of them, glad they are out and able to get on with the busines of living.

It was hard to get accustomed to them in the beginning, and now its hard to remember that peacetime (?) is back again.

Friday Waterloo October 3, 1947 One of the things I miss about 'Dega are the "bull sessions"—gab fests. A lot of others were filled with talk about women or the fellows, but very seldom did ours get off on those subjects. We tore the world apart & put it back together. We decided what was wrong with Greek-letter organizations (we were Greeks, too) & what must be done to improve them. And so they went. They might start late at night & continue until dawn or they might begin on a Saturday afternoon when no one felt like doing anything and the girls would gather.

For some unexplainable reason my room was very popular for gathering of some of the girls. They'd come in to fix their [hair] or to iron a dress or to talk & before we knew it, my roommate & I had been all but pushed out of our room. But, they were great fun. . . .

Sunday Waterloo October 5, 1947 Baseball games can be exciting and the world series even more so. This year the series have had more than its share of thrills. Listening to the game today, I was on edge & all but biting my nails to the nibs the whole time. I am for the Dodgers this year (mainly because they had the courage to demonstrate the democratic spirit). When Gianfreddo caught Di Maggio's seemingly homer, I was so excited I couldn't sit still. And when the double-play ended the game, I was too exhausted to cheer anymore.

Both teams have been neck & neck with each other. They have attack & defended with skill. Sometimes the breaks were with one & against the other. Yet, the fact that most of the time, skill & a good spirit (something Iowa's football team needs) is there, shows in each team's playing.

Tomorrow's game should be anybody's game.

Monday Waterloo October 6, 1947 My little sister, Becky, is not only highly interested in dolls, but also in lipstick, powder, perfume, & pocketbooks and all other items reserved for the women.

Becky has quite a collection of old, battered purses gathered from her other sisters or from the Sitterly girls who live across the street. She has boxes filled with old lipsticks, perfume bottles, powder puffs, combs, & rouge. By wheedling & begging her sisters, she manages to add to that collection. Not only does she have lipstick, but she uses them. She can apply lipstick like a veteran. Once in a while, she must apply her make-up, carry one of her many purses and be a thoroughly grown-up woman.

She, also, has a collection of jewelry and, seemingly, she puts most of it on at these times.

Children love to pretend & being "grown-up" seems to be more exciting to the imagination than anything else. Oh, if they only knew that they were in the happiest time of life. . . .

Friday Waterloo October 10, 1947 Today I noticed I've been writing November in here. I wonder what makes people do things like that. Freud says it's no accident that we do things that seem arbitrary. Oh, well, maybe I [am] just losing more of my mind.

Today is my mother's birthday. Gee, it doesn't seem possible she's as old as she is or, maybe, it's that I'm as old as I am. Daddy will soon be nearing 50—a half century. People begin to round that age before you know it. My mother never could hide her age. We always knew it—better than she could. We used to buy her present—it took a lot of thought shopping to find the right one. Most of the time, we try to get something personal—something not for the house. Sometimes that's hard on our meagre supply. One year our card may be sentimental, another funny. This year's was a killer. It was made out of sandpaper & on the front said "Another birthday"—& inside "Rough, ain't it?" Muddie said, "It certainly is." But she thought it was funny.

Saturday Waterloo Oct. 11, 1947 Homecoming at Iowa U. An exciting time. It's been four years since I've been here for a homecoming.

The crowds & crowds of people. The mums—all golden. The big monument on Clinton street. Seeing old friends. The big game (and what a game), the victory whistles, almost deafening you. Then a dance. going to a frat dance is fun. Hearing them sing their songs. Then to a few private parties. Get something to eat & home.

Homecoming is like no other time. No one studies—who could at a time like this. It's too exciting. There are crowds & crowds of people & noise everywhere.

The football team tries to do its best. And this year Iowa outdid the outdoing. During the half-time, the band welcomes the grads back & cuts amusing capers.

When it's all over, we all say "What a good time we had."

Sunday Waterloo Oct. 12, 1947 I spent the day in Iowa City. After the excitement of yesterday—all was quiet. We went to the Union to a tea dance. It was downstairs in the River Room. It was a lot of fun watching the kids dance. They dance so differently from us. Most of them hop about while we glide. All colored people don't dance well, certainly, but they do dance differently. Most of the kids I knew don't jitterbug any-

240

more, either. It's all slow dancing. (Jitterbugging is too much for my tired bones.)

We finally figured out that the white kids danced on the off-beat & that was why they hopped. Some of them whirled & whirled.

Another thing—they like a different kind of music. We didn't dance much because of the type of records they had. Dancing & record-likes & dislikes are one area where whites & Negroes differ. I wonder why. Yet, when whites are around Negroes they learn to dance the same and vice-versa. More association would help, I think. . . .

Thursday Waterloo October 16, 1947 There is a lot of fun in driving a car. I like to drive. I just got my license this summer, maybe that's why. But, my pet bugaboo is driving at night. You can meet enough impolite drivers in the daytime, but at night—oh. Some people evidently don't know what a dimmer is for. And it's so nerve-wracking to meet a car with glaring headlights. After two or three, your eyes hurt and you can hardly see. Then there are the drivers who are always in a hurry. They dart in & out of traffic, pass you & then slow up, pass on curves or hills & do anything else foolish that can be done. It's enough to make you wish the horse & buggy days were back. I wonder why people do these things. They can't seem to see that they may be the next victims. You begin to feel that they have no value on their lives, let alone any others. Driving—and especially American driving—is good evidence of the lack of social responsibility in humans.

Friday Waterloo October 17, 1947 There's a fellow who is East High's star football player. He's colored, a good student & very popular with his fellow students. But, that's no story. The amazing facts are found in the boy's background. His father is what is known as no-good altho he has worked hard, yet at one time he was a bootlegger. His mother could do nothing about it. Two of the children, an older boy & girl, didn't finish school. what will happen to the others is only a guess. One of the younger boys seems to be a half-wit. This boy, the football star, grew up in an environment that nurtured no ambition, no dreams of achievement, no desires for education. And yet, this boy desires to go to college, he has practiced faithfully & earnestly to be a football player, & he dreams of a future. What has caused this one child to be like that? What one or maybe many small factors in his environment led him to be an earnest, sincere lad? What in his heredity? He's not an angel, as a boy he was part of many pranks, some of which could have meant a reformatory—& yet with a little help & encouragement, he may realize his dreams. What is most important heredity, environment or personal will? I don't know. . . .

Wednesday Waterloo October 22, 1947 This week I have been helping in my father's office. I have ~~always~~ helped there before & I have
always been intrigued by the ability of the ~~strangers~~ people waiting to talk
to each other. Seemingly, waiting in a doctor's office has the same effect
as traveling. Perfect strangers will converse as though they were old
friends. They will tell each other all their troubles & their life histories.
European's have often said that this tendency for ready conversation with
strangers is only to be found among Americans. Many think it is good,
that it shows the trust & friendliness. I think it's foolish. I'd just rather
watch people than find out about them. It is very annoying to me to have
some stranger telling me all his troubles, when I'm not interested in
them. But, then I always say to myself that perhaps it makes them feel
better. So I nod my head & murmur sort "yes's" & think about something else.

Thursday Waterloo October 23, 1947 Today really seems like Fall. It's
raining. It's cold. Everything is dripping. And it feels good. It's dreary.
It's damp. And it's fall.

This is the kind of day that really gives you a lift. You want to work.
Your spirits rise—at least mine do—rain or no rain.

The rain started this evening and I had to drive to Cedar Falls. That
was quite an experience. I thought about slippery roads, blinding rain,
glaring headlights (they reflect on the pavement) & I got nervous. That
was the first time I'd driven ~~up~~ in rain, but it wasn't as bad as I'd imagined. The day I learn to drive on slippery roads, I'll really feel like I know
a little about driving.

Yep, today is a beautiful day in Iowa (even though some people
might disagree with me).

Friday Iowa City October 24, 1947 Tonite I heard a jazz concert. It
was the "Jazz at the Philharmonic" group sponsored by Norman Granz
who had sponsored many of these in Los Angeles. Granz felt the "jam"
sessions of jazzists should be lifted out of the gin mills & taverns & onto
the concert stage. So he got together a group of jazz artists who gave jam
sessions in a concert hall. These concerts were recorded, although the
musicians didn't know it. On the records you can hear the audience's
applause & the remarks the musicians make to each other. They decide on
a piece & who will follow who on the solos. And that is all. After playing
the piece once all together, they begin, as the slang goes, "to riff." That
is, they play whatever comes into their heads. A good jazz musician can
really demonstrate his imagination & skill here. Well, the concert at Iowa
U. was, as slang says, "real gone." The artists were among the names in
jazz. Some of them were not as well known to the general public as others

like Coleman Hawkins. The group was mixed (white & colored) & the music was "fine." They played "Body & Soul" & it was beautiful. They swung out on such pieces as "Stuffy" & "Flying Home." And each one tried to outdo the other on solos. When you hear men like these play, you begin to appreciate the training & background they had to have in music before they develop into good jazz artists. Jazz is gradually becoming more than a whim, more than something to sing or dance to. It is an expression of a race, an era, a country & eventually, will be considered a part of the long historical development of expression through music. . . .

Sunday Waterloo Oct. 26, 1947 For some unexplainable reason I wanted to see a movie. So I went. The picture was typical Hollywood. An attempt to be realistic (like "True Story" magazine is). Dorothy Lamour & Alan Ladd were the stars. All the men were rough, tough & ready seasonal workers. The women were "dames." Dorothy Lamour led to trouble, between wild beatings of the heart & looks that were sparks of fire between she & Ladd. All in all, it would have been better if Hollywood had never made it. And that is true of most movies. They are very seldom what they pretend to be. They are filled with all the best propaganda techniques, they idealize everything while they are trying to be realistic & a story must ~~never~~ always have a love interest, even if only implied. Once in a while, someone out there forgets about making money & turns out a good picture.—And they have the nerve to make fun of radio!

Monday Waterloo October 27, 1947 It's funny the type of conversations a bunch of kids gathering together can get into. Last nite there were some over here. We sat around our kitchen table, eating popcorn & drinking lemonade & talking. A lot of it was crazy. Nonsense, that's all. Telling tales. We talked about sports announcers, football, basketball & inevitably, school. We discussed music—songs we liked & didn't like. We discussed bands—likes & dislikes. Sometimes our gab had a touch of seriousness. We talked about the House un-American Comm. & what a farce it was. We discussed the Four Freedoms. (One of the participants had to write a paper on it & that is how it came up). Sometimes I like to sit back & listen to the drift of "gab-fests." It's amazing how they can change. From one subject to another without just the smallest effort. I like sitting around our kitchen table & talking like that. It's one of the best ways to spend an evening.

Tuesday Waterloo October 28, 1947 Have [you] ever sat in a room & listened to people talk or stood somewhere & suddenly got the feeling that you have been here before & done this very thing with these same people? I often get that feeling and it is one of the most wierdest things to happen. Out of the clear blue sky, that feeling will hit you & you can never figure out why. You know very well that you haven't been here before & yet you cannot shake it off. You wonder if you dreamed it or what. Sometimes you want to run away, it scares you. It's that great, mysterious thing that comes from the mind. It is a reaction that has not been explained, as yet. Freud might say that it is your subconscious mind pushing a similar experience to the fore. It is one of those things that makes you realize there are greater forces than man in this world of ours.

Wednesday Waterloo Oct. 29, 1947 Our priest was by tonite. He was telling us about Communist China (he was a missionary there until Pearl Harbor). Naturally, he holds the Catholic viewpoint about the Communists. He's "agin 'em." Myself, I don't know. It's something I have to see for myself. The way Father talked, the nationalists were good, the Communists & Japs about equally bad. Yet I have read books such as Theodore White's & Annalu Jacoby's "Thunder Out of China," which showed the Nationalists no better. The world is divided between two theories of government, two ways of life. The Russians have security, but no freedom (as we see "freedom"). We have freedom (at least we think we do, but right now that is in danger), but no security. I had a teacher once who always used to ask: "Which is more important, freedom or security?"

Anyway, I think the common people are being fooled. They are listening to men shout & rant about beautiful ideas. Men who are afraid of losing their power & wealth. I'm Catholic, but the Church has led to decay in Spain & Mexico. It has promoted ignorance & poverty. Under its strict moral code can be found the worst of morals. The world is in a period of great change. Something is happening. We are gradually leaving the Middle Ages behind & catching up with science. There are men (as there are always) who are trying to stop it. But it's too late. Two wars have broken it down. We can't stop it. Maybe we'll have that world of brotherhood & humility dreamed of by Jesus, & the other utopian thinkers. . . .

Wednesday Waterloo November 5, 1947 Today I had to make a speech—horrors, I got roped in on that. Anyway, I was to tell the group (a Ladies' Aid Group who had suddenly discovered that race relations were a part of "Christian Education") about the Negro in the South today. The talk was composed of a few formal notes to keep me on a track of some kind plus a few meanderings & mumblings of Talladega, etc.

I hope those women really realized what race relations & minority problems are. I doubt it, it's too remote from them. One of the ladies, did, though, mention the fact that it had occurred to her that her grandparents had once, perhaps, been a minority here in America (she is Danish). She is beginning to have an inkling of what it means. But, unlike the Italians & the other Latin-Europeans, her ancestors were of Germanic stock which was not too strange to the Anglo-Saxons & so they probably never felt like too much of a minority group.

I hope my little effort brought the women a knowledge of what Negroes (some, anyway) are thinking & to make them gradually realize that a man is a man no matter what his external problems. But, if the old folks (as I told them) be quiet, the young people might work it out. . . .

Saturday Waterloo November 8, 1947 I should be a cake of ice. We went to Madison, Wisconsin for the game. Iowa lost (as we said Wisconsin—46, Iowa fights). Anyway Johnny Estes got a chance to show what he could do. Too had he didn't have a clicking team playing with him. He did most of the offensive quarterbacking. But, it was so cold. Flurries of snow, icy winds & I froze. Not used to this kind of weather yet.

We saw Wisconsin's Union. One thing I really liked about it. Beer is sold there—have a room called the Rathskeller room. Very lovely atmosphere. Madison is a pretty town. Johnny Estes' parents & sister went with us, also, some other friends. The girls all rode with Mr. Estes—that was fun. Coming back, Johnny drove. We put Mr. Estes out. We sang all the way back—we had some very fine harmony, too. Even sent ourselves, but good. After we left Independence, John passed Daddy (he was leaving) & we scooted for home. When we got here, we hurried out of our things. Daddy wasn't too far behind but we wanted to pretend we'd been here a long time. Didn't fool them, though. After we ate, we went to Charmaine Richardson's house for a "get." This was a really fine day. . . .

Monday Waterloo Nov. 10, 1947 Today looks like Christmas. It has been snowing all day. Everything looks so pretty & white (but, oh, what a foreboding of the winter to come). Fresh snow always reminds me of Elinor Wylie's poem "Velvet Shoes." Today the snow was falling so softly—everything looked so pretty. I can just imagine walking through snow in "velvet shoes." Miss Wylie caught a mood there using such simple & concise expressions.

I always like the first snow of the year. It covers a drab landscape with magic. Everything appears to be so different. I missed it at Talladega. We used to have one or two a year, but they would barely last a day. It always amused me the way kids from Florida used to act when they saw it for the first time. Naturally, we Northerners always had to tell about real snow—with slight exaggerations.

But, snow has reminded me that a long, hard winter is ahead. Brrrrr!

Tuesday Waterloo November 1, 1947 Today is Armistice Day & my reaction is "So what?" I think it is time (as does the Des Moines Register) we stop commemorating this day. It was not the day the war ended in 1918. And the commemoration of it each year did not make for peace. What had happened in 1914 to 1918 was soon forgotten, in the "velvet" days of the 20s & the harsh days of the 30s. Then, as now, people turned to their own little petty tasks & fears & worries, ignoring what was going on in the world. Today the world is in an even greater turmoil. And we are still being hoodwinked by the politicians who seem to want to ignore our part in the world. These same politicians are shouting loudly against Russia, while they, undercover, are grafting. Americans haven't been taught to see things as they are. We haven't been shown how to examine a situation & really look under to find what is what. If we can all wake up to the implications & causes of the conflicts & disturbances in the world today—eventually, war as a means of getting what the other fellow has will not be the politician's method.

Wednesday Waterloo November 12, 1947 I am supposed to be direct-ing a play for the Youth Council. (They think I know how—joke). Any-way, the play is by Langston Hughes. It's very interesting. Named "Don't You Want to Be Free," it is the history of the Negro from slavery to now. It's written in episodic fashion & is only an hour long. If it is done correctly, it can be effective. I only hope this cast will hurry & learn their lines—so we can start whipping it into shape.

Play rehearsals are fun. I enjoyed them at 'Dega. Being in the play & on stage isn't half as much as being at the rehearsals. More funny things can happen—& they always seem twice as amusing as ordinarily. There's a certain comradeship that comes in, too. Then in dress rehearsal & the actual performance, things happen that at that time seem great tragedies. Then, when you look back, it is funny.

But, being director, I have to calm the antics of the cast down—I have to have a little more authority & get tough with them. I only hope that the play will look halfway good—.

Thursday Waterloo November 13, 1947 In reviewing today, I find no brilliant, philosophical thoughts to record or can I discover any historical happenings. So another day has passed. . . .

Monday Waterloo Nov. 17, 1947 The last night of the quarter. Hoo-ray.

I washed my hair tonite—It is such a task to get down to and then when it's [done], you feel so good. Think I'll get a wig. Much simpler that way.

There's a nip in the air tonite. Christmas is nearer, too. All the stores are getting out their tinsel, bells, & holly. It won't be long, before 1948 will be here. Wonder what it will bring?—or am I being too forward?

Journeys

3

This chapter focuses on eight diaries by women who, for one reason or another, were writing in an unfamiliar setting and whose
perspective was that of the observer. In certain cases, such as those
of Isabella McKinnon, Sarah Pratt, and Jane F. Grout, the diarist is
literally moving from one country or state to another. Other
diarists, such as Emily Quiner and Agnes Barland McDaniel, write
of their experience as nurses living in cultures unknown (and perhaps unknowable) to them. Three diarists, Alice Gortner Johnson,
Gwendolyn Wilson Fowler, and Ruth Van Horn Zuckerman, write
travel journals that, to varying degrees, contain not only narration
and description but also reflection and introspection.

In each case the diarist's tale follows the pattern of the quest:
she leaves home and travels through unfamiliar and/or foreign ter-
rain. Sometimes she meets a friend or guide along the way—someone with whom she can share her experiences. The quest/journey
stories in these diaries, however, differ from traditional quest narratives in one significant respect: they do not always end with the voy-
ager's triumphant return home. Diaries do not always reveal how
their writers' journeys concluded, or, for that matter, whether their
journeys concluded. Nor do the diarists always presume that returning home is the desired or necessary conclusion to their journeys.

Shaping each diarist's entries are her prior experiences as well as her assumptions about both the environment from which she has come and the environment into which she has entered. In each case the concept of journey denotes the act of travel or passage from one literal place to another and at the same time connotes the rite of passage from one way of seeing and understanding to another.

The Diary of Sarah K. Pratt, 1844

Sarah K. Pratt was born in 1819 to Betsy (Sherwin) and Phineas Pratt. Sarah lived with her parents, six sisters, and one brother on a homestead located on Pillar Point (now known as Phillips Corners), New York. Like her siblings, Sarah Pratt had only a common school education; at the age of fourteen or fifteen she began teaching school to help support the family, and her younger siblings, Semantha, Parthena, Amanda, and Collins, were among her pupils.

The first member of the Pratt family to migrate west was Jane, Sarah's older sister, who married Ira Washburn in 1838 and moved to the Wisconsin Territory shortly thereafter. Because Ira Washburn worked as a steamer captain and was often away from home, Jane, lonesome in her husband's absence, soon invited her sisters Sarah and Susannah to join her. Their journey to the Wisconsin Territory began on a steamboat in September 1844. That journey became the impetus for Sarah's diary, in which she wrote not only of the journey itself but also about her sadness at the separation from the rest of her family and her desire to grow spiritually as the result of her life experiences. After arriving in Wisconsin, Sarah, then about twenty-five, continued keeping her diary and teaching; her first school was in the town of Union, Wisconsin. In her free time Sarah, along with Susannah, often spent time with their sister Jane on the homestead near Afton, Wisconsin, that Ira and his brother William Washburn farmed.

Phineas and Betsy Pratt and their younger children also came west to the Wisconsin Territory. At that time members of the Winnebago Nation were being removed from Wisconsin as more and more Euro-American settlers moved west. Sarah K. Pratt's diary,

248

which she kept until her death from consumption on September 22, 1847, reflects the events that mark her journey and three years in Wisconsin. Like many diaries of its time, her diary reflects a fluidity in sentence structure, spelling, capitalization, and punctuation. The diary was not only a place where she could describe people, places, and events on her journey west from New York but where she could ponder her station in life and meditate on her spiritual growth. After Sarah's untimely death, her sister Susannah continued writing in the diary, recounting details of the final months of her sister's life and creating a memorial to her.

1844. This book is intended to copy a brief sketch of the occurrences of scenes which transpire through the remainder of my life. I often feel to regret that I have not commenced to pen down things which occurred since I was educated enough to write and form sentences; therefore many things which perhaps might be worthy of note for my aid and counsel will be erased from my memory for it is or seems to be almost natural to all mankind to forget counsels and instructions that have been given. Many, very many that I have received as it were but for a moment now is gone. Could I but have it here inscribed I might read it here and perhaps receive instruction. Many are the kind dealings of a kind providence. Will they be forgotten? I fear many will. I pen these lines not for the instruction of any other person nor for their perusal but it is to peruse myself that I may, should I [be] permitted to remain an inhabitant of this earthly ball here, look back and recollect this time and perhaps strive to derive counsels from all instructions given in future.

I was born in the year of Our Lord eighteen hundred and nineteen in the town of Brownville, County of Jefferson, New York and at the age of three years my parents removed from that place to the town of Ellisburgh in the same county. there we lived and the family of children which consisted of seven children received a good chance for education for people in moderate circumstances. indeed our parents took great pains to keep us at school as long as the school continued which probably averaged about nine months during each year. it was seldom that any were kept from school except in case of sickness, though their circumstances or means would not allow of no greater advantage than a common school which is surely greater than many poor children receive whose parents are wealthy. Many parents realize not the worth of an education and care but little whether they use means for the education of their children or not. I have often felt thankful that I was blessed with parents that took such an interest in the welfare of their children. . . .

Our family consisted of six daughters and a son of which the boy was the youngest. We were all blessed generally with good health and all were permitted to enjoy each others society till my eldest sister married and moved to Wisconsin Territory. It truly was a cause of grief to us that we could not live in her society. They had a great deal of bad luck and came very near losing their lives on the journey. but they, through the kindness of their Heavenly parent, escaped from the destruction of the watery element by losing all their goods and the most of their clothing. and they were obliged to experience the hardships of a new country without them, which they must have realized a great privation. We often heard from them by letters. . . .

My sister that lived in Wisconsin and her husband felt many anxieties to see their friends and they wrote a number of times for some of our family to come and spend a season or two with them. Accordingly my sister Susannah and myself came to the conclusion that we would go and spend the winter with them. We started with deep feelings of regret suffering many anxieties about the troubles on our journey besides the parting with numerous friends and friendly relatives.

September 3, 1844. I left home. I started about 3 o'clock P.M. intending to start out the same evening on the Lady of the Lake, a steamer which we expected according to usual custom to leave Sackets for Oswego about nine oclock. Never shall I forget the feelings which I realized when parting. I realized I was parting with my dear parents, sisters, and brother to go to a foreign land. There I should be deprived of the counsels of my best earthly friends. It was truly a solemn thing for us to part with all our dear relatives and other dear friends. Some [who] came to take a parting had been with us at my fathers. We were met by some at the ferry. I thought I was bidding a final farewell to many of them and perhaps to all. O, who can realize the feelings which are realized under such a scene but hose that have tried the test. nothing hardly came to console me but the thought that I was doing my duty to go, realizing my sister had been gone from us a great while and doubtless it would be consoling to have some of her dear friends with her for a short time.

We came in company with Mr. Fall and his family at the ferry. they were going to the same place or near; it was in the same county. Mr. Vanpatten's family had gone over in the ferry and we met them at Sackets. I truly felt thankful that we had so many of our acquaintances to start with us, though the most of them we were but partially acquainted; but here is the place that a person will be anxious to have a friend to converse with, O, a person whose countenance is familiar, a person that you can recognize you know their name and place of former residence; does not seem like a stranger.

We crossed the ferry. We had a rough time crossing the ferry. Many were seasick, my sister Susannah and Mrs. Fall. It truly seemed discouraging to think of going such a long journey on the water when so little swell will cause so much disagreeable feelings. I truly almost felt as if we had undertaken more than we could perform and perhaps lose our lives before we arrived at our place of anticipation. . . .

The steamer arrived about eleven and we went on board but there was considerable sea on the water and they waited till one before they left Sackets. I cannot describe the sensations of sorrow that we realized when I thought with what rapidity I was going from most all I hold dear in this life; yet the seasickness occasioned by the dead sea rolling from the lake soon put all those tender feelings from our minds; we had enought to think of besides it seemed like a long night to the sick ones; for many cried, how far have we to go before we get to Oswego—There were a great number of females on board. All that was under my observations were sick and a great many males. They all acted like drunkards. I almost though[t] they were trying to have a little fun and mock the drunkards but when I got on my feet I found if I tried to go one way I would another and could not walk any better. It was something new for me to experience such a scene and I am sure it would be as much a sight for a person to look into a room of people that were seasick as a caravan or a circus. We arrived at Oswego about sunrise.

I now purpose to write a journal of the voyage as I copied it. Sometimes I was in quite a comfortable place for writing, at others I was standing up, and never was I at a place where I could not hear a great many talking; therefore I could not write. . . .

Sat Morning Sept 7th [1844]. We had our berths put up last night We were all made much more comfortable than we any of us expected We soon went to bed and when all were quietly at rest they began to ring the bell loudly which started all the passengers Every one was awake I cannot express the feelings which I had when I realized I was going away so far on the broad lakes and in the night I had many fears that I never might reach the end of the journey but a storm might arise and all hands might be lost I thought I should be seasick as the boat was on the move without fail but I designed to keep my berth as long as I could but in that I was disappointed We had an excellent time there was not one sick on board though there were so many on board.

We found all hands well in the morning and truly a delightful morning it is. I truly feel thankful that we have such a pleasant time. When we went to bed we expected they would stop at Sodu; but in the morning we found ourselves far beyond: The wind was fair; the country at a distance appears to be almost a wilderness. there is now and then a solitary dwelling. though were we near the prospect would be very different. I find much to interest me as I am not used to journeying. we expect now to get in the [Erie] canal this evening. I find this boat much more comfortable than the Lady of the Lake, though I presume it is owing to the weather chiefly. I do not now feel a mite dizzy from the motion of the boat . . . I cannot write and have my sentences very well connected when there is so much talking. There are a great many passengers on board. the berths are as thick as they can conveniently stand, both in the steerage cabin and also in the other, and on an average 3 deep all through the boat; a person that never saw such a sight it is quite new to them: we all thought we could not rest at all last night but they did the most sleep well. The boat did not rock to disturb any one. . . .

We are now in sight of a very pleasant country. I should like to be nearer so I could have a better prospect of the surrounding country. It is I believe what they call the Genesee country. Our vessel moves very rapid and there is but one way you can look to see any land; We have fine breeze and I feel very thankful that we remain well all hands; for there is not seasick people on board, but I don't expect it will be so through the voyage. I think to have so fine a ride as we have had during the day and last night is worth all it costs just to see what there is that presents itself to our observation. . . .

Tuesday, September 10th [1844] It is now Tuesday about ten o'clock, the Land Lady says We are at the extremity of the canal where it is intersected with Lake Erie. We are soon to go on the propello again, and soon to be on Lake Erie. . . .

It is now Tuesday about sundown. We have had an excellent time on Lake Erie so far. the wind is fair and there is none too much of it. there has been no seasick people on this lake. I feel rather more encouraged than I did when we were on the canal we are about out of sight of land but I cant say but what I feel safe for I think they have a good set of hands and a good Capt. that understand their business well.

Susannah and myself are on the deck besides a great many others. I cannot write much about the country about here for we are not near enough to see it. There is as usual all sorts of business going on. Some are talking about the Scriptures. others are playing cards. Others are preparing their victuals. I think with but a few exceptions we have the first rate of passengers; for they are all very obliging. I have got considerable passengers well acquainted with a number of the passengers. I think I never shall forget many of them and perhaps I shall ever remember all their countenances; for I think now I know them all now by sight, though I have not learned their names and now we are not halfway; there is said to be about one hundred and thirty passengers; besides all their luggage and the wood which completely covers the deck; there is now and then a vacant place that a few passengers can sit without getting on the boxes and goods that are on the deck. I thought when we first started it would be impossible to sit on deck. I imagined it would be so rough it would be quite unpleasant. but I think it is the most pleasant part of the boat and I sit here generally all day unless it rains.

I almost dread to have bedtime come it is so warm and sultry in the cabin and so many to occupy the room that we are in . . . some of the crew were very unkind last night and would not have the window open. Others were so warm they were obliged to get up and go to the doors and windows to breathe; but I hope we shall not suffer as much with the heat as we did last night. but I cant see to write any more for it is dark. . . .

Wednesday morning [September] 11th [1844]. . . . I feel considerably refreshed this morning for I slept quite well last night. We had the door open and we were on the lake where we could get a fresh breeze and it seemed a great deal more pure than the air did when we were on the canal.

I cant say but what I had much rather be here than there, yet when I realize with what rapidity this boat is carrying me from my dear friends, it seems as if I could not help from bursting into a flood of tears—knowing and realizing my dear friends are at this very moment perhaps thinking with deep anxiety about us, and wishing most ardently that Providence would lend a kind and protecting hand and guard and watch over us that no harm may befal us. Oh those friends are not forgotten by us though there is so many around us that it would seem almost impossible to cast a thought on the past time. but care and troubles will only make a person think the more of their absent friends that they have left behind. Shall I ever forget the kindnesses of many of my dear friends that I have left behind as well as those on board this boat for they are very friendly indeed here. . . .

Thursday [September 12, 1844]. We arrived at Cleveland safe and had a very pleasant time. I went off the boat a few moments while the pro-pello called at the wharf. we had not much time to see the place but I should judge by what I did see it is a place of business. there were plenty of melons, apples, pears, peaches, plums, bread and almost every thing heart could wish was brought on the boat for sale. Some were brought by little boys—I should not think they were over five years old and some was brought by women. the company on board purchased a great deal of provisions and supplies themselves with provisions through the voyage. the great box that belongs to the deck was filled to supply the cabin with provisions. it was very large. but it was well filled with various kinds of garden sauce and fresh meat and fruits. The passengers eat a full supply of fruit while they called at Cleveland. we did not think what might be the consequence.

But after we left Cleveland we had been from the port about 2 hours and the wind blew quite fresh, the boat began to rock some; and the people in every corner of the boat began to be dreadful seasick. those that could walk enough to get on deck went there, but others remained in their berths. It was a very unpleasant season for all till about daylight. I became sick after I saw so many in every corner of the cabin that were seasick. They all acted and I believe felt like people intoxicated with Spiritous Liquors. I am sure I never wish to feel so again, but after I got over my sea sickness I rested better than I have before on the propello excepting one night. I was sick but a short time. Sister Susannah was in the same berth with me. She was quite seasick and went on deck. I felt considerable seasick when she first got up but I thought I would remain where I was as long as I could. I stayed I should think about half an hour and then I thought I would get up and go to see about Susannah. As soon as I raised my head from my pillow I was as sick as the rest; but by staggering considerable I managed to get on deck. I found her in a safe place where she would not fall over board, but she was sick enough. I staid there till I felt better and on account of the cool air and having not my cloak there I went down and remained in the berth till day light and I got to sleep in a few moments and rested well. We did not consider it in the least dangerous but it was some rough. Susannah went to bed and slept though not all night for she felt seasick again before morning.

It was really fun to hear the observations of some on the boat before they began to be sick, making fun of others and it would not be a moment before they were sick enough themselves. It is dangerous to laugh at seasick people, for if you do you will, with out fail, feel as bad as they do. I am sure a person that never saw a room of seasick people would laugh if they were sick themselves to hear so many odd expressions as were made by some of the passengers.

but we all got over being seasick, the cabin cleaned out, and our breakfasts ready about Eleven O'clock and we went on deck to eat it. Our company, I mean those that were at our table, could do very well after we got to the table, excepting Mrs. Fall. She could not eat much. William Washburn was not sick at all on the journey, neither was Mrs. Vanpatten. they do not know how nice a person feels but perhaps they will find out before they get to their journeys end. . . .

Monday afternoon [September 16, 1844]. We had a favourable time last night and to-day so far. we expect to see the end of our journey on the water tomorrow, if we do not get a storm to drive us back; we are all blessed with good health—all on the boat—and all seem to be much animated with the thought of getting through the end of their journey soon on the water. I presume we shall all feel lonely after we leave the boat for awhile, and should we ever meet the passengers, it would seem like meeting with old acquaintance. I often hear the people inquireing of the others where they are going and often hear them wishing to live [as] neighbours when they get in the Western country. I hope I shall not have to wait long at Milwaukie, for it seems as if I was now more anxious than ever to see my friends. O how anxious must Sister Jane feel for she has been absent a great while from all her fathers family.

We are out of sight of land on Lake Michigan. the wind blows fresh though not enough to make the boat rock. they are not seasick on board but all are able to eat their allowance if they can get it cooked. They have a busy time till they get their meals. There is as many as 20 families and all cook by one Stove.

Tuesday Morning [September 17, 1844]. It is a fortnight to-day since I left my parents residence. It seems as if I now could realize in a measure the great distance that separates me from my friends. O let us realize though so far separated from each other we are under the superintendence and kind care of a Heavenly parent that does order all things for our benefit. And could we look without selfishness on the dealings of providence, we should refrain from murmuring. But to take a sense of the goodness of kind providence in thus protecting us through dangers, seen as unseen.

We are now in sight of Milwaukie. I cannot express my feelings of gratitude that I have thus been protected; and many, very many have expressed the same in my hearing on the boat. it is much better than we could expect. I expect we shall be at Milwaukie in about an hour and a half. O could our friends all know we are so near our journeys end, it would be a great satisfaction to them no doubt. Mrs. Vanpatten and her family have stood their journey remarkably for so large a family of children. they were some fatigued as well as the rest. but it is over with and they feel in good spirits. Mrs. Fall likewise is well. I have not been deprived of writing a day since I started, which was far beyond my expectations when I started.

It is now Tuesday about 5 o'clock. We are now in Milwaukie in the Washington house. we arrived at this place about eleven this morning. They seem to be very friendly people indeed. we do not know how long we shall wait here. I feel something of an anxiety to be on the road where I can get to a resting place. We have had our dinners and suppers at this house. before tea we took a walk through the different streets. it is truly a thriving place for a new country and a great deal of business is carried on.

Things, many of them, are full as cheap as they are East. There are several families at this house from the propello; they are waiting, as we are, for an opportunity to get their goods carried back into the country. They are very friendly indeed but I expect to part with them soon. I should really be happy if I could see them after we get to our place of residence.

Thursday night [September 18, 1844]. We have stopped at a tavern kept by a Mr. Goodrich. I am now going to retire but I will write a few lines first; the people all are very friendly and we found them so last night. I think Wisconsin affords some first rate of inhabitants at least. but they are crowded with passengers. I neglected writing yesterday, or as I was situated I could not write . . .

We passed through some beautiful country. I could hardly believe I was in a new country. The farms truly look like old farms that have been settled a great while excepting the buildings. they all look new and with the exceptions of fruit too. And to view the prospect of the farms at a distance you truly would think you were surrounded with large Orchards: A great deal of the timber is low trees, as scattering as trees would be that have been set out for a fruit orchard. Those trees are principally oak or walnut. Some of the timber was different. The roads we passed with the exception of about 12 miles from Milwaukie, were of the best kind. they were very smooth though the land is somewhat rolling; and to be on one side of a hill though not a very high hill and look around you and see the gradual elevation of the surface and the flowers that nature has planted, it looks pleasant. They told us about the 12 miles woods in coming from Milwaukie and about 2 oclock the first day we started, I inquired how far it was to the 12 miles woods; and to my surprise they said we passed it that morning. it was settled all along the roadside and every mile or to there was a sort of a tavern. We passed some elegant buildings and several villages yesterday. I imagined we were going in a wilderness but in that I am disappointed. I see many good gardens and many large pieces of wheat and we pass some places where they have a great many stacks of grain, and we saw many farmers that had as good buildings as any one need to have. others still lived in shanty. I presume we passed many where they had just moved for some were building fireplaces and some were digging wells. The water is good in all the wells I have seen yet . . .

I feel really thankful that we have been thus preserved. I have heard it remarked by a number of the passengers we all out to have a day of Thanksgiving that we have been thus spared, for I presume our lives were in peril when we were on the water. For our boat was so heavily loaded. the decks would have had to been cleared of their contents. And the passengers would have died, I fear, perhaps some would have gone over board, had a storm put the tempest in motion. Had the passengers known with what reluctance the Captain left Oswego with his boat, we should have felt worse than we did. He said afterwards it was far beyond his expectations to arrive at Milwaukie with all hands alive. And wanted the overseer of the boat to release him, but he would not. The Capt. was very watchful of the wind and weather. He seemed to like his boats crew, for he said he never saw so many together where they were so well united. I never shall forget how they used to sing on deck to divert themselves. There was not a day passed but what some sang and sometimes all that could sing. It truly seemed as if then we could almost then forget all danger though the passengers suffered but little through fear. for we did not know till afterward but what they generally loaded as heavy.

There are a great many settling through various parts of Wisconsin I am sure it will not be long before it will all be taken up. for we see teams after teams loaded with people and their luggage going from the seaport back. but I cant write any more for I must retire. Susannah is already asleep. I expect we shall start early in the morning. We hope to get through to my sisters, though our hope is faint. For our team goes very slow indeed. . . .

[October and November 1844]. . . . Since I came to Mr. Washburns I have had many things to attract my attention. It is not exactly here as it is in [New] York state. It is a common thing in the fall of the year after the frost kills the grass and verdure to see the prairies on fire. it is some what pleasant to view the scene; but here is considerable danger of farmers losing their grass and grain. Many I have heard of have lost all the provisions they have procured. To cast an eye around on the prairies after they have been burnt presents quite a different prospect from what they did before. I have been to Beloit 3 times since I came in the Territory to meetings. and in going there we passed a large prairie. The first time I went was before it had been burnt over. the prospect was fine for the prairies were crowned with beautiful flowers as fine as you would ever wish to see, but when I went to Beloit the next time the fire had swept everything from the prairies; to cast an eye over the prairies after they have been burnt presents the appearance of a large lake and [as] the hills gradually rise they have the appearance of swells. The Prairies are not entirely destitute of timbers but every new and then there are groves of timber and the fire does not entirely destroy the timber and that has the appearance of Islands.

I engaged a school about 14 miles from Mr. Washburns; I left Mr. Washburns the first day of December to go to my school and went to Mr. Boyces; they lived in the district; I got there about dark. I did not commence my school the next day; but I went about 8 miles to be inspected and I then passed many thousand acres of land which was new to me and

I might say to every one for there was not much marks of settlements some of the way;

The same evening after I got back I was carried to Mr. Pierce's in order to commence school on the following day: They lived in the district quite near the school house; They were people that I had formerly been acquainted with. and their children had been my scholars in [New] York state. It truly seemed like meeting my old friends to meet with them.

I commenced school on the third of Dec 1844; I had seven scholars on the first day and the next I had 8. I have a very pretty school but it seemed rather more lonely than schools in usual, East. My school has been 8 in number and no more. I taught every day that week and the two following weeks till Saturday. I went and spent Saturday with Mrs. Boyce; and Saturday evening I took a ride with Miss Sarah Vanpatten, Mr Boyce, and Mr. Town. We started to go to a singing school which was about 5 miles from their house, but when we got there, there was none. So they went and spent a few hours to Mr. Warrens and I with them. it was a beautiful evening and there was a little snow—just enough to get along comfortable with a sleigh; we passed two small lakes and the prospect was beautiful to me to view those lakes by moonlight. . . .

The Diary of Isabella McKinnon, 1852

The diary kept by Isabella McKinnon tells the story of her family's emigration from Findhorn, Scotland, to Otsego, Wisconsin, in 1852. Isabella McKinnon was born at Findhorn on March 30, 1833, and she was eighteen when her family left Scotland for America. Her parents, Colin and Jean McKinnon, had seven children: Margaret, Agnes, Ellen, Isabella, John, Jean (also called Jane), and Colin. The entire family immigrated to the United States together. Sometime later, Isabella married Francis Ritchie.

The diary is a coverless account book measuring approximately three inches by five inches. The diary contains nearly twenty pages of entries telling of the family's journey, which began on March 31, 1852, and ended when the family arrived at their destination, Otsego (about eighty miles from Milwaukee) on June 4, 1852. Diary entries are in pencil; many are quite faint and difficult to read. Included with the diary entries are a poem, several recipes, and a list of letters that Isabella wrote to her friends in Findhorn. The original diary and a typescript copy were donated to the State Historical Society of Wisconsin by Richard and Russell Lewis, her grandsons, in 1957.

March 31st, 1852. Left Findhorn for America, Wednesday morning 7:00 o'clock A.M. arrived at Inverness 11:00 o'clock A.M. after a pleasant passage. Thought little of the Capitol of the Highlands except a few public buildings.

April 1st, 1852. Left Inverness for Fall of [illegible] through the Caledonian Canal 6:00 o'clock A.M. enjoyed the scenery very much. Had very agreeable company. Landed at Fort Augustus visited the Fort. Proceeded to Banarie visited Loch Tabor Hut at the foot of Ben Nevis. The inhabitants in one end, the horse and cow in the other. Arrived at Glasgow 6:00 P.M. Spent a very happy week with kind friends and acquaintances. I thought a great deal of Glasgow. Visited all the public buildings, the Necropolis, Royal Exchange and all the rest of the public buildings.

April 8, 1852. Left Glasgow 3:00 o'clock A.M. arrived at Greenoch 5:00 o'clock P.M.

April 9, 1852. Left Greenoch pier "Sara Mary" for New York. Did not proceed further than the Bay of Greenoch. Captain Brown delivered a lecture on board to the passengers from John 6-

April 10, 1852. Passengers examined by the Doctor and Government inspector. Eight of the passengers rejected. The sugar condemned by the Government Inspector. Superior returned. Left the Bay of Greenoch at 5:00 o'clock P.M. Wind unfavorable. Towed out to Sea by a steam tug. One of the passengers an Irish woman got drunk and disorderly and was put in irons for some time.

April 11th, 1852. Becalmed—spent a very unprofitable Sabbath. Captain [illegible] distributed Tracts to the passengers. Wind the greater part of the day.

April 12th, 1852. Rules of the ship read, A committee of the passengers formed to keep order and observe cleanliness, One of the rules, To rise at 7:00 A.M. To be in bed at 10:00 P.M. to be strictly obeyed. A fine day, wind favorable. took the last look of Scotlands hills at 10:00 o'clock A.M. A little sick, soon got better, employed the day in sewing, crocheting and reading. An alarm of fire, nothing serious. A fair wind, all sails set. Going at the rate of 8 knots an hour. A dance, to the music of the Bagpipes, Fiddle and Tambarine, got up amongst the passengers. A beautiful night. On deck all the evening.

April 13th, 1852. A strong fair wind. Sick all day.

April 14th, 1852. Still continuing a fair wind. Very sick.

April 15th, 1852. Sick till 12:00 o'clock. Took nothing the last two days except a little brandy and Laudanum. Went on the quarter deck at 12:00 o'clock Was much refreshed with the fresh air. A fair wind, a great swell on the sea. Ship going at the rate of 8½ miles an hour. Ship rolling tremendously. Every one more afraid than another. Passed a wreck in the morning. Too lazy to get out of bed to see it. . . .

April 18th, 1852. Public worship on the quarter deck. A good attendance, very impressive on the mighty deep. Spent the afternoon reading.

April 19th, 1852. A beautiful day, very little wind, but fair. On the quarter deck knitting. Took dinner on the quarter deck.

April 20th, 1852. A very fine day. Calm. The Atlantic like a loch. Wind rose at 3:00 P.M. A strong breeze with rain at 7:00 o'clock P.M. Ship going at a good rate. On deck at 9:00 o'clock, looking rather stormy. Stayed on deck an hour with very interesting company.

April 21st, 1852. Very stormy all day. A high wind with showers of rain and hail continued very severe all night. Thought we would never see morning. Water rushing into the steerage.

April 22nd, 1852. Storm somewhat abated, wind contrary.

April 23rd, 1852. Passed a ship in the morning, another in the forenoon. The "Falcon of Newcastle." On deck at 9:00 o'clock. Pouring of rain.

April 24th, 1852. Passed "The British Tar of London" 16 days from Newcastle for Quebec. Wind unfavorable, on deck at 8:00 o'clock. Listening to the Music of the Bagpipes.

April 25th, 1852. Public worship in the cabin. Raining all day.

April 26th, 1852. Rain and sleet. Wind contrary.

April 27th, 1852. Very cold—supposed to be on the banks of New Foundland.

April 28th, 1852. Very calm. A ship in sight. Wind arose at 10:00 o'clock. A strong fair Wind accomp. by heavy rain in the evening. Ship going at 9½ miles an hour.

April 29th, 1852. A fair wind and rain., changed at 2:00 o'clock on deck at 9:00 o'clock. Passed by an American mail steamer. A beautiful calm moonlight night.

April 30th, 1852. Wind contrary all day, wind fell in the evening.

May 1st, 1852. Very cold. Wind contrary.

May 2nd, 1852. A fine day. Attended divine service in the Cabin. A fair wind arose at 3:00 o'clock P.M. Two Lads fighting. The one in fault was put in irons for an hour. A very rainy night.

May 3rd, 1852. Wind contrary all day. Turned fair in the evening. Ship going at the rate of 11 miles an hour. A very rainy night.

May 4th, 1852. A fine day. Wind moderate and fair all day. A Steamer "The Asia" within a short distance another ship in sight. Three men fighting all three put in irons for an hour.

May 5th, 1852. A fine day, wind unfavorable.

May 6th, 1852. Wind continuing the same.

May 7th, 1852. Seven ships in sight, fishing for Cod, Passed close by one. Some one with the life boat went and brought some cod, part of which Captain Brown distributed to the passengers gratis. The deck very much resembled a fish market with every one crowding to get their share. Wind somewhat favorable. 16 miles from Sable Island   400 from New York.

May 8th, 1852. Wind contrary all day.

May 9th, 1852. Wind contrary till one o'clock.

May 10th, 1852. Attended devine service in the Cabin. Very little wind but fair.

May 11th, 1852. Continuing the same. A Beautiful day. A ship in sight.

May 12th, 1852. A delightful warm day. A fair wind. Five ships in sight going to America. On deck at 10:00 o'clock. Very dark. The water round the sides of the ship as if on fire. Very beautiful on the gulf stream of Mexico.

May 13th, 1852. Wind continuing fair, a very misty day, with rain. "The Emily of Halifax" passed us in the evening. Captains spoke to each other. They left New York on Saturday bound for Halifax. Contrary and light winds all the time. Thundering through the day. A great deal of lightning.

May 14th, 1852. Very misty and rainy. Wind favorable.

May 15th, 1852. Wind continuing fair. Very misty.

May 16th, 1852. Misty in the morning, cleared up in the forenoon. Attended devine service in the Cabin, wind favorable all day. On deck at 9:00 o'clock A fine starry night. A ship passed within a few yards of us. The Pilot expected every minute.

May 17th, 1852. The Pilot came on board at 10:00 o'clock A.M. In sight of Long Island at 5:00 o'clock. A very welcome sight. The steam tug came along side at 12:00 o'clock. Coming up the River was the finest sight I ever saw. The scenery exceeded everything I have seen. Off Staten Island at 2:00 o'clock. A very pretty place. The doctor came aboard. The passengers all on deck and examined in less than five minutes. The Doctor said he had never examined a more healthy good looking set of passengers. Arrived opposite New York at 3:30 P.M. The first thing I got belonging to America was a new Testament, which a gentleman came aboard and kindly presented to the passengers. A very amusing sight to see friends meeting friends. Lay out in the River a long time.

May 18th, 1852. The Steam Tug came out for the passengers and the luggage. Left the "Sarah Mary" at 1:00 o'clock P.M. Remained in New York all night. A very fine City. Saw the place where Kossuth the Hungarian General landed [the political reformer visited America around 1851]. Saw a good Number of the "Sarah Mary's" passengers.

May 19th, 1852. Had a long walk through the City. Crossed the river to Brooklyn in a Yankee Steamer. Returned in an hour. Went down to the

Quay and took my last farewell of the "Sarah Mary" passengers to leave her. Left New York at 6:00 o'clock P.M. Came up the Hudson River a distance of 20 miles to Mospier. At 9:00 o'clock P.M. left by the Erie Railway for Dunkirk a distance of 500 miles at 10:30 o'clock. Slept a good part of the night.

May 20th, 1852. Got a fine view of the city from the carriage window. Very much disappointed with the look of the country. Some of the "Sarah Marys" company still with us.

May 21st, 1852. Arrived at Dunkirk [on Lake Erie near Buffalo] at 4:00 o'clock P.M. Took lodgings in a house kept by an Irishman. Very kind people. Had a walk through Dunkirk. Visited the light house, about 2 miles walk by the side of Lake Erie.

May 22nd, 1852. Left Dunkirk at 2:00 o'clock P.M. Per Steamer Niagara up Lake Erie slept all night.

May 23rd, 1852. A beautiful Morning. Some fine villages on the side of the Lake. Arrived at Cleveland at 9:00 o'clock. Some of the "Sarah Mary" passengers who had taken up their abode in Cleveland of the quay, meeting us, took us through the town. A very fine place and beautiful buildings. Far surpassing any I have yet seen in America. Streets so wide and trees growing on each side. Left Cleveland at ½ past six o'clock P.M. by the "Steamer Detroit" for Detroit. A very rainy night. Had a conversation with a Negro rather an intelligent man.

May 24th, 1852. Arrived at Detroit at 4:00 o'clock A.M. Went to a Roman Catholic church, a very large fine building, very strange ceremonies. Stayed only a few minutes. Went to a Methodist Episcopal church. A beautiful building, very clean, never saw a more respectable looking congregation. Took a walk through a part of the town. A pretty place and fine buildings. Left Detroit by railway for Chicago at half past 5:00 o'clock. A beautiful night. Very warm through the day. Trees and fields looking so fresh and green. Fruit trees laden with blossom, filling the air with a fine fragrance.

May 25th, 1852. Arrived at Chicago at 7:00 o'clock A.M. Took lodgings in the Temperance Hotel. Took a walk in the evening through the town. A large town and a great deal of traffic carried on in it.

May 26th, 1852. A very warm day. Took a walk to the railway station a distance of about 3 miles along the side of Lake Michigan.

May 27th, 1852. A very misty and rainy day. Case of Cholera in the town.

May 28th, 1852. Cholera spreading. A very warm day.

May 29th, 1852. Left Chicago at 8:00 o'clock A.M. Per "Arctic Steamer" for Milwaukee. A beautiful day. Arrived at Milwaukee 4:00 o'clock P.M. Apparently a fine place. Took lodgings in the "Wisconsin House."

May 30th, 1852. Took a walk around the town, a pretty large place.

May 31st, 1852. Went to the Congregational Plymouth Church. A large fine building. Went in the evening to an English Church.

June 1st, 1852. Left Milwaukee at 10:00 o'clock for Otsego, a distance of 80 miles. Proceeded about 40 miles and stayed all night at a tavern by the way.

June 2nd, 1852. Passed through Watertown in the forenoon. A very nice little place Arrived at Lowell a small village and stayed all night. An awful night of thunder and lightning. Never saw anything like it before. The sky all in a blaze for two hours.

June 3rd, 1852. Left Lowell early in the morning and were detained in Columbus by a thunder storm. A nice little place. Proceeded to Otsego and were overtaken by another Thunder Storm and heavy rain. Were obliged to remain all night in the "Prairie House" about 5 miles from Otsego.

June 4th, 1852. Arrived all safe at Otsego in good health not without a good deal of fatigue on the 4th of June 1852.
    Colin McKinnon and Jean Ross McKinnon
        Margaret McKinnon
          Agnes and Ellen McKinnon (Twins)
            Isabella McKinnon
             Jane McKinnon
             Colin McKinnon

Queen's Cake. One pound of flour one pound of sugar eight ounces of butter, one pound of raisins one gill of brandy one gill of brine, one gill of cream, four eggs and one nutmeg.

Mush. One pint of milk, one teacupful of yeast. Mix it thin; when light, add twelve ounces of sugar. Ten ounces of butter, four eggs, flour sufficient to make it as stiff as bread. When risen, again, mould and sponge upon tin.

The Diary of Emily Quiner, 1863

Emily Quiner was born on January 26, 1840, the oldest child of Edwin and Jane (Phelps) Quiner of Milwaukee, Wisconsin. In 1850 the Quiner family moved to Watertown, Wisconsin, where Edwin Quiner published the *Democratic State Register,* later known as the *Watertown Weekly Register.* In 1858 the Quiners moved to Madison, where Edwin Quiner worked as a claims agent during the Civil War. Emily's younger siblings were her sisters, Maria, Fannie, and Nellie, and her brother, Charles.

The Quiner family was living in Madison when Emily began keeping this diary on April 14, 1861, following the firing on Fort Sumter that marked the beginning of the Civil War. Emily's eagerness to contribute to the war effort began to grow, and during the summer of 1863, when she was twenty-three, she and her sister Fannie volunteered to go to Memphis to serve as nurses in the Gayoso Union Army Hospital. In her diary, which she called her "faithful friend," Emily Quiner often wrote lengthy, introspective entries. Those written during the summer of 1863 reflect the grimness of the hospital environment as doctors and nurses tended to wounded, sick, and dying soldiers. Upon her return to Madison at the end of August 1863, Emily faced a difficult decision: whether to return to the Gayoso Hospital in Memphis or remain in Madison, at her father's behest, to assist him with writing *A Military History of Wisconsin* (1866). Ultimately, her father's will prevailed.

She lived and taught in southern Wisconsin for a number of years, then taught for more than twenty-five years in the public school systems in Chicago and Denver. On October 23, 1919, when she was seventy-nine, she died in Chicago and was buried in the Quiner family plot in Forest Hill Cemetery, Madison (for her obituary, see the *Wisconsin Capital Times,* October 28, 1919). Emily Quiner may well have kept other diaries during her lifetime;

this one, dated 1861 to 1863, is the only diary known to exist. The eight-by-eleven-inch manuscript diary, kept in a cloth-bound volume with lined pages, is housed in the Edwin B. Quiner Family Papers at the State Historical Society of Wisconsin in Madison.

Saturday, July 4th [1863]. Independence Day! and we floating down the Mississippi! Who would have thought it, on such an errand too? It was very warm this morning. I sat down immediately after breakfast and wrote a long letter home to be mailed at Memphis, After this we went up to the pilot house and had a good view of Fort Pillow which we passed about ten o'clock. It looks like a very strong point indeed, Very high bank surmounted by a high board railings, with one or two guns visible from the river, is all that meets the eye now. hardly a vestige remains of what must have been a formidable looking place, We passed island No. 10, in the afternoon, It is garrisoned by negro troops. New Madrid is also quite a large place on the river, which has been the scene of a hard fought battle, A lady who came down from Cairo with us, and who is commandant at the New Madrid, got off here, In a short time after this, we got a view of Memphis from a point in the river which is about four miles from the city, where the Mississippi bends in an abrupt curve, It looked beautiful in the light of the setting sun, and was quite a welcome sight to us when a few moments after we found ourselves approaching the scene of our future labors, It is situated on high banks overlooking the river, and has many fine public buildings, We went immediately to a boarding house on our arrival and retired to rest, or rather to try to rest, for the house being nearly full, four of us, had only a single room, with a bed and a lounge as sleeping accommodations, We had quite a celebration on board the steamer to-day, The gentlemen got a flag and unfurled it in the cabin, and then drew up resolutions, sang songs, and had a general good time Jenny & I were appointed as committee with three gentlemen to draw up resolutions, We had quite a celebration Met Paulus Adams & Rebels on the boat to-day they are going to Lake Providence. . . .

Wednesday, July 8th [1863]. Started immediately after breakfast to see Dr. Irwin Surgeon General of Hospitals here, he immediately engaged us, for hospital duty, and gave us our papers. We visited the Jackson Hospital, and afterward the Gayoso, where we were engaged. We found Mrs. Wemple, a Wisconsin lady and Mrs. Green a sort of under matron here, very pleasant, They told us some very discouraging things, and for some time I felt rather <u>blue</u> over the prospect, The surgeon is in charge, Dr. Hartshorn came in and assigned us our wards. Fannie's is next to mine on the same floor. The wards are long rooms containing from fifty to seventy beds, Each one has a surgeon, a ward master and four nurses beside a formula nurse, Dr. Nelson the surgeon of my ward seems to be a very pleasant man, There are some very sick men in my ward, and being an entirely new business to me, I went at it rather awkwardly I expect, but I shall soon learn how to work, I hope, Mr. Smith & and another gentleman came to take us to walk in the evening, We had ice cream, sat a while in the park, and then came back, and I went to bed feeling sensibly the oddity of our situation on our first night in the Hospital.

Thursday, July 9th [1863]. Rose this morning at the sound of the bugle at five, dressed and went down to my ward. went around and said 'good morning' to all my men, attended to the giving out of the breakfast fed one man, there are some who are very sick. One man was having fits when I entered the ward yesterday, he had them at intervals all through the night, and they think that he will not live through the day. After breakfast the surgeon came, and I made out the diet list for the day under his directions I staid in my ward nearly all day, at night I was so tired and my feet were so swelled, that I could not sleep. There is a great deal of noise in the street, and sleeping in dreary rooms is not just the thing for nervous people.

Friday, July 10th [1863]. Dreaded to go to my ward this morning, the air is so bad there, There are some very sick men here, and they require my constant attention, I already feel very much interested in some of them, some who are very sick, Wm. Clark a boy of about 19 who has chronic diarrhea. I am afraid he will never get well. I feel very badly about him, and shall do all in my power to help him, he is very low, however, and there is but a bare possibility of his recovery, There are several other cases of the same disease, all doubtful. One man Alfred Rest, about twenty I should think, and from Ohio, is very low with fever & debility, I am afraid that he cannot recover. I was very tired to-night, [Note written sideways in left margin]—10th young men died on Louise's ward. I felt very sorry about it. His name was Martin. . . .

Monday, July 13th [1863]. Rained this forenoon made it very cool. Went to my ward as usual. Men getting along very well, Did not go out to-night, One of my men very sick. He cannot live. He is an Ohio boy, he is a very fine fellow, about 20 years old, I would almost give the world if he could live. I wrote a letter to a cousin of his in the army at Vicksburg. telling him how he was, and asking him to write home, and inform his friends. He is very grateful for anything I do for him. and though he never says much, his eyes follow me everywhere, He is very home sick, How my heart aches when I think that this is the way that the flower of our country's youth are perishing in this cruel contest I am thankful that God has given me the opportunity to do some good, and pray that he will give me strength to do my duty faithfully in the fear of His Holy Name, Tired out to-night. went to bed, with a heavy heart, almost expect to find Kent dead tomorrow morning.

Tuesday, July 14th [1863]. Pleasant & cool this morning. Men about as usual. Kent is better this morning, Ate quite a breakfast, I do wish he would get well. Clark is getting better slowly, I think he may get well. He seems to be in better spirits. Jennie & Lou went up town this morning. Mr. Smith & Mr. Hayne called in the evening Tired to-night To-day as I was sitting by Kent, Dr Nelson came in with a passion flower, which he got at the Jewish cemetery. I pressed it.

Wednesday, July 15th [1863]. Warm to-day, In my ward all day, Mr. Smith & Dr. Sweetland of the Adams Hospital, came this afternoon to have us up to the Officers' Hospital to see a Wisconsin captain. I did not go the rest of the girls did, I feel too anxious about my men to go any-where, there are three or four that may die any hour, Kent is very low to-night. I have sat by him all the afternoon, he is very quiet. It seems as if I could not bear to see him die the Doctor will not let me tell him that he must die for there possibly may be a chance for his recovery. he says, I have no hopes of it, God pity his poor old mother, and God pity all the mothers whose hearts will ache, through the terrible consequences of this unnatural war. Went to bed tired enough.

Thursday, July 16th [1863]. A warm day, it rained about noon and cooled the air somewhat a real tropical shower it was, the rain coming down in sheets, I enjoyed it but I guess some of the boys who lay under the ventilator <u>didn't</u> for the rain came right through, In my ward all day. Kent has been stupid all day. Had no appetite for food, could hardly rouse him to take his wine, I felt very bad about him. he will not live through the night, I fear, God have mercy upon him, poor fellow, I would do any thing in my power to give him back the lost life power. but alas, human arms are too short, and human effort, too weak to help in such cares. There is another man in my ward whom I fear will die to-day, I wrote to his wife yesterday. 9 o'clock P.M. Kent is dead, He breathed his last a half hour ago. I closed his eyes they prepared him for the grave and took him away, I shall never forget the sorrow I felt for his death, he was so young a patient, so lonely and homesick and so grateful for every-thing, I did for him, I shed as bitter tears over his dying bed as I ever wept in my life, it is so hard to see our noble boys, die here alone so far from friends who would give their lives almost to have been with them in their last moments, I shall write to his mother. The saddest duty of our position is this, breaking the tidings to anxious loving hearts at home, God give you the strength to bear it poor, loving, mother, My ward will seem lonely after this. I have watched him, and fed and cared for him for so long. that the sight of his poor, pale, face on the bed, seemed a part of my life. poor fellows, so they die. . . .

Tuesday, July 28th [1863]. A warm day, We went up to Mr. Smith's office to get some things from a box which came from Wis. The man whose mother I wrote to last week, died to-day, he was not quite sensible when he died, He wished very much to see his mother. I expect she will be here soon.

Wednesday, July 29th [1863]. In my ward early, Immediately after breakfast the ward master came to tell me that there was a lady below who wished to see me, I went down and found it to be the mother of the man who died yesterday. she was almost inconsolable when she found that he was dead, I had to undertake the task of comforting her. with poor success I fear, for who can comfort or console such broken hearts, he had died without a word for his friends, and she an old lady, had come this long distance to see her only son and found him dead, I could not find words of comfort for her, only begging her to look to God for consolation in her hour of bitterest need. . . .

Wednesday, August 5th [1863]. In my ward all day, A man who is in Ward D, Lou's ward died this morning, immediately after having an arm amputated, His father and mother have been here for some time. Went up to the Officers Hospital to-day with Mr. Smith. Saw Major Rusk, of the 25th, who has been very sick, is getting better, also. Adj't Shafer and Capt. Berry also were there very sick There are quite a good many Rebel officers in this Hospital, and we met a large number of ladies from the city. with baskets. and I presume all manner of good things, bent on deeds of charity to the secesh. It made my blood boil when I thought that it was such as these who had caused and were still causing all the misery, that we were encountering daily, in our life in the Hospitals. . . .

Monday, August 10th [1863]. In my ward and Ward B. all day, There was a boy about 19, in Ward B. who has been under the influence of opium for two days so that he was perfectly stupid and could not be roused The Dr. told me to give him strong coffee every half hour, all day, I did so but it did no good and about 8 o'clock, in the evening he died, I felt very badly about it, as I believe he died from an overdose of the drug. . . .

Sunday, August 16th [1863]. Very warm indeed to-day. Went to church, this evening for the first time in my stay in Memphis. went to the Union Church. it used to be a Methodist Church unfortunately with southern principles, so that Uncle Sam thought it would be about the right thing to <u>confiscate</u> it which was done accordingly. It looked rather queer to see a church decorated with pictures of Washington and Clay, and festooned with flags but, I am getting used to almost anything.

Saturday, August 23rd [1863]. . . . We had a grand supper in the dining room, after which we enjoyed ourselves, according to our tastes. Dr. Nelson & I walked through the grounds. He told me the names of all the trees with which I was not familiar, and we collected quite a bouquet of rare leaves and grasses and flowers, There was a cotton field near the grounds, which we visited, and I saw for the first time a cotton boll and the cotton plant growing with its flower I had some to bring home with me, I enjoy the society of the Doctor very much he takes such an interest in every thing that I like and I believe him to be a noble minded, honorable man I would like an opportunity of being better acquainted with him, but he is going away in a week or two, and I presume we shall never meet again. . . .

Tuesday, August 25th [1863]. We went up to the office immediately after breakfast, to see what the prospects were for going home, Mrs. Brake went with us, Mr. Smith said that it was very probably that we would go to-night, we made a few purchases in town and then returned to prepare for our journey. I packed my trunks and dressed myself after dinner and then went to bid the boys <u>good bye</u>, Went through Ward I first Poor boys, some of them cried, at parting with me I have been up there a good deal, and it seemed very hard to go away and leave them so sick, I went through Ward B. and also the Kitchen and shook hands with all the boys, before going into my own ward. I felt so bad at leaving my boys that it took away all the pleasure I had felt in the prospect of going home, some of them wept when I bid them good bye, and all seemed to feel sad at the thought that I was going to leave them poor fellows they are so grateful for any kindness shown them, I was glad when I had got around, I shall miss my ward, and my poor sick boys, whether they do me or not, I had not much time to spare, I had a long talk with Dr. Nelson, in which he very kindly advised me in matters affecting my interest, and whether I take the advice or not, I shall always be grateful to him for the interest he has taken in my welfare, He has been very kind to me and I shall always remember him as a true hearted gentleman, He gave me some cotton flowers to bring home, and also another rare flower whose name he did not know, and also a book which he had lent me. He asked me for my address, and gave me his promising to call upon me in Madison, on his way home if he possibly could. We bade all our friends good bye and started for the boat about half past four. Mr. Tatt, Mr. Cotton & Dr. Nelson accompanied us, The boat was almost ready to start, and we bade them good bye and shortly after standing on the guards saw the houses and spires of Memphis receding from our view. I stood on deck until the city was lost to my view behind the winding banks of the river, and then went into the cabin. I felt sad to night, and for several reasons. The principal one was leaving the boys sick in the hospital most of them I shall never see again. if any. I felt sort of presentiment when I came away that I should never return, however that may be. The God who careth for us all, keep them in His kind guardianship. We took passage on the <u>Platte Valley</u>. not a very large boat but a good sailor. Went out upon deck after supper but could not remain long on account of the chilliness of the atmosphere Retired early. . . .

Friday, August 28th [1863]. Rose early this morning. after a passable nights rest. dressed as well as the motion of the cars would allow and went into the other car. It is very cold indeed not much like the weather we have been having in Memphis . . . Arrived at Madison at three o'clock, P.M. not having stopped since we left Chicago, It rained heavily, but it was the best looking place I had seen for some time. Folks all glad to see me, of course, Alice & Charley were in the country, so that I did not see them, Pa was very much relieved and I guess a little surprised to see me at home safe again. They are all unwilling to have me go back. Several friends came to see me to-night. I was very tired, and went to bed early. . . .

Monday, September 27th [1863]. Rose early this morning. Got ready, and went to the German recitation this morning. They were reading <u>William Tell</u>. Commenced French or rather a review of my French Grammar with the class this morning. When I came home at noon, Nellie met me at the gate telling me that Pa had received our transportation papers, I was very glad to hear it at first, and went to work immediately to get my trunk packed ready to start. Pa was very unwilling that I should go, however, and after getting my things all ready, and the time nearly at hand to start, I yielded to the persuasions of my friends and concluded to remain at home, Pa wants me to write for him on his history, and though it is very hard for me to give up going when I have thought and planned so much about it, I do not know but my duty lies in this direction, I could not go away to be gone so long, possibly never to return, and leave such hard feelings as I felt he would have behind me, I went down at about nine o'clock in the evening, after I had decided not to go, to tell the girls of my determination. Fannie & Ma went with me, we met them a little way from home, and went back with them. Fannie & Lou went to see if Miss Boardman would go in my place, she willingly consented, and said she would be ready at the time, Saw the girls finish packing, get ready and start in the omnibus for the depot. I felt so badly, all the time, that I could hardly keep the tears, back, and when they were really gone, it seemed as if I could not bear it. I cried all the way home, and would have given worlds almost to have been with them. I did not sleep much that night. It seemed as though I had almost committed a crime in not going I shall never forgive myself if it should prove that I was needed there, for not going, I am so miserable about it, I have always longed so much to be able to do something in this great struggle for the life of the Nation, and now that an opportunity offers, I have thrown it away. Yet God knows it was not for myself, I would willingly bear any amount of inconvenience or hardship knowing that it was in good cause, and that it was soothing some pangs caused by this war, and I never knew so much real happiness in my life as I experienced in the few weeks which I spent by the bedsides and ministering to the wants of the sick and dying in the Hospital, It is being deprived of this happiness, perhaps more than anything else, and the feeling that I was at last able to do something of actual good to my fellow men that made the dissappointment so keen, and now thinking of it when it is past and impossible for me to go it seems as though I could not bear it, There is another things which also adds to my sorrow, which I must record in you faithful old friend, as being a part of my life, and which I may wish to remember in the future that is, that the old sorrow pressing so sorely on my spirit for so long a time seemed almost light when I was away, my mind being so fully occupied, and my sympathies so fully excited for others. I had little time or opportunity to think of myself. At home now in the comparative quiet of the life I lead it comes back upon me with all the old pain, and like the opening of an old wound, bleeds afresh. this more than any thing else makes me sad and heartsick now, and I think of it and of my dissappointment so much that it seems sometimes as if I should go mad, I cannot help thinking of it. and to-night I believe. I can say truly is the most miserable of my life. I am sad when I think that the last page of my journal, should be made to chronicle such a fact. It is true, soon I shall bid you adieu faithful friend, after having gone in your company for nearly two years and a half laying you away among the relics of my <u>dead past</u>, no more to look upon your pages, save as reminders of what I have been as chronicled, in you, and what I shall be no more forever, Thirty months seems a short time looking back upon the, but when I think of what I was then, and what I have been in them and what I am now, They are not to be counted by days of months, God has prospered us greatly in these months, His blessings have not been few nor small, and although looking back on myself at that time, I see a lighter heart, a more youthful face lit with far more hope for the future and joy for the present than it would be possible to find in the one now bending over these pages, yet I am sure that were it possible I would not exchange the one for the other, The discipline which contact with the world, rough though it may be together with that chastening of the heart, which sorrow gives has I hope not been lost upon me, and now writing these last words of my life record as far as this book is concerned, I feel that if a sadder, I am also a wiser woman than when I began. I feel now that although it is a thing sad and terrible to be robbed of the hopes and promises, which early youth holds out for the future, and to be made to feel that life instead of being a flowering path, down which we can go with winged feet, and joyful hearts, it is oftener strewn with thorns which piercing our feet, leave stains of our own blood to crimson the pathway, yet the pain and heart weariness, if it be borne bravely, will prove a greater blessing in the end, and lead our lives to higher walks and purer aims than mere pleasure and happiness in the present could do. I began this record in April when the young leaves were springing, and the infant year was just girding his loins with the green robes of festal gladness, eager to run the golden round of the seasons. To-day as I write, the leaves touched by the white fingers of the frost, have turned to gorgeous tines of gold and scarlet, of purple and crimson arrayed for the last time, in State robes, ere he puts on that last white garment, which will cover the naked boughs, and wrap them for the sleep of winter. Farewell my Journal, thou hast chronicled many pleasant scenes, thou bearest on the pages the names of many friends dear to me in the past. Keep them sacredly. I give thee them in trust.

The Diary of Jane F. Grout, 1873

Jane and Thadeus P. Grout, both native New Englanders, moved to Columbia County, Wisconsin, in 1855. Their children, Fannie, Ambrose, and Effie, were born in Columbia County. In the spring of 1873 the Grouts; their Norwegian servant, Elsie Ellens; and their friends, the G. H. Hentons, began their journey west to Minnesota.

Jane Grout's diary recounts the story of this journey from Fountain Prairie, Wisconsin, to Luverne, Minnesota, in a covered wagon. The manuscript diary, recently bound with a brown cover, measures five by seven inches and contains sixty bound pages and

Jane F. Grout. Courtesy of the Minnesota Historical Society.

six looseleaf pages. The diarist used an old composition book; she crossed out old entries and began writing new ones. She single-spaced her diary entries in pencil with no margins and wrote each day for thirty-four days until June 18, when the family arrived in southwestern Minnesota.

On June 18, 1927, after rereading her journal of fifty years earlier, Jane Grout wrote an addendum:

On our wagon trip from Wisconsin over here to Minnesota, I picked up a <u>cast off Composition Book</u> & wrote each day what we saw & did—for my own amusement & to tell my friends when I wrote to them—never thinking to keep the record all these years—but the younger members of our emigrant train have asked for it, & have typed it to keep for themselves, even tho' it was not in very good condition. My own daughter, who was then only five years old, can remember enough of the trip that she wants to reserve the Original for her own. . . . I am now eighty seven years old & have seen—Luverne, the end of our trail—grow into a beautiful thriving little Rail Road city & the entire broad prairie of beautiful Agricultural Rock County, dotted all over with fine houses & barns, surrounded by groves which here become useful for not only their lovely shade, but an <u>occasional</u> stick of timber. Also many thriving villages have grown up with their necessary high school buildings, which have been liberally patronized. Every family of our Emigrant train has high school graduates & College graduates among their children & Grand children.

The original copy of Jane F. Grout's diary was given to Theodore C. Blegen, dean of the graduate school at the University of Minnesota. He donated it to the Minnesota Historical Society and included the diary in his book, *The Land Lies Open* (1949).

Thursday May the 15th 1873. Left our old home about nine o-clock accompanied by Br. John. Sad at parting with old neighbors. Reaching Father Hentons at the next town we concluded to lighten our load by taking out the bureaux one chest and several farming tools   we then packed up again. Father Hentons folks having very kindly prepared dinner for us we partook & about one o-clock started on our journey again. We stopped at Rio to see some friends but did not find them at home. We reached Wyocena about five o-clock where we parted with Br. John & Father Henton (who had accompanied his son) They returning home. We traveled about two miles farther where we found a nice camping ground & put up for the night. It seemed like camp meeting. We slept nicely until about two o-clock when an ambitious whip-poor-will succeeded in waking us, the birds sang so among the trees we could sleep no more. We lost our canary bird before we reached Wyocena & John took the cage home to Jessie.

Friday May the 16th 1873. Arose early prepared our breakfast. Family worship conducted by Sister Henton. Had a call from the lad who had provided us with the necessary accommodation for the night. We then moved on toward Portage. Just as we reached Portage Mrs. James (Henton's sister) missed her pocket book containing twenty dollars. We all halted & Br. Henton took one horse & went back in search. Providentially he only had to go about half a mile before he found it in the road, In the midst of the city we found E.H. Bronson & family & Orvie Taylor waiting to join our company. We camped for dinner about a mile out of Portage. This afternoon our road has laid along the Wisconsin river. The river is dotted with rafts of lumber. The scenery quite varied & beautiful. Cherry trees in bloom. Commenced looking for a camping place about four-o-clock but traveled until seven before we could find hay & barn to put up our teams. Camped about thirteen miles from Portage on the river. The wind blew quite hard while we were preparing supper & we looked for rain.

Saturday May 17th 1873. We did not get to rest very early last night, but slept nicely while we did sleep all except E.H. B's family who had not got things very well arranged yet. We set our tables around the camp fire for breakfast & then had family worship Scripture read by Orvie Taylor prayer by G. Henton We started on our journey about eight o-clock reached Delton where the scenery is beautiful & winter greens plenty a distance of about six miles about ten o-clock stopped awhile in town drove out about two miles & camped for dinner, near an English family. Started out again about half past one drove out about three miles when little Beauty (the pet dog) being out to play & run, was run over by the loaded team & died in a few minutes. The children all cried bitterly, & felt very sad all afternoon. They carried him along to our camping ground & there buried him. We camped about four o-clock to prepare for sabbath. The men got some boards & crotches & built a table large enough for the whole co. & then drive down some crotches for a fire place, & when our supper was ready & we surrounded the table one would think of camp meeting. . . .

Tuesday May 20th 1873. It rained most all night, but our family slept in our wagons & did not get wet any. We all took breakfast at Davidsons Our bills quite light. No charge to E. H. B. because he was a minister reached Mauston before noon mailed some letters, bought some feed for the teams &c then drove out six miles & a half & camped for dinner near the house of Mr. Goodenough where I baked my bread that I sponged last night. We cooked out dinner by the road side washed up our dishes & packed up to start. Just then quite a campany of indians came up with ponies well loaded. My team was afraid of them & had to be led past Both of our teams acted badly as we came along past the cars. About nine miles from Mauston is a tasty looking village by the name of Lisbon, on the Lemonweir river, a sawmill doing considerable business We drive out about five miles farther (passing a little place called Orange) & then finding good hay camped for the night, about half past five o-clock.

Wednesday May 21st. We arose in good season cooked out breakfast by the road side The hogs showed their appreciation of victuals by taking a ball of butter out of my basket. reading of scripture & prayer by Mrs. James. After our usual work of dishwashing & packing we started off. Hiram Trip's train [was] passing just before Augusta. After traveling out two or three miles we came to the junction of Camp Douglas the rail roads M. & St. P. & West Wisc. near which are some of the most magnificent bluffs I have yet seen surrounded by pines. we passed near one I should think to be 150 feet high Thaddeus is abed in the wagon sick, was sick most of the night. The day is a beautiful one but the country through which we pass is poor. Now & then a tamarack swamp The pines are small but now and then we find a decent farm with good buildings. We camped about twelve after driving over nine miles of sandy & rough roads found a well of soft water cooked dinner & did some washing Reached Tomah about five o-clock after riding some ways in a very hard rain. They run the wagons under the shed & put the horses in the barn at the Grant house. Walked out all looked at the town in the evening.

May 22nd 1873. Thursday half past eight. We drive out a few miles & got breakfast & fed our teams, before breakfast was quite done it commenced raining so we ate in our wagons taking our family in the light travelling wagon started for Sparta a distance of twenty miles to visit brother Albert Ingalls. It rained very hard for about an hour & then cleared up. We passed the dividing ridge through which a tunnel eighty rods long is dug for the cars to pass through. Next of note was a little place by the name of Lafayatte in which was a steam saw mill. In the suburbs of Sparta was a little place called Angelos. We reached brothers home about one o-clock, feeling sadly disappointed at finding him absent, We had an excellent visit with his wife & her brother Mr. Lockwood. About six o-clock our company drive up & camped near brothers on the green In the evening Mrs. James Mr. Lockwood, Fannie Annie & I took a stroll around the city, first we visited the Artesian well with a fountain situated in the courthouse yard, then another Artesian well in the park. Sparta is beautiful.

May 23rd 1873 Friday. The morning was beautiful. Our Co. breakfasted early & started off for Lacross We stayed behind to prolong our visit. I did some washing & cooked some beans to take on the road. After dinner we took our lieve of brothers family & started on expecting to camp with our Co. tonight. We found the roads good & the country very pretty. Out about two miles from Sparta to our left is a pretty little village by the name of Bangor nestled among the hills. Out three miles farther another village by the name of Salem. on the rail road very thrifty looking were three nice little churches. We overtook out Co. seven miles from Lacross went on a few miles farther & all camped on black river, purposing to get an early start in the morning so as to cross the Mississippi in the first boat.

Saturday May 24th 1873. We were all awakened about four o-clock by G. H. Henton prepared ourselves as soon as possible & went into Lacross a distance of about three miles Stopped in town to get our mail & some bread. Rode five miles on the mississippi, landed a few minutes after nine on the Minn. shore. Lacrescent is a little village not far from where we landed. We found the country very hilly after we left the river for about fifteen miles. We climbed one fearful hill, it seemed nearly a mile from the bottom to the top. In this region there was no wells cistern water scarce & at noon we had to buy water for our teams & for cooking. We were obliged to travel late at night before we could find water & hay & grain for our teams, but finally we got in with a baptist man where the accommodations were good. A nice little Grove back in his field, with a well near by. The young man brought out an accordeon & entertained us finely with music in the evening. We are so nicely situated for the sabbath we think it a blessing from the hand of our Father. . . .

Tuesday 27th (of May 1873). We rested well last night, all slept in our wagons except Mrs. James & Libbie. We cooked our breakfast in the house. Had family worship by wagons, reached St. Charles about ten o-clock & Mrs. Henton & Mrs James left our train & took the cars for Rochester to visit some friends After we left St. C. we found the deepest mud we have yet seen Passed through a little village called Dover Camped about twelve o-clock & cooked dinner & I baked bread. It commenced raining about the time we were ready to start & rained furiously. We found the worst roads I ever saw, no exceptions. We passed one little village this afternoon. The country is really beautiful through which we have passed to day. Got the privilege of camping in a grove on the farm of a young man by the name of Pitcher. It was a pretty place. We traveled about twenty five miles to day

Wednesday May 28th 1873. Did not get a very early start this morning were up late last night cooking meat & sauce. Reached Rochester between nine & ten o-clock & mailed some letters bought bread &c. G.H. Henton here left us, joined his family & went to visit his brother who lives out ten miles from Rochester We met his brother after we left him. We find the roads very bad. Camped about half past eleven under a pretty line of willows. In the afternoon we found a beautiful country but roads bad as before. One curiosity between Rochester and Mantorville which is a big stone perhaps 15 feet high & no other stone to be seen any where. We also met with an accident   Got into a bad place in a slue a[nd] broke a whiffletree [the swinging bar to which the harness is attached and by which the wagon is drawn]   About ten miles from Rochester up on the prairies to our left stood a little village called Byron. Very good buildings around here surrounded by the white willow in almost every case. This is all the timber you will see in going from Rochester to Mantorville, a distance of seventeen miles, except when within three miles of Mantorville we came to a beautiful piece of oak timber in which we camped for night. Traveled about twenty miles

Thursday [May 29, 1873]. Last night it rained terribly, but we all slept in our wagons & did not get wet. We did [not] get a very early start in the morning as it was very wet & some rainy. We reached Mantorville middle of forenoon while it was raining   Stopped & got some bread & enquired the way to Andrew Curtis' whose residence we reached about eleven o-clock, where we were all taken in & hospitable entertained. The weather was cold & we felt thankful to get in by the fire. Cousin Esther in tears told us of her recent affliction in the loss of her darling little baby nine & a half months old. At times she receives it as from her Father's hand for her good, then again she murmers & thinks it so hard. Soon comes in Ella Snyder with her two little ones who I have not seen since she was five years old. I did not know that she lives so near to Esther. Esther got us a good nice dinner. It seemed a luxury to have our dinner in the house & cooked without ashes or sand in it. Libbie & I washed considerable in the afternoon. It did not rain. Esther is anxious that we all stay over until monday hoping the mud will be dried up. The report is that the slues ahead of us are impassable. Think we shall accept their invitation to stay over sabbath. . . .

Saturday [May 31, 1873]. We had a good nights rest, breakfast at six & quarter o-clock. Thadeus does not feel any better this morning. Cous Milton made Thadeus a pair of whiffletrees & then took us back to cousin Esther's. Thadeus then felt so bad that I went to work & gave him a good thorough sweat with hot corn. Br. E. H. B. treated him with quine powders. We had promised to visit an old acquaintance this afternoon N Grams & Thadeus felt a little better & thought we had better go & leave him in the care of Grandmo Curtis. Esther Andrew & I went & had a pleasant visit with the old gentleman & his maiden daughter who seem to be very happy in each other's society. his farm is beautiful the prairie & heavy timber meeting on it. A good house & splendid spring as ever graced a farm. When we returned we found T P better. Libbie & I ironed until quite late. Libbie & Elsie have been at work hard all day. Orvie took Fannie & Ida over to Uncle Nicks after we came back to stay all night. Charley Cowan came down from Owatonna this after noon. I have not seen him since he was about five years old. . . .

Monday June 2nd [1873]. We arose in good season & although rainy made preparations to start on our journey. Our things were badly scattered so that it took us some time to get ready Ells Snyder & Charley Cowan are going with us up to Owatonna. We bade adieu to our friends & started off. Traveling over very pretty country but the worst of roads as we soon reached places where there had been heavy showers. Traveled about ten miles & then camped for dinner. About the time we were ready to start it began to rain & the roads were very bad. We had to double our teams to get through the slues. E H B's team got stuck in a slue just before dinner. We camped quite early got our supper & I arranged so as to lodge Charley Cowan & Ella & her two children.

Tuesday June 3rd [1873]. We had a very hard rain last night & it rained this morning so that we took a lunch in our wagons & did not try to cook breakfast. Old Rover feels so sober after laying out in the rain that we can not get him to even wag his tail. It is the most lonesome & tedious day we have yet seen We took a lunch for our dinner & it as it still rained we got the privilege of going into the house. we cooked our supper in doors. E H B brought in his bed but the rest slept out in our wagons. Charley Cowan made up his mind to leave us & take the cars at Claremount a distance of five miles. I made biscuit for supper & after Supper fried a mess of cake. Our hearts were made to rejoice about six o-clock by the king of day making his appearance. . . .

Thursday [June 5, 1873]. E H B's family, Ovie Taylor & our family breakfasted with Cousin Charley Cowan & then want over to Alethera's to make a forenoon visit. Cousin Ella Snyder was there. we had a pleasant time. After dinner we took our leave of them & in company of two other cousins started for Aunt Jemimas who had cordially invited us We had not got far from Owatonna before it began to rain & rained very very hard for about an hour, & the roads were awful. We reached & greeted our Uncle & Aunt about five o-clock Fount Aunt in very poor health but glad to see us. . . .

Saturday June 7th [1873]. After breakfast and prayrs Libbie Elsie & I went to ironing & did not get through until most night. Auntie & hired girl Fannie tended to the work. The men got ready for threshing in the forenoon & in the afternoon finished up Uncle's threshing which was left on account of the Epizootic among the horses last fall. About five o-clock we were gladdened by the arrival of G. H. Henton's family who left our train at Rochester They had much to tell us of their perils in mud and slues.

Sunday June 8th [1873]. Last night it rained again very hard. We have had no rain for two days. This morning it is pleasant but the wind blows very hard. We got ready to go & hear Nelson Liscomb preach. (an old acquaintance) But were too late, & the neighbors invited E. H. B. to preach in some of their houses. It was decided that he should preach here at Uncles at five o-clock. We had a good congregation & a good sermon. At the close prayr by T. P. Grout & G.H. Henton It seems more like sunday to have preaching.

Monday June 9th [1873]. It rained hard most all night & some this morning. We did not resume our journey until after dinner. Romey piloted us out about eight miles from Uncle's & within one mile of a village named Wilton we met with a sad accident. Our heavy loaded team leading the way got into a very bad slue & got down. E H B quickly unhitched his team from his wagon & went to the rescue. letting his team stand alone a few moments They took fright at the floundering of our team in the slue & ran away. They ran some ways & then came back to the wagons just hitting H Hentons team & rushing past a buggy where Elsie was standing knocked her over & ran over her. She got up alone, walked a few steps & then sank down again. We thought her hip or back broken. We took her up & put her on a bed in the wagon. Then she had a piercing pain in her side. We bathed her in a strong camphor & thought to have a doctor see her at W. but before we reached there she felt so much better she would not have a Dr. We camped at Wilton & got her a bed in the hotel. We bathed her with Arnica & got her in bed feeling quite comfortable.

Tuesday June 10th [1873]. The morning is gloriously bright the night moonlit & cool well calculated for tired ones to rest & those thrown into nervous headache by yesterdays accident are healed. Elsie walked from the hotel over to the wagons before we got our breakfast ready. Feels sore & bad with quite a headache but is much better than it seemed possible she could be when we think of those horses running directly over her. God has seemed to care for us all through our journey. We started off again about half past eight, traveling over a very level tract of country new because owned by speculators. We found many wet slues. Camped

281

about noon, cooked dinner in a little house (paddie house) started again about two o-clock getting out on a prairie all boundless except at a great distance off on one side a little crooked piece of timber. Here we came in contact with the little Cobb river & soon after crossing E H B got his horses down in a soft miry place & had to take them off & put them on the back end of the wagon & draw it out. E H B left one chain & had to go back after it. After going a mile or so farther we crossed another stream along which were many mounds supposed to be an Indian burying place. We forded another stream. E H B got stuck again toward night we found bad slues. Camped about seven, in front of a mans house under some nice cotton woods of about nine years growth. We got a bed for Elsie in the house She has felt pretty bad today.

June 11th Wednesday [1873]. Arose about four o-clock but we did not get started until seven. Found the roads improving in the beautiful sunshine which has blest us since monday & yet some very bad places. To day we see timber which follows the big cob river. We do not see timber only along the rivers. Camped about noon with a sabbath school Supt. of the M. E. Church. Had a very nice place to set tables among the willows & cooked dinner in the house. This camping place was about two miles west of Minnesota Lake a small village on the lake. We found the roads worse in the afternoon having often to double teams. Thadeus & H. Henton went off the road to look at a cow the wished to buy & got into a bad slue with a light wagon. Then toward night we crossed a mice high prairie near Delavan & then a large march. G. H. Henton got his team in badly & the others had work to get through. It was so late we had to camp as soon as we came to a house. The first house we came to was a Methodist preachers. They took Elsie in &did all they could for us. Their name was Nock E H B's left us this PM. & went on to Winnebago City to visit some friends.

Thursday June 12th [1873]. This morning we cooked breakfast in the house with the ministers family & all went in to attend prayers. We expect to renew our pleasant acquaintance ere long as Br. Nock goes onto a claim near Worthington this fall. As we got into our wagons & turned our horses to the road we saw the cars for the first time this week. They were passing through Delavan a nice little prairie town. Just before noon Orvie got his team down in a slue. We have had to double our teams several times. We were welcomed into a baptist ministers house to cook & eat our dinner on his table. After dinner we pushed on to Winnebago City finding several places we could not get through very easy. Winnebago is a nice enterprizing looking place. Good buildings & in good repair. We were made glad by letters letters from Brs. Eli & Cyrus Hen-

ton at this place. Leaving W. City we passed through a nice piece of timber in which lays the blue earth river which we crossed by ferry boat. We
camped with ferryman near by. It rained very hard for an hour after we
camped. Elsie took a bed in the house, & in the evening she fainted away
& did not come to herself in some minutes. We thought her dead. But
she came out of it & rested well all night. . . .

Saturday June 14th [1873]. We got up early & got started about half
past six, cheered on by the music of the hungry mosquitoes. in the
forenoon we had very good roads the sluey places were only wet not
miry. We camped again at noon on the Elm Creek. cooked our dinner in
a kind lady's house whose husband was Justice. In the P.M. we traveled
quite fast over good roads, until night we came to a bad place where the
water covered the ground. our team got a little out of the road & got in.
We have traveled all day out of sight of trees except along Elm creek.
They are setting little slips around their sod houses. This afternoon we
came to a sod house & all got out & went in to see how it looked. We
were none of us charmed however I think. Orvie is quite sick, we feel
considerably alarmed about him. It appeared very much like a hard storm
& we camped near a small frame house which looks rare for many miles
surrounded as it is by little sod ones. We are thankful to get shelter &
wood & milk & oats & all we <u>realy</u> need out on this almost wild prairie
to night. . . .

June 16th Monday [1873]. Got up before four o-clock cooked our
breakfast in the house. Prayrs conducted by G.H. Henton. We did not
get started until seven & half o-clock. The country looks better as we
advance Though not a tree to be seen of any size. We see more frame
houses than sod. When within about five miles of Jackson we met the
grasshoppers which are coming from the west where they have done
much damage. Just at the foot of a steep hill lies Jackson on the Des
Moines river a little sprightly looking village with a nice court house. We
drove through the village & camped for dinner on the banks of the
De. M. When out on the prairie again we could see three trains of emi-
grants besides our own. one train of eleven teams. The country is very
pretty. the roads are very good excepting some bad slues. We camped ten
miles out of Jackson at what is called the ten mile house. Libbie has been
very sick this P.M. Nellie's eyes & very bad. Orvie does not get well yet.
Elsie is very faint & tired Every night it is hard to keep her from fainting
away some times. . . .

Wednesday June 18th 1873. Started out about seven o-clock   soon
reached Worthington a lively village out on the prairie of two years

growth. The wild grass growing right up around the houses. Our train stopped some time at Worthington to get supplies & as we sat in our wagons a gentleman came up to enquire about another emigrant train, who taught the Milford school in Jefferson co. Wis. last winter. He said Alice Ingalls my niece went to school to him. I like the country around Worthington very much but the farther we go the better I like it. We camped for dinner fifteen miles from Worthington at the half way house. After dinner we traveled about four miles when we came to the Kanaranza a beautiful stream with a hard pebble bottom, quite a treat after ploughing slues to ford it. After crossing the Kanaranza the country is perfectly beautiful. We found when out seven miles from the Kanaranza that G. H. had lost his dog. So we went back after it about two miles could hear from it but could not find it. The rest went on & we over took them at Luverne. We crossed the rock river in boats at Luverne but the teams come through without any trouble. We found Br. Eli Jennie Grout & Abbie waiting for us on the other side to welcome us. Our family went on to Eli's, E H B's to uncle Williams, G.H. Hentons to Cyrus Hentons. We Got to Luverne about sundown & did not get to Elis until after dark it seemed an awful long five miles.

There we rested for the night. Our trail ended.

The Diary of Agnes Barland McDaniel, 1923

Agnes Louise Barland was born on April 21, 1891, in Eau Claire, Wisconsin, to Dora (Schlegelmilch) and John C. Barland of Eau Claire. Along with her siblings, Margaret Dorothea ("Thea," excerpts from whose diary appear in chapter 2), Thomas Gordon, Charles Herman, John Howard, and George Clarence, Agnes Barland grew up in Eau Claire. After attending the Normal School there, she taught country school in Seymour, Minnesota. She graduated from Oberlin College (also her sister's alma mater) in 1914 and taught English for a time in Fergus Falls, Minnesota, before moving to New York City, where she earned a master's degree from Columbia University Teachers College. During World War I she completed preclinical work in nursing in preparation to be a military nurse. The war ended before she completed her work, however. In 1921 she earned a degree in nursing from the Johns Hopkins School of Nursing.

The following year she traveled to Chiang Mai, Thailand, then known by most Westerners as Siam, to work as a missionary

Agnes Barland McDaniel. Courtesy Thomas H. Barland.

nurse for the Presbyterian Church. On March 22, 1933, she married Dr. Edwin B. McDaniel, a medical missionary, and helped him operate his mission hospital and leprosarium in Nakhon Si Thammarat, Siam. In later years, following her husband's death in 1938, she taught nursing in San Juan, Puerto Rico. After her brother Thomas's death, she returned to Eau Claire to take over the T. G. Barland insurance agency. During her later years she lived in the M. B. Severson Home in Eau Claire. She died on June 5, 1982, at the age of ninety-one.

Her cloth-covered diary is a small National Date Book, three and a half by six inches. It has lined, dated pages, with twenty lines allotted for each day's entry. The diary is primarily a descriptive record of its writer's sojourn in Siam; at the same time it offers glimpses into the cultural assumptions and beliefs that shaped the direction of her work as a nurse. The diary runs from January 1 until February 27, 1923. After a break, it concludes with an entry dated March 18, 1923. It is housed in the Barland-Schlegelmilch Family Papers at the State Historical Society of Wisconsin Area Research Center in Eau Claire.

January 1, 1923. At midnight we were preparing to leave Prae for Nam with 36 carriers and 56 baskets. Mrs. Taylor and Mrs. Ferry were carried in basket chairs and Irene, Dr. Perkins, Mr. Henry and I rode horseback. The moon was shining brightly as we left the compound about 3 A.M. At 3:20 we came into a little village named Long Quam, entered the bamboo house of a Dane of the East Asiatic company [to which she subsequently refers to as E.A.]. The boy put up our saleed and mosquito nets and we had supper as the sun was setting.

January 2, 1923. This morning we were up at 4. Our 36 carriers and we on our 4 horses started out about 6 o'clock up thro the beautiful foot hills, the bamboo jungle valleys covered with a riot of flowering vines— tinted mountain walls sometimes blanketed with lavender heliotrope and great red—and—white trunked trees every where. Once we saw two elephants with turbaned keepers. At 9 A.M. we turned off to a little E.A. bungalow Axel—Margarethe of Denmark had written names on wall-fire-tiffin—On we led—Horse—foot—in strange talk by stream supper— candlelight.

January 3, 1923. Today we saw a tiger trap and heard the wild "huis" of the monkey. We started out at 7:30 A.M. We on horses turned aside about

5 kilos to see a mineral water falls with wonderful lime formations. Then on we galloped. My horse knelt down in the water and I fell over his head full in the water. At 3 P.M. we arrived at an old saz with elephant mounts and tiger stories galore. We had supper on the porch by candle light with the moon rising full behind the jungle.

January 4, 1923. Up this morning at 6 A.M. "Oh!" said Mrs. Taylor, "we'll have to hurry or we won't finish today's trip until after dark." We started out up—hill and down—then over the mountain and through "the valley of the shadow"—a dark, moist narrow passage. It wouldn't take much imagination to see a tiger there. Then we came out on level woods stretches and finally across a rice field with threshers on each side into the little village where we were to spend the night at the christian chapel which was simply a substantial little building open on one side. Dr. Taylor appeared to meet us on his motor cycle and we all had an early supper with several bloodcurdling tiger stories as appetizers.

January 5, 1923. Up at midnight and out under a foggy moon across the plain. The fog was so thick that my sweater was covered with droplets and our hair was dripping. At one place we dismounted and built a small fire to partly dry ourselves. Toward morning we walked when cold. The country became more wooded. We passed the spot where Dr. Taylor had seen a tiger cross the wood and he told us of a village a little farther on where 42nd 5 men were being taken every month. After a long debate we decided to wait until we got home before having breakfast. We galloped into the city—elephant pagoda—river—girls' school—pancakes—syrup—coffee—fire—unpacked—slept.

January 6, 1923. This morning I got into my uniform and Dr. Perkins and I walked down the river to the hospital after opening a box of gauze, sheets, pillow slips and old clean rags that Dr. Perkins' church had sent out. We did a "salvarsan" at the hospital [a treatment involving a toxic powder then used against syphilis and a tropical disease called yaws], went thro' the operating cupboards, cleaned up the sterilizing room and came home to a lunch of rice and curry—lettuce—bread—butter—baked bananas & milk. In the afternoon I took an inventory of hospital linen, bathed our three bed patients, got one of them out on the porch in the sun, made a pneumonia jacket for one and came home at 5 PM—dressed in green organdie and played tennis. As we called the watchman to take us home—Irene and I rode to the girls' school—Dr. Taylor told us how two years ago, he had looked over the porch railing straight into the eyes of a tiger. The tiger of course ran but Dr. Taylor had not allowed Mrs. Taylor to sit on the porch after dark, since.

Journeys

January 7, 1923. A quiet Sunday—Dressed in my blue polka dotted dress from home—Sunday school at 9:30 after a breakfast of pankakes, sausage, eggs and coffee—church—Dinner of chicken—potatoes—chinese cabbage—baked bananas. Read "without Benefit of Clergy"—wrote letters.

January 8, 1923. This morning Dr. Perkins and I went down to the hospital I sorted out the instruments and tore up old linen for binders, etc. In the afternoon we examined all the school girls, bathed four patients, set a fractured femur and made some applications for the hospital.

January 9, 1923. This morning we did three adenoidectomies, two salvarsan treatments and wrapped a burned child with picric acid dressings. In the afternoon I bathed four patience—made up solutions for the operating room—fixed up Balkan frame for the little girl with the fracture and dressed two ulcers . . . This evening Dr. Taylor told us that he had seen tiger tracks around the Boys School this afternoon.

January 10, 1923. This morning we took out a sebaceous cyst, and cleaned up 2 cases of long drawn out ulcer. One of the patients, a little boy, had his body almost completely covered with scabby old ulcers. Then we did a salvarsan treatment after which we were informed that there was a baby elephant in the yard which had been bitten by a Tiger. Dr. Perkins chased it all over the compound squirting zotol on it. This afternoon the church had its Christmas celebration with one of the trees growing in the yard of the Girls' School decorated as a Christmas tree. A big feast followed of rice & curry and cakes.

January 11, 1923. Last night—the thermometer went down only to 57. It has been going down to 52 & 50. Dr. Perkins did an eye an ear and a nose operation this A.M. I dressed 5 incisions. The little fellow with the ulcers all over his body we put into a tub of salt water. In the afternoon I bathed 3 patients, dressed a burn, filled the sterilizer, went home and dressed and played a game of tennis. This evening Mr. Perry got out his Chinese puzzles. Irene and Mrs. Perry both have colds.

January 12, 1923. This morning I showed Chum Pen how to take temperatures, got the boys started at fixing bottles for rubber goods, put some sulphur ointment on a child with scabes, got things ready for the extraction of a sebaceous cyst and helped with the operation. Dr. Perkins let me make the incision and cut. When we got down aways I let him do the cutting. Then we did a salvarsan. I irrigated an eye and then we came home to lunch. This afternoon I bathed the child with the fracture gave the little fellow with the ulcers a continuous tub in bichloride, helped with two dressings and took temperatures.

January 13, 1923. Today the men put my rubber goods over kerosene oil—temperatures taken—I bathed 2 of our 9 patients—massaged Ut De helped with the 10 dressings. An enema was given and the morning was gone. This afternoon the hospital was closed—rested—bought a rin—45 tics [a tical or baht] two Nan scarves—14 tics—a skirt—5 tics—a vest—11 tics—a table cover—3½ tics—tennis. This evening I played dominoes with Dr. Taylor & Mr. Perry and on arriving home found an exquisite crocheted yoke from Yawt with the wish for a Happy New Year.

January 14, 1923. Quiet Sunday. Went to the hospital after breakfast, and then to Sunday School and church. In the afternoon, I read and wrote letters. This evening we had an old fashioned sing.

January 15, 1923. Today was Irene's birthday and at breakfast her plate was piled high with gifts, & beautiful Lao skirts—note paper—brushes—suitcase—candy, etc. I gave her a piece of nature silk from Chieng Mai. The morning was a busy one—a salvarsan—dressings—etc. In the afternoon I took an inventory of our drugs and in the evening we had a big birthday dinner.

January 16, 1923. This morning I gave Ai Ma an injection of milk and helped with dressings, etc. Examined about 6 patients. In the afternoon a woman came with complete prolapse of the uterus. I sent a note up to Dr. Perkins who came down & replaced it. We then irrigated and sent her home.

January 17, 1923. This morning Dr. Perkins left for Chieng Mai. I was called out to a heart case on the other side of town. I gave her a hypo of atropine, digitalis, and nitroglycerin, and then gave her a bath. This afternoon I gave a patient an injection of emetine—a beri beri patient a massage—compresses on a sore arm and went to call on our coolie who has gastric ulcers.

January 18, 1923. This morning we had the usual cases in for examination—poor, trusting people. I have wished a hundred times that I had a good Dr. here. Do you people at home realize that the only person to meet the physical needs in a city of 18,000 with a surrounding population of 50,000—is your nurse with your spirit in back of her? This is the missionary work of which you dream. Need on every side and all you can do is to keep smiling and say "I will at least try to do this."

January 19, 1923. This afternoon at 5 P.M. as I was following the river road home a thin little woman with a baby in her arms ran down from a little bamboo house and said, "O Meleon, won't you help me? I have no money left and no food with which to feed my three children tomorrow." At home such a woman might find work but here there are no factories or offices or stores. I told the woman to come up to the Taylors and if they thot she really needed it I would help her. I found that her only source of income was 5 tics $20.00 a month to feed herself and 3 children.

January 20, 1923. This afternoon I had my first obstetrical case on a bamboo floor in a little dark windowless room. The baby was a beautiful little brown, however, and the mother is getting along beautifully. I had sterile towels and boiled instruments already ~~so~~ we can do that even [in] the tiger jungle of Siam—so at least we are not looking for infection and the baby's eyes have had silver nitrate in them and the care which every baby ought to have.

January 21, 1923. A day of rest indeed! This morning I went to the hospital and as all the patients were quiet I went over to Dr. Peoples' old home which has been closed since the Dr's death two years ago. It is a beautiful old house with spacious ground and a riot of rose bushes as high as your head over in one corner. I picked a bunch of long stemmed beauties and took them over to my patients. Then came Sunday school and Church with a long afternoon of rest for the new week. I am to take my first Sunday school class next Sunday.

January 22, 1923. This morning I thot I would get the drug room cleaned but instead I was deluged with patients—two babies with high fever—a little brother had died during the night—a woman with ulcers all over her legs—a man with rheumatism—a gynecology case—a boy with a huge splinter an inch long in his foot—a woman with pain in her shoulder—a young boy with a history of T.B.—a man with a tumor and no one to operate—aborted baby etc. This P.M. I had my first lesson in Siamese since coming to Nan. In the middle of it the home mail came and Oh how I wanted to open it. Then just before the lesson was over there came a call to see a patient and I didn't have a chance at my letters until evening. Thea—an operation! She may all be glad that she is in a Christianical country where such things are possible. Out here she would have just gone on and died.

January 24, 1923. This morning in the midst of examining my patients, I was called down to see the Siamese commissioner's wife who has a large abdominal tumor. On returning to the hospital I found among the waiting patients an old white haired woman with inflamed eyes. Kneeling on the floor she begged me to help her and when we had washed her eyes with boric and put on copper sulphate she almost wept for joy thinking she was cured. This afternoon I studied Siamese.

January 25, 1923. This morning when Dr. Taylor stepped into the hospital the place was crowded mostly with babies. One had very sore buttocks, another had a cyst, still another was burned, etc. It seems as though we had our hands full. The afternoon was full with my Siamese lesson and with getting the mail off. Our mail comes in on Tuesday and leave on Thursday so our letter days are busy days and Tuesday is a real red letter day. In the evening we played dominoes.

January 26, 1923. This morning was a quiet one at the hospital. I had time to massage Ut De and to give Jun Khee a colon flushing. She has dysentery. This afternoon I went over to see Maa Hum who was complaining of "Jep Tong." My lesson in Siamese came also. In the evening I went down and massaged Ut De. After dinner we played dominoes.

January 27, 1923. A busy morning at the hospital. Every Saturday is busy because as at home all the country people come in on that day. They knew we close on Sunday. This afternoon just as I was finishing my lesson our coolie came busting up stirs and said that one of our Christian natives had been carried off by a tiger. He had gone with his 15 yr old son and his brother out in the country to work in his rice field. At noon he told the other two to go down to a little stream near by and catch some fish for dinner. In about an hour the fishermen returned to find him gone. They found his knife and bloody panong, at which they became panic stricken and ran for town. Dr. Taylor got about 20 men and went out but could find nothing in the dusk. They returned home about 10 P.M. Irene and I had already gone over to our rooms at the school but hurried back to the Taylors when we heard the men galloping into the yard.

January 28, 1923. This morning at dawn the men went out again. I met two of our teachers on their way out as I walked over to breakfast and told how glad I was they were going. "You do not have tigers in America?" Questioned one—"To Take me as a food!" he added disgustedly. The men returned at noon. They had traced the tiger to a spot where they found a piece of the man's blouse and his hand and foot. Tracks of three other tigers approached the place. The Buddhists here believe that these man eating tigers are spirit tigers and so make no effort to kill the beasts.

January 29, 1923. This morning I played dentist and pulled a tooth—my first experience as a dentist. I also pushed back into the rectum of a baby a small tumor which will have to be taken off later on. I can't do it alone. Then Ut De and my three other women patients were bathed. Ut De had a massage and Kun Kheo had a colon irrigation and murphy drip. In the afternoon after my lesson we went up the river in a boat to the barracks where we played tennis with the major and the "ampere" or city mayor and others. The mayor played in bare feet but played splendidly. The soldiers band came out and played squatting on the grass. Among other selections they played Columbia, the Gem of the Ocean—Mine Eyes have Seen the Glory—Yankee Doodle and other American Selections in our honor. We glided back home in the twilight with a big moon above. The natives were out fishing and having the jolliest kind of a time. We found our mail waiting for us and Oh, it was so good. Grace has a baby girl, Beverly Jean. There was a long letter from Ethelyn, two from Aunt Louise, one from Rella Howard, and two Leaders. The whole family played dominoes in the evening after supper.

January 30, 1923. Here my diary is running over the space assigned but there is so much to tell. This morning I found that three of our thermometers had been taken so into the storeroom went everything that couldn't be locked up outside. After temperatures were taken and the patients bathed and Ut De massaged and Kun Kheo irrigated a call came to a patient across the city. She will be brought into the hospital tomorrow.

January 31, 1923 /February 1, 1923. Elder Pun says that every morning someone comes in and asks for a salvarsan treatment. The only needle I could use is broken so I am sending to Bangkok. The need is here and I am the only one to meet it. Ut De and Kum Keo seem to be getting better, slowly. This afternoon during my lesson a great crowd of boys gathered around a little raccoon out in a tree just as the boys would do at home. At 4:30 P.M. we all went to prayer meeting which was in reality a funeral service for Tum who was taken by the tiger. One dear old Elder said that Tun reminded him of Moses because no one knew where either was buried.

Tonight Dr. Taylor and Mr. Perry are going to watch for tigers in a tree down by the tiger spring where the tigers are said to come every night to drink. This morning at 10:30 o'clock I ushered my second baby into the world, Chum Pe Ng's baby boy. This afternoon I went back to the hospital and gave Ut Me her massage and Kun Keo her irrigation. At 5 A.M. the men went out to their "hang." In the evening we four remaining women played dominoes.

February 2, 1923. This afternoon I went to see Chumpeno's wife and baby. They seemed both to be doing well but I had just arrived home again when Chum Peng came running and said the baby was choking to death—was blue in the face, etc. I hurried down to find the baby peacefully sleeping. We played rook tonight.

February 3, 1923. A busy day! Maa Cot came and I gave her a good massage with eucalyptus and mentholatum and a good colon irrigation. That in combination with my other work kept me busy. In the afternoon I went back to the hospital and gave Ut De a good massage. In the evening I went to the prayers at the school and then to bed. Kru Vant led prayers.

February 4, 1923. This morning I was wakened at 6 o'clock from a sound sleep by a voice beginning Kam Meleon. It was only the arrival of a new baby. That makes the third one in the month since I have come. At church a woman with a huge abscess below her ear made arrangements for its lancing. I went down to the hospital and gave Ut De a good massage before dinner, then over to see that Chum Peng's and the new baby were all right. After dinner a little girl came running to ask me to come and see "Muenchi" who had fever. "Muenchi" proved to be the little brother. A sponge and some quinine with plenty of water is, I hope, bringing down the fever.

February 5, 1923. My fever patients are better. This morning I called on one immediately before breakfast and on the other immediately after. Then on the way to the hospital I called on the baby who arrived yesterday morning. After giving 6 injections of emetine and milk, one vaginal douche and one enema I lanced an abscess and gave a massage. I was in the midst of this when a hurry call came to an obstetrical case—a retained placenta. After lunch the mail arrived [with] a card from the Iversons—a letter with snapshots from Dr. O'Brien—a paper from Cora May Walton—the Oberlin volunteer Leaders and fire Leaders—no letter from home. After my lesson I went back to the hospital where I gave two baths one massage and a colon irrigation. I was on my way home when I was hailed by a woman to come and see her baby. I found the baby a feeding case—terribly emaciated. They will bring it in to the hospital tomorrow.

February 5, 1923. This morning I had barely reached the hospital when they brought the baby in. I started a morphy drip on it immediately and put it on regular feedings. It's such a pathetic little youngster. Then another baby came in with fever. We gave him a bath for he was very dirty, gave him quinine-santonin and castor oil and put him to bed. After

293

bathing the patients and massaging Ut De the morning was gone. In the afternoon Sa came in making 11 hospital patients. The baby with pneumonia seemed a little better.

February 7, 1923. This morning we were busy with the babies, Sa and all the rest. Kun Keo has fever but Maa Jum is better. A little woman brought me five eggs as a gift which I turned over to our poorest patients. I pulled another tooth. The baby with pneumonia seems about the same. I love my work here.

The Diary of Alice Gortner Johnson, 1933

A native of St. Paul, Minnesota, Alice Gortner was born on April 20, 1917, to Ross and Catherine (Willis) Gortner. During the summer of 1933, as part of a group of Camp Fire Girls and counselors, Alice Gortner, then sixteen, set off from Camp Ojiketa on an adventure to what is now the Boundary Waters Canoe Area in northern Minnesota. The group went north toward Duluth, then on to Grand Marais, Minnesota, along the north shore of Lake Superior. From there they traveled inland on the Gunflint Trail to Camp Kiwadinipi, a private girls' camp operated by Winifred Bailey of Wellesley College. Next, the group traveled southeast to Little Marais, Minnesota, also on the north shore, then down Highway 61 to Duluth, and eventually back to the Twin Cities. Before the journey, Alice decided to keep a diary of the group's journey which, according to a newspaper clipping found in her papers, also marked a rite of passage for her and her companions: "Each one of this group has passed the gypsy test, the highest national rank in camp craft, and also an advanced swimming test."

After returning home to St. Paul, she continued her commitment to the Camp Fire Girls. By 1938 she had served as a counselor at Camp Ojiketa herself. She attended the University of Minnesota, from which she graduated in 1939. Some years later, after her marriage to Al Johnson, her daughters, Linda and Sarah, also became Camp Fire Girls. Once her children were grown, Alice Gortner Johnson worked as a buyer for the University of Minnesota Bookstore until her retirement. She continues to live in St. Paul, where she enjoys traveling, is active in social clubs, plays golf, and skis.

Alice Gortner Johnson, 1931. Courtesy Minnesota Historical Society.

Monday—Started out from camp with high hopes. We got as far as Chisago when Roberta Simonson got terribly sick. We took her to a doctor and he told us we couldn't take her so Miss Mildred came in and took her back to camp. Too bad, after Roberta had worked so hard for her gypsy. We started again about 9 o'clock. We stopped at Carlton for gas and as we left we lost Miss Mary Lou. Stopped in Duluth for gas and purchased some meat. We got hamburgers which were the best I'd ever eaten. Just out of Duluth we heard a terrible bumping behind and we realized our trailer was broken. We spent two hours by the roadside while Miss Evelyn went to and from Duluth. Miss Evelyn acted the good Samaratin and brought us food while we waited for the trailer to be fixed. (Later we found out that Miss Mary Lou also had another flat tire.) We drove on to West's cottage at Beaver Bay and were welcomed by a worried reception committee. They have a lovely cottage, so rustic and all. It is right in the heart of the woods with pines all around which give off such a fragrant odor. We had a lovely stay which was much to short for all the keen places there were to see. Miss Mary Lou drove on ahead to make a fire for us at the tourist camp at Grand Marais. On the way to Grand Marais we stopped at the Aztec hotel. It is a funny affair along the way, famous for its homemade ice cream. It could be lovely if they wouldn't mix ideas so. Soon we traveled on to Grand Marais. We roamed around town trying to find the camp and when we finally found it they had the fire made for us. We ate supper which consisted of roast corn, ribs, bread twists, tomatoes and nectar. Everything went keen until Jo Burns filled her bread twist with mustard instead of brown sugar. She surely had a mouthful. Miss Louise washed the dishes and all our hands for us and we climbed gayly into bed. We slept wonderfully. It was a flat place and covered with hay so you can guess we did.

Tuesday—We woke up all rested from the nights rest. We hurried about and got our blankets rolled before breakfast. Some were faster than others and we or they (which have you) started making breakfast. We had pancakes, syrup, bacon, cocoa and oranges. Mary Fran and Jo went to church only to find that it was held an hour later so they walked back to camp. Later we heard the bells and they started out again. The rest of us went to the Coast Guard station and first we climbed the small tower and then the high 85 foot tower and were my knees shaking when I got to the top! It was a hard climb down but I got there. We went across the swinging bridge and started on our way up the Gunflint Trail. It was a beautiful drive and I loved the smell of the pines so much. We rode in the rumble seat (Jo, Mary Jane and I) behind the other cars and we suffered terribly from the dust. We stopped at Bearskin Lake for lunch and we had Club House sandwiches and some mores. We went swimming and got

296

cleaned off. While doing the dishes Miss Louise was throwing the plates
to Miss Jack to put away and one of them dropped in the lake. Miss
Louise went in after it up to her knees but it sank and she only got her
pants wet for the reward for her effort. We got a good picture of her in
the process. After clearing it all up we continued on our way. The roads
resembled a roller coaster all the way. We had loads of fun watching the
car ahead bob up and down. We detoured from the trail to see Gateway
Lodge on Hungary Jack. It is a beautiful lodge and is so rustic looking.
All the furniture is made of wood, the lamps of birchbark trimmed with
pine cones, rugs of rag which were woven wonderfully well etc. All in all
it was the best place we have seen so far. We went on to Gunflint Lodge
where we got ice cream cones and all. This is the only place on the trail
where you can see Canada. Bill Kerfoot was the guide there and he asked
about Aiken and Will. From here we went on to Sea Gull Lake, the far-
thest lodge on the Gunflint Trail. The lake was gorgeous which had hundreds of tiny islands scattered around. From a high rock we could see for
miles down the lake. Everyone was so friendly to us and we enjoyed our
stay a lot. We couldn't stay long so we turned around and started down
again, hoping to reach Camp Kiwadinipi by evening. The camp is about
half way between Ely and Little Marais. On our way back we stopped at
Clear Water and we went past Lake Duncan. Between Clearwater and
Grand Marais Miss Evelyn hit a bump which knocked us into loose
gravel. This threw us back into a post and so on. Jo and I were sitting in
the back with Majel, Mary Jane and Miss Evelyn in front. Jo and I hit the
top a number of times and Mary Jane and Majel hit the glass. We ended
up in a ditch with two flat tires, a bent axle, the brakes locked, wheels out
of line, fenders bent but otherwise O.K. Our tire let out a "ssss" sound
and we thought the car was on fire or else acid was spilling. We jumped
out of the car as fast as we could. My head was killing me and I thought I
must have broken something but I didn't. We honked at Miss Louise as
fast as we could but she didn't hear and although we sent a car after her
they couldn't catch her in time. Miss Evelyn was terribly worried as it
was her first accident as well as the rest of us. Men from the CCC [Civil-
ian Conservation Corps] Camp came by and helped us get the car on the
road by used [using] a log as a prop. They also fixed the car as much as
possible but it all took time. Jo's and my back and head were killing us so
they made us lie down by the roadside. Fortunately Miss Mary Lou's car
was yet to pass us and when she came she got help at the camp for us.
Miss Mary Lou hauled us to the CCC Camp and from there they phoned
Miss Louise in Grand Marais. They told her we had had car trouble and
were being hauled in. She was terribly worried but calling her helped. On
the way home we had to get out several times and push the cars up the
hill. My back was about broken when we arrived at the tourist camp at

about 1:30 A.M. They had our beds made for us so we climbed in. We were just getting to sleep when a rain came up and we had to move into a cook shack. There was hardly room for us and lots had to sleep on tables and one on the stove. Oh it's a great life. In the morning it was still raining when we woke up. A man came to get wood and when he looked in he gave one snort and ran!

Wednesday—When we got up we rolled our blankets and made breakfast. and were we hungary after not having any supper!—also tired for four hours sleep wasn't enough for us. Some of us started out for Camp Kervadinipi and the others were left until the next load. Think of going over 100 miles three times—up and back and up again. The girls that were in the rumble seat were wrapped, pinned, tucked and just squeezed into the back with blanket rolls at our feet. Never have I had such a hard ride. It was a long rainy ride, the only stop being at Little Marais. The cabin we are in is brand new and they have four double deckers (I sleep on top) and two single beds. We went to dinner shortly after arriving and was it ever a wonderful meal. Afterwards three girls did the dishes and the rest of us made candlesticks—or at least three of us did. They are out of birchbark and are so cute. Then we came back to the cabin and some slept while I wrote in here. Just before supper we went in swimming in the Stoney River. It was cold but refreshing. We ate supper and I helped with the dishes. We were out walking for a time and helped the chore boy gather kindling. He is the only fun around here since the girls are away. Later they showed us moving pictures of the camp but we went to bed before the end. About 10 o'clock the rest of the kids came and we made our beds and went to sleep.

Thursday—We got up at 8 o'clock and went to breakfast. We had fish, cereal, cocoa, muffins, and apricots. Three girls helped with the dishes and Jo, Majel and I went outdoors to help the chore boy haul canoes for us to take. He took us for a short ride and then we hauled the canoes up to the trailer and then we took them in the car to a lake nearby. We had loads of fun kidding him along. We all hiked over to the lake and got in the canoes—they were so awful I could hardly call them canoes for one of them we had to sue oars on and the other had such long paddles we could barely manage. We found after we got out a ways that the boats were too hard to handle and that there were so many logs and rocks that we could make hardly any headway so we turned around and came in. Instead we took a long hike through the woods. It was nice to hear the wind through the trees and it surely was dense. We had to come back shortly for lunch. There were some guests there and "Jennie" from school was one of them. I certainly was surprised to see her. After dinner

298

we all lay down to sleep. We slept for about two hours and then we could have slept more. Everyone got up except Miss Karen. It seemed nice to have all of the previous sick ones up (I forgot to tell you that half of us were in bed on Wednesday morning.) We went to the handcraft cabin and walked around after supper until bedtime. During the night Dorothy Peterson got sick but didn't tell anyone.

Friday—We got up at seven o'clock and got our blankets rolled before breakfast. after breakfast we packed the trailer and some of us did the dishes—and were there loads of them. I've never seen so many dishes used for breakfast in my life. After many goodby's we drove off and started up the Finland Trail. It was terribly rocky and curvy—almost right angles every time. I think this stretch and the Gunflint Trail are the prettiest things we've seen so far. The trees are just gorgeous. Our first stop was Halfway Camp on the Kawishiwe River. We got out and took several pictures (resting our legs in the mean time). We drove on to Ely where we got gas and candy. People got a big kick out of us here for they surely gave us funny looks. Right outside of Ely we found a road taking us to Burnside Lodge so we drove in. It was a beautiful lodge overlooking the river. It had a huge living room with rustic furniture. Every lodge so far has had some thing rustick so far! We got stationary and postcards and sent some of them. From there we went to Tower where Jo met her father and mother much to her surprise. She just walked into a cafe to find out where the depot was and here they were. So was glad because she didn't have to go over to Isle of Pines alone, like she had planned, before she met them. We ate lunch at the Vermillion Tavern and then some of us went with Jo down to the boat. At the dock we found out that we could have a short ride in the speed boat for 25 cents so we all piled in and had a ride. It was loads of fun and the spray was a grand feeling when we all were so dirty, although some of us did get pretty wet. The lake was beautiful with its many islands. Coming in the channel we saw a beaver and a blue heron. We went from Tower to Virginia. Coming out of Virginia Miss Louise felt a knocking at her wheel and discovered it was a broken spring. We (Mary Jane, Majel, and I) were in the car when it happened. We have been in everything so far. I guess we are the "Jinks." Miss Louise went back and the rest of us went on to Hibbing. We went all over the town trying to find a place to sleep and finally we ate anyway. Miss Louise came shortly and some counsilars went to the police dept. and he gave us permission to sleep in a public park in the bandstand. The ground was too cold and we found out the next morning it was 39 degrees outside the night before. To get to the stand with the trailer we had to turn around in a graveyard because we couldn't back up! When we got there we found that there were lights all around us but we didn't even mind we were so tired. Nor did we mind making our beds almost in the dark, for bed making is becoming a habit with us. I forgot to tell you that Mary Jane had expressed her desire for eggs in the morning so when Miss Louise went to town after supper she obligingly brought us the eggs, which in the mean time had been sat on and scrabbled by Miss Florence. It got all over the car and jackets but now that it is cleaned up it strikes us funny. Miss Florence surely is having her fill of jokes, the other night she brushed her teeth with vanishing cream instead of tooth paste. She thought it tasted funny and was quite put out when she found it was cream. We surely had loads of fun! Well to go back to our bandstand. The floor was hard but to add to our troubles we had a couple in back of us on a bench who were keeping us awake with there "aaze is aooze" and all.

Saturday—When we woke up we all took pictures of the beds and then we washed and packed. I'm afraid when I get home that I will begin tearing my bed apart in the morning or else sleeping out in the back yard as force of habit! We ate at our farmer place and took several more pictures, some unexpected ones. When we were all packed Miss Karen discovered she had lost her pen and we had an awful time finding it but we finally did in the back of Miss Mary Lou's car. We went from here to see the iron pit by the tourist park. It is said to be the largest iron pit mine in the world. It was a real thrill for me since I had never seen one before. We decided after seeing this one that we would drive over to see the deeper one. It was 220 feet deep. Miss Jack took a picture of it on the camp Kodak so I hope I will get one. We left Burnett Park and went to see the $5,000,000 Hibbing High School. First we saw the auditorium which is nearly as large as the Northrup auditorium and it is just grand. Then we saw the study hall, library, gym, swimming pool, boys gym and shower room. We also saw the Home Economics room. All the decorations are hand painted. The rooms are huge and so well lighted. It is a grand school in all and something everyone ought to see. I can't see it being wasted on those foriegnors who don't appreciate it. The flagpole alone costing $5,000 and being of pure marble.

We had to journey on over though we didn't want to. When we left Duluth we lunched at Joe's Pickwick Tavern and we all had fried chicken, corn fritters, and boiled potatoes. Discussed going to Brainard but Miss Karen had to be back by supper so we decided not to. Instead to spend some time we went down to watch the boats come in. We saw the largest aerial bridge and we saw a big boat pass a smaller boat and come in. The new cars were coming from Detroit and they passed right by us. We were standing on the point on the side of the canal where the lighthouse was to watch it. Then we went over to where they were loading butter on a ship. They were to be loading for twenty four hours and in the end were to have 350 box cars full of butter. We left Mary Matt and Mary Francis at the Union depot, for each were to leave us there and while we were parked Miss Louise got "told" not to park double like that. We drove on to Moose Lake for cones and gas. Between Pine City and Rock Creek we (the three of us) were again riding in Miss Evelyn's car when something in her motor went wrong. We stopped to see what was wrong and we three changed with Naomi and Dorothy. As soon as we got in Miss Louise's car she couldn't start her engine. It began being funny about this time and we had a hearty laugh over it. At Rock Creek, Miss Evelyn found out it was a value spring that was making her "alarm clock" so we had it fixed and started out once more. We had no more trouble on the road and Majel and I were talking so hard that we were at Chisago before we knew it. Driving into camp was so exciting! We honked the horns all the way up to the lodge and we were yelling at the top of our lungs. We went swimming while some of the others took showers. At supper we laughed so hard my stomach ached and all of us talked at once. Later around the evening fire we told some of our adventures and then we went to bed for a much needed rest—and so ends our trip of 850 miles!

Girls who went—
Mary Francis McCarthy, Josephine Burns, Mary Mott West, Naomi Briggs, Majel Espland, Mary Jane Hagen, Dorothy Peterson, Alice Gortner, Karen Daniels (Miss), Mary Lou Bryant (Miss), Louise Larson (Miss), Florence Jauss (Miss), Evelyn Lundquist (Miss), Ruth Toogood (Miss)

The Diary of Gwendolyn Wilson Fowler, 1936–1937

Gwendolyn Wilson was born on December 8, 1907, in Dard-enelle, Arkansas. In 1913 the Wilson family moved to Des Moines, Iowa, where her father, a physician, opened a practice. After attending Des Moines West High School, Gwendolyn attended Freedman Russ College in Holly Springs, Mississippi, which was the first college built for African Americans after the abolition of slavery. Upon her graduation from Russ College in 1926, Gwendolyn enrolled at the Drake Des Moines College of Pharmacy, where she earned her degree. She became Des Moines' first African American woman pharmacist.

During the 1930s, at the height of the Great Depression, she

Gwendolyn Wilson Fowler. By permission of the Iowa Women's Archives, University of Iowa Libraries.

moved to Chicago to look for work. She found none and returned to Holly Springs, Mississippi, where she taught seventh grade during the 1930–1931 academic year. After that she began earning her living by waiting tables. At a wedding at which she was working, she met Winnie Ewing Coffin, a wealthy Iowa woman who hired her to keep her apartment in order. When Mrs. Coffin decided to take a world tour to buy various art objects for the Des

Moines Art Center, she invited Gwendolyn Wilson to accompany her as her assistant. On this world tour Gwendolyn Wilson began the diary from which the excerpts here are taken. The world tour was cut short when Mrs. Coffin suffered a stroke, recovered enough to continue on the trip, then died in August 1937, while the two were traveling in Japan.

Following an eight-year marriage, Gwendolyn Wilson Fowler was employed from 1945 to 1955 by the State of Iowa as a pharmacist's clerk, then as a chemist. During the 1950s President Eisenhower appointed her to the U.S. Foreign Service, and she worked in Viet Nam for nearly five years, becoming the first African American woman from Iowa to be appointed to such a position. When she returned to Des Moines, she accepted a position at Broadlawns Polk County Hospital, where she worked until her retirement in 1974. According to an article that ran September 22, 1995, in the *Commentator*, a multicultural daily newspaper published in Des Moines, Gwendolyn Wilson Fowler was a lifelong member of the NAACP, was active in the American Association of University Women, volunteered for the American Red Cross, and served on numerous public commissions. In 1987 she was inducted into the Iowa Women's Hall of Fame. She was ninety when she died in November 1997.

The diary is formatted as a one-year diary, and it measures about four inches by five inches, with the remains of a broken lock and key. The diary contains a number of full-page entries, along with some shorter ones, a number of blank pages, and several snapshots inserted between pages. Gwendolyn Wilson began making entries in her diary on November 20, 1936, when she was nearly twenty-nine, and continued doing so throughout a good part of 1937. At times she wrote daily entries, while at other times she wrote sporadically or not at all. Her diary provides a glimpse of a world traveler's observations about cultural differences and race relations.

November 20, 1936. To night at 12:30 I set off on a journey of about 15 to 20 thousand miles of pleasure and what have you. It is a with a sad heart that I get on train but after a nice rest and sleep until 12.35 Sat. I am happy as a lark. . . .

[During December 1936, Gwendolyn traveled to Seattle, Vancouver, and Victoria, British Columbia. She wrote that her ship went out to sea in mid-December, that she was seasick at first, and that

she soon felt better than most of her fellow travelers. The ship's
first port of call was Honolulu.]

Thursday, December 24, 1936. To day is Xmas Eve on ship board
wrapped my presents and also those of Mrs. Coffin. Decorated our
rooms with holly and evergreen. Had a cocktail party to serve in the Mrs.
rooms. There were 11 came down stairs to a nice dinner of fowl. Wrote
some letters. Read my self to sleep with the book Lives and Times of
Edgar A. Poe. Clocks back 40 min.

Friday, December 2, 1936. Awake at 5 oclock to morning had a sad
feeling thinking how far away I was. Opened my presents from Agnes
and Mother. A diamond ring from Mother and cologne from Agnes.
They made me very happy. Went to Mrs. Coffins room and she gave me
$25.00 for the purchase of some thing I should like and a box of
hankies . . . . played bridge with my Chinese friends and had a lovely dinner of turkey and all the trimmings. To morrow we land in Yokohama.
Every one is happy about that. It is quite cool! Retire feeling I have had a
nice day. . . .

Thursday, December 31, 1936. A few more hours now and the year
1936 will be over. It has been a happy year and a very interesting one for
me. I spent 3 months at home. The 1st of the year in California for 4
months and Thanksgiving there. Summer at Spirit Lake and Xmas on
high seas and New Year's day in Hong Kong. I have had good health and
so has Mother. I want to offer my thanks and a grateful prayer to my creator. I met a American negro on ship to night from Shanghai on his way
to Marriliu. [He has] lived in Europe for the last 15 years and speaks
French and Italian. Looks like a Hawaiian. He let me know quietly who
he was and gave me a letter to some friends of his in Hong Kong. The
Chinese Doctor, The Indian and the French art and myself played bridge
to night to see the old year out.

Friday, January 1, 1937. Up early to get breakfast and get off at Hong
Kong. This is a lovely harbor. One of the prettiest in the world they say.
It is raining. We see lots of high mountains. We land at Kowloon which is
the main land and take a ferry over to Hong Kong which is an island. It is
lovely with the little Chinese sail boards made of paper very strong and
painted. Lots of British war ships here. This being a English city. We go
to the Hong Kong Hotel which is full. Lots of ships in to day. We come
to the Repulse Bay hotel. It is beautiful. Very high up in the mountains
over looking Repulse Bay. One of the worlds prettiest spots. I stroll take a
few pictures of it. Shanghai is a international city. All different settlements

and then a Chinese town and Grenhisburg from the city. It is very wicked. It is raining here. a bad day. . . .

Sunday, January 3, 1937. Mrs. Richmond out for the day. Mrs. Coffin and I went on the tram up to the peak. It goes straight up and back down. It is steep as any roller coaster I have been on. When we got to the end of the tram we took 2 chairs and 4 coolies took us the rest of the way. It was a beautiful sight. The harbor, the Island of Hong Kong and Kowloon. All at your feet. The ocean lies peaceful and calm the sun bright, the sail boards with orange sails dotted around and around you hills streets, homes dotted here and there. The view was great. It was nice and warm. No fog, a perfect day for the trip. We went looking in the windows and back to Repulse Bay. Saw lots of East Indians and their girl friends in bright colors dress, veils, and togas. Saw the governor-general's house.

Monday, January 4, 1937. Moving day again. We move into the Hong Kong Hotel this after noon. The rooms are larger. They have verandas and long doors. Talked to the Dixie Sister. Went to a movie to night to see Carole Lombard in My Man Godfrey at the Queens. Lots of sailors there. Sail from here 3 weeks from to day on a French boat for Saigon. . . .

Wednesday, January 6, 1937. Went to the Kings to see the Dixie Sisters show. It was great. They are very good tap dancers. Have lived in Europe for 3½ years. Home in Shanghai and will be leaving for home 16th. Had tea with them and back to work. . . .

Monday, January 18, 1937. Went to Canton to day. The largest Chinese owned city in China. It was really a revelation. The train there is less than a 3 hr ride. It is owned by British and has 3 classes 1st 2nd 3rd the British ride in 1st or 2nd the Chinese mostly 3rd. It makes 2 stops between H.K. and Canton. Shek Lung is one. This is where the train caught fire Sat and burned 77 Chinese to death and injured 300. We go to the Victoria Hotel in the British section and have lunch. . . .

Wednesday, January 20, 1937. To day I had a visit with Palmer Johnson by phone and he also called to see me in the late after noon for tea. We had quite a chat. It is nice to see one of your own race some time. Went to the movie that night to see an English picture. Operatic movie of "Hearts Desire." Very good. . . .

Thursday, January 28, 1937. [On the ship "Jean Laborde enroute to Saigon"] It is hot as hades. I could not sleep well. The French are so romantic so I must lock my door nights and it keeps out much air. The Hindu gives me a farewell buffet supper with every thing to go along. 1 French, Chinese, Hindu and my self.

Friday, January 29, 1937. Land at Saigon at 5 o'clock A.M. Make first stop to pick up pilot as the river is very dangerous where tide is not right so ships are always piloted in harbor. get dressed. get all bags packed and we get off at Saigon the wild, strange, wicked city of the world. Say good-bye to my Hindu friend. Lots of ricksha await us on the outside of ship. We take them to the Hotel Continental Palace. It is French and get to our rooms. I unpack, It is then the time for lunch. Have lunch in a large open dining rom where a mixture of French Italian, German, Indians, English and my self eat, happily receiving all the Chinese [food] put before us. It is the custom to sleep in the after noon until 3 every thing is closed from 11-3 for the heat. At 3:30 I go out walking go in some little shops, get a bracelet. Go to a side walk cafe and sit and sip ice cream soda and watch this folk. . . .

Tuesday, February 2, 1937. Up at 6 oclock breakfast and start for Ang Kor. Had a nice days driving. It was through dense jungle across the river Me Kong by ferry and stopped at a bunk house for tea. Arrived in Ang Kor at 1:45 o'clock. Have lunch, rest, unpack and get dressed for evening. We went to Ang Kor Wat at 8:30 P.M. for the Cambodian dances. They were grand. They were done in the same style and color that they were said to be done during the time of the Khmers (kings). They can get their fingers and feet in the most unusual shapes and yet it is very pretty and full of rhythm. They are made up and wear jewels in toes and top and bottom of their arm. They dance with a queer lifting slow rhythm not common to any other race unless it is the Balinese. The little boys meet you at the gate with fire torches and light your way to the palace. They are called flambogis. . . .

Sunday, February 7, 1937. Up at 3:00 get ready leave for Bangkok at 5 oclock by motor to Aranya the border town and get the train to the end of our journey We get to the border we were stopped by the Siamese customs agent. He was having his shower It was 7:30 oclock and much to all's disgust but we all waited. One man said to Mrs Richmond that you will have to wait and the less said the better, because you are in their country now. When the officer appear he was very good looking and young. He was very nice didn't open every thing and had quite a chat with me because of my color. We went to train put on luggage went to hotel had breakfast I went over to the little train (run on wood and runs very fast stops often) to see how the compartment was and the young gent came over to train and sat and chatted until train pulled out. The pass port official was ½ Jap and ½ Siamese. He came back to the compartment & stayed a long time and kissed my hand. We arrive in Bangkok at 5:10 hot hungry and tired. dry dusty trip.

I am asked a lot what I am. When they see an American passport they next think I am from Manila. When I say no they can't believe it. I have lots of fun with the natives because this is a colored country with colored officials everywhere. It is an agreeable change from so many white faces in America.

The people all look alike it seems. Women all have short hair (Siamese custom) Lots of cocoanut trees around. I saw lots of monks out today gathering in their food. They wear bright yellow draped robes heads shaven clean. Everything is given them. Their are 10,000 here. Went back in China town. Tomorrow every thing will be closed because of Chinese New Year. . . .

Friday, February 12, 1937. Up at 7 oclock get dressed to go visit the Palace of the King. The King a 12 year old boy is in Europe going to school. His father was forced to abdicate in favor of his son after they caught him as a traitor to the Siamese. The palace is beautiful. Here is a large building done in red and gold the throne room where large receptions are held, dressings rooms, red carpets, mother of pearl doors. Gold temples. lots of color[ed] mirrors, glass, etc., bronze marble . . . Saw the kings small reception room.. The Buddhist temple. It was lovely . . . In the Temple they have the famous Emerald Buddha 60 cm height. It is lovely. . . .

Sunday, February 14, 1937. Had a wonder nights sleep sans mosquitoes. I don't guess there will be anymore insects like Bangkok. The towns along the line have such queer names. Taking, Chan Junet, Tung Song. This is a pretty place from the train. A very large tall gold temple looks up in the back ground. We reach the border at 2 oclock this afternoon or 13.55 train time. Here time goes from 1 to 24 hours. Malayan time is 20 minutes faster than Siamese time. The Malaya states are federated and the races are much confused. You see Indians a plenty, Burmese, Ceylonese, Japanese, Chinese a plenty and of course Malayan. They all are much darker races than I have seen all along the way. In fact they are black 75% with very straight hair. The Indians and ones from Ceylon (men) wear their hair in a knot on top of their head and they wear the prettyish bright color sarongs. We arrive at 6 P.M. Take a ferry boat over to the island. . . .

Wednesday, February 24, 1937. Singapore. A Hindu holiday. I tried to get in an American office to get my toothe fixed but could not every thing closed. Everyone here celebrates everyone's holiday. bought some film met a nice Indian and others too. . . .

February 24, 1937. Singapore. A Chinese girl who run a shop, Rachel, came to see me. we had a long chat. She asked me to her room for afternoon tea. I went. The tea was good. Went down town for a ride. Mr. Hernand the Indian came to visit to night. He is very interesting and was full of information . . . We went to a garden party a feast and show. He a great lover. Weakens me. I bought a charming lacquer what not. . . .

Friday, February 26, 1937. At Singapore. Up early. Pack and get on ship for Sumatra. Leaving on a Dutch ship. Sailing at 10 oclock. It is a very large ship. very well built and is going to Amsterdam. It is full of Dutch. They are very rude people and are very fat or very tall. Not good looking and eat like animals. . . .

March 8, 1937. A stormy day. Every one in 2nd class sea sick except myself and 2 Dutchmen. One of them is quite charming with me. We had a long talk and exchanged views about the Dutch and American. We had some drinks before dinner. Hungarian wine. very good. Stayed up on deck until 10:30. We passed the straits and the active volcano on the Indian sea. It was some large affair setting out in the middle of sea. I was very glad to be away from it. I saw lots of flying fish.

March 9, 1937. Land at Java at 6:30. It is a lovely island. I went up on deck at 5 oclock to watch the sun rise and see us come into the harbor. It was a beautiful sight. The colors change so quickly a painter could not catch them. You can only remember their loveliness. We are at the Hotel Des Indes. . . .

Friday, March 27, 1937. Good Friday. To day at about 8:30 oclock we passed the island of Timor. A partnership island of the Portuguese and Dutch. It is very mountains and has several volcanic mountains on the isle. [The] length of the island is 20 miles . . . A few missionaries are there of course. It is noted for its little horses. . . .

Friday, April 2, 1937. Arrived at Brisbane to day at 3:30 . . . . I went ashore to see Brisbane. There was not much to see. A large spread out town. Houses built on sticks like the native houses, because of the terrible heat. Bought some flowers, and a few books. Went up on the highest peak of Brisbane and had a good look at the town. It s a great tea center and also wool. It was funny to see white people working and loading and unloading the ship after seeing natives do all of this work for so long.

They work here by union and system, no over time. They start at 8 and stop at 5 5½ days a week—no Sunday work. When I was going ashore 2 reporters stepped up and asked me for a picture. I refused. I guess they thought I was a news hound. . . .

Sunday, April 11, 1937. Had a nice taxi ride. Saw some more of the town. I have seen 6 colored people since I was here. I have found out there are many aborigines here in a camp. Lots of half castes are here. They are very ignorant. But I don't blame them. There are no schools open to them like are open to the Am. Negro. They can't be other wise. . . .

[The entries in the diary become shorter and more sporadic in April and May 1937, with some days passing with no entries.]

May 12, 1937. Coronation Day. Sydney. George VI. Went to the movie this after noon to see Greta Garbo in "Camille" with Robert Taylor. It was very good, but not so good as when Norma Talmadge played the leading role in the good old days. This evening I saw the huge fire works of the N.S.W. Celebration from the roof of the Australian Hotel. The bridge was lighted and the whole harbour and all the battle ships and ferrys. It was a beautiful display fire works a plenty. Huge rockets and cannons. A life size fire frame of the King and Queen was also displayed. Very good view of the entire city. The sun building was beautiful . . . The entire city was illuminated so that you thought you were on the great white way. Came down to my room and listened to the ceremony and felt happy and sad that so much care and responsibility may be thrust on 2's shoulders whether they like it or not. . . .

Friday, May 14, 1937. I had a long talk today with a real Australian full of real Australian phrases here are a few used in her conversation.

I'll spit me death	I'll beware
me face	my face
under done	rare meat
bushman	country people
sleep out	sleeping porches
domain dassers	bums

Thursday, May 20, 1937. Mrs. C Birthday. I gave a white chrochet bag. I made. She was quite pleased. No one else gave or said a word to her about it. It must be terrible lonesome for one to have so much money and no near friend to say happy birthday to you, yet they don't wish her a happy day. they just sit and wait for her to die and leave some thing to haggle over. She is one who has had so much money. never wanted for any thing, now a lonesome old lady. no one left, but she still keeps going. A brave person. . . .

Monday, May 24, 1937. Mrs. C. has a slight stroke and paralyzed her face on one side. It will be 6 or 8 weeks before she can leave the Dr. says, and she must be massaged 2 daily. B.p. 230. So we won't sail. Man can plan but God designs.

Saturday, May 29, 1937. To day was to be my sailing day, but instead I am caring for Mrs. Coffin who is here for 6 or 8 weeks from facial paraliss

[Gwendolyn Wilson made few entries in her diary during the spring of 1937. When she did make an entry, it tended to be only a few lines. In July 1937 her first diary entry gave one explanation for her inability to write regularly in her diary.]

Thursday, July 1, 1937. It has rained 41 days and 41 nights here now. To day is the 1st day of Mo. and first day of sunshine through out the day. I to day fainted. I have not gotten over that food poisoning of a fort night. The 3 Harmony Kings of Shuffle Along fame are here for an engagement. . . .

Saturday, July 17, 1937. Depart from Sydney. Leaving Sydney Australia after almost 4 months, on board H.M.S. Phangte. A very nice clean ship and a very nice bunch of folk in the 2nd class. A lady broke her arm as ship was leaving port. She is a very nice person too. Sorry to be leaving now. I was going strong in Sydney. Made a lot of friends and really enjoyed my stay, but for so much illness. . . .

The Diary of Ruth Van Horn Zuckerman, 1967

A native of Kalamazoo, Michigan, Ruth Van Horn was the daughter of Samuel Hale and Laura Mills Van Horn. Ruth had a younger sister, Marian, and a younger brother, Wesley. Ruth attended elementary school in Kalamazoo and graduated from Kalamazoo Central High School. After earning her bachelor's and master of arts degrees at the University of Michigan in Ann Arbor, she completed postgraduate work at Columbia University, Stanford University, and the University of London.

Ruth Van Horn Zuckerman, 1962. Courtesy Jerome Zuckerman.

In 1942 Alan Swallow, the founder of Swallow Press, published Ruth Van Horn's first book of poetry, entitled *Crooked
Eclipse,* and she began teaching English and humanities courses at
Western Michigan University. During World War II she worked at
the U.S. Army Signal Corps in Washington, D.C. After the war
she returned to Western Michigan University, where she continued
to teach courses in English and the humanities.

On October 20, 1962, Ruth Van Horn married Dr. Jerome
Zuckerman. In 1964 the couple moved to Mankato, Minnesota,
where they lived for more than twenty-five years. A prolific poet,
Ruth Van Horn Zuckerman published her work in such venues as
the *Denver Quarterly,* the *Nation,* and the *New Republic.* She and

her husband taught courses at Mankato State College, and she was active in community organizations, including the American Association of University Women.

Over the years the Zuckermans traveled widely in Europe, Asia, and the Caribbean. She often kept diaries during their journeys, and the excerpts printed here come from the journal she kept while they traveled in England in August 1967. Ruth had traveled and lived abroad; this was, however, her husband's first trip to England. Throughout their journey she penned a number of descriptive and introspective diary entries of one to three pages each. Many entries comment on visits to historic places and offer playful comments on her husband's reactions as a first-time visitor to England. Ruth Van Horn Zuckerman was a keen observer of people, and in her diary she often reflected on the nature of human beings and on her relationships with others. Her diary, a Standard Miniature Blank Book, measures about five by seven inches and contains 152 lined pages, nearly all of which are filled with neatly written entries.

In 1984 *From the Ravine,* the second volume of her poems, was published. The title poem reflects many of the same themes about which she wrote in her 1967 England diary:

> The poplars extend their fingers,
> witch-like, to a dimming sun.
> Except for one slim maple that
> staunchly holds its burnished leaves
> in silent protest of the season,
> the trees in the ravine are showing black, foreshadowing sharp winds
> and tricky ice.
>
> Even now I seem to see a northwest wind
> begin to swirl the maple leaves'
> false summer into the leafmould ground.
> The sun slides to another hemisphere.
> From the ravine, I learn there is a time for letting go.

After a long illness Ruth Van Horn Zuckerman died on November 2, 1991. Her diary remains in the possession of her husband, who gave his permission to include these excerpts in this collection.

Merrie Olde England (Or Beloved England), August 1967

Dartmouth House English Speaking Union, London. August 1, 1967. Jerry is ecstatic! He is in England, now hoping he will hear a nightingale sing. He is more likely to hear an elevator come gasping up on the other side of the wall near his bed. It sounds exactly like a person getting ready to vomit.

We spent most of the day preparing for and succumbing after a fifty-five minute flight from Amsterdam to London. The KLM airport in Amsterdam is large, modern, and beautiful. It has the best duty-free shopping center on the continent. I bought a newspaper and six postcards with our remaining coins.

Then we got into a tourist plane with a Globus Tour from the U.S. A very nice high school boy from a town near Mankato sat with us. But we were mobbed in getting our passports stamped and there was much confusion in finding our bags and getting on a limousine after J. had got our English money. It was raining but very warm. Another struggle for a taxi before we reached Dartmouth House. . . .

Jerry just wondered what I had to write about because "we just wasted a day in travel really." But now he wants to live in England; this morning he would have settled in Amsterdam. Now he thinks England is more "civilized." Fortunately, he likes the English-Speaking Union and claims the dinner we had in the dining room the best we've had in Europe, though there were a couple other meals that were good.

Our room is spacious, on the fourth floor and at times a walk-up because someone hasn't closed the elevator (lift) doors. We are hearing an accordian, instead of nightingales, playing Charmain. Down the street is a pub called Samuel Pepys. And so to bed.

"You're in London, Jerry. Pinch yourself."

ESU, London, August 3. When we set out to buy an umbrella yesterday morning, it was raining, and we walked. Britts had been recommended to us, but the umbrellas started at £12; so we found a lady's umbrella at Fortnum and Mason's for around £7.00, which I still think is too much to pay for an umbrella. This is a neat little black affair. I bought Jerry a guidebook of London at Hatchard's. It is not too helpful. The movie of Joyce's Ulysses is playing here. As it is widely censored in Minneapolis and plays only a few days at a time, we decided to get tickets for today. We finally had to take a cab to the Academy Theatre and then have the driver bring us back to Dartmouth House. We went to the Snack Bar at Concord House and then slept.

There is a little mall near here and I took two Ektachrome films over to be processed and we had tea at a little shop there. Jerry likes cress sandwiches and was delighted when the maker of them called him "dear." He was shocked today when another barmaid called a man "Love". . . .

Then we walked to the Academy, where we saw <u>Ulysses.</u> The acting was excellent and one felt a good deal of sympathy for Leopold Bloom and Stephen Daedalus. Jerry did also for Molly though he agreed with me that her soliloquy was too long. He did not think it a "dirty" show. We were both disappointed. I followed the story better than I had anticipated, for I have not read the novel in years. Bloom and Stephen were very realistic and I could mostly tell what was actually happening and what was stream-of-consciousness. The movie was more comic than the book, but the tragedy was also there. For me too much was left out. I think the lead was given too much to Bloom, especially in the brothel scene, and not enough to Stephen.

We were out about five-thirty and walked through Soho. Carnaby Street is now the fashion center of London, that is for the teen-agers. I must go back to take some pictures, for no one in his right mind could imagine the strange get-up, the absurd and horrible mixture of colors. We saw a good many long-haired, bearded boys in Amsterdam, but their hair is conventionally cut compared to many I've seen in London. While girls' hair may be straight, the boys are wearing theirs long and curled. I swear many of them wear wigs. . . .

E.S.U. London, August 4th 3:00 P.M. Jerry and I just returned from a bus tour to Sloane Square and a walking tour through Chelsea. I took pictures of eight different houses on or near Cheyne Walk. No. 4 George Eliot died; Rossetti and Swinburne lived in No. 46. We went through Carlyle's home at No. 24, Cheyne Row. It is one of the few houses that has been restored with the writer's own belongings. I was there long ago with Marion Terpenning, who is now dead, as is Walter. I remember how fond of Carlyle Mr. Sprau, my old English teacher, was. . . .

We nearly took Bus 19 the wrong way, but an old man overheard our conversation and told us the stop was across the street. We got off at Green Park and stopped on Landsdowne Row at The Nightingale for tea. The woman who called Jerry "dear" remembered him and asked if we were having a good holiday.

E.S.U. London August 5. 9:30 P.M. We have been going around honoring the dead and now, with peculiar poignancy, I am going home to it. I wish I could write as well as Keats though I certainly do not belong to the romantic school. Keats is one of the few who could write of their own emotions without becoming sickeningly sentimental or self-pitying. This morning Jerry and I took buses to Hampstead Heath to see Keats House, the last home in which he lived before going to Italy to die. It is in a beautiful setting and has many of his own books and manuscripts. Jerry feels his spirit hovers over the house.

We came back to the E.S.U. to find an airmail letter from (Mother) Marian peculiar mistake. I fingered it while Jerry was looking for dinner here and said, "I hope it's not bad news." Jerry said, "I don't know why it should be." It was the letter, in Marian's very concise style, which I have been expecting all summer. Wes couldn't reach Mother on the telephone and called Marian and Jim. "We went down, found her in the bedroom dead."

In a sense she has been dead for nearly two years, but the realization that she isn't is difficult to grasp. Jerry offered to give up the remainder of our trip. I said, "No, we'll go on as we planned, but I will have to go to Kalamazoo when we get back to Chicago." He said he would go with me. For some time I couldn't think what I should write Marian . . . After dinner we got a stamp from the desk and walked over to the post office. . . .

E.S.U. London Monday, Aug. 7. This has been a long, drizzly day. At least I dragged about. We took a bus to Bloomsbury and walked some distance to the Dickens House on Doughty Street. I saw the Dickens House several years ago. There is something vulgar and common about it compared with the Keats House. I saw Bradford Place, where I spent a month in August 1951 and met Gordon and Robert Thomson. It looked to me as though all those buildings had been torn down and new ones built in their places. The pension at which I had stayed had been bombed. Theobald Road, which had been badly destroyed is more spacious, with new buildings. I am very conscious of change in many facets of life right now. Jerry went through the Dickens House but I sat in the parlor. I saved two shillings and several staircases . . .

Wild Boar Hotel, Crook. August 11, 1967. 10:30 P.M. Jerry and I have not seen any Americans all day . . . The bus was crowded, but we were fortunate enough to get a front seat. The countryside is "gorgeous" . . . great rolling expanses of green grass and trees with occasional fields of burnished yellow grain.

The rest stop, where Jerry bought sandwiches, was a barren and cold spot but we saw how the busing population of Yorkshire travel—with bags and parcels and children and dolls.

The Windermere stop was merely a covered sidewalk. Jerry stayed with the bags while I crossed to the railway station to inquire about trains to Chester on Sunday. As I had expected, there is none. A taxi driver had greeted me cordially. When I said I was from the States, he answered, "I had gathered that, Madam." I went to another bus station and learned we would have to take a bus to Liverpool, where we change for Chester. I

315

suppose we could get a train from Liverpool. The taxi driver brought us, about ten miles, over to the Wild Boar Hotel, a spreading white stucco affair built on a split level. Our room, a small one with bath, is in the back so that we see only hills. . . .

It has rained off and on all day with a rare, dim sun. The sun was shining when we woke up so we dressed and took a delightful walk down a lane which had a brook babbling beside it and little springs gushing into the stream.

We dressed and had dinner after eight. Poor Jerry spilled gravy from the lamb onto his gray suit and is in despair. We had Poached Eggs Florentine and I must try to make them. They were served on a sea shell with spinach and a cream sauce. Delicious.

Wild Boar Hotel, Aug. 12 9:00 P.M. We caught a bus outside the hotel and went to Bowness, which is on Lake Windermere, at 9:21 this morning. Then we had to bus to Windermere, wait some time and take another to Grasmere. The little towns and the mountains and water are "gorgeous," as the English say nowadays about everything lovely or interesting. Then we walked to Dove Cottage, where Wordsworth lived with [his sister] Dorothy and his wife Mary. The place has changed considerably since I first saw it and seemed to have more of his things in it. We also visited the museum, which had many manuscripts and first editions of not only Wordsworth's writings but also those of Coleridge. It had been raining with few "sunny spells" until we came out of the cottage. I took a few pictures. Then we walked to the center of Grasmere and had pork pies at a Red Lion pub. Sat in a green and watched some canary-like birds and took a bus back to Windermere and another to Bowness, where we had tea at The Spinnery. For over an hour we sat on a bench with some Boy Scouts, waiting for the bus back to the hotel. It came, changed its signs further down the street, turned around, picked up some people and disappeared up a side street. We chased around the launch or excursion office and could get no information, so we took another bus back to Windermere, where fortunately there were taxis and after a few trying moments we finally got back to the hotel, where we had a delicious dinner. . . .

The Mitre Hotel, High Street, Oxford, Aug. 17. . . . Now I am writing in a delightfully large room, which Queen Adelaide, the consort of King William IV, used to inhabit when she visited Oxford. The room is in the 17th century style, the fireplace probably being the original. The fireplace is grey stone, eight to ten feet wide, now with a little electric inset which I have enjoyed, for the air is chill. The entire room is paneled in black walnut, with stucco approximately two feet from its beamed ceiling.

There are two beds, five chairs, a sofa, two wardrobes, a chest, a dressing table and a writing desk and full length standing mirror beside the tables. Still we did not feel crowded; so one has some conception of the size of the room. One end of the room is almost given to two windows over which hang rich brocaded red curtains with a valence.

Tuesday night—when I left off—we saw Paul Scofield and Vivien Merchant, Harold Pinter's wife, in <u>Macbeth</u>. The witches and the opening scene were marvelous and frightfully convincing. At first I did not like Lady Macbeth; later she seemed better, but I do not think she was an entire success. At times Scofield was excellent, but I liked him better as Sir Thomas More in <u>A Man For All Seasons</u>. Some people think the halting way he read the lines was not his natural style but the fault of the director, Peter Hall. Nobody at the Haytor, whom I overheard, was completely satisfied with the performance. Jerry thinks many of the faults lie intrinsically in the play. . . .

Wednesday morning we walked to the bus station and took a bus to Coventry. We had already discovered the Cathedral was very near. It was our extreme good fortune that the sun came out as brilliantly as it has any time since we've been in England, and I took a number of pictures of the exterior of the new Cathedral and the interior of the walls of the old bombed one. The two have been so spaced that they make a complete and harmonious whole symbolizing the great tragedy of our suffering from war today and man's persistent attempt to gain peace . . . the tall shafts of heavy stained glass inside, the chapel of Gethsemene, where one looks at Christ through a wrought iron crown of thorns is shattering. The entire Cathedral is <u>gorgeous</u>, in my strong, reserved meaning of the word.

Jerry's reaction surprised me. He said nothing has moved him so much since Hiroshima. . . .

Chose Hotel, Ross-on-Wye, Sun. Aug. 20th. We awoke to fog but fortunately it cleared early and we had sun most of the time, for the first time since we reached England. This was certainly an easier Sunday than last, for we left our bags here and are spending our second night in Ross. We spent most of the day riding through pastoral lanes, very green fields and forests with sheep and cattle grazing, hedgerows at the sides of the narrow, curving roads. First we drove through Hereford and crossed the Uze River into Wales. Very narrow tall bridges. . . .

After lunch, I talked with a rather plump, gray haired but attractive woman from Durban, South Africa. She had never heard of Nadine Gordimer. I asked her about conditions in South Africa. She said everything was quiet there, implied newspapers give false information, only the very lowest class cause trouble, the Negroes are well-treated and well-fed, working in white homes. They are a happy people but need to be educated. Their hygiene is bad. She is surprised to see other whites carrying burdens here. In South Africa the Negroes do that. Although she implied that there is no intermarriage, she spoke of "coloreds," who I have always understood from my reading are mixed races. She spoke approvingly of apartheid and Molly Outhwaite, from New Zealand, said there was no difficulty in New Zealand and there is apartheid. I made no comment but said I didn't know what was to be done about the race riots in the States. I don't.

The South African woman is traveling with a good looking older man who appears very stately. He also always sits by the window and I have never heard him utter a word. She has a very cultivated voice. Someone told me he is her "friend," so I don't know whether they are married or not. He took off his suit coat this afternoon and there is a large tattoo on one of his arms. We have had less contact with them than with anybody else. . . .

Now we are almost packed to leave for Bath tomorrow. Jerry is very happy about this tour and likes everyone on it. That is always a relief to me, for he is impossible when he doesn't like people . . . He is sorry that two days are over of the nine, and hoping people think he is very British. Actually he is just Jerry.

Smithbourne Hotel, Bath, Mon. Aug. 21. This is the best day that I have had in England. There has been sun all day and I've been warm. We had breakfast with the same people whom we were with last night . . . We took a motor boat trip in an old boat through rather muddy water. The most interesting part of the trip was the guide, who couldn't have been much over fifteen. But he spoke very well. He lingered around there until eleven and then drove to Chepstow for lunch. Just before we got there we passed the ruins of Tintern abbey, which Wordworth wrote about. Jerry's usually hot hand became very cold and he said later a chill went through him. The standing walls with the empty spaces where the stained glass was at the altar end was very impressive. . . .

This is definitely a working man's tour. On the Galleon bus there are the letters WTA and Betty asked us yesterday if we booked through the Workers Travel Agency. We are very careful not to tell Jerry's occupation . . .

Bay Hotel, Falmouth, Aug. 24. I was awake and kept Jerry awake most of the night. He should write this day's episode, for more happened to him than to me. I didn't get up for breakfast and spent most of the day in bed. Jerry went with the group to Lands' End, St. Ives, etc., but did not seem to find the scenery especially exciting . . . I tried to sleep but didn't more than half an hour. Then I began trying to pick up some threads in my Yugoslavian journal. I reread parts of the Viennese accounts and found myself a rather horrid person. Well, I feel horrid!

It was a gray day but about four o'clock the sun began to shine dimly. I dressed, took my camera and went out the back way . . .

Rembrandt Hotel, Friday, Sept. 1 4:15. Mother would have been 87 today if she had lived, Father 92 tomorrow. What distresses me most about her death is that she really never had a <u>good</u> life.

Yesterday, we took two buses to get to the British Museum. We looked at only the Elgin Marbles from the Parthenon. Jerry never gets the least bit enthusiastic about them, and I wished I didn't take him there. I tried to imagine them back on the Acropolis, where they rightfully belong.

We ate at the Museum Tavern, where I went for so many meals in 1951. The downstairs looked the same but the upstairs restaurant, where we ate, seemed very drab. Another example of lost magic.

Then we walked some distance to find the Russell Square underground and got to Leicester Square, where we saw the movie of Sidney Poitier and Rod Steiger in <u>In The Heat of the Night</u>. A little disappointing, for in it the whites are prejudiced against and the Negro is the hero, a police officer from Philadelphia, who finds himself arrested for murder in a little back-water Mississippi town. There are more good scenes, but the plot is too contrived. . . .

Rembrandt Hotel, Sat., Sept. 2. . . . Today, Saturday, I dragged Jerry to Westminster Abbey and the Tate Gallery. He was glad he went, for we found T.S. Eliot's grave in the Poet's Corner, ironically buried near Tennyson and Browning. One has to pay to see the Royal Chapel, where the kings and queens are buried and tour groups were lined up. I refused to go, for I have little sympathy with the egotism of royalty. . . .

The following quotation from <u>The Four Quartets</u> is on Eliot's burial stone in Westminster Abbey: "The communication of the dead is tongued with fire beyond the language of the living." . . .

Rembrandt Hotel, London, September 4. This is my last entry in this journal, for we leave before noon tomorrow for the States. The plane leaves at 12:30 P.M. . . . It was a beautiful fall day with brilliant sunshine such as I have seldom seen in England. The Odeon is near Hyde Park and it was unusually beautiful . . .

So farewell, England. I'm going home and another era of my life begins with the end of this journey.

Home, Work, Family
4

This chapter includes diaries that describe the daily lives of women from various economic classes and from a variety of geographical locations, work environments, and family settings. Several of these diaries (those by Antoinette Porter King, Lillian S. Carpenter, Maud Hart Lovelace, Ruby Butler Ahrens, and Juanita Ahrens) recount daily work within the home, on the farm, at the office, store, or school. Others (those by Maria Morton Merrill and Carol Johnson) explore family relationships, and several (those by Jennie B. Andrews, Martha Smith Brewster, and Sandra Gens) have their genesis in the death of a family member and the effect of that death on the survivors—the diarist herself and those around her.

This chapter also includes diaries kept as various kinds of family or communal records. Two diaries (those by the Eliza and J. Talmai Hamilton family, and the Lucinda and Edward Holton family) were undertaken with the intention of creating family chronicles, and the Wisconsin families who kept these diaries were conscious of their texts as collaborative efforts that would be shared among family members. Two diaries in this chapter are chronicles (also called annals) kept by orders of religious women living and teaching in two small Iowa towns; one diary was kept by the School Sisters of Notre Dame during the mid- to late nineteenth century, and the other was kept by the Sisters of St. Francis during the latter part of the twentieth century. These diaries were also meant to be communal texts, shared by the members of the family of women religious who lived, worked, and prayed together.

The diaries included in this chapter have one common thread: the transmission of family and cultural values among a family or community's members and the survival of those values from one generation to another.

The Diary of the Eliza and J. Talmai Hamilton Family, 1837–1851

The Hamilton family diary represents a cooperative effort by several members of a Wisconsin family to create a record of their family life that would span several decades during the nineteenth century. Marianne Eliza Neill was born in Lansing, New York, on March 8, 1818, to Elizabeth (Jacobs) and Tillyer Neill. When she was ten, her parents separated, and she went to live with an aunt, who helped her get an education. At seventeen Eliza Neill began teaching school and working in a mill to help support her family. She began keeping a diary just after her nineteenth birthday. Five years later she married John Talmai Hamilton, who was born in Lansing, New York, on September 15, 1815, to Elizabeth (Bower) and William Hamilton, also of Lansing. Eliza and Talmai were married on September 25, 1842, at the Methodist church in Lansingville, New York.

On June 5, 1843, the Hamiltons headed west to the Wisconsin Territory and, upon their arrival, settled on eighty acres near Whitewater and began to farm. Four children were born to them: Frederic Brown, Philena Gould, Talmai Neill, and William Tillyer. Eliza Neill Hamilton died on October 20, 1851, of "enteric fever" (typhoid fever). She was thirty-three. Her widower remarried on January 21, 1855, at Whitewater. His second wife, Amelia (Dubremont) Pinkerton Chamberlain, had two sons from a previous marriage. Amelia and Talmai Hamilton had three children of their own: Rea, Eliza, and Dewey. On January 3, 1900, Talmai Hamilton died in Harvard, Illinois, at the age of eighty-four.

The Hamilton family diary begins with a preface by J. Talmai

Hamilton in which he addresses his children, explaining to them that, four years before she died, their mother had begun to keep a record (as a continuation of her long-time diary) of family activities so that, when the children were grown, they would have these memories written down. The hardbound book in journal format measures approximately eight by eleven inches and contains 523 pages, all filled with single-spaced handwritten entries in ink.

My Dear Children,

A little more than three years previous to the death of your dear mother, she commenced keeping a brief record of the most interesting and important occurrences that transpired in our little family. The chief design in doing this was that, when you were grown up, you might have some knowledge of what you said and did when you were little children, and also to present a brief history of events, as they took place in the family. After she commenced doing this, your Father suggested the idea to her, of having a short history of our lives written in connection with what she wrote in the form of a diary, or daily journal. She approved of the plan without hesitation, but it was procrastinated and consequently was not done while she was living. And now that she has been taken from you, when you were so young that you will have little or no knowledge of her in any other way, your Father feels it to be of ~~some~~ great importance that a history of her life should be written for your sake especially; that you may know what an excellent mother you had and be made acquainted with the intense anxiety which filled her mind, that you might be good, useful and happy. In this way, though she is dead, yet she will speak to you with more than an audible voice . . .

In the month of March of the year 1837, she commenced keeping a register of her daily thoughts, together with the events of her life, which is copied in this place, as it will give a better history of her life than can be given in any other way.

Tuesday, March 21st, 1837. This day I commence to continue through the year, a register of thoughts and events, thinking that it will be both for my improvement and pleasure, in future years (should I live) to look on this little manuscript, and recall thoughts and feelings, and events, long forgotten; and which, perhaps, could never have been recalled, but for this little memento. Attended this afternoon, a little party at Mr. Morehouse's, consisting principally, of my former schoolmates. Had a very pleasant visit. Before we left, Miss Bates remarked that this was the first time that her scholars had, so many of them, met under her roof, and it would probably be the last time, that we should all meet under similar circumstances, and she admonished us in view of the transitory nature of earthly things, to do our work while the day lasted, and always to be ready, not only to do what our duty bid us, but to be ready to leave those duties, whenever God was pleased to call us from them. Attended a lecture on Slavery, this evening, and joined a society which was instituted for the diffusion of light on the subject of Slavery, and for a union of influence on that subject, which may operate on the minds of slaveholders at the south, and the friends of Slavery in the north. The question often arises in my mind, when about to join any such society, What good can I do? How can I forward the cause? Can I a poor, lone individual, by the magic of my name, induce any one to flee from error, and to embrace the truth? But again, I recollect, that the world is composed of individuals, and that the union of individual influence, is the great moral machinery, by which any mighty revolution in public sentiment, must take place, if it ever is accomplished. For it is public sentiment, with which such associations have to do. And even if the society fails to accomplish its object, yet if that object be a good one, I cannot think of any culpability in trying to promote its interests.

[Eliza Neill's diary entries continued for several months during 1837, then ceased for a time. According to her husband, in 1838, when Eliza was twenty-one, she was saved; a year later she joined the Presbyterian Church. She began teaching sabbath school in Ithaca but soon went to the town of Ludlowville, New York, to work at the loom and teach at a small school until April 1840. She met Talmai Hamilton on December 14, 1839, and they soon began their courtship.]

Monday, June 8, 1840. Received this afternoon a visit from T___ H___ who professed an affectionate interest in my welfare, and laid before me a most important subject, for my consideration. O may the Lord show me my duty, and direct me in the way of all truth. O Lord I would commit my ways to Thee, and do Thou direct my steps. I know thou wilt, if I will only trust in Thee, and do my duty. . . .

August 29, 1848. A few days ago, our little son Frederic met with an accident, which I fear will injure him during life. He was so naughty as to have some contention with another boy, who kicked him, or hit him in some other way so severely, as to cause a rupture in the lower part of his abdomen. May my little son learn from this, that it is dangerous to quarrel or to fight, and may he never again raise his hand, or his foot to do another harm. May he remember that God loves those who are mild, and peaceable, and kind, and may he look to the Lord for grace to become so. . . .

Sept. 20, 1848. The birth-day of our little Philena. She is now two years old—a lively, affectionate child,—but she does not try to talk much yet. If a question is asked her, she gives her affirmation in a whispered "heh" (yes). But if the subject displeases her, she can give a most emphatic "<u>No</u>." Ah may we have grace so to train her, that as her years pass successively away, we may see that she has improved, both in mind and heart. . . .

Jan. 14, 1849. Freddy and Philena are both improving rapidly. Freddy has become quite a reader. He can now read little stories for himself without much assistance, and he has lately read several little books through; from which he has obtained many important ideas. I am laboring assiduously to impress religious truth upon his mind. He understands much about God, and his duties to God and to his fellow creatures, but I am afraid this knowledge does not much affect his heart. O may the Holy Spirit impress truth upon his heart, and lead him early to the Saviour. Philena can now communicate nearly all her ideas in an intelligible manner. She imitates all that she hears her "<u>bullah</u>" (brother) say, and they take much pleasure in repeating sentences after one another, or in concert . . . .

January 1851. "The sun shines bright, The moon makes it light, The hills and rocks, and mountains are so far away, Don't you want to go to that Heaven, pretty place."

The Diary of the Lucinda and Edward Holton Family, 1845–1904

Like the Hamilton family diary, the diary of the Lucinda and Edward Holton family represents a cooperative effort by several individuals to create a record not only for themselves but also for future generations. Edward Holton, born on April 28, 1815, was one of eight children in the family of Mary (Fisk) and Joseph Holton. Lucinda, born Lucinda Millard on August 28, 1824, was one of twelve children in the family of Jessie and Lucinda Millard. On October 14, 1845, Lucinda Millard and Edward Holton were married. Shortly after their marriage they made a joint decision to begin keeping what they called their "Family diary," in which they proposed "to record and make memorandum from time to time of such events & incidents as may occur in an individual or united history." In the diary they recorded births, deaths, family activities, and genealogical information. The Holtons lived in Milwaukee, where their three daughters, Alice, May, and Harriette, were born. Over the years both Lucinda and Edward Holton continued to make entries in the diary. Eventually their daughters too began writing in the family diary, which continued for more than sixty years, from 1845 to 1909. Diary entries were made periodically and generally marked events that were considered milestones in the family's life.

On April 21, 1892, Edward Holton died in Savannah, Georgia, while returning from the family's winter home in Florida. His obituary stated that he had come to Milwaukee in 1840 and worked for the Milwaukee and Mississippi Railroad as manager and fiscal agent. From 1852 to 1861 he was president of Farmers' & Millers' Bank. He was also the vice president and manager of the Northwestern Life Insurance Co. His obituary described him as a staunch abolitionist. He was survived by Lucinda, his three daughters, their spouses, and several grandchildren. Members of the Holton family continued to make entries in the Holton family diary until 1909.

[1845] . . . After mutual consultation we have concluded to commence this book calling it as for its label upon the back "Family diary" in which it is proposed to record and make memorandum from time to time of such events & incidents as may occur in an individual or united history. [entry by Edward Holton]

Jan. 4, 1848. Tuesday Evening. This is a most important epoch of time in our family history. By the good providence of God it commemorates the time of our becoming parents. Two well formed and beautiful female children each weighing eight pounds and looking singularly like each other were born to us but one of them however it is painful to add lost its life in the severe struggles of nature which it encountered in the birth. [entry by Edward Holton]

Jan. 25, 1848. Lucinda rode out today for the first time since her sickness, baby doing well—no name for the baby yet. It seems to be a difficult matter to fix upon the name. [entry by Edward Holton]

March 1848. Weigh the baby tonight—weighed 15 pounds being eight weeks old this Evening. Is a healthy and thrifty child—without a name. [entry by Edward Holton]

We are enjoying a fine run of sleighing the first we have had this winter! Also a very pleasant visit from Mr. Shales of Green bay. Took the baby out to ride for the first second time called at Mr. Goodalls and Mrs. Loves . . . [entry by Lucinda Holton]

[April 1848] Baby ten weeks old today weighed 15 pounds, sleeps in her cradle at night getting up but once to nurse. We conclude to call the baby Alice Millard [entry by Lucinda Holton]

Aug. 26, 1849. [Our daughter Mary] was born on the morning of the 13th of May 1849 from a comparatively easy & rapid confinement . . . The family physician Dr. Bartlett administered ether to the mother which was regarded as a very valuable agent in assuaging the pain and aiding nature in this most severe of all the conflicts she calls her children to pass through . . . The child weighed seven pounds. [entry by Edward Holton]

Feb. 24, 1851. Lucinda gave birth at 2 past 2 pm to our fifth child & third living child. I was away ~~from home~~ three miles & was unable to reach home until after the birth—a healthy well formed fine looking female child. [entry by Edward Holton]

Feb. 23, 1852. After a long and unusual neglect of this journal I again resume it . . . It is late in the evening. My children are sleeping and in perfect health. Oh what gratitude I ought to feel for so many blessings. I often think there was scarce ever an individual who had so many blessings. What a contrast in my estimation to that of a poor slave mother who is obliged to relinquish her hearts treasures to the mercy of a cruel and oppressive master. How long shall the vengeance of Heaven sleep over such inequity? [entry by Lucinda Holton]

Jan. 21, 1853. At 3 o'clock PM of this day Lucinda gave birth to a daughter. Dr. Bartlett the officiating physician. Sister Sarah Millard the Mrs. Kilmer assisting. The infant weighed 6 1/2 lbs and slight in its formation but very pretty in its features irregular in its formation. Ether was administered to the patient with gratifying results. Lucinda doing remarkably well— [entry by Edward Holton]

March 3, 1853. " 'Tis but a step from the cradle to the tomb." The last record made in this book was of the birth of an infant. The next is of its death. She was left with us but four weeks sufficiently long however to have entwined herself closely in our affections. She was a beautiful flower but frail and delicate. Inflammation of the lungs caused by a sudden cold was the cause. Her sickness was very brief but one day. Though young it is a great loss particularly to me as I had almost the entire care of her from her birth. But I feel that it is infinite gain to her having escaped the contamination of this world while pure and sinless. She died on the 1st of March. [entry by Lucinda Holton]

Jan. 24, 1869. On this quiet, neutral gray Sabbath Day, I came across this Family Diary and for an hour or two have been lying here, reading it. I find here a record of my birth. Seventeen years ago I opened my eyes to look life in the face. Seventeen years, bright, beautiful and happy years, clouded to be sure with passing shadows, but so slight that in the retrospect they seem nothing. What have I to record? Nothing very eventful has ever happened to me. School and parties, friendships and all the commonplace et ceteras of a schoolgirl's life fleck the pages of my life history. In turning the leaves, one page always arrests me with its brightness. It is the page telling of my year in Europe. It was a beautiful year and the happiest of my life.

I have lived all my life in this beautiful city of Milwaukee. I love it and never want to live anywhere else. —Harriette Holton

Oct. 14, 1870. The twenty fifth anniversary of our marriage! How the years have flown! Freighted with the various experiences of life. But the joys have far outnumbered the sorrows and to night we have to return a thank offering for a married life filled up with unnumbered blessings from our kind Heavenly Father. What will the next twenty five years bring to us? We know not; and tis well we do not; but we will go forward trusting to His guidance and fearing nothing while thus led. [entry by Edward Holton]

Aug. 28, 1904. I am eighty years old to day; a long life has been granted me, and it has been filled with blessings immeasurable; few I think have had so much sunshine in their lives as I. It could not be otherwise, with such a husband & such children as were given me. May I be enabled to spend the residue of life in gratified fidelity to my Heavenly Father the giver of all good. [entry by Lucinda Holton]

The School Sisters of Notre Dame, 1865–1894

The School Sisters of Notre Dame (SSND), dedicated to the education of poor girls, was founded in 1833 in Neunburg, Germany, by Sister Mary Theresa of Jesus (born Caroline Gerhardinger). In 1847 Mother Theresa brought Sister Caroline Friess and four other sisters to the United States to teach the children of German emigres. The order began teaching in parish schools throughout the eastern United States; soon the sisters' work spread to Milwaukee, where their first North American province was established. Mother Theresa returned to Germany. From the SSND Motherhouse in Milwaukee, Mother Caroline Friess traveled throughout the United States and Canada, considering missions in which the sisters might teach.

One of the first SSND missions in Iowa was established at St. Donatus, a small village settled primarily by Luxembourger immigrants and located along the Mississippi River, a dozen miles south of Dubuque. Several School Sisters of Notre Dame left Milwaukee, arriving in St. Donatus on October 27, 1865. The chronicle kept by the school sisters during their work in St. Donatus (1865–1968) was intended to be a communal record of the religious community. Customarily, one sister would write entries in the chronicle throughout the school year.

Entries describe the sisters' arrival at St. Donatus, the challenges of their first decades of teaching, changes in staffing as sisters were transferred in and out of the parish, and occasional power struggles between townspeople and religious. The chronicle, one of the best historical sources on the village of St. Donatus, includes detailed accounts of the deaths of two beloved figures—the long-time parish pastor, Father J. M. Flammang, and Sister Superior Mary Sebastiana, who had devoted herself to making the mission at St. Donatus a thriving religious community. The handwritten "Chronicle of the School Sisters of Notre Dame at St. Donatus," and a typescript, are housed in the regional motherhouse in Mankato, Minnesota.

Oct. 27, 1865 set out from Milwaukee Rev. Father Krautbauer, Sisters M. Mathara, M. Joseph von Cupertino, Candidate Wilhelmina Wehrheim to Freeport, Il, to Galena, crossing turbulent river to Dubuque . . . Then a wagon drawn by two white horses also appeared. Two trunks were loaded on the wagon. The other two were kept back until Monday as it happened to be Saturday. We placed ourselves on the wagon with the trunks. The priests went in a buggy and so we drove to St. Donatus.

When the Reverend Father Bonaventura, Cap, who was conducting a mission, and several parishioners noticed the vehicles at a distance, several cannons were fired. At good last, about 3:00 p.m., we reached the Sisters' house, which, however, was not complete, so only one story could be used. Around the house everything was wild and called for attention. Sunday at High Mass, Rev. Father Flammang gave a short address of welcome to the Sisters in the name of the parish. Then Father Krautbauer delivered the festive sermon. After the high Mass, the procession wended its way to the convent which reverend Father Krautbauer blessed. Then followed the Te Deum, after which the people went home. Monday, Reverend Father returned and left the Sisters at their new mission. On account of the jubilee celebration and the mission, the opening of school was postponed and we decided to open school on November 13. This was done and the enrollment numbered 54 pupils, boys and girls.

One morning the Sisters were waiting for the bell to summon them to Holy Mass, but in vain. Reverend Flammang had ordered no bells to ring for low Masses. So that morning, the Sisters had no Mass, though there had been three celebrated. Missed it because they were strangers. Another time, they missed High mass on Sunday, November 26, because every four weeks the pastor said Mass at St. Nicholas Church.

At Christmas, the sisters brought joy to the whole parish. They had prepared a Christmas tree for the children. But oh, how all, old and young, came to see the Christmas tree of which they had heard, but had never seen.

January 2, 1866 the Sisters had the happiness of having High mass in their convent for the first time.

February 3, 1866 the men sang the first Requiem Mass in the chapel.

February 26, 1866 the Sisters opened the public school. They received the certificate without passing an examination. Likewise, they were happy to say the Stations on Mount Calvary. The first Friday of Lent they had the pleasure of kneeling in the snow which was several feet deep. On the second Friday the weather had changed and they knelt partly in water and partly in mud.

April 26, 1866 Susanna Lingden from St. Nicholas Parish came to us as candidate . . . poplar trees were planted from the convent to the street and a so-called promenade started.

Sunday, July 3, 1866 about 9 o'clock, Reverend Mother M. Caroline and Sister M. Theophile, in company with Reverent Hattenberger, came to St. Donatus. After expressing her satisfaction, dear Reverend Mother left for Fort Madison, July 5, at five in the morning.

January 24, 1867 Johanna Sandt entered with us as candidate from St. Nicholas Parish. The altar in a classroom on second floor was moved to first floor and placed in a room prepared for same.

May 1, 1867 This room was blessed and the first Mass celebrated. Henceforth this was to serve as an auditorium.

May 5, 1867 On May 5, three orphans from St. Catherine Parish were brought to us: Frances Debra, 13 years old, Catherine, 12, and Magdalen, 7.

August 10 [1867] Sisters Felicitas P, and Sister Leonissa, Novice, made the retreat with us conducted by Father Flammang. This morning after renewal of vows, they returned to Galena. Retreat was from August 20 until August 27. At the opening, during, and closing of the same, Benediction with the Blessed Sacrament was given. . . .

April 1, 1868 Theresia Bohn, a poor orphan child for whom the Reverend Father pays board, came to us.

August 3, 1868 Sister M. Leokadia came from Belleville to take Sister's School.

August 28, 1868 Sister Johanna and M. Anno came from Milwaukee, Sister Johanna for the boarders, Sister Anno for the kitchen.

September 19, 1868 Sister Euphrosina and M. Hyronima came, the former as needlework teacher for the boarders, the latter to take charge of the wardrobe and assist with the general housework. So the beginning was laid for the Institute, which Reverend Flammang had planned and suggested for years. This circumstance, however, required much expense which was defrayed by the order. Piano, bedsteads, chairs, tables, cupboards, bedding, etc., etc., were necessary. Since the opening of this mission, Sister M. Mathara had made many and great sacrifices and therefore enjoyed the respect and love of both parents and children.

1869. At this time, too, Sister M. Leokadia took seriously sick and good Sister Mathara took care of her day and night, so she too became run down and sick, and unable to do her own work. This necessitated help. Mother Caroline could not leave the Motherhouse at this time. Therefore she appointed Sister M. Ildephonsa as visitor who would at the same time make arrangements regarding the newly-begun institute, send Sister M. Mathara to the mission at Teutopolis, and if possible, bring sick Sister M. Leokadia to the Motherhouse. Meanwhile, dear Reverend Mother called Sister M. Basilia from Baltimore and sent her to St. Donatus to replace Sister M. Mathara. This was January 3, 1869. Sister Basilia took the upper grades and Sister M. Euphrosina the lower. Sister M. Odilo came to take charge of the needlework. During Lent we said the Stations on the hill, but always had bad weather, deep snow, and often bitter cold. In May 1869, we received a good piece of land which we used as a vegetable garden.

August 1869 Sister M. Basilia went to Milwaukee for final vows. On her return she brought with her Sister M. Didaka to take Sister M. Europhrosina's class. The latter went to Galena in November.

1870–1872. During the month of May [1870], the children had examinations and exhibits which proved very satisfactory. September [1870] to May [1871] we had 17 boarders. In August [1871], two novices, M. Anno and M. Hyronimo, went to Milwaukee for profession. Sister M. Odila, likewise, went to Milwaukee. On account of illness, Sister M. Anno did not return. Sister Jamblica substituted for her and took care of the kitchen.

July 28, 1871 Sister M. Albina came to conduct German class with the boarders and upper grades. Sister M. Jona came August 3 to take care of the barn and assist with the house and garden work.

November 22, 1872 Sister M. Johanna left the order. Mother M. Seraphine, who had been delegated by Reverend Mother, came November 30, 1872, to settle affairs. With her came sisters M. Hygine, M. Baldomera, and a candidate, Mary Ann Wright.

1873–1875. Sister M. Hygina replaced Sister Johanna. Sister Baldomera was in charge of the wash. The candidate taught English to the children.

February 12, 1873 Sister M. Didaka and Sister M. Hyronimo left the convent and returned to the world.

In the spring of 1875, scarlet fever raged throughout St. Donatus, and several school children died. Mary Linck, a boarder, also took sick and after two days died—15 years old—having been fortified with the holy sacraments.

331

August 1875 Novice M. Jamblica went to Milwaukee for profession, but did not return on account of ill health. Sister M. Gotta took her place on August 28. At this time, too, Sister M. Prudentia and a house candidate, Mary Ryan, came. Sister M. Prudentia took the place of Sister Albena, who left for Milwaukee in September.

August 1876 Candidate Mary Ann Wright went to Milwaukee for reception.

September 8, 1876 Minnie Flynn entered the candidature. We sent six candidates for reception. The number of boarders changed from year to year. Exhibits were always kept in May or June. The same were always satisfactory. The number of school pupils generally came to about 150. Sister Ermelinda came September 20, 1876, to take the place of the candidate.

October 12, 1876 Sister M. Sebastiana and Sister M. Chionia came to St. Donatus, one to replace Sister M. Basilia, and the other to see her good, pious mother once more.

October 17, 1876 Sisters M. Basilia and M. Chionia, and Candidate Minnie Flynn went to Milwaukee.

August 6, 1877 Sister M. Jona and Candidate Mary Ryan went to the Motherhouse. Sister Jona took vows and returned September 1 to resume her regular work. September, Sister M. Viatora substituted. Sister Paladia went to Belleville.

August 16, 1878 Sister Prudentia and Sister Viatora went to the Motherhouse, the latter to take vows. She returned September 3 to resume her work. Sister M. Prudentia went to Chicago and was replaced by Sister Norberta from St. Louis. The three candidates, Mary Kirpes, Lena Schaefer, and Anna Heiar, went to the candidature in Milwaukee.

April 24, 1879 A great celebration took place here on April 24, 1879, the silver jubilee of Reverend Father Flammang. His three sisters, Sisters M. Irene, M. Chionia, and M. Agape, came to complete the family circle. Sad to say, the mother had died the preceding February. The opening of the festival began the evening before with the firing of several cannons. A very beautiful vestment had been presented by Reverend Mother M. Caroline. The solemn High mass was at 10:00 a.m. The two oldest men of the parish presented Reverend Father with a costly gold watch and a gold-topped cane. At 2:00 p.m., the school children acted their parts in the decorated school. At the close, Reverend Father expressed his surprise and heartfelt thank you.

May 12, 1879 61 children received their First Holy Communion and on the 17th, His Excellency, Bishop Hennessey, administered Holy Communion. Until the present, we had pleasant occurrences, but now came a change. Reverend Father Flammang felt his health failing. To improve the same, he left the parish on May 28 for a trip to Europe. Meantime, Reverend Father Anler took charge of the parish.

September 5, 1879 Sister M. Hilaria came from Milwaukee to give some assistance and enjoy the country air.

October 31, 1879 we received a surprise visit from Reverend Mother Caroline. November 3, Reverend Mother's nameday, several men fired a number of cannons and in the morning, Reverend Bessler said Holy Mass and the Sisters received Holy Communion in the chapel. A solemn High Mass was celebrated by the Reverend Anler and assisted by the Reverend Schulte and Reverend Bessler. Reverend Mother invited the reverend clergy for dinner in the convent. Reverend Mother left for Galena on November 6, and Sister M. Hilaria accompanied her to the depot and from there went to Peoria.

December 2, 1879 Sister M. Norberta was transferred to Red Wing, Minnesota, and Sister M. Eulalia came to take charge of the sewing and needlework. Meanwhile, nothing happened except false reports were rumored for the return of the pastor. Yet, June 5, a telegram reported his arrival in New York. Immediately, the news spread and arrangements were planned for a welcome return. Decided: At 5:00 a.m., all bells were to be rung and cannons fired. When the signal was given, all came and gathered in town and went to the next parish, St. Catherine. Here a halt was made and the pastor welcomed home. Some people went as far as Dubuque to welcome him on his return.

The health condition of the pastor, Father Flammang, was fairly good for some time. In November, however, he again took sick. His condition therefore was doubtful and the sisters missed many a Mass. On Christmas Day, the Reverend Haxmeier said his first holy Mass. He celebrated his first High Mass December 31, which had been postponed until then. Father Haxmeier took the sick pastor's place until February 1879.

May 24, 1879 was First Communion Day for 44 children. The exhibit was held in June.

June 9, 1879 Sister M. Crescentia from Galena came to us and remained two months to recuperate and then was transferred to Teutopolis.

July 13, 1879 Reverend Father Flammang started his second European trip for his health. Meanwhile, Reverend Schulte from St. Catherine's took care of the parish. Towards the end of July, Reverend Father Knapstein came to us. We were very happy to have a resident priest with us again.

Our regular retreat began August 22, conducted by the Reverend Father Theodore, Franciscan. The Sisters of Galena, as usual, made it with us and returned home August 28.

Our school reopened in September with High Mass in honor of the Holy Spirit.

1880. During the stay of Rev. Kampstein, all went well. He was a peace-loving, zealous priest, a real friend of the children, gave them many pleasures, and regarded them richly. He visited the school daily, and the children loved him as a father. . . .

Our retreat opened on August 18, and with us the sisters from Galena. A Franciscan, Rev. Clemens, gave this retreat, after which the Sisters from Galena returned home. The first Monday in September, our school reopened with High mass and a brief address to the children. The number of Sisters remained the same. . . .

Toward the end of September, there was quite an excitement in the parish. Rev. F. Kampstein was to be transferred which came rather unexpectedly and unfavorably for the parish and us likewise. A petition to keep him with us was sent to His Excellency, but in vain. On the Feast of the Holy Rosary, he left for Springbrook—eighteen miles from here. In his place came the Rev. Schulte who lived here and took care of his former parish, St. Catherine, at the same time. He was not liked as well; nevertheless, everything went along nicely when the people became acquainted with him. He was like his predecessor, a friend and a father to the Sisters. Not once was there a disagreement; rather, he anticipated our wishes. Rev. Schulte came to school almost daily and gave instructions to the upper grades likewise, and taught singing even after class hours. He worked hard to instruct the children in singing—even Vespers and Latin hymns.

1881. The Feast of the Ascension, May 18, was First Communion Day, which was made very solemn. The parishioners and communicants started in procession from the convent to the church. The Pastor had previously blessed the scapulars and presented them to the communicants, and also had them renew their Baptismal Vows. In the afternoon, during the May Devotion, the children offered their candles to the Blessed Mother, at which time they received their scapulars.

After this, the older children remained home to help with the work. As usual, school was kept going until June 7. This year, too, there was no exhibition.

In gratitude for the year's good work, Father Schulte prepared a little feast for the children, after which he gave them his blessing, and school closed for the year. Vacation would last until the first Monday in September.

1882. Our retreat this year, 1882, began on August 21, conducted by Rev. F. Nerr, CSSR. The Sisters from Galena also made the retreat here. Otherwise, everything else was the same as always. School opened in September as in previous years. On September 28, Sister Eulalia went to Milwaukee. On the same date, Rev. Father Flammang returned from Europe. Since it was late in the evening when he returned, the children had a welcome of verses and song for him the next morning.

Although Father Flammang's health was not good, never the less, he worked as before for his beloved parish. He was forced to admit that his health was not in good condition; worry bothered him, and he spent his days lonely, not even his dear school was visited.

1883. Against all expectations, on December 6, 1883, news came of the death of Reverend John Michael Flammang, one of the first zealous, active, spiritual, and energetic men of the Diocese of Dubuque. His death day was his 58th birthday. Reverend Father Decker from St. Anthony Parish, Milwaukee, and a sister and brother brought the corpse to us. At its arrival, the parishioners manifested their mourning in loud lamentations.

The funeral took place on Monday, December 10 . . . The Funeral Sermon was preached by Reverend Decker, his friend. In deep and impressive words, he described the life of Father Flammang as an energetic, true, and faithful priest—not only toward the laity, but also the priests. With touching words, he described the blessed and fruitful life of the strict, self-sacrificing and energetic man, words of advice and edification not only for the laymen, but also for the priests. Many an eye was filled with tears, many a sob escaped from a heavy breast.

After the absolution, they brought the corpse of the departed to the cemetery, near his co-laborers in the vineyard of the Lord. With the sad tones of the "Miserere" and the mournful sound of the church bells, the procession, following the cross bearer, moved to the grave. First came the school children, then the girls dressed in white, and behind them, the priests with the corpse. Then followed the relatives, the choir, and the mourning parishioners. Not only his own parishioners, but many people from the neighboring parishes attended the Mass and accompanied the corpse to the cemetery to await the Day of Resurrection, next to his dear Mother who went to her eternal reward only a few years before him . . .

After Reverend Flammang's death, the pastor of Spruce Creek took care of the parish without, however, having been appointed pastor. On the first Sunday of every month, he went to Spruce Creek to give his parishioners services. He, however, and the Superior were not acquainted with the order of the parish; therefore, disorder and misunderstanding crept in. Hence, many of the people wrote to Mother Caroline petitioning her to send Sister M. Sebastiana back to St. Donatus.

Finally, the pressing request was granted, and unexpectedly, on April 30, Sister Sebastiana landed at St. Donatus. The good old priest was happy to have someone to acquaint him with the customs of these Luxemburgers. Peace and order were restored.

1884 . . . On July 20, thirty-six children received their First Holy Communion. . . .

On September 12 [1884], the most Reverend Bishop appointed the Reverend Ulrich Frey as successor to Reverend Father Flammang. Accompanied by the Reverend Father Bies, he visited the school during the afternoon where the children welcomed their next Pastor with song and verse. Until the arrival of the new pastor's housekeeper, he was boarded by the Sisters for two weeks. On the Feast of the Holy Rosary, the Rosary Society celebrated its Silver Jubilee. The church was decorated its very best for the occasion. The Reverend John Koch, the brother of Venerable sister Sebastiana, happened to be visiting at this time, and a Jesuit Father had also been invited to the celebration, so there was a Solemn High Mass. The choir consisted of all male voices without organ accompaniment, so the pastor asked the Sisters to let the children sing with organ accompaniment. This proved satisfactory, and the Sisters were asked to keep it up for a month. Finally, with permission of Reverend Mother M. Caroline, the choir was taken over by them for a remuneration of $100 a year.

In November, 1884, a fourth of the roof was newly covered since there was not enough money to cover the entire roof at one time. Therefore, only the most necessary was done at this time . . .

September 8 [1885] Sister Superior M. Sebastiana celebrated her 25th anniversary. It was a double feast because we had the honor of a visit from Father Spiritual, M. Abbelen, who came with Reverend G. Haxmeier at nine o'clock in the morning. His fatherly admonitions enhanced the day, and all were sorry at his leaving on the following morning for Springbrook.

Our joy was not to last long. Sister Pauline was not happy with her obedience to remain at St. Donatus. Due to dissatisfaction in the house, she was called to the Motherhouse on October 15.

1886. On Tuesday of Easter Week, three candidates were sent to the Motherhouse—Barbara Leiszt, Margaret Wagener, and Johanna Fisch. . . .

On October 19, His Excellency, Bishop Hennessey, came to St. Donatus to administer the Sacrament of Confirmation . . . After the noon meal, the Bishop promised to pay us a visit sometime during the year to clear up a misunderstanding which had occurred on account of school money. With him were the Reverend Father Johannes, Fathers Bies, Knaepple, Frey, and the Superior, Sister M. Sebastiana. The Bishop, in his talk said, "Father Frey will tell the people and you, Sister Superior, may also tell them my decision is: All money for school must be paid to the sisters, <u>not</u> to the priest. Every year the people should pay two months tuition for every child, 50 cents per month. All money, after you have your $400 salary, should be used for wood or whatever is necessary. Surely, the people do not expect the Sisters to keep their house in repair, buy their wood from the $400 salary. How can they live? My opinion is that the people of St. Donatus should thank God that they have so much money from the state to keep up the school, and have only two months to pay tuition. No other school that I have come in contact with enjoys this privilege. Other Catholics must pay for the entire year. They must also pay their taxes, and support their priest. I hope the people will now be satisfied, and cause no more trouble. Tell them that this is my wish, and these are my orders for the welfare and upkeep of the school that the good people of St. Donatus will fulfill the wish of their Bishop. They have asked me to settle this affair, and bring order, and so I trust in happy results."

The bishop's message was given verbatim, so that later on, no misunderstanding must be straightened out.

On December 28, 1886, at about 2:30 in the afternoon, fire was seen on the roof [of the school building]. The cause—a faulty chimney which had started already in the morning. As soon as the good people of St. Donatus noticed the fire, they rushed to help. No less than 100 people tried to save the building, not however without great difficulties. The loss was $225, which was paid by the insurance. After examining, they found the other chimney faulty, also. New Chimneys were put in. The expenses were paid from the surplus school money, and Reverend Mother Caroline allowed the Sisters to add $20 thereto . . .

[No entries were made in the Chronicle for 1887–1889. Only one brief entry was made in 1890, none in 1891, a brief one in 1892, and none in 1893.]

1894. In January of 1894, Ven. Sister Superior M. Sebastiana took sick. This had been the case for four years at the same time. By April, however, the doctor diagnosed heart trouble, and a serious illness was to follow. He expected dropsy, and a cure could not be expected. The last of April, the dear Sister received Holy Communion for the last time in the chapel. Henceforward, the illness increased rapidly. By Pentecost, May 14, the dear patient was helpless. Gladly the Sisters vied with each other to nurse the dear patient. As the doctor was two miles distant, Rev. Mother was so kind as to send us Ven. Sister M. Kiliana as nurse. She arrived here on May 25. On Sunday within the octave of Corpus Christi, the dear patient received fully conscious, with great devotion, yes, joyfully, the last Sacraments. During the ensuing night, her condition became aggravated, yet as a good Mother, she was concerned about the Sisters, especially at the loss of their night's rest. She evinced a marvelous patience. Oftentimes as she would say, "Oh, what must Reverend Mother have suffered!"

Tuesday, May 29, was the day when good, dear Jesus came to take home His Bride. About 5 p.m., the pains were exceedingly great. We telephoned for the doctor and called the priest. When asked whether she still recognized the priest, a painful "Yes" was answered. Now the agony began. Repeatedly the priest gave her general absolution, while the Sisters praying, surrounded the deathbed. At 7:40 p.m., the dear Sister went to the good Lord in her fifty-fifth year.

Nineteen years Sister had worked zealously and successfully on this mission.

The funeral took place on June 1. Seven priests and the entire congregation attended. The celebrant of the solemn Requiem was the Reverend Father Koch, brother of Ven. Sister M. Sebastiana. Thirty young ladies in black dresses and white veils alternated carrying the corpse. St. Joseph's Sodality considered it an honor to wear their insignia for the first time at this occasion. The young men, her former pupils, sang the Misere and the De Profundis on the way to the cemetery. The gratitude of the people manifested itself principally by the large number of stipends given for Holy Masses for the repose of her soul.

The Diary of Antoinette Porter King, 1866–1868

Antoinette Louise ("Nette") Porter was born on December 12, 1833, in New York City, to Selah and Cornelia Porter. Her father was a printer who, along with his wife and children, and two of his brothers and their families, moved to the Wisconsin Territory in 1838. On March 27, 1856, Antoinette Porter married William

Antoinette Porter King, 1865. Courtesy Ruth King Freymann.

Vipen King. In October 1866 the Porters and their children
(Selah, John, Willie, and Nellie) left Wisconsin by Conestoga
wagon for southern Minnesota, settling near what would become
the small town of Jackson. The traveling party also included
Antoinette's two brothers, Lib and Irve Porter; William's three
brothers, George, Robert, and Albert King; his two sisters, Nell

King Porter and Eliza King Barney; Eliza's husband, M. S. Barney; their friend, Charles Heath; and all their children.

Antoinette Porter King's diary recounts the family's journey as well as their first years in southern Minnesota. Initially, they lived in a log cabin on the prairie; in 1872 they moved into the village of Jackson, where she was active in civic affairs for the rest of her life. She kept this diary from 1866 until 1874 and a second volume from 1888 to 1894. She died on March 26, 1896, and is buried, along with her husband, in Jackson. Her tombstone bears the inscription, "Here is sweet rest."

October 1866

Tues 2nd Packing up. Preparing to move. Bid good bye to the Cook farm. Fine weather.

Wed 3rd Nell, I & the children went down town. I intended to have the childrens pictures taken but the Artist was not at home.

Thurs 4th A beautiful morning. Started for our new home in Jackson, Jackson Co. Minn. Lib & Nell went with us as far as the Turtle. At night camped side the road . . .

Fri 5th Quite cold this morning. Camped at night in Albert Lea. Came across Rob and Albert. They will go to Jackson with us.

Sat 6th A fine day. Camped at night in a straw stack somewhere on a prairie.

Sun 7th Traveled all day. Camped in the woods on the Blue Earth River. Rained a little at night. Took dinner at Rice Lake. . . .

Thurs 11th Have not come very far today. Got set in a Slough this morning. Broke the wagon tongue. Had to unload and had bad luck generally besides being very cold. Camped on Ten Mile Creek.

Fri 12th Arrived at our new roofless home about 10 PM. dirty tired & hungry & wind blowing a hurricane. . . .

Wed 17th At work on the house & looking for the cows. They went away on Monday. . . .

November 1866

Sat 10th Robert in search of the cows. Lib & Mitchell moved today. Cold. Tuttle helping break up a little to get sod to build a stable.

Sun 11th Rather cold. M.S. Elisa, Nelly, G & I went to meeting over to Belknaps. Charlie's horse fell in the well. Very foggy this morn. Albert got home with the cows. Found them about thirty odd miles from here. . . .

Sun 25th Very windy. Wanted to go meeting but could get no one started to drive the team. Wm & A got back from W—City. Brought wheat, flour, lard, mutton, codfish &c. Cold.

December 1866

Tues 4th William drawing hay. Lib & R gone trapping. Albert at work at Ashley's mill. Nell & I went up to E Heaths. Very sloppy.

Wed 5th Trying to be sick. Elisa came over and done up the work. Will gone for load of wood.

Wed 12th Colder than ever. Thermometer 10 below zero. I am 31 years old today. Sent letter to Irve. . . .

Tues 25th Merry Christmas. "Santa Claus" came but was not generous. Charlie's folks, M.S. folks, Lib's folks & the boys here to supper. Libs, M.S. & the boys went up to Thomas's to a dance. Not very cold today. . . .

Fri 28th Rather cold. "Picked turkey" & fussed around all day.

Sat 29th Nell came over staid a while. Said she would take "turkey" over to her house & bake it so we concluded we would all go over & take supper with her. Had a very pleasant time. Charlie & Elisa came over in their carriage which was a lumber wagon & one horse. . . .

January 1867

Tues 1st Robert started for Wisconsin. Not quite as cold as usual. Wm & Charlie started for Austin. Tuttle & Hinckley visited over to M.S. I went over a little while. . . .

Sat 5th Quite pleasant. Lib & Alb went fishing but did not catch any.

Nell came over. Made "corn bob." I wish William was at home. I would like to go to meeting tomorrow. . . .

Tues 15th Lib went for a load of wood. All went to town. Lost three hens last night. Froze to death. Snowed & blowed worse than ever. . . .

Thurs 17th Albert drew a load of wood for E Heath. Wm & Charles not come yet. Feel very much concerned about them. Pretty cold.

Fri 18th Rec'd letter from Vie. [Viola Cornelia Porter, Nette's twenty-four-year-old sister-in-law, who lived in Whitewater with Nette's father.] The boys did not come last night. Lib came up to chop wood for us. Tolerable cold. The boys got home today about 4 o'clock & want [weren't] we glad to see them. They was detained on account of bad roads. Left a part of their goods at Blue Earth City & Fairmont.

Sat 19th Set up our new stone Homestead. Like it very much. Not very cold today. . . .

Mon 21st Elisa came over early this morning to help me make my dress. Little Selah & Alice very unfortunate. Selah set down in a pan of hot ashes & little Alice scalded her hand in a cup of hot coffee. Albert broke through the chamber floor but did not hurt himself much. take it all around it has been quite an unfortunate day. . . .

Wed 23rd Invited up to Charlie's to eat turkey but was cheated out of it. Company came & had to stay at home. Had a pleasant time however. . . .

Tues 29th Wrote to Vie & Lucy. Charlie lost one of his horses. Quite a loss for him just now. . .

February 1867

Fri 1st Very warm & pleasant. E.H. came over. We went over to M.S. Had a pleasant time. Wm. drew hay. . . .

Fri 8th Quite cold. Commenced blowing & drifting in the afternoon. Never see it blow & storm so before could not see three rods from the house. . . .

Fri 15th Snowing & hailing. Not very cold. Wm & Albert went to the woods this afternoon. Cooking beans. Going to have fish for supper. . . .

Fri 22nd Pretty cold. Lib hens all dead. Killed by weasel.

Sat 23rd Weasel dead. Killed by trap. Cold as Greenland. . . .

March 1867

Fri 1st Cold as Greenland. Wind blew hard. . . .

Sat 9th Wm came home this morning from Fairmont. He was lost last night. staid in Cloughs haystack. Fortunate it was not very cold. He was very tired when he got home. . . .

Mon 18th Cold & windy. Wm gone for load of wood. Albert gone to work on the bridge. Weather moderated considerable since morning. I finished Nellie's nightdress. Snow about 2 feet deep on an average. . . .

Thu 21st Cold & disagreeable. Wm went for a load of wood. Irve came had a cold & tedious journey. Left Whitewater on the 27th of Feb. Brought us some very nice presents from home.

Sat 23rd Snowing blowing & drifting as usual. No signs of Spring yet. Cold as fury. . . .

Sun 31st Very pleasant. Thawing slowly. The cow has got a little bossie. MS & E came over. Staid to sup.

April 1867

Sun 14th A gloomy day. Snow about gone but the ground is nearly all covered with water. All the sloughs are full & running over. Wm gone to Mankato to see about raising funds for the relief of the poor. A great many destitute families in this county. . . .

Wed 17th Not very pleasant. Roads bad. Little George Irving born this morning. A promising little bud. Lib & Nell very much pleased with their young son. Hinckley here at work on the yoke. Hard rain towards night. . . .

Mon 22nd A little more Spring like but very backward. William came home today from Mankato. . . .

May 1867

Tues 28th Robert came. Warm & pleasant. Old Jim got in the Slough last night & the wolf eat a great place on his side. I guess he will die. . . .

Fri 31st Getting ready to commence breaking [sod]. Warm & pleasant. . . .

June 1867

Sat 8th Windy. Appearance of rain. Hard shower at night. Boys been looking for oxen all day.

Tues 11th Alb & John gone to Canfield to break. Old Jim the ox died today. Very warm. Wm. got home. . . .

Fri 14th Wm. breaking over to Canfields. John planting corn. Eliza & I went to town. Staid all day. Bought Nelly a dress & myself an apron.

Sat 15th Rather cold. Nell helped me make Nellie G. a dress. Wm. planted potatoes. . . .

July 1867

Mon 1st Rained quite hard this morning. I washed. Will made a milk house. Alb & John breaking for Mrs. Somebody. . . .

Thurs 4th Spent the Glorious Fourth at home. Wm. & Charlie drew house logs for Lib. Very warm. Hard rain at night. . . .

Sun 7th Very pleasant. Organized Sabbath School last Sunday at our house. Had six scholars. Had ten today. . . .

Sun 21st William very sick today. Made six cheese. Cut one today. It was very good for a green one.

Sat 22nd During this month have been busy breaking, hoeing, haying. Stacked hay today. . . .

Wed 31st Irve, Albert, Nellie g. & Effa Heath started for Wisconsin. Hope they will stand the journey well. Feel so lonesome without my little Nellie.

August 1867

Fri 2nd Very warm. Not much air stirring. Swarms of mosquitos. William trying to break [sod,] Willie holding plow. Elisa here to dinner. Had chicken-pot pie. . . .

Fri 30th Windy & every appearance of rain. Awful dark nights. A little cooler than it has been.

Sat 31st No rain yet. Everything in need of rain.

September 1867

Sun 1st Rather cool. Charlie came for me to go & spend the day with them. Mrs. Thomas, Nell & Dr. Eaton there & about Six PM another gentleman came—a little stranger but I guess it wont take us long to get acquainted with him. . . .

Sat 7th Wm. went to town on business. Charlie Heath cut hay for us in the afternoon. I came from Charlie's. Been up there most a week. . . .

Mon 9th Wm. & Lib stacking hay. went up to see how Elisa & the baby was getting along. . . .

Thurs 19th I went up to Eliza a little while. Eighteen years today since my dear Mother died. . .

Sat 28th Wm. went to the mill for a load of slabs. Very pleasant. Keep up I am going to have a new shanty. . . .

Mon 30th Made tomato pickles. Very pleasant. Wind all day "over the left"

October 1867

Mon 7th Cold & windy. Wm. looking for the cows. Could not find them.

Tues 8th Raining a little. Wm. looking for the cattle. Did not find them until most noon. Went to town in the afternoon. Rec'd letters from Albert. Lib & Geo came home. . . .

Mon 14th William started this morning. Dont like to have him gone from home so long. A very pleasant day. I went up to Heaths, staid until after dinner. Came home & wrote of some town business. Four long lists—the names of the voters in the town of Desmoines. George staying with me. . . .

Tues 22nd Willie & I dug the potatoes. Had three bushel in all—a heavy crop. So much rain in the fore part of the season it drowned out nearly everything. Rec'd letter from Sister Vie with sad news about Father. He went East on a visit for his health. Came back as far as Corfu (NY). Was unable to come farther alone. Telegraphed for Irve to come for him. Poor poor father, his stay with us will not be much longer. How well I would like to see him once more. . . .

Thurs 24th Have been so lonely all day thinking about Father. A dreary day. William got home tonight with Albert & Lona. Was so glad to see them but they brought me more bad news. Albert was at Father's on the 18th. Father had got home. Was failing fast. The doctors had given him up & said he could not live twenty four hours & that it would be impossible to get home in time to see him. It seems I cannot have it so—that I must go home anyway.

Fri 25th A pleasant day but O how gloomy to me. I feel that my sorrow is more than I can bear. I want to be alone for everyone around me seems so happy but I cannot be. This life is made up of trials & afflictions, sorrow & tears. . . .

November 1867

Sat 2nd Since last Wm. & Albert have been busy building sheds &c. Wm. went to town this afternoon. Rec'd letter from home confirming our fears. Yes poor dear Father is at rest, gone from this world of sin & sorrow I hope to a better land. But O how hard it is to give him up. If I could only have seen him & heard him speak once more. What a satisfaction it would have been. Eighteen years ago my dear Mother was taken from me & now my dear Father is gone. The Lord gave & the Lord has taken away but can I say blessed by his holy name. He died Sunday morning Oct. 20th 1867. . . .

Sat 10th Awful windy & cold. Charlie came for me to go & see their baby. It is sick. Stayed all day. Came home with William in the eve. Very pleasant. . . .

Thurs 28th Thanksgiving today. Made supper. Company present—Heaths, Porters, Barneys & Kings. Turned off very cold towards night. . . .

December 1867

Wed 4th William went to the mill for lumber. Two Norwegians staid here all night looking for sheep.

Thurs 5th Wind blowing strong from the south. Nell & I went to Mr. Sandons visiting. Was treated to green Wisconsin apples. . . .

Thurs 12th Snowed a little last night. I washed. I am thirty two years old today.

Fri 13th Expecting Wm & Alb home today. Not very warm. Snowing & blowing a little. Willie cleaning up snow out of the chamber. I must go to ironing. Wm. & Albert got home this afternoon. . . .

Wed 25th Christmas day. Albert, Leona, Nell & Eliza here to supper. Cold & windy.

Thurs 26th Went to town with Eliza to have her tooth extracted but the Dr. could not do it. . . .

January 1868

Wed 1st A very pleasant day. All invited to Charlie's to supper, had a very pleasant time. . . .

Sat 4th Mitchell & Albert digging the well. Eliza & Lona here. Eliza cut my dresses. Wm. went to Thompson's to attend the suit. . . .

Mon 6th Wm. commenced his school, has not taught since the winters of 1855 & 6 . . . Very cold, ther. 15 degrees below zero. . . .

Sat 18th Albert & Lib went to the woods. I went over to Mitchells in the afternoon, had a nice visit. Hard walking. Road drifted full of snow.

Sun 19th Not very cold. Weather moderate. Went over to Libs, staid to supper. Lost my breast pin. It made me sick. . . .

Tues 28th William came home tonight. Wm. started for his school this morning but came back again, so very cold & stormy he could not go. House came near catching fire by the stovepipe. Scared Willie & I most to death. . . .

Fri 31st The last day of January 1868. Quite pleasant. Thawing some in the middle of the day. Sewed 1 lb of carpet rags today. Made an apple short-cake for supper, it was real good, I thought. Ther. 6 degrees below early this morning, at sundown tonight 50 above.

February 1868

Sat 1st Snowing & drifting a little, not very cold. Thermometer 18 above z. Lib Nell and I went up to Heaths. Met Mrs Tuttle there . . . adjournment the school meeting. Blowing & drifting pretty bad all the eve. . . .

Sat 8th A terrible day, blowing & drifting & cold. Wm Alb & Lib went to School meeting. Wm fixed the stable. . . .

Wed 19th Blowing some all day. Nell & I went over to Tuttles for garden seeds. rec'd a letter from Vie tonight. She feels somewhat despondent by the tone of her letter. O how well I would like to see her. . . .

Fri 21st Somewhat chilly but not very cold. Lib, Nell, Albert, Lona & I went to Thomas visiting. Were not very warmly received although invited. Strange people in this world. Went to school meeting in the eve. . . .

Sat 29th The last day of Feb. A cold chilly S.E. wind all day. Nell came over & sewed carpet rags. Lib here to Supper.

March 1868

Sun 1st Came in like a Lion. Hope it won't be like this all the month. Cold wind from the East. Albert sick with a cold. Lib had a very poor spell this morning. Spit up about two large table spoonfulls of fresh blood. He looked terribly. Feels a little better this evening. I hope he wont have any more such spells. He is troubled with heart disease. . . .

Thurs 5th Washed a bedquilt this forenoon. Done up my work & then went over to see Elisa. She is not very well. Took her some toast & cheese. Went over to Nell's staid to supper. They had souse, potatoes, raised cake etc which was very good. . . .

Tues 10th Very pleasant this morning. Went visiting to Mr. Johnsons. Staid to go to Singing school. Got as far as the river but dare not cross. Call on Mrs. Eaton—found her sick abed.

Sun 22nd A beautiful spring day. Lib & Nells wedding day. All went over there to supper. Had lots of goodies. . . .

Fri 27th Twelve years ago tonight, away in Wisconsin, in the old log-house, William & I were married & here we are tonight, away out in Minnesota. Oh! What changes in those few years. A dear Father, brother & other friends have passed away to the Spirit Land since that never to be forgotten night. This afternoon E. Heath, E. Barney, N. Porter & L. King have been here sewing carpet rags for me & their respective husbands came to tea. Have had quite a pleasant time. . . .

April 1868

Wed 1st Very windy. Wm helping M.S. I went up to Heaths for some milk& butter. Growing cold fast. Thomas sent for Wm to do some writing for him. . . .

Fri 3rd Windy & cold. Froze in the house last night. . . .

Mon 13th Wm busy with the taxes. Cold as Greenland. I have been over to see Elisa. She is quite sick. Wm gone up to Mr. Heath. Dark & cloudy, appearance of rain. Bosh has got a little calf.

May 1868

Sun 3rd Awful windy. Landon here. I went over to Alberts a little while. Nell has been quite sick so that we had to wean Georgie. He is getting along famously. . . .

Sun 10th Wm gone up town again. Awful lonesome. Went over to Nells a little while. . . .

Sat 16th Mitchell & Albert been at work here nicely all the week. Plowing, dragging, planting broom corn, potatoes, &c. Wm made a little fence. Getting ready to go to Mankato to attend law suit. Chamberlain has sued him for the Auditors office. Irve & Lib came this afternoon. Took M.S. cow one day this week, Thurs or Fri.

Sun 17th Wm started for Mankato this morning. . . .

Sat 23rd Warm. I washed, ironed, baked, mopped &c planted melon seeds. Looking for Wm. Windy all day.

Sun 24th Windy & appearance of rain. Lonesome. Wm got home tonight. Trying to rain. . . .

Wed 27th Wm planted corn, melons, squash &c. Quite pleasant after the rain. Very warm.

June 1868

Mon 1st A hard rain this morning. Wm went to town to sell delinquent lands. . . .

Fri 12th Went visiting with Lib & Nell to Mr Thomas. Very warm. Indications of rain. Commenced raining about 4 o'clock. A terrible storm of hail & wind. Rained nearly all night.

Sat 13th Started for home bright & early. Had to stay at Thomas last night on account of the storm. Found the corn & gardens pretty well destroyed by the hail. Mr Lyons & Savage called.

Sun 14th A lonesome day. Sent for Lib & Nell to come over to tea. Little Georgie not very well. The last time he was ever here. He was taken sick shortly after they went home so that we had to go for the doctor. The doctor came about ten o'clock. Said he had the bloody dysentery but thought he could help him. I stayed all night with him.

Mon 15th Very close & sultry. Lib quite poorly & little Georgie not much better. Lib had a fainting fit this morning. We thought he was dying. Oh what trouble we are having. . . .

Wed 17th Georgie growing worse all the time. 5 o'clock in the afternoon we thought he was dying. Excessively hot weather. A hard shower in the night. . . .

Thurs 18th Morning—fifteen minutes past 8 and little darling George is no more. Gone home to die no more.

Fri 19th Quite cold, cloudy & dreary. Buried little Georgie this afternoon. He was fourteen months old. the funeral was held at the house of B.H. Johnson.

Sat 20th Cold & dreary & very lonesome without our baby. Lib & Nell feel very sad & lonely.

July 1868

Fri 3rd Albert Lona & I went gooseberrying up to the other Mill. Pretty warm. . . .

Sun 5th Went to Meeting. Very warm. During this month it has not been as warm as usual. The boys have been busy breaking [sod]. Have nearly finished. . . .

August 1868

Sat 1st Will & Alb are harvesting. . . .

Thurs 6th Lib has been very sick lately. He is talking of going to Wisconsin to be doctored. . . .

Sun 8th Well we are all going to meeting today & Vie too. It seems so strange to go to meeting with her again to think we are out in Minnesota. I am so glad she came with Elisa & little Nellie too. I have not seen her for a whole year my little blue eyed girl. . . .

September 1868

Sun 27th Well August & Sept are gone & they have both been disagreeable. Windy & rather cold. Vie dont think much of Minnesota weather. Today it is cloudy windy & lonely. On the 6th of this month Lib & Nell started for Wis. I hope he will regain his health by going down home. Vie & I have commenced to cut the broom corn. Wish it was all done. Do not find time to write in my journal. Wm busy haying hope he will get through before Christmas. Irve & Albert trapping. Albert is living in Lib's house. . . .

October 1868

Wed 7th Blowing & snowing & very cold. Alberts folks have got a little baby girl born this morning.

Thurs 8th Getting ready for threshers. Vie & I went over to see Lona & the babe. Coming back I scared Vie most to fits with a snake.

Fri 9th Threshers are here. Vie & I cut a little broomcorn. Quite pleasant. William went to Fairmont to attend convention. Eliza has another little girl born this eve. MS disappointed because it was not a boy. . . .

Tues 27th Making preparations to go to Spirit Lake tomorrow. Cold & disagreeable.

Wed 28th Have given up our expedition to the lake on account of the weather. Feel disappointed. . . .

November 1868

Tues 3rd Election. Company today Mrs Johnson, Mrs Radford, Mrs Baldwin & Mrs Barney. A very pleasant day. . . .

Sat 7th Have been busy all this week getting Vie & Irve ready for their journey. They started for Wisconsin this morning. Not very pleasant. Wm & Woodward gone to Petersburg. Melissa Ullis visited here this afternoon. Rainy. . . .

Thurs 19th Storm abated a little can see Mitchells house this morning the first time since Sun. Lost 10 or fifteen chickens in the storm. . . .

Thurs 26th Thanksgiving. Spent the day over to Mitchells. Had a very pleasant time. A fine day. . . .

Sun 29th Awful lonesome day. Thawing fast.

December 1868

Tues 1st Not very cold. Appearance of snow. Wm gone to town about the suit. MS scraping broomcorn. I have been trying to sew on the machine. Vie left her machine with me but I am such a goose I am afraid I shall not learn very fast. Juna came up & brought me some buttermilk also a short note from Eliza. She wishes she & the children were on top of Mount Ararat. What a wish & how funny they would look up there. Her ideas about "Love in a cottage" with little brass are somewhat like mine. What you might call humbugish.

Wed 2nd Cold raw wind. Wm gone to town again wonder if he will have to go tomorrow. I have commenced to run off my luck. Expect it will freeze up solid tonight. Elisa has been over this afternoon. she made most of Nellie's apron on the machine. She is a good little body. I received a letter from E J Allen last night. Father King sent some eye water to Willie which we got tonight. . . .

Fri 25th Christmas Day. Mitchell's folks & us spent the day at Alberts. Had a very pleasant time.

The Diary of Jennie Blair Andrews, 1876–1877

Jennie Blair was born on January 12, 1851, and married her husband, Orlando J. Andrews, on May 5, 1874. The young couple began farming near Ono in Union Township, Pierce County, Wisconsin, not far from River Falls. The first diary kept by Jennie Andrews begins on March 1, 1876, and appears to have been occasioned by the death of her six-month-old son, Hiram, on February 26. The diary, which measures three inches by four inches, has no cover; it is constructed from a railroad agent's account book and has been hand stitched. In her diary she began to grieve and come to terms with her loss as she and her husband worked hard to make a home. Most entries are short and descriptive of daily work on the farm, visits from family and friends, and bouts of illness; on occasion, however, the young mother's sadness is interspersed with her record of daily work and activities and with her acknowledgment of loneliness and loss. Eventually, Jennie and Orlando Andrews became the parents of three more children, Edna, Sarah, and Ward. Jennie Blair Andrews died on October 10, 1900, at the age of forty-nine.

Wednesday, March 1, 1876. Striving to forget the crushing sorrow of the past few days & begin a new journal. Sunday morning my darling went up to Heaven. We layed him in the grave Monday afternoon. I am alone today. Have been gathering up his little things that I may not see them. The gentle wind seems to say gone gone. Good bye my darling pet. By the help of God I'll meet you above. . . .

Friday, March 3, 1876. I washed all my dirty white clothes. Orlando worked for Mr. Brisbine for Shaker. Lonesome afternoon.

Saturday, March 4, 1876. I went to Irenes & O & Albert went up to Rock Elm to buy seed wheat. I walked to the corners & got a ride with a

Jennie Blair Andrews. Courtesy Sam and Judy Gerrish.

wheat team. got their seed wheat for 95 cts. Per bu. O took the stove top to get straightened. Orlando came home & fetched in the clothes & brought the plow & stove piece & came home with Albert. Brought me a new black calico dress. We had squirel at Irenes. Albert brought us home. Sunday night. How lonesome. Stove top did not fit good.

Monday, March 6, 1876. O started for Decks corners with the stove top & left me in bed. got home 12 o'clock, snowing fast. Stove top fited little better. O brought drag teeth & payed Doctor bill. Albert Baker & wife came in afternoon. A.S. Brought them over from his house. . . .

Wednesday, March 8, 1876. I washed calico clothes in forenoon, baked cookies & moped & sprinkled clothes in afternoon. O cut & hauled barn logs. Cloudy & windy. Mr. Shafer came in the even to get him to work in Brisbines Mill for him tomorrow.

Thursday, March 9, 1876. Alone all day. Uncle S & Aunt Lib went to Ellsworth. We sent our deed & assignment & satisfaction to be recorded. I ironed, & layed away my little Angel's clothes.

Friday, March 10, 1876. Rained most all day. O hauled logs all day. Had veg. Soup for dinner. I baked pies & tart crusts. . . .

Thursday, March 16, 1876. Stormed all day. O choped. I sewed on the skirt of my black dress. Jim Shelito came in evening. Dry throat sore. . . .

Wednesday, March 22, 1876. We went over to aunt Lib's with the oxen. Ned came up in the afternoon & brought me a pattern from Mrs. Holt—a loose bask for my black calico. Uncle Simeon had gone to the Rock with the preachers father. I wrote aunt Lib's family record down in her big bible. We came home after dark & hoped into bed. . . .

Saturday, March 25, 1876. Warm & pleasant. I moped & sewed on dress & melted snow to wash most. O went over to see prin Shelly tonight. A new cat has come to us lately. Big gray & white.

Sunday, March 26, 1876. Pleasant & warm. rough roads prevented us from going to meeting. We went over the fallow, first time I had been out there. Lonesome in the afternoon for my darling baby. read library books.

Monday, March 27, 1876. 2 hrs. I baked bread . . . cooked beans & prepared coffie & pie & cake from the raising. O visited his help & layed foundation.

Tuesday, March 28, 1876. Raised our barn . . . We had baked beans & meat & potatoes & pork & turnips & butter & coffee & pie & bread & beet pickles. They were here to dinner & supper had come for supper. Irene & Albert stayed all night. . . .

Saturday, April 1, 1876. I baked, sewed & melted snow for Monday. O. framed his rafters & cow came in. . . .

Sat. April 15, 1876. Alone all day. O went to Fritz Whites raising a log barn. I embroidered the covers for our red round cushions. Was lonesome. John Shelito came for our milk. . . .

Monday, April 24, 1876. I did not wash. O began sowing wheat. . . .

Wednesday, April 26, 1876. Finished sowing wheat. I mended my wraper. O went over to Uncle Simeons to get his seed oats, but left the oxen for Uncle Simeon to use.

Thursday, April 27, 1876. Rained. A Norwegian stoped here to dinner. I made a comb case for Aunt Lib. O split rails. . . .

Sunday, April 30, 1876. We walked in the woods & the winter wheat & on fallow. Got some leeks for din for trial.

Monday, May 1, 1876. Chilly & cloudy. I washed in forenoon & drove oxen for O to plow the houseyard in afternoon. Jim called. . . .

Thursday, May 4, 1876. Cold. I cleaned & baked & ironed. Had dried corn for dinner. O sowed oats frost last night. Expect Pa & Ma.

Friday, May 5, 1876. Two years ago was our wedding day. Time flies like a bird on wing. . . .

Wednesday, May 10, 1876. O made Pig pen plowed one onion bed & sage in trough. . . .

Friday, May 12, 1876. Irene & Albert came & Alice came with Chat who went to milk. I went home with Irene & stayed all night & I visited Mrs. John Van. Irene & I had greens for din. Albert & Ernest went to Lake City to get Pa & Ma & the goods. Came about ten. . . .

Wednesday, May 17, 1876. O & Albert went to Maiden Rock to get more things. Ma & I went down to the Duncan place & got cow slip greens. Pa is lonesome & disoriented. An extreamly unpleasant day. The trees are just putting on a coat of green. . . .

Friday, May 19, 1876. We sowed oats & peas & carrotts & planted sweet corn & beans & potatoes & set out onions & set our two crab apple trees & set out some rose bushes. Rained afternoon. We set a pen, sowed lettuce. . . .

Thursday, June 1, 1876. Rained. We set out cabbage & tomato plants, took kittens out of the cellar, put soap down cellar.

Tuesday, June 18, 1876. O went to Mr. Campbells raising. I cooked beans to bake & baked bread & dug some nerve root. . . .

Friday, June 23, 1876. Not well. Pa came over. O rested. Pa bought the 40 acres in front of Irenes, very warm. . . .

Wednesday, June 28, 1876. Made soap. O plowed his corn & potatoes with Jims horse. . . .

Saturday, July 7, 1876. O went to Maiden Rock with Jim Shelito got some sugar & coffee & lemon extract. Pa & Ma came at twilight. Ma & O went to meeting in evening. Sick. . . .

Monday, July 24, 1876. O commenced cutting his winter wheat. Ma baked. Sick. . . .

Sunday, July 30, 1876. Ma & O went to meeting. Sick. Ma stayed all night. . . .

Tuesday, Aug. 1, 1876. O cut oats. Feel better today. Ma & I walked up in the other garden.

Thursday, Aug. 3, 1876. O commenced cutting his spring wheat. Feel pretty well today.

Friday, Aug. 11, 1876. I worked some, picked pickles. Consequently was sick. . . .

Monday, Aug. 28, 1876. Been sick abed for two weeks, not able to turn in bed. Lived on starch, oat coffee & slipery elm. O went to Ma's in Rock to see the Doctor. Got some medicine. Doctor came next day, left some medicine. Just able to write now. Very weak. Pa & O went black berying got half a bushel in three hours. We thrashed last Thursday. Had 160 bu wheat, 166 bu oats & some barley &c. Ma did all the work. O went to Maiden Rock today with grain & got 80 cts for wheat & 65 cts for barley. Mailed a letter to Mich. . . .

Sunday, Sept. 3, 1876. Had two partridges for breakfast. Went hunting after breakfast. Had pidgeons for din. All went over on the fallow & to the spring. Pa shot a pidgeon. . . .

Tuesday, Sept. 5, 1876. O, Ma & I went over to Irenes, we looked through the old house. Pa came home & fixed up & left a line, stating that he had gone to the centeniel & would be home in three weeks. I stayed with Irene Wednesday & Thursday. Albert brought me home Thursday night & took ma back. My cut a bu. of apples to dry.

Tuesday, Sept. 12, 1876. O thrashed for Mr. McMan. Alone all day. . . .

Thursday, Sept. 21, 1876. Aunt Net came at seven oclock, Riner came, we had chicken din O plowed Plenty of melons. . . .

Saturday, Sept. 30, 1876. I sewed, Ma knit. O finished plowing ten acres, dug potatoes afternoon. Had onions for dinner. Cloudy. . . .

Monday, Oct. 2, 1876. I washed & worked butter & boiled hog potatoes &c. O dug potatoes. The leaves are falling. Ma came just at night to get ready for Weyauwega. O & I went back with her & stayed at Alberts al night. Me went up as far as Lake city with Ernest. Aunt lib & I & O went to Maiden R to trace some. Albert went to take honey for Snow. They got home about noon. . . .

Tuesday, Oct. 10, 1876. O cut turnips. I made apples, sweet pickles. Uncle Simeon came over to tell us about the meetings this week. . . .

Sunday, Oct. 15, 1876. We went to meeting heard a powerful sermon. Meeting every night.

Tuesday, Oct. 17, 1876. I baked pumpkin pies & set bread. O finished the privy. We went to meeting. . . .

Thursday, Oct. 19, 1876. Minister wrote all day. I cut apples. O thrashed for H. Wood. We went to meeting but had some trouble to get ready. O went across from thrashing. O & Albert sat up with Jim Brisbines dead child & I stayed with Riner all night. . . .

Sunday, Oct. 29, 1876. I was to tired to go to meeting. O got up early & took the horse & wagon over for the Minister to go to Maiden Rock. Got back before I got up. Mrs. Fred Hayes & four children came. Stayed all day. Not welcome visitors. . . .

Wednesday, Nov. 15, 1876. O & Pa went over to the Grey place to get lumber to make a bedroom upstairs. O mended his shed. Trades Jerry & Bright for Toms horses. . . .

Thursday, Nov. 24, 1876. We killed our pigs. Pa helped.

Saturday, Nov. 25, 1876. I fryed our lard cleaned some &c. Charles Morse & wife called to borrow some salt. . . .

Wednesday, Nov. 29, 1876. I made mince pies & burned my arm with a hot pie. O over to Irenes underbrushed. Pa went. . . .

Tuesday, Dec. 5, 1876. I washed. O cut & hauled wood. Ernest called. Uncle Westby stayed to dinner. . . .

Friday, Dec. 15, 1876. I commenced to brush the horse & Irene came to go to Annie Campbells. Orland, Charley S & Albert, went hunting. Wind blew furiously, blew off some of Campbells house roof & the stove pipe down. Albert came after us. Charley stayed all night. Pa came after dark. Very cold. . . .

Saturday, Dec. 23, 1876. I baked. O fixed sled. Fritz payed our tax. Looked for Ma all day.

Monday, Dec. 25, 1876. We spent the day at Alberts. . . .

Sunday, Dec. 31, 1876. At home all day. O had tooth ache. . . .

Sunday, January 14, 1877. At home all day. Somewhat lonesome.

Monday, January 15, 1877. I sewed some on my dress. O. hauled logs to the mill.

Tuesday, January 16, 1877. I baked bread. I sewed. O. hauled saw logs to mill. Jim called in even.

Wednesday, January 17, 1877. I sewed on dress, had onions. O. hauled some logs.

The Diary of Martha Smith Brewster, 1876–1879

Martha (Mattie) A. Smith, the daughter of Caroline (Jordan) and John Ketner Smith, was born on February 7, 1839, in Newport, Pennsylvania. She spent her childhood in Pennsylvania and later moved to Indiana, where she lived with her uncle, Dr. Lewis Jordan.

Martha Smith Brewster, 1878. Courtesy of the Blue Earth County Historical Society; E. F.
Everett, Mankato, Minnesota, photographer.

On October 14, 1869, she married George H. Brewster at Delphi, Indiana. They came to Mankato, Minnesota, where Brewster was a partner in the firm of Hall & Brewsters, abstracts and titles.

Martha and George Brewster became the parents of two daughters, Carrie, who was born on December 23, 1870, and who later taught at Mankato High School; and Grace, who was born on August 15, 1880, and who cared for her mother in her old age. The Brewsters' infant son, George, Jr., died on September 6, 1875. Martha's husband, George Brewster, died on November 4, 1901, in Mankato. More than twenty years later Martha Smith Brewster died on April 25, 1925, at the age of eighty-six. She is buried in the Brewster family plot in Oak Lawn Cemetery in Mankato.

Like the diary of Jennie B. Andrews, the diary of Martha Smith Brewster appears to have had its genesis in loss, specifically, the death of Georgie. The first entry in the diary reflects the diarist's struggle: her prayer is soon interrupted by the language of grief. She then crosses out several words that refer to her baby's death, resuming the stylized, formal language of prayer. The diary of Martha Smith Brewster, which contains sporadic entries during the next few years, probably once contained more entries. Pages have been cut from the diary, leaving what remains as a truncated record of the diarist's recovery from grief and loss. The original manuscript diary of Martha Smith Brewster is housed in the archives of the Blue Earth County Historical Society in Mankato, Minnesota.

Of Such is the Kingdom of Heaven

"Our Blessed Master while here upon earth taking little children in his arms blessed them and said suffer little children to come unto me and forbid them not—or such is the Kingdom of Heaven. ~~Four weeks ago on Sabbath night my little boy~~ What a comfort this assurance of the saviour is to us when we are called upon to part from our little ones—to feel they are "safe in the arms of Jesus safe on his gentle breast." How much nearer Heaven seems—how much happier it appears to us"

February 7th 1876. at 8 o'clock in the morning George and Carrie and myself started from Mankato to visit in Indiana came to Logan & down to Delphi, left Geo. in Chicago & he came to Delphi Thursday the 10th. Friday 18th we left D. in the morning came up to Logan at 2 took the train for Kokomo then waited there on the platform for 2 hours for the hack it came at last & we started for Burlington Oh what a ride, expected to be tiped over in the mud, but did not. Carrie is so happy here. I think I never saw her quite so happy away from home.

Sunday 27th , 1876. This morning I woke to find Carrie crying I suposed she was crying in her sleep & asked what is the matter was you dreaming she said I want my Papa.

March 2nd 1876. Last evening we all gathered in the dining room after tea & Carrie played untill eight o'clock. She dressed up in her Grandma's calico wrapper & was the kittens mother then when she called it precious darling she saw some of us laughing at her she said now don't you look at me & laugh. She is happy, never thinks it is time for bed. Today Mrs. Stockton & family will all be here to spend the day. Yesterday Grand Pa Stone gave me Grand Ma's & his own picture. He misses her very much. He gave some of his hair too it is such a beautiful white. I felt it is my last visit with him, but how bright he is, and so very strait he walks. And his mind is good but his memory fails him some, but he enjoys the children and always has a pleasant word for them, but the noise hurts his ear so he does not stay with them long at a time. When Carrie gives him a good night kiss he always wishes her pleasant dreams & she thanks him. the first time he expressed such a wish when we came to our room she said, Mama what did Grand Pa mean. Grand Pa seems so happy & he says every day he thanks God he has such good children & they are <u>all</u> so thoughtful of his comfort. it is beautiful to watch them to see how all try to do for him & make him happy.

Friday March 3rd, 1876. Yesterday afternoon Grand Pa came over to the dining room said Carrie had been visiting him & brought the kitten with her for the baby. Then she said well I must go for the children at home are getting sleepy & hungry so she went home. Grand Pa said I never saw a child that could play old lady as well as she can. He went through all her performances by tossing her head &tc.

She is willing to divide all her friends with Morton except her Grand Ma she went over to M. to she says he has one GrandMa & this is her own.

Aunt Jane & her Mother started to Ohio this morning to visit a sick sister. I was unfortunate enough to lose my knife. George gave me. I feel real sorry about it.

March 4, 1876. Saturday evening. This evening Carrie & Uncle Pratt was out at the store & she saw some bracelets but Uncle told her they were to large for her sometime he would try to find some small ones. And after I put her to bed tonight she talked of the B____, said we can get some tin ones at the tin shop but I don't like that kind I like gold ones best but we have to go up <u>North</u> to get them. I asked "Who said so," Uncle Pratt. I said tell him we don't have gold at Mankato. She said but we have to go up North to Winona to go to California.

This evening Mother went to sit up with Mrs. Brown [who] is very sick. The boys & I looked over <u>their</u> Sunday School lesson some. Eddie's eyes filled with tears sometimes. . . .

March 14, 1876. Today when we was all sewing Grand Ma Brewster told Carrie to take some things to her across the room & she was so slow. G—Ma said you are like your Father, never in a hurry. She said when he was little she sent him for a skimmer & he came to slow she said to him, "Georgie you are never in a hurry, are you"& he answered, "No and I never intend to be" & she says I don't know but he sticks to it. And when he was not three years old Mother was teaching him his letters & pointed to W. but did not tell him what it was only asked, "What does that look like" he said "Fawress." And when he was a very little boy he always wanted her to go with him up stairs & one day she said to him, "Georgie when you are 21 will you be so you can go alone," he answered "I guess I can with a candle." Somehow I feel sad & lonely this evening. I can't write nor work guess had better go to bed. I've worked real hard to fix Lulie & expect its a thankless work if not worse. I go away from here next week, and perhaps for the last time.

March 28, 1876. Tuesday morning. Here it is almost the last of Mar & we are at Burlington yet. It will be six weeks Friday since we came & we only expected to stay ~~five~~ at the most, but I told Uncle Pratt this morning I thought he might count on us for six weeks more from present appearances. For we have a regular Minn Blizzard this morning. This morning Grand Ma said to Carrie her Papa used to be troubled when a little boy about his cloaths. "What he would do for cloaths to fit him,"for he expected some morning to wake up & find himself a man or at least to large for his cloaths. Guess he has come nearer seeing that time since he went to Minn than when a child.

Grand Pa feels bad when he is housed up so much because he has no exercise. He says when it gets to be pleasant again he thinks we shall be able to know some thing of the feelings of Noah when he cameout of the Ark.

Yesterday Uncle James gave Carrie a blue plaid dress like the one I made for Lou. And last Friday Uncle Pratt gave her a white one. I forgot to tell you my book about Geo. drinking tea. He used to go to Grand Ma Stone's & she gave him cream & sugar with a little tea in so he passed his cup back & said please I will take some tea with a little cream & sugar in.

Apr 1876. Mr. Lafayette preached for us today. text John 12.24 Except a corn of wheat fall into the ground & die. It abideth alone. Death is the ~~necessary~~ needful condition to the large broader life beyond. Comparison of our life & Death & life hereafter to the Mediterranean sea Strait betwixt it & the Ocean. Die unto him that may life unto God & would with him. Was at Sunday School taught Mrs. Bridges class met there Etta Bowen one of my old infant class scholars. After lesson I spoke to them of missionary work. Tomorrow is the first day of May.

May Sat 6, 1876. One o'clock. Carrie and I expected to go to Delphi yesterday but it rained all day & this morning it rained but it is clear now & hope it will be. Expect snow to go Monday morning.

Yesterday I did not want to go very much for Grand Pa was very sick but is better today has just walked out. Wednesday we went to Mrs. Stockton's & made calls as we came home. Thursday made calls & took tea at Uncle James's. Uncle J gave me a pair kid gloves for to wear home. I hope to be at home again one week from today. I do enjoy our visit but I feel now its time for us to go home & I am anxious to go. . . .

October 13, 1876. the ladies held a missionary convention at same time of synod.

Friday 14, 1876. organized a Presbyterian society.

October 18, 1876. Today Auntie Hall came & I drove out to the country I planted a snowdrop at the head of Georgie's grave in center a sweet sented Jonquill at foot a scarlet Tulip all at the top of grave. I put a bunch of flowers on. Tomorrow is his birthday. He would be three years old. . . .

October 20th 1877. Dear Georgie's 4th birth day. Auntie Hall, Carrie & Myself [The remainder of this page is missing.]

Sept 16th, 1878. It is a long time since I last wrote in this Book & today I have to record my Father's death. He died Sep 10 but I only received the letter today. Some time ago he [The remainder of the page is missing.]

Nov. 13, 1878. Georgie Paul Ray has gone to be with our Georgie. he was only 4 years & 6 months. In life our Georgie loved Georgie Ray & would put his arms around his neck and kiss him.

In the few months or weeks past how many of our Sabbath school have passed into Eternity.

Christmas 1878. Was a beautiful day. Geo was at home & we had a good quiet time. I surprised Carrie with a "camp rocker" and Geo thought it would be a nice thing to surprise me with a nice large rocker & it was a surprise that pleased me very much   [The remainder of the page is missing.]

~~Jany 1st~~-1879   The New Year has come with its Joys & Sorrows, too. Geo. is away from home. It is a beautiful day but cold.

Jany 3, 1979   had teachers meeting at our house.

Jany 4, 1879   It is not so cold today. Carrie says the Thermometer was 4 from zero the other day.

September 1879. at rest. Oh how thank ful I feel for such a message from his death bed & now he has entered that rest. It does not seem possible he is gone for 15 years I have not seen him but always thought I should not now that can never be in this world. but I may hope to meet him on the other shore with the many loved ones gone before. The 6 of this month it was 4 years since Georgie left us. Father was 70 years old last Apr & is buried at "Mount Carmel," Fulton, Mo. I do not know if Mt. Carmel is a cemetery or a church yard.

Oct 20, 1879. Georgie's 6th birthday. It is a beautiful summer day so warm. This year I have had a dollar for Missions for Georgie's birthday gift again. Dear child how distinctly I can remember him both from voice & expression of features. Carrie is going to school at the Normal & learning so fast she never went to school untill she was 7 years old but she is up with those who went much sooner.

The Diary of Abbie T. Griffin, 1882–1885

Abbie T. Griffin was born on October 16, 1851. When she began keeping her diary, she was thirty and working as a seamstress in Minneapolis. In her first entry Abbie wrote about caring for her sick mother and added, "I am very tired." She continued making daily entries averaging four to eight lines and wrote about her daily work, the weather, her mother's health, financial worries, and her recurring bouts with migraines and exhaustion.

In June 1882 Abbie T. Griffin met Samuel C. (Clint) Dike, who would become her suitor. Clint Dike worked as a teamster, packer, and machinist, according to Minneapolis City Directory entries. In September 1883 he brought his nine-year-old daughter, Etta Dike, who had been living with her aunt and uncle on a farm in Sherburne County, Minnesota, to board with Abbie and her mother, Mrs. V. R. Griffin. On January 20, 1885, Abbie T. Griffin married Clint Dike. Abbie's mother died two weeks later. After 1885–1886 neither Clint nor Abbie Dike is listed in the Minneapolis City Directory, and their whereabouts are not known. I continue to search for information about the family's life after the mid-1880s.

The diary of Abbie T. Griffin is a hard-bound volume that measures eight inches by ten inches and has seventy-seven lined pages. The first sixty-five pages are filled with entries over a three-and-one-half-year period. Her work as a seamstress required long days, yet she managed to keep her diary on a daily basis throughout most of 1882, with a break in late summer and another in early fall. She was forced to stop writing in her diary for nearly a year, from November 1882 until October 1883, because she injured her eyes in an accident. When she resumed writing in October 1883, her diary entries became more sporadic, and the final entry was made on May 25, 1885. The original manuscript diary of Abbie T. Griffin is housed in the archives of the Minnesota Historical Society in St. Paul.

January Sunday 1st, 1882. The new year comes to us with a fresh fall of snow, but only an inch. The weather has been lovely all through December, no cold no snow, but sunny & warm. Mother has been very sick since November 19 and as yet is not able to be dressed or to sit up long. Ma and Mrs. Hill called today and brought her a nice piece of venison. I am very tired. . . .

Saturday 7. Still pleasant. I have been so busy all day long, baking, ironing & cleaning. Mrs. Coe is making me a dress, my old brown made over & trimmed with a shaded brown stripe. Gus came up in the evening. . . .

Tuesday 10. Mrs. Coe went to see about work. Mother had a hard night, another abcess opened. I had no sleep until four oclock A.M. and today I am all tired out. Received a letter from Mary Day. . . .

Saturday 14. Warm again. Mrs. Coe went away this morning and I have been busy all day. Baked read and a cocoanut cake, worked on the table cover. In the evening began knitting a hem edge which is very pretty. The Fairport paper came today. . . .

Tuesday January 17, 1882. Down to twelve degrees below zero this morning and a high wind. Finished my table cover and went down with it seemed so nice to get out once more. Mrs. Thorp called to see mother. Have baked three mince pies since I came home. . . .

Monday 23. Cold yet. Went down town this afternoon and met Gus and Nellie. Gus came home with me and staid all night. We had a fine time. . . .

Friday [February] 3. So warm and sunny, also sloppy. Went to town this morning to the store and to Mr. Tonsley's another real estate agent. Brought home two letters to work. This afternoon worked on Mrs. Symes table cover. Received my books from Cinda. . . .

Monday 6. Warm and so muddy. Worked the letters. E & H on black with shaded red filling silk. Went to the store about three. Nellie came up at night. . . .

Friday February 10, 1882. So much like spring, the sun is so hot and there is no snow. Went to town this morning and brought home a letter to be worked on a towel. Received a Floral Guide from James Vick of Rochester. Mr. & Mrs. Clark & Eddie have gone to Farmington on a visit. . . .

Wednesday February 15, 1882. Cloudy but pleasant. Went to the store this morning and carried my letter. Am feeling much better have been working in Mrs. Syme's table cover and mother's dress. Mrs. Thorpe came to sit with mother awhile. . . .

Wednesday March 1st [1882]. So warm that we have had the front door open nearly all day. Have been making a lambrequin for a bracklet of Aida canvas and working it with the same design as the border of Mrs. Syme's table cover. . . .

Friday 3. Dull & cloudy, signs of a storm. No Nellie, no mail, and so lonely. Have finished the table cover and it is a beauty. Sent a card to cousin Kate. The morning paper brings the news that Queen Victoria of

England was fired at by a fellow named McLean, last night at Windsor Station. No one hurt. . . .

Tuesday 7. Cold and cloudy. The mail brought me a card from Nellie mailed the 3d. She is too sick to come. Have been busy all day. . . .

Thursday 9. Am so tired but have been at work on my letter all day. Am so anxious to get well. . . .

Sunday 19. Such a lovely day. Almost like summer. Have been in such distress for breath all day. Oh if only I can get well again. . . .

Wednesday 29. Still warm. Have been busy all day. This morning sewed my brown and blue rough straw turban over into a small poke, trimmed it with the bright plaid from my winter bonnet & a navy blue plume. It looks very nice and is becoming. Then made some silk mats for a lace sett. . . .

Sunday [April] 9. Such a storm, rain, snow & wind. Am nearly down sick, my head aches as if it would split. A sorry Easter. . . .

Tuesday 11. Went to town & brought home a pink brocade silk kerchief with a light blue border & a letter new wheat to be worked in pink etching silk. . . .

Monday 17. Warm but not a leaf to be seen and not much grass. The spring is so backward and work is so dull not a thing for me to do, so I am improving the time for myself. Am making me a cloak out of father's grey coat. It matches my flannel dress. Mrs. Kilgore called. Mr. & Mrs. Ellis have brought up their dead baby, it was only nine months old. . . .

Sunday April 23, 1882. Warm. I have had a fine time today, went over to Foss church this morning and her [heard] Prof. Johns of Hamline University preach. In the evening went with Mr. Clark to Centenary church. Dr. Van Anda is a fine preacher, the young people's meeting is very fine.

Friday 28. Wednesday I went down to Nellie's & found her sick, not able to go to Lodge so I staid with her until today. A terrible thing happened here on fourth Ave S ~~here~~ yesterday a man Frank McManus decoyed off a little daughter of Jason Spear & outraged her & at night a group of vigilantes took him out of jail & hung him up.

Saturday 29. So cold & raw. Went down for work but did not get it so dull now. Spend much of my time trying to sell this place. . . .

Tuesday [May] 2. Warmer, but the wind does blow so hard. Mrs. Clark and I went to town, no work yet, but ma sold some hens so we had some money for a load of wood. $1.30 for a load of green gang. While I was gone Mrs. Dennison & Mrs. Phillips called. . . .

Wednesday 17. So fine. Have been so near sick that I could not go down town, but have worked at a little of my own work. Mr. Farrier brought a man here to see the house. . . .

Saturday 20. Cold and rainy. Have been busy baking and working about. Mrs. Burns sent for me to help care for Willie.

Sunday 21. So cold and windy. Went up to Mrs. Byrns soon as I ate breakfast and found that Willie Melrath had died during the night so I found plenty to do until afternoon. Then came home and went with Mrs. Clark to see Dr. L. Hall about her swelled face, then home to supper & up to Mrs. Byrns' again and after all was ready for the night home again, tired out. . . .

Saturday [June] 3. Such a tiresome day. Got up early to work on my blanket and finished it. Mr. Ellis came on the morning train, then Finley & Priscilla McNeil came & we had a busy morning, then we all went to town & I had a good many errands. Bought me a pair of grey cloth & glove kid buskins. The price was $3.50 but on account of their being an unusual size they were put down to $1.50 and are a perfect fit. Bought four yds of light grey woven for a petticoat and a veil for mother of silk tissue at 35 cents. . . .

Thursday 8. Washed. Mary Mills brought me two skirts to embroider and they are a grape leaf design and a forgetmenot vine for Mrs. Coykin-dall. Mr. Gold called to see our place today. . . .

Sunday 11. A lovely day so warm and sunny. Had made no preparation for church so did not go. Sewell Patten & Henry Tyler called. Afternoon Mr. & Mrs. Little & I went up to Lake Keegan & Medicine Springs and had a pleasant walk. In the evening Mr. Denman called & brought a friend of his a Mr. Dyke. I've never seen him before. They did not stay long. . . .

Tuesday 20. Rainy. Have had a hard day. We hear of a cyclone that has nearly destroyed Grinnell, killing many people and wounding many more. We are afraid for our people there. Mr. Connor called to see the house, for a friend.

Wednesday 21. Very pleasant. Mr. Denman carried mother down to Mrs. Montgomery's to dinner. They were gone until two o'clock. Meanwhile I had worked very hard at my work & tonight I have finished. Mr. Dyke called and staid until nine. . . .

Sunday 25. A lovely day. Mr. Dyke called for me to go to church and we went over to Foss M. E. [Church]. Mr. Berry preached a fine sermon. He seems to have returned from California refreshed in body & mind. Ma & I had a long quiet afternoon and then at night Mr. D. came down from his brothers and we went to hear Mr. Macquesten, who did preach a beautiful sermon. . . .

Monday 26. A perfect summer day. Got my wash out early & had the afternoon to work on my dress. After tea I hoed five rows of potatoes. Mrs. Dr. Hall called & Mrs. Rohan came to see if we would rent some part of our house. Received a card from Mary Parks saying that they were all safe & their property not damaged. It is such a relief to us all. . . .

Saturday July 1 1882. So cool & pleasant. Baked, did so many little odds and ends of work, trimmed my hat with a large satin bow of delicate cream with a tiny vine of cardinal & a long navy blue tip. Prof. & Mrs. Macquesten called on us. She is very nice & we like him much as ever. Louise came down to trim her hat. The morning paper brings the news of the execution at 12:40 P.M. yesterday of Chas. J. Guiteau at Washington D.C. for the murder of President Garfield whom he shot last July.

Sunday July 2. Such a lovely day so cool & pleasant until evening when it rained some. At seven o'clock AM. Mr. Dyke and I started for the Red Rock camp meeting & had to walk to the Milwaukee station, there we met Mr. & Mrs. Chas. Dyke and went with them. At nine o'clock we were at a class meeting, at 10:30 there was a general meeting. At noon we ate our lunch & then strolled about, then came to hear Rev. Thomas Harrison & Rev. Mr. Harrison [who] is an odd man but has wonderful power. We came home at seven. . . .

Tuesday July 4. So beautiful, no dust and not too hot. Mr. Dike came at night and we went down to the motor took it & went to Calhoun, had a nice time there, went through the cemetery, took a boat & rowed all around the lake, walked all about & thoroughly enjoyed ourselves. Came home at six. Mr. Denman came to tea, later Mr. Marsh & Miss Clark called. In the evening we watched the fireworks. . . .

Saturday 8. Cloudy & threatening. Took my spread down to the store and finished it there but it took me all day long. Came home tired out. Called to see Mr. Macquesten and Mrs. McCay on my way home. . . .

Tuesday August 1, 1882. Rainy in the morning but cleared at noon and the sun came out quite hot. Had to go to the store early but came in without any work. Have had so much pain in my ear all day and for some time past. Am working on Miss Bowman's hunting dress. Mother went to a prayer meeting at Mr. Little's tonight, led by Mr. Macquesten. . . .

Monday 7. Hot until noon and then a shower cooled the air. Went to the store early and worked hard at the dress all day. Began at four o'clock this morning. Mr. Dike saw me safely home. He goes with Ettie in the morning to Dodge county Minn. . . .

Thursday 24. Still melting hot. Have been at the store all day long, commenced a table cover with a heavy couching pattern, worked a watch pocket and brought home a skirt to embroider with lilies of the valley and a heavy scallop. Three gentlemen called to see the place and the firm of Place, Wetmur & Kees submitted me an offer of $1700.00 cash. Received a letter from Mr. Clark. . . .

Tuesday 29. So nice & cool, showers all the morning. Ironed all the clothes and had the afternoon clear. Received a letter from Mr. Dike. He is coming home. . . .

Friday September 1, 1882. Warm. Have been rushed all day and tonight am so tired. This is mother's birthday, she is sixty four years old. I am so sorry not to be able to give her a treat.

Saturday 2. Hot. Was so hurried to get the skirt done but I finished it & went down after dinner, brought home a stripe for an afghan, peacock blue felt to be embroidered with wild roses, commenced. . .

Thursday 7. Warm but fine. Have had a very busy day, worked a spray of jessamine on a black cashmere collar & three letters in the fern daisy letters. C.E. N. in cardinal on wattered blue ribbon. Priscilla has been learning. Called on Mrs. Bowman. Received a letter from cousin Maria Kellogg & sent one to Mr. Dike. . . .

Friday 15. A busy day. Have had so much to do. Mr. Dike called having just come home. He looks well.

[Abbie Griffin made no further diary entries until the beginning of October 1882.]

October 1, 1882. A lovely day but still dusty. I have not written much of late, as we have been so busy cleaning house. Have done so much and on Sept. 26th Ettie Dike came to board with us, and will stay for the winter. Today we three went to church and heard a beautiful sermon from Mr. McQuesten. At three we went to Sunday school and in the evening Mr. Dike and I went out again.

Monday 2. Misty. I took Ettie to school and then came home and helped clean the pantry. . . .

Sunday October 8, 1882. Rained all day long. We have had a lazy day did not get up until late and it was eleven o'clock before we were through breakfast. Mr. Dike came after dinner and we had a quiet after- noon. This evening I am writing, mother reading and Ettie looking at pictures.

Monday 16. My thirty-first birthday, and I have celebrated it by staying quietly at home and working at that abominable blue felt stripe covered with wild roses. Katie Ward arrived yesterday from Main and we have vis- ited today. . . .

Sunday 22nd. Lovely. Got up early and put all to rights & then attended to [Mrs. Kelsey's] baby. Mother and Ettie went to town church in the morning and I staid at home. Mr. Dike came up after dinner and in the evening we went to church. It is Ettie's birthday she is nine years old, and I made her a birthday cake and we had it for tea.

Monday, October 23rd. Lovely. Have had a fearful headache and could not get up to breakfast but felt better after dinner. Went to town and did some trading for Ettie. Brought home dress to embroider. A lady called to see the place this afternoon and Mr. Lichlider on the same errand this evening. Dr. Hall came and vaccinated Ettie tonight. Katie Ward called and I was over there. Received a letter pattern from Priscilla.

Wednesday November 1st, 1882. Pleasant. Am just about down sick with a cold and am in such a hurry with my work too. Have a child's yoke of garnet merino embroidered with daisies of garnet, and it is awful.

372

Mr. Dike came to see us tonight and found Ettie working away at a tiny cloth etching three little girls on each end. . . .

Saturday 4th. Warm. Got up early and worked before daylight at my work finished it ready to go down at three o'clock and Mrs. little & I went down town & came back in a fine rain. Sat up late and worked on Ettie's dress, but did not finish it but made her a pair of flannel panties, very pretty ones of red with a little frill embroidered with black. . . .

Saturday 11th. Rainy. Finished my work about ten o'clock and then had to go to town with it and also delivered a handkerchief with Jack on it. Came home and brought me an afghan with Baly to be worked in it. Bought me a pair of new shoes. paid two dollars for them. Mr. Dike came up in the evening.

Sunday 12th. Cold and blustering freezing and the first day any thing like winter. Did not get up until late and then was busy trying to get things in order for cold weather. We have had a very quiet day, no one here and we have been home all day long. . . .

[No further entries appear in Abbie T. Griffin's diary until October 16, 1883.]

October 16th, 1883. It is nearly a year since I have written in my Journal and so much has happened of interest to me. I will note a few of them.

The last day of November I poisoned my eyes with the stamping liquid and for the rest of the winter could not see to read or write or sew. Mother was so sick all winter too and has had such a hard summer. In March we sold our home to G.C. Rodells of J. D. Blake for $600 in April I bought Lot 2. Block 3. Third Ave. Addition of J. D. Blake for $6.00 & Charlie Jones built me a house, a cottage of four rooms. We moved here June 3rd and are here now.

This day I am thirty two years old and a quiet day it has been. This morning I did up my work, bought eight bushels of Beauty of Hebron potatoes, and this afternoon bought 22 tons of nut coal & 2 ton of Ill. Lump. Of W. W. Fuel Co. Went over to Nellie's & she cut me a velvet vest for my black broadcloth jacket. This evening I have written to Julia Dickinson & Nonotuck Silk Co. It is a cold stormy, windy night. . . .

Friday 19th. So cold and windy. Went to town and stamped a sack, made me a black velvet turban. Saw a lovely banneret of dogwood blossoms on sea green plush a wedding present for Miss Annie Tuttle of Norwich, Conn. . . .

Sunday 21st. Snowy, cold & raw. Mother is much worse and is threatened with pneumonia. Ella Carr called and Mr. D. . . .

Thursday 25th. Cloudy. Ironed, baked apple pies & fried doughnuts. Mother is much better. Miss Partridge called & in the evening Mrs. Smith called. . . .

Saturday 27th. Cold & raw. Have been sick all day and have hardly been able to keep up. Embroidered two wild roses in natural colors on light blue cashmere.

Sunday 28th. Cloudy & misty but warm. Have had a nice day. Went to Simpson M.E. church in the morning and heard an excellant sermon from Rev. Mr. Teter. Mr. Dike came up in the afternoon. . . .

[No further entries appear in Abbie T. Griffin's diary until August 1884.]

Friday August 1st, 1884. Resolved that I will write in my journal & stick to it and not leave so many unfinished things. Have been so busy sewing all day & my machine broke down entirely so that I had to sew on Mrs. Flemings. Am working on some little Mother Hubbard dresses for Mrs. Tenney.

Saturday 2nd. Showery. Finished a little dress for Mrs. Tenney then went up town and came home at one o'clock and went right to work. Wheeled mother over to the meat market & had her weighed. Sixty pounds. Received a letter from Mr. Dike from Norfolk. . . .

Tuesday August 5th, 1884. Cool. Worked at my sewing after breakfast until dinner and then the neighbors began to come over. About four oclock I started out with mother down Third Ave. to thirty eighth street then we came up to Portland Ave stopped at Smiths greenhouse enjoyed seeing the flowers so much. The little girl gave mother a lovely boquet. Edna Morse called & brought mother more flowers and some pears. . . .

Sunday August 31st, 1884. Such a lovely day, so bright & nice. This has been a busy week. On Monday I did some emb. On Tuesday I wheeled mother up to see Anne Patten & gave them such a surprise, on our way home called on Jessie Collum & Mrs. McIntyre. Thursday Mrs. Smith called & directly after Custar brought up Annie. He brought mother a big watermelon.

Monday, September 1st, 1884. Mother's birthday and such a nice day if only the wind did not blow so. I have washed & ironed. . . .

[No further entries appear in the diary of Abbie T. Griffin until January 26, 1885.]

Monday Jan. 26th, 1885. I have determined to write a Journal once more & record many transactions. Last Tuesday night at 11:50 P.M. we had a very interesting ceremony here. For two weeks mother had been very low and on that night we gave up all hope of her and feeling her end was approaching she felt as if she would like to see me married. Clint went directly up to get cousin Ed and they went together to get a lisence came back hunted a minister and were ready. I had only a common dress and it was a dark grey trimmed with pipings of crimson, just a full skirt & slashed basque. The Rev. Archibald Hadden transformed me from Miss G. to Mrs. S. C. Dike. Mother has been very low and is so still. Last night was the first night for eighteen months that I could sleep all night. Mrs. Hull came & watched with mother. Nettie Sullivan wrote us a letter today and I received one from Poughkeepsie.

Tuesday, ~~27~~ "Feb. 10" Since I last wrote have passed through a very trying time. Jan. 29th I just gave out & had to go to bed & have the doctor. My hands & limbs swelled to an immense size & I had a good prospect of inflammatory rheumatism, but with a good girl in the kitchen good care I am at last up again.

Dear Little Mum has gone through & I am so lonely without her. She went to Father last Thursday morning, Feb. 5 at 3:45 A.M. and went triumphly. I was able to see her but not able to sit up on Saturday at the funeral or to see her but once after she died. Ettie came home to me on Thursday.

Monday May 25th, 1885. How can I help getting well in such a lovely day, all nature seems to rejoice after the rain. I have been writing to aunt Mary today but it has been a long hard letter for me. How much have I missed mother today. Ettie has gone over to see Laura and Mrs. Clark. Mrs. Fleming gave Ettie a bird today and she is delighted. I hope to write more now.

Sure Lemon Pies. 2 large lemons. 1 cup water, 1 cup sugar, 4 eggs, 2 tablespoons cornstarch or 3 of flour. Grate the yellow rind of one lemon, squeeze out the juice & pulp, removing all seeds. Add the sugar and water, separate the whites from the yolks. Beat yolks well and add to the lemon, stir well & place in a steamer over a kettle & steam until hot.

This will make 2 large pies. While steaming bake the crust being careful to make 2 or more holes in crust to prevent blisters. Then mix the cornstarch with half cup cold water & stir into the lemon, let it cook until the crust is done. Then fill the crust with the lemon place on top the whites of the eggs beaten stiff froth with 8 spoonfulls of sugar return to the oven to brown.

Warmed Potatoes. Chop five and to two cups allow ⅔ of a cup of milk 2 teaspoon salt 1 heaping teaspoonful of butter cut fine & 1 egg. Mix and Heat gem pans hot butter well, fill, flour & brown.

Waterproof Clothing.

No. 1. Make the cloak coat or trousers of linen, soak them well for a day or two in boiled oil, then hang them up in a dry place until perfectly dry, without wringing the oil out. Then paint them without turpentine or driers being in the paint, any color, put on thin & let dry. Seaman's method.

No. 2. Make the garment of strong unbleached cotton, hang it up in a dry place, and with a brush give it two coats of boiled linseed oil, a pint will be sufficient for a cape or pair of overalls. Canvas may be prepared in the same way.

No. 3. Oilskin coat or wrapper. If a stout one is wanted, let the material be strong unbleached or brown calico. If a light one is wanted use brown holland. Soak it, then make in hot water & hang it up to dry, then boil 10 oz. of India rubber in one quart of raw linseed oil until dissolved (it will take about 3 hours), when cold, mix with the oil so prepared, about half a pint of paint of any color.

Paint with a brush a thin coat, brushing well into seams. Hang up to dry in a current of air. Give three coats and dry well.

The Diary of Maria Morton Merrill, 1890–1899

Maria Catharine Morton was born to Judith (Packard) and John Morton of Monson, Maine, on March 21, 1832. The sixth of eight children, she worked as a textile laborer before becoming a language teacher in the Gainesville (New York) Female Seminary in 1858. She remained there one year, then came west to Jackson County, Wisconsin, to be near her sister, Augusta Morton Merrill, the wife of Chauncey Merrill, who farmed near Sechlerville. Maria Morton taught for a time; then, after her sister's untimely death in 1869, she married her brother-in-law on July 27, 1871. She became the stepmother of her nieces, Eva, Gertrude, and Clara Merrill. A son, Waldo Morton Merrill, was born to Maria and Chauncey Merrill on September 1, 1872. Chauncey Merrill died

Waldo Merrill, with woman believed to be his mother, Maria Morton Merrill, ca. 1890–1900. Courtesy Horace S. and Marion G. Merrill.

in 1882. Maria Morton Merrill died on January 26, 1904, and is buried in the cemetery at Sechlerville.

Maria Merrill began keeping this diary in 1890, while she was in her late fifties and living on the family farm near Sechlerville, ten miles from Black River Falls, Wisconsin. In 1895, after a trip to the World's Columbian Exposition in Chicago, Waldo, then thirty-two, decided he wanted to attend Winona State Normal School. Maria Merrill leased the farm and they moved to Winona, Minnesota. After graduation Waldo taught school at Eyota, Minnesota, for a time; then he and his mother returned to the family farm near Sechlerville. In 1903 he married Myra Elizabeth Curran, and they became the parents of three children: Gertrude Lydia, Philip Chauncey, and Horace Samuel Merrill. Maria Merrill lived with her son and his wife until she died.

Her diary reflects her reliance on faith to help her cope with family problems and the infirmities that come with age; it also describes the difficulties of midwestern farm life at the end of the nineteenth century. A typescript of the diary of Maria Morton Merrill was donated to the State Historical Society of Wisconsin La Crosse Area Research Center by her grandson, Horace (Sam) Merrill, and his wife, Marion Merrill.

January 10, 1890. Waldo has been to Black River Falls today and has brought me a new blank book and I suppose I must keep a record of passing events which concern our business and our everyday affairs generally. He went out with Mr. Curran to help drive some cattle which he had sold. he sold him our old red cow which we have had nearly six years. He got but $12.81 for her. Cattle and pigs and all kinds of farm products are exceedingly low; the lowest I have ever known. We are having a very mild winter, scarcely any snow and very little cold weather. We killed a beef the 7th, sold one half at three and three-quarter cents. Would like to sell another quarter but beef is very plentiful so I suppose we shall have to eat it if we can. We had a somewhat dull Christmas though we got some presents from Gerty. She sent me $5.00 and a book and presents to the children.

We milk but three cows now, but will have another soon. We have fifteen head of cattle now, besides a little calf. We have watered the cattle at the creek till within a few days. It's quite a job to pump water for them all. Waldo started going to school this week and has been two and one-half days. Not a very good beginning. . . .

February 6, 1890 Thursday. We have been having some very warm weather for winter. All last week was warm and nearly all the snow is gone. There is some ice left yet but the sleighing is very poor. Tuesday quite a good deal of water came into the cellar. We had to dip it up and carry it out. I took out 17 pailfuls. Cherry had a heifer calf the 26th of Jan. It is rather small but we are going to raise it since it is a winter calf. Then we shall veal all our late calves. We milk three cows now. The weather is colder yesterday and today. Waldo has finished drawing ice today. Mr. Preston will finish packing in a day or two. Waldo drew a load of sawdust Monday—paid $1.00 for it. Will Pillsbury was down the 25th of Jan. He was going to start for Colorado the 28th. His family will not go out till fall. I am sewing patchwork as I haven't much sewing on hand. I got an egg today; haven't had any for two or three weeks before.

February 27, 1890 Thursday. It has been so long since I have written in my journal that I don't know where to begin. In the first place I have

had the grip. Was taken the 9th. Was not very sick. Did not last but three
or four days but it left me in bad condition. Had no appetite and very little power of digestion, had quite a cough and have been a good deal
troubled with weakness and lowness of spirits and I have not yet recovered my normal vigor of mind and body. In the meantime Clara has had
quite a severe bilious attack and also an attack of toothache and Waldo
has been suffering a great deal from neuralgia and toothache so that altogether we have had and are still having quite a dubious time. Waldo has
got all his wood drawn and Albert Lowe helped him draw the rest of his
clover hay and Mr. Preston helped him draw logs for a thousand feet of
lumber from Pine Creek to Ed. Holmes' sawmill. Laurie had a calf last
Monday. We have had but little snow this month till the 25th [when] we
had about 3 inches of snow and last night we had some more snow. . . .

March 21, 1890. I am fifty eight years old today. Am in quite good
health for a person of my age. Have great reason to be thankful for the
mercies of the past year. Have had no very great troubles since my last
birthday. We have to work hard and economize to get a living but the
world is full of people less favored. I feel to praise the Lord that He has
spared all our lives and surrounded us with many comforts and blessings
of which we are not deserving. Trials, cares, and difficulties beset the
paths of all and we have no more than our share. May God make us
thankful for the mercies of the past and help us to do better the coming
year. I had a letter from Gerty last night. She has left the apartment and is
going to keep house a few weeks for a friend. She intends to come home
the first of June. We have had another cold snap since I wrote last week.
The thermometer dropped to 18 below zero. We have had little snow-
storms. There was one today but it is warm and pleasant this afternoon.
Lizzie Maule was here for a visit yesterday. Waldo has all his wood sawed
and about all split and has been hauling manure. We are getting quanti-
ties of eggs now. . . .

May 29, 1890. I have been so overwhelmed with work that have made
no entries for a long time. The spring has been very cold and backward,
yesterday being the first really warm day. The weather was very dry till
about a week ago it began to rain and we have had an abundance since. It
rains every day. The trees are scarcely in full leaf yet. The apple trees are
in bloom. The pastures are so short that the cattle have scanty rations.
Waldo finished planting corn the 27th. Have planted but few potatoes
yet. He has gone to the saw mill for lumber today. Gerty was married the
18th of May to Charles T. Dodds of Chicago. They came here the 21st
and left for their home in Chicago yesterday. Her husband seems to be a
very nice young man. We all like him very much. They made a very short

Home, Work, Family

visit as he could not be spared from his business any longer. We feel very lonesome, but life is full of lonesome places. Care and work will soon drive away loneliness. Providence has wisely ordered that most people shall work for a living and work is a good tonic for a wounded spirit. I have set two hens today and had one come off with ten chicks.

August 5, 1890. A month has gone since I have written anything. The first part of July we had rain enough, but the last half of the month was very dry and hot which injured small grain considerably. The 2nd of this month we had a much needed shower, but it was accompanied by a fearful wind that did some damage to the grain by [illegible]. On the third, we had another about as severe with much more rain. Now it is cool and pleasant and farmers are cutting their grain in all directions. Our winter wheat is stacked. The spring wheat was ready to stack when the rain came. Now it will have to dry out before it can be stacked. Our oats are ready to cut. Corn is looking well. Waldo cut a large amount of clover hay and secured most of it without much injury by wet weather. He is hauling manure today. We picked quite a good many blue berries last month and I have canned 30 or 40 quarts. I had a letter from Gerty some time ago. She is housekeeping and they are enjoying themselves very much. They invited us to visit them.

October 31, 1890. I am getting very negligent about writing in my journal. The last day of October, and it has been snowing. We have had a very unpleasant fall, a great deal of rain and cloudy weather and cold as well. Waldo stacked most of the grain himself, help was so scarce. We threshed the 21st and 22nd of Aug. We had 128 bushels of wheat and 542 bushels of oats and about 50 bushels of potatoes which were very poor. Our corn is good and yields well. We have not got it all husked yet. It is not very dry this year. Waldo had to build a new crib to hold all the corn. We have sold all the hogs, except four little pigs, and we bought a sow for breeding purposes. We got for the hogs we sold $61.69 and paid for the sow we bought $4.72. We have sold one cow for which we got $16. Feed is high, consequently cows are very low. We have had a boy working for us one month this fall. His time was out a few days ago. The plowing is not all done yet and there is a good deal of other work to do. It is very cold now and I am afraid it is going to freeze up. Clara has been husking corn a long time and I have done the housework. Am trying to do a little sewing now. People around here have raised quite a good many potatoes this year and are finding it quite profitable. We intend to plant more next year. Grain of all kinds brings a good price. Eggs are $.17—cream 18.

August 13, 1891. Nearly ten months have elapsed since I have recorded anything in this book. I am thankful that we are alive and that we are still in fairly good health, though my own health has been rather poor this summer. I am not able to do much hard work, but keep onward. We had quite a mild winter with but very little cold weather. The spring was very late indeed and cold as well. The summer has also been cold with a few exceptions. The first of the season was exceedingly dry and the prospects were very poor for crops, but after a drouth of about 2 months, we had abundant rains which improved pastures and meadows and all other crops. Winter wheat is mostly threshed and is generally good. We got 208 bushels from about 9 acres and the quality is excellent. Waldo has cut nearly all the oats. He thinks they are very good. Corn owing to the cool weather is very backward. The frost will have to hold off very late to give us a crop. At present we are having another drouth. the ground is so dry that it is nearly impossible to plow. We are longing for rain. Our crops last year were very good and prices were also good. We sold 200 bushels of corn for $.40 and I think about as many oats for the same price. As we had a little money to spare we bought a few things that we needed very much. We got a new top buggy with shafts and pole-and whip for about $80.00. We have also plastered three rooms in the house and painted and papered and made other improvements. We also got new chairs for the sitting room and bought two new bureaus. I am having new carpets woven for two rooms. We have worked very hard to get the house in order and we have got mostly through. We traded the old mare and two little colts for a self-binder. Now we have but the team and a yearling colt left. We bought a clover seeder with one of the neighbors which cost us $400. Waldo got a man to help him and moved my sister's remains from the grove where she was buried to the graveyard where Chauncey and Eva are buried. We have paid out a good deal of money this summer but it has gone for things that were very necessary. We lost one more cow this summer. Have seven left. Cream has not been below $.14 this summer. Eggs have been 12-1/2 cents most of the time. We have had our trials, annoyances, and aggravations like other people, but we have had a great deal to be thankful for. . . .

September 4, 1891. We had a big frost this morning. Corn and everything else that could freeze is killed. I presume we shan't have an ear of hard corn but I am thankful that we have wheat enough to eat. The crops in Europe this year are so short that there is not near enough to bread the people and I suppose we ought not to complain because we have lost our corn.

Waldo is sowing winter wheat today. He cut some clover for hay yesterday. We have but little hay this year and we are anxious to save all we can. I am feeling a little better now. . . .

September 9, 1891. Since my last entry the weather has continued about the same with warm days and very cool nights. The frost did not kill the stalks of the corn and we are hoping it will ripen some by standing. The nights are so cold that it does not improve very fast. Waldo will finish sowing winter wheat today. Farmers will be behind with their work this fall the weather has been so cold. The land is too dry to plow and most corn is not ready to cut, and will not be much before October. The County Fair opened yesterday at Black River Falls. Will hold four days. Waldo intends to go tomorrow and take our wool to the carding mill and get our new carpet that we have had woven. Our cows do not give very much milk now though we feed them twice a day with fodder corn. Our hens lay very well indeed. . . .

October 7, 1891. We had another hard rain the 3rd and the ground is pretty thoroughly soaked. Waldo plowed two days and Ole is plowing today and Waldo and Clara are husking corn. The corn is pretty poor, the frost having killed it before it was ripe though we shall have some good corn. The weather has been cold and cloudy since the rain. We haven't been selling our cream for a week or two. The ice gave out so I set the milk in pans and churn the cream. Shall sell some cream again when the weather gets cold enough. . . .

October 30, 1891. Two weeks have passed since I have made an entry in my journal. We have had some cold disagreeable weather and some quite warm and pleasant. For two or three days the weather has been quite nice. They have got two pieces of the corn done and Clara is husking on the third. Most of it was not cut ripe so it will not take very long to husk it. The boy's time was out last Monday. They stacked the shocks that day. We also sold a cow the same day for $15.00 for beef. Sold the hogs Saturday for $3.75. they weighted 1110. We went to a sociable at Edwin Bradbury's yesterday. It was Mr. Well's seventieth birthday. There was quite a crowd. About forty were there to tea. He got $43.00.

November 9, 1891. They finished husking corn the 7th. We sold the corn from the last piece to Sechler for 45 cents a bushel. The yield was very poor. The dry weather and the early frost about ruined it. Waldo is plowing the land where it grew now. The weather is quite mild and I am in hopes we shall get the plowing done before it freezes up. We have a great deal of work to do both out of doors and in the house. Prof. Rogers of Galesville was up the first day of this month, both morning and evening. He made a public announcement of the severing of the pastoral relation between Mr. Wells and the Presbyterian church of this place. Mr. Wells is seventy years old and in consequence cannot sustain the pastoral relation to a Presbyterian church any longer. Besides he is too feeble to have the care of a church. The Presbytery is trying to get another minister for us. We hope they succeed. . . .

December 11, 1891. I am all alone tonight and feel pretty lonesome. Clara left for Chicago the 3rd. The day was rainy and disagreeable. Gerty sent us a card the next day saying that she arrived safely. The 4th was a very squally, windy day and quite cold. Since then it has been quite warm and for two days very warm and pleasant for December. My health is very poor indeed. I get very tired doing the work. I got some flannel yesterday for shirts and drawers for Waldo and have been trying to sew a little today but I am too weak to sew. I suppose I shall have to work as long as I have an ounce of strength left. Waldo has gone skating this evening. He has left me alone every evening this week but one.

December 24, 1891 Christmas Eve. They are having a Christmas tree at the M.E. Church tonight. Waldo has gone but I did not feel able to go. The weather has been warm since my last entry. It rained the night of the 21st and is storming a little tonight but is above freezing. Waldo killed the steer the 16th and our little heifer came in the same day. She gives a nice mess of milk. Waldo sent to Chicago for an organ the 8th. It did not get here till today. I suppose he will commence taking lessons next week. I have heard from Clara twice. She is enjoying herself very much. I presume she will come home next week. We have but ten head of cattle this winter besides a little calf. We have no hogs, two horses and a colt coming Sat. and ten sheep and about sixty hens. . . .

January 5, 1892. A kind Providence has spared our lives to commence another year. Though I have not escaped sorrow the past year I have had many blessings. Take the year together my health has been poor. I do not expect ever to have very good health again. Cares and sorrows and hard work have about used me up but I am very thankful to be able to be around. Clara has not returned yet. We have had some pretty cold windy weather, but it is quite milk now. Looks like snow. We have not had snow enough to make sleighing yet. Waldo has commenced taking music lessons. I doubt very much whether he does much at it, he is so indolent and fickle. Though it has been quite a sacrifice, I thought I would give him a chance so if he does not learn no one will be able to blame but himself. We are expecting our new preacher this week. I shall be glad when he gets here. . . .

January 31, 1895. Three years have passed since I have written in my journal. That I am alive and able to be out of bed I have to thank a kind Providence. I have been an invalid since early in March of 1892. I had a relapse of the grip and was in bed several months. About midsummer I rallied and got able to be around and to do a very little work but had a pull-back in the fall, but gradually got over that. We got a coal stove and burnt coal the following winter and though quite feeble I got through the winter quite comfortably. In April I had an attack of neuralgia. Had the doctor and got over that after a while. My health improved slowly through the summer and fall as I did quite a good deal of work. Waldo went to the World's Fair [Chicago] in June. After he came back he began to talk about going to Winona, Minn. to the State Normal School. I could not see how he could be spared as there was no one to run the farm and besides my health was so poor I did not like to have him away from home, but he was determined to go and I finally told him he might try it one year. We let the farm to Albert Lowe on terms far more favorable to him than to me. Together we staid alone, Clara doing the chores at the barn and I attending mostly to the house. The experiment was not a paying one. The summer of '94 being the severest month ever known in those parts. The crop of oats was good but even potatoes and hay were nearly a failure. Having passed through one year of the Normal course Waldo was very anxious to continue his studies and go through the entire course of four years. Since it did not pay for us to keep house on the farm for three years for the sum of [illegible] per year and all the taxes paid by the man hiring the farm. It was a great sacrifice for me to break up my home where I had lived so long and go among strangers in my feeble old age, but I thought that perhaps I ought to give him all the chance I could for an education. We came to this place the last of August in '94 and the last of September I took cold and got sick. Was in bed several weeks. Clara came to take care of me the 10th of October after which I was out of bed and have been up and down ever since. I don't expect to improve much till warm weather and may not then. I can't say that I have enjoyed life much since I have been here. It seems as if it would be all that I would ask in this life if we could all be back on the farm again and have everything as it used to be, but since it cannot be I try very hard to bear it patiently, knowing that my time of sojourning here cannot be very long at best and in the far away future of the next world it will make no difference whether I die in Wisconsin or Minnesota.

February 28, 1895. Another month has passed since my last writing. The first half of the month was frightfully cold and the last half very warm for winter. There has been but little sleighing this winter. Not more than two or three weeks but the snow is all gone now. I presume we shall have more cold weather but we cannot expect much sleighing. My health has not improved much the past month. The first of the month I seemed to lose strength but for a week or two I have been improving a little. I took cold last week which made my cough quite bad, but I hope it will be better when the weather gets better. The winter term of school will close one week from today. Waldo is doing quite well in his studies. He is attending a course of lectures on English Literature delivered by Prof. Norton of the University of Chicago. He likes them very much.

March 21, 1895. Sixty-three years ago today I first saw the light. Sixty-three years seems a long time to look back upon and yet, when viewed in the light of the great hereafter it is exceedingly short—all too short to fit the soul for its future career. A life of usefulness is the only life worth living. To overcome the selfishness of the heart and strive day by day to live for the good of others and trusting in the Lord's power to help us, repenting of all our sins and serving Him faithfully praying for guidance in the smallest concerns of life, these are but the duties of all Christian people. though I have a great many trials and a good deal of sickness during the past year yet I have received a great many mercies from My Heavenly Father. My health is slowly improving and I hope to be able to get back to Sechlerville before many weeks. I have no home there but I hope the Lord will induce some kind hearts to open their doors for me till I can find a permanent place to stay. Before another year has rolled around perhaps I shall not want an earthly home. Life hasn't many attractions for me and yet there are many pleasant things that I did not observe when I was younger. The beautiful sunshine, the changing landscape, the growth and decay of vegetation, the lovely flowers and a great many other things that once seemed common place, I now contemplate with interest. . . .

December 25, 1895. Winona, Minnesota 468 Center St. Christmas has come around again and found us all alive though my health is still poor. My cough is very severe, my digestion is rather better than last fall. I am able to be around and sew some and do a few chores and read a good deal.

We came to this place the 18th of September. We have a good sized house in a very good location. We rent one of our rooms to two students. It is now vacation and nearly all the students have gone home. Waldo has gone to visit one of his student friends so Clara and I are alone. I don't go anywhere at all as my lungs will not bear the cold air. We are having very nice warm weather which has continued for more than two weeks. Yesterday we got some presents from Gerty. Waldo got a necktie and Clara and I some books. This is Waldo's third year at the Normal. I shall be glad when he gets through the whole course which will take him one year after this. It is somewhat doubtful whether I shall live to see him through. I hope his education will be worth the sacrifice made for him to obtain it.

March 21, 1896. Winona, Minnesota. I scarcely expected to see another birthday one year ago. My health has been very poor through the entire year. the 13th of January I had an attack of something similar to the grippe. I was not so very sick, but I have been slowly failing ever since. I have lost nearly all my flesh and am very weak. I sit up about five hours a day. I have been having neuralgia lately which is very hard to bear. We have two young men occupying the room joining my sleeping room and they talk so late nights that I don't get much rest. I don't expect to see another birthday. I can't say that I want to since my home was broken up; that home that was so very dear to me I have scarcely any real interest in life. We often hear of broken hearts. I think the breaking up of my home broke my heart.

I dislike this place very much. We have run across a few very kind people but nearly all of them let us severely alone.

I feel to thank God for his goodness to me and my daily prayer is that He will prepare me for what is before me and give me grace and patience and courage to take me through to the end.

December 25, 1896. Christmas has come around again and I am still in the land of the living and my health is much better than it was when I made my last entry. Last spring after warm weather came I began to improve and though I was feeble all summer I was able to keep around. Through the fall I have been quite a good deal better. Have gained some flesh, though I have but little strength. My cough is quite severe but I have got so used to it that I don't mind it so much as I did. Waldo has gone up to Wisconsin to spend a part of the holidays. I suppose he will graduate in the spring. If he can get a position, he wants to teach a while. I suppose he will have his own way as he generally does, but I very much want him to go back on the farm. Indeed, I have such an intense longing to get into my old home again that it seems as if I cannot be denied the privilege, but I try very hard to leave my future in the hands of my Heavenly Father who will surely do what is best for me. I think I feel truly thankful for the mercies of the past year and I pray god to continue His mercies to us all through the remainder of our lives.

March 21, 1897. Three hundred and sixty-five days have completed another circle of my years and I am still here to record it. Each day has brought its joys and its sorrows, its cares and its comforts, its pain and its rest, and a kind Father has presided over them all. My general health is better than it was a year ago, though my cough is no better. Though we have had some very cold weather, on the whole we have had a mild winter. This month has been somewhat rough, and a good deal of snow has fallen. There is a great deal of snow all through the Northwest and there is a good deal of anxiety lest there will be heavy floods when this great body of snow melts. There have been already great floods in the lower Mississippi and other large rivers.

Waldo hasn't got a situation as teacher yet, so we don't know much about our future destiny. I know where I want to go, but very likely that will not be where I will be forced to go. Spring will soon be here and I think we shall all hail it with joy, for winter at best is a dreary season and to an invalid it is doubly so. I do not go out at all and very few people come here. Clara has very little interest in things that interest me and it never occurs to Waldo that I have any intellectual needs to be supplied. He not only will not tell me anything that he learns, but he does not want me to tell him about anything that I read, so I must keep my mouth shut and be satisfied with what I can get from books.

November 25, 1897. Thanksgiving Day Eyota, Minnesota. Waldo got the Principalship of the graded schools of this place last spring. He graduated from the State Normal School of Winona, Minn. last May. We came to this place the first of June. After we got settled he went to Hixton, Wis. and with Mr. Apple as partner bought blueberries and shipped them all over this part of the country. He was gone two months. He didn't do extra well. This school commenced the 18th of September. the school is very difficult to manage, but he gets along as well as one could expect. I don't like to live here very well though there are some nice people here, but I want to go back to our old home on the farm, but Waldo didn't want to live on a farm because he will have to work, but I don't think he will get through life without work, at least, I hope he won't. My health is about the same as it has been for a long time. I have done quite a little sewing this fall but not much house work. I read a good deal, but forget about everything I read. We have a good house and are very comfortable. I have a great deal to be thankful for, and I think I do feel in some degree thankful.

December 25, 1897. Eyota, Minn. I write in my journal every Christmas if no more. Waldo has gone to Wisconsin to look after our interests there. He has but one week of vacation which will not give him much chance for rest. We find this part of the country very cold, much colder than at Winona. We find it difficult to keep our rooms warm enough for comfort, though we consume nearly double the fuel that we ever have before. My cough is quite hard this winter, which of course I ought to expect. I spend a large part of my time in reading. At present we have the two dailies, three weeklies, and one, and I shall have two, monthlies, besides Waldo has numerous educational journals and more or less transient literature. I never go away from home and I find life somewhat monotonous. But I am not unhappy. I seem to have passed beyond the scenes of life and to have entered a kind of border land. This is a somewhat narrow tract of land covered with grass that is short and smooth and always very green. The ground is level and there are no trees. The sun is always shining, but it is not too warm, neither is it cold. On the one hand the whole world is spread out before me like a panorama. I can easily see to its remotest bounds; its oceans, its seas and rivers, its continents with its lofty mountains and its extended plains and all its marks of civilization; its highways and its railroads, its warehouses and its factories, its churches and its institutions of learning, its broad fields of waving grain and its orchards burdened with fruit, its beautiful flowers and its pleasant homes. All of these I have left behind and they seem to me like the toy imitations that we buy for our children. On the other hand is a river whose waters are nearly level with the grassy banks on which I stand. It is a broad, placid stream, flowing on with scarcely a ripple. The opposite shore is seldom visible as there is a heavy mist resting upon it. Sometimes when I have gazed a long time upon it the mist lifts and I catch glimpses of that wonderful city whose builder and maker is God, but it is only for a moment. The mists return and shut out the view and I resume my walk back and forth on the banks of the river, waiting for my Pilot who will soon appear with his boat to take me across to that blessed land of rest. But I am not impatient. I am not weary. I can wait. I feel no disposition to return to the world, yet I do not bear it any ill will. I have simply weighed it in a balance and found it wanting, and now I am waiting for transportation to the city that hath foundations.

March 21, 1898 Eyota, Minnesota. God has granted to me another return of my birthday. I am sixty-six years old today. I feel to thank a kind Heavenly Father for the mercies of another year. I have been fed, and clothed and sheltered, and, though I have been far from well, I have not been a great sufferer. My cough at present is quite troublesome, but it may be somewhat better when the weather gets settled. We have had a very mild winter since December. Farmers are beginning to think about the spring work and I suppose they will soon be very busy. Waldo has made up his mind not to teach here another year. The school is a very difficult one and he feels that he is not giving satisfaction. He talks now of going back on the farm, which, of course, I would be very glad to have him do, but the prospect looks gloomy to him. He dreads the hard work. I am afraid the education he received at the Normal weakened rather than strengthened his character. He seems to shrink from everything that requires great effort, either mental or physical. If he does not rise above these fatal tendencies he will make a total failure of life. I am tired of moving around and I long for a permanent home for the few remaining days of my life, but it is my constant prayer that I may be willing to follow any path through which the Lord leads me, however thorny it may be. I still read most of the time. I am now reading the history of Europe from 1789 to the rise of Louis Napoleon. I find it quite interesting. To appreciate the blessings of civilization and peace one ought to read the history of the past. Human life must have seemed as insecure during those stormy times but the nations of the earth are far from being at peace with one another yet. To all appearance, the millennium is still a long way off, but I feel sure that God will bring all these things about in his own good time.

I suppose we shall leave this place in a few weeks and where ever we go we shall have to experience all the horrors of moving, which generally make me ill.

July 4, 1898. Sechlerville, Wis. Well, I am back in my old home again and very glad I am to be here. We got here the 22nd of June. Waldo did not like teaching very well and he did not like Eyota at all, so we have come back on to the farm. Of course he does not work it this year. He and Mr. Apple are buying blueberries at present. My health is very poor indeed. I don't get up till about eleven o'clock and then I sometimes have to lie down before night. My cough is not so very hard, but my digestion is very bad. I am losing flesh right along. I am troubled to get a suitable diet. The old place looks quite natural; the trees have grown beyond all belief. My flower garden is all grown up to grass and weeds, but I don't know but it is just as well since I am too feeble to take care of flowers. There have been quite a good many changes in the neighborhood since we lived here. Some have died and several young men have married and settled on the farms, though I have been living where I saw a good many more people than I see here, but I don't feel at all homesick. I hope I shall not move again till I make my last journey. . . .

December 25, 1898. Sechlerville, Wisconsin. When I was a child the circle of a year seemed of a gigantic size, but the path of each circle has been getting shorter and shorter till now that I am nearly sixty-seven years old, the path from one to the other can be covered by a single step. But where will the next step land me? Will it be here in my earthly home, or in the great "beyond" where unkindness, care, and sorrow, sickness and pain are unknown; where I shall meet the many friends who have gone before and above all the Saviour whose birthday nearly all the inhabitants of the civilized world celebrate today. The past year has been one of very great trial; the most unhappy year, with one exception, of my past life. For a little while the load has been partly lifted but I tremble all the while lest it will fall again with a still more crushing weight. But my prayer is that I may be prepared for what is before me and that I may bear all the ills of life with faith and patience. Today is very fine, bright and sunny, but quite cold. Very little snow has fallen this winter so far. There will be a Christmas tree at the Presbyterian church tomorrow night for the children. But two more years and the nineteenth century will be ended. One hundred years seems a long time, but it is not so very long. My father was born in March of 1793, one-hundred and six years ago when next March arrives. Two lives more than cover the whole space.

March 21, 1899. Another birthday has arrived and I am sixty-seven years old. My health has been very poor during the past year but I was getting through the winter better than I expected till the first of this month, I was seized with the grippe, which has nearly used me up. My cough was very hard at first but it is much better now, but my digestion is very weak and my flesh has about all disappeared so that I haven't much chance to recover my strength. Starvation is my chief danger. If I can hold my own till I get the grippe poison out of my system I may regain my strength. Perhaps my last birthday has come. If so, I pray god to receive my soul cleansed from all sin into His glorious Kingdom to go no more out forever. I feel to praise Him for his great goodness to me. He has cared for me all my life, though I have been an unworthy servant, and since His promises are sure, I believe He will care for me to the end.

Nearly all this month has been unpleasant; cold and stormy. Tonight a great deal of snow has fallen. Sleighing is good at the present time, and the weather is really very cold for the season. I long for the spring sunshine and the warm breeze, but I suppose they will come in their own good time.

The Diary of Maranda J. Cline, 1906–1907

Maranda J. Cline was born in Columbus, Ohio, on April 1, 1833, to Matildia (Emmons) and George Cline. Maranda was one of nine children born into the family. They left Ohio in 1837, traveling down the Ohio River and up the Mississippi River to Burlington, Iowa, where they remained for four years until 1841. On July 17, 1856, when she was twenty-three, Maranda Cline gave birth to her first child, Henry Berdette Cline. On December 21, 1865,

Maranda J. Cline. Courtesy Patricia Lorentzen.

she married John McLaughlin, and they had two daughters, Bertie Georgia McLaughlin, who later married Robert Shellady, and Gertrude Ingemisca McLaughlin, who later married Joseph Stover.

After Maranda and John McLaughlin divorced in the late 1860s, she took back her maiden name. In 1870 she bought a farm in Johnson County, two miles south of the town of Hills, Iowa. She lived there until 1900, then moved in to Hills, where she had joined the Presbyterian church two years earlier. While caring for her youngest grandchild, she became ill and died on January 20, 1907. She was seventy-three. Her obituary notes: "Full of years she was gathered like a ripened sheaf among the garnered."

Like many farm women's diaries, the one kept by Maranda Cline reflects its writer's limited formal education in its fluid sentence structure, spelling, capitalization, and punctuation. This diary, kept by hand in a large notebook and based on the "line a day" principle, may require what Elizabeth Hampsten has called a "special inventive patience" for readers, who must pay attention not only to what is on the lines but also to what is between the lines. The spare style of Maranda Cline's diary says little directly but implies a great deal about the nature of the hard life that she faced in her later years. Her daughter Bertie Shellady inherited the diary three days after her mother died, then wrote retrospectively in the diary from January 6 through January 31, 1907, the last entry. The excerpts here are taken from the diary entries that Maranda J. Cline and Bertie made during the final months of Maranda's life.

December 1906

1   Mrs. Henry Eirhart Died yesterday at 10 oclock
2   a cloudy Day but sunshined at 3 an warmed the air
3
4
5   I fetched my Bed down stairs
6   I sent to Ward Montgomery & Co for 3 pair of skates
7   George Emmons was struck with palsy
8   Our Bazar was held in Hirts Hall we cleared 111
9   Rods an I went to Jo Stovers
10 the Stud hors trial the Draker Boys Knox an Fred Cline an Aers
11
12 Jo Stover bete Cox in the stud horse trial

13 the indevering Society had a play an cleared 35.23
14 Knox sawed 12 hours wood for me to burn in the kitchen
15 I put 100 dollars in the Bank at Iowa City
16 I wrote Fred Fesler a letter to Minesota
17 I got Blanch a finger ring
18 Charles Mancer finished laying the Blocks of stone for his house
19 Schmiah Snair had a sale an wil move to Kalona
20 Berdett sent me 15 lbs of venison from Aitkin
21
22 Cousin George Browns Daughter Lulu Died
23 the Iowa River froze over in many places
24 I caught a mink in my buggy shed
25 Christmas I eat oysters an turke at Visa McLaughlins
26 I went to Robs, Herbert Ashdown moved in Hills
27
28 Malinda Cline Flakes Baly Died at 3 to Day
29 Charles Mander covered his Block house, north of me
30
31 On the 19th I sent J. N. Walschmitt his note   it was paid

January 1907
1 Jos Stovers an Knox Clines Eat dinner with me
2
3 [. . .]
4 I paid Rev Luce the last $2.00 of my 10 dollars subscription
5
6
Bertie G. Shellady fell Earr to this book   I came posessor of
Mothers dira Jan. 23, 1907

[The remainder of the entries for January 1907 were made by
Maranda's daughter, Bertie.]

7 took Berdett Stover to Hospital at Iowa City
8 Mother went up to J. E. Stovers to help care for Ira
9 Rob an I went up to Joe's in afternoon to see Irr
10 Mother took Pluracy. I went up next morning to Joe Stovers
11 Bertie to see Mother   the Dr. to see Miscas baby an Mother
12 I come home, Blanche and Cloyd to Iowa City to see Berdett S.
13 we to church
14 Mother took worse
15 I went back to stay with Mother, stayed untill she died

393

16
17   Berdett got into Iowa City at 9 oclock at night
18   Berdett and uncle Fred come to see Mother out at Joe Stovers
19   Aunt Moll Cline come to J. Stover, Rob Blanche and Cloyd to Joes
20   Mother died 23 minutes of 9 oclock Sunday morning at J. Stovers
21   Uncle Fred Fesler Aunt Mollie Cline Berdett Cline Bertie Shellady
      and Children allstayed at Mothers house in Hills untill after
      Mothers funeral.
22   buried Mother
23   Divided Mothers bedclothes Berdett, Misca and Bertie
24   Berdett went to Iowa City came back at night
25
26   Sold Mothers house and Houshold goods, house $905.00, Goods
      $80.00
27   Uncle Fred Fessler hear, Berdett went to Hills
28   Apointed Berdett adm of Mother Est. Berdett went to Aitkin
29
30   put up Ice at Chas Shelladys job, Earl Bryant and Bertie
31   John Douglas killed at lone tree

The Diary of Lillian Stephens Carpenter, 1934

Lillian Margaret Stephens was born on March 17, 1904, in Omaha, Nebraska. In May 1915 her parents, Annie (Olsen) and Marshall Stephens, moved their family to Minneapolis. The oldest of four siblings, Lillian quit school when she was sixteen to go to work. Her first job was at Mazda Lamps, located near the family home on Monroe Street. According to her younger sister, Pearl (Pet) Stephens Ginthner, Lillian later worked as a telephone operator, along with her lifelong best friend, Sylvia (Begin) Tomalie.

On July 26, 1924, Lillian married John (Johnnie) Wesley Carpenter, and the couple lived in a working-class neighborhood in northeast Minneapolis. She worked briefly at a bakery; then, in the mid-1930s, she began working for American Farm Machinery in the mailing and advertising department. In 1939 the Carpenters purchased a cottage at Briggs Lake, Minnesota, where they spent weekends and holidays.

After her husband's death from heart disease, Lillian Carpenter kept working until her retirement. In her final years she entered the Minnesota Masonic Home in Bloomington, Minnesota. She

Lillian Stephens Carpenter. Courtesy Pearl Stephens Ginthner.

continued crocheting and kept her diary until December 3, 1981, when a stroke prevented her from writing again. Her final diary entry concludes with the words, "Alone evening." Lillian S. Carpenter died on September 18, 1989, at the age of eighty-five.

The sixteen volumes of her one- and five-year diaries contain brief daily entries about her activities as a housewife and employee as well as information on daily work activities, wages earned, social activities, family visits, family events, and weather conditions. The following excerpts from the first diary, kept during 1934, provide glimpses into the life of a Minneapolis working woman who, along with her husband, was facing the uncertainties of day-to-day life during the Great Depression.

January 1, 1934. Went down to Mothers. Had dinner at Olives and Roy's.

January 6, 1934. Went downtown in afternoon, then to Mother's. Gave Pet her bag for birthday Club in the evening at Ruth and Russell's. I won booby prize, the knife set.

January 10, 1934. Went down town then to Co-Workers at church. Had dinner at Florence and Bens.

January 18, 1934. The whole Club bunch went down to Elsie and Rueben's for the evening Johnnie booby prize. Hankie, me booby prize powder puffs.

January 20, 1934. Had Club at our house. Also Sylvia and Andy. Served Chili Carne and Upside down cake. Elsie and Ruben.

January 21, 1934. Stayed home. Had Company, Sylvia, Andy, Babe, Grace, Jimmie, Marion and Don. Olive and Roy and Barbie came in for a few minutes.

January 22, 1934. Started work at American Farm.

January 26, 1934. Stayed home. Bert and Archie were here for the evening.

January 27, 1934. Fell down and hurt my ankle. Went out with Sylvia and Andy in the evening to Fisher's. Saw Gretchen & Dick.

January 28, 1934. Stayed home. Sylvia and Andy came over in the afternoon and spent the evening.

January 29, 1934. Stayed home and ironed. Myrtle came up for a little while.

January 30, 1934. Stayed home. Florence & Karl spent the evening with us. Johnnie wraped the pkg for Mildred. Raymond come down and asked us to dance at Columbia High School. Didn't go. Foot too sore.

January 31, 1934. Pay day. $20.26, 50 cent raise. Had dinner at Mothers. . . .

February 3, 1934. Went to town with Mother, got new drapes. Club in the evening, at Cliff & Alice. Got home about 4:30. . . .

February 5, 1934. Stayed home, washed clothes. . . .

February 15, 1934. Had dinner home Mother & fixed it. My mother and Mrs. Amble stoped in for a few minutes. Stayed home all evening. Brought car licence $7.75. Pay day $31.42. . . .

February 21, 1934. Stayed home. Mine C came up for a short while, also Olive, Roy and Babe. Sylvia got laid off. . . .

February 25, 1934. Stayed home all day, went out with Sylvia and Andy in evening, went to Fisher's, Pine Tavern, The Point and Northern Light. . . .

March 10, 1934. Went down town with Sylvia. She got new dress. Went to Fisher's, and Hillard's Inn with Sylvia and Andy. Eva got laid off. . . .

March 15, 1934. Went to Mothers, Sylvia and Andy's from work. Had dinner at Florences and Ben's. Went for ride in their new car. Paid day $31.42. . . .

March 17, 1934. Had lunch at Mother's. Got new bag from Mother and Pet. Went to Saint Patrick's dance at Portland Ave Arena with Sylvia & Andy . . . Got home about 2:30. . . .

March 23, 1934. Went down to Babe & Grace's, Sylvia & Andy & Mothers. Spent evening at Mothers, then went over and made date with Sylvia & Andy for Sat. Johnnie started work at American Farm. . . .

April 2, 1934. Had dinner home alone. Went down to Myrtle's for the evening, Johnnie come down later. Rain all evening. Johnnie brought new suit. . . .

April 18, 1934. Had dinner at Myrtles. Went up to Annie's and Scottie's after Johnnie come home. Sylvia, Andy, Myrtle, Art were there. Got laid off from American Farm $7.25. Took Mother C. pillow to her. . . .

May 4, 1934. Cleaned house. Went down to House of Faith Church with Mother & Pearl to supper and 1 cent sale. Johnnie met me at Mother. Johnnie got paid $16.00. . . .

May 11, 1934. Hung clothes, clean house, ironed and mended. Andy came for a couple minutes. Johnnie paid $16.00. . . .

May 19, 1934. Got up at 3:30 A.M. went fishing at Twin Lakes with Sylvia and Andy. Andy caught 3 fish, Johnnie 1 and me 1. Got home about 6:30. Archie came for a few min., also Sylvia and Andy on way to Anoka. We drove out to Hillside and Fisher's. . . .

May 31, 1934. Stayed home all day. Hottest day since 1931—T. 107. Johnnie worked 12 hr for Crown Sidewalls $1.25. Walked over to Florence's, weren't home. Went to Bernice's for little while. David started work at Imperial. . . .

June 8, 1934. Stayed home all day. Ironed clothes. Sylvia and Andy came up in evening. Also Myrtle and Howard. Planted tomatoes and pepper plants. Johnnie paid $20.80. . . .

June 16, 1934. Pearl & Harriet came up for little while in morning, also David went down town with Johnnie, he brought new watch chain. Had Chown Mein. Sent flowers to Carlie & Betty for 6th Ann. Went there in evening, had a good time, got home at 4:30 A.M. . . .

July 4, 1934. Went fishing at Rush Lake with Mattie, Ray and girls. Caught sunfish, perch, and bullheads. Got home at 11:30 P.M. . . .

July 16, 1934. Johnnie didn't work, rained all day. Went down to Mother's from there went down town. Sylvia and Andy came up in the evening. David came up for dinner. Got China Closet. Strike started. . . .

July 26, 1934. Stayed home all day. Ella, Gordon, Myrtle and Howard came up in evening, went to Chris, Anns with them. Martial Law was declared at 12:20 P.M. David came up with Irvin's letter. Jensen went home. . . .

August 8, 1934. We down town with Bernice and Toots. Had lunch at the Russian Bear, had my fortune told. Then went to the Lyric and saw "He Was Her Man." Went to Sylvias in evening and went to Mike's with them. . . .

August 27, 1934. Had birthday lunch for Mother. Grace and Pet stayed for dinner. Went down to Mother's for a few minutes, then to Walkathon with Mattie and Ray. Saw Lill, Gus, Rose and Tom there. Gave Mother robe. . . .

September 9, 1934. Canned peaches all day. Went to mother's in evening, took babe, Grace and kids home from there. . . .

September 23, 1934. Canned tomatoes. Sylvia & Andy came up, went out to the heights to look at some dogs. Bought sandwiches, came home. Ella & Gordon come up. . . .

October 7, 1934. Went down to Myrtle's, worked on scrap book. Canned tomatoes. Went to Heights Theater with Myrtle & Howard. Saw The Thin Man. Johnnie worked all day & all nite.

October 20, 1934. Johnnie & Andy went hunting. 10 squirrels & 4 rabbits. I went to Mother's, Bobbie took me to town. Bought new shoes. Sylvia, Andy, Ella and Gordon came up in evening, went to Chris Ames. Four of us went to Central Café to eat. Ray stoped for minute. Sylvia and Andy stayed all nite. . . .

October 30, 1934. Sick all day. Myrtle came up for the afternoon. Stayed home in evening. Ella & Gordon stoped for few minutes, just as we were going to bed. . . .

November 9, 1934. Went to work at Gutegsell's. Went down to Sylvias, went to Andy's Place from there. Johnnie paid $25.45. Me paid $2.40. . . .

November 29, 1934. Thanksgiving. Washed clothes. Went down to Mother's in evening. . . .

December 8, 1934. Worked 2 day. Came right home. Connie came and cleaned. Got phone put in. Stayed home all evening. Connie washed my hair. 6 calls. . . .

December 13, 1934. Stayed home. Laid off from Gutegsell's. Paid $13.20. . . .

December 24, 1934. Went down town with Mother. David came over in afternoon and had dinner with us. Ella & Gordon stoped for couple minutes. Went to Mother's for Xmas Eve. Gave Mother ring. Johnnie gave me Robe. Last day Johnnie work.

The Diary of Ruby Butler Ahrens, 1942

On April 2, 1911, Ruby Alma Butler was born to Lucy Ellen (Parmley) and Robert Lee Butler on the family farm near Grinnell, Iowa. One of nine children, Ruby Butler attended country school as girl and Grinnell High School for two years. In 1929 she married Stanley Ahrens, whose family lived on the farm adjoining the Butlers'. Ruby and Stan Ahrens became the parents of five children: Paul, Raymond, Norma, Donald, and Mary. Ruby and Stan Ahrens remained on their farm outside Grinnell until they retired and moved into Grinnell; their son Donald took over the family farm operation. In 1993 the Ahrens farm received a Century Farm Award.

As an Iowa farm woman, Ruby Butler Ahrens worked with her husband. In her spare time she enjoyed gardening, sewing, quilting, and craft work. In 1940 she began a series of five-year diaries, which she continued until 1988, when she became ill. She died of a heart attack on September 25, 1989, at the age of seventy-eight.

During a forty-eight-year period, Ruby Ahrens wrote daily entries in three-by-five-inch diaries. Like Lillian Carpenter, Ruby Ahrens adhered to the five-year diary format, writing four-line entries in which she commented briefly on farm work and prices, the weather, visits to and from family and friends, and her daily work. The entries included here are from 1942. During this wartime year, buying defense bonds and rationing sugar and gas, along with butchering hogs, making hay, and canning pickles, became routine aspects of an Iowa farm family's daily life. The original manuscript diaries of Ruby Butler Ahrens remain in the possession of her son and daughter-in-law, Paul and Juanita Ahrens. (Juanita Ahrens also is a diarist; excerpts from her diary appear later in this chapter.)

Ruby Butler Ahrens and children, 1945. Courtesy Juanita and Paul Ahrens.

January 1, 1942 Terrible blizzard. Had planned on company.

January 2, 1942 Shoveled snow all day. Snow plow went by at noon.

February 2, 1942 Bert and Folks came out and we butchered. Hogs hit $12.50 top.

February 7, 1942 Saturday. We went to town. Rudkins took 1st eggs at 37 cents a dozen. Johnny and Evelyns little girl is Patty.

February 13, 1942 I made Norma a new dress for her birthday. Blue top and plaid bottom. She will be 8 tomorrow.

March 3, 1942 Stan hauled straw and wood. Worked in the grove cleaning up wood. I helped. I made doughnuts and tea towels. A lovely day. Hogs are $13.35.

March 12, 1942 Cleaned parlor paper and pantry. Stan sold 3 hogs. Telephone meeting at night. Nice day. Bought 1 defense bond.

March 18, 1942 Stan went back to work at church. I stayed home with Raymond. Had some sort of breaking out. Made Norma a skirt.

March 30, 1942 I got my chickens. Stan went to Gilman for telephone poles. Worked on line in afternoon. I papered John's room. Got birthday present from Merle. It snowed some today.

April 9, 1942 I painted floor in our room and cleaned upstairs. Dad was out and poisoned gophers. Stan sewed oats around brooder house. Disc garden, and hauled manure. It is clear and cold today.

May 1, 1942 Set out some flowers Marie gave me. Stan took 2 cows to sale barn. Paul took exams. I made me a new dress. Louie and kids were over in evening.

May 6, 1942 I went to home nursing class. I registered for sugar rationing. Stan and Harlan went to town.

May 19, 1942 I washed out feed sacks. Jock and Marie were over. Jock helped Stan fix the rotary hoe.

June 8, 1942 First day of bible school. I picked strawberries over at Larsens. Marie and I went to town. Marie told me her news.

June 15, 1942 I washed. Bible school. Stan made hay at Louis. Yesterday was Lillian Davidson's wedding. . . .

July 21, 1942 Sold old sows. I ironed. Jock and Walter were over to fix tires on hay rack. Made hay in afternoon. Got Tippy. Went over to Widdels in evening.

August 9, 1942 Church and sunday school. Jock and Marie and Stan and I went to town for dinner and to see "Gone With the Wind". Elizabeth kept the children.

August 19, 1942 Had hogs vaccinated. I canned pickles and beans. Stan mowed schoolyard. Jock and Marie came home from vacation.

August 22, 1942 Hauled manure. Took Louie's stack back and then we all picked Button weeds. Folks took Aunt Ella to Ames.

September 5, 1942 Paul is 13 today. I washed and ironed. Jock and Marie were over for dinner

September 21, 1942 I washed. Finished hauling lime. Folks were out. Got chickens. Jock came over and helped scrape dirt.

September 29, 1942 Jock and Grandpa and Stan shingled the dog shed. Marie and I went to Elizabeth's and made sauerkraut.

October 9, 1942 Stan cleaned hen house. Grandpa and Grandma were out. Marie and I went to town and had our hair set. Teacher director and banquet tonight.

November 8, 1942 Entertained soldier boys at church. . . .

November 12, 1942 Gas rationing began. Stan and boys went to Newburg for lumber. Jock came over and told us about Darlene Luella Plum, 8 pounds, 9 ounces. Ervins and us went to Widdels and made benches.

December 16, 1942 Cleaned my house. Kept Darlene while Jock and Marie and Stan went to town. We went to FREE show at night.

December 25, 1942 Christmas Day at folks. Boys got train and I got a vacumn sweeper.

The Diary of Maud Hart Lovelace, 1953–1955

Maud Hart was born on April 25, 1892, to Thomas and Stella (Palmer) Hart of Mankato, Minnesota. When she was five, Maud began writing stories; poems and plays soon followed. When she was ten, a collection of her poems was printed, and by eighteen she had sold her first short story to the *Los Angeles Times*. After she graduated from high school in 1910, her family moved to Minneapolis, where she attended the University of Minnesota and traveled throughout Europe until World War I began. In 1917 she married the journalist and author Delos W. Lovelace, and both husband and wife worked seriously on their writing over the next years. In 1926 Maud Hart Lovelace's first novel was published. In 1931 the Lovelaces' daughter, Merian, was born.

The stories about her childhood that Maud Hart Lovelace told to her young daughter became the source material for the well-known series of Betsy-Tacy novels that Maud Hart Lovelace published, beginning in 1940. In writing these young adult novels, she drew not only on her memories but also on letters, photographs, and other mementos she had saved. Throughout her life she kept diaries in which she described daily events and family activities as well as her progress with her writing. She used a series of diaries (such as the Standard Diary and the Daily Reminder) with lined, dated pages that measured five and a half by eight inches and contained twenty-five lines per daily entry.

From 1953 to 1955, shortly after she and Delos moved from New York to Claremont, California, Maud began writing *Betsy's Wedding*, the final novel in the Betsy-Tacy series. On occasion, a daily entry in her diary would begin with a notation at the top of the page (such as "Dictate 11," "Polish 13," or "Mail 13, 14, 15"), defining her expectations for that day, sometimes with a prayer that her progress on the day's work would fulfill her hopes. An added influence may well have been the marriage of Merian Lovelace to Engelbert ("Bert") Kirchner, which occurred while her mother was writing this novel.

After Maud completed *Betsy's Wedding* in 1955, the Lovelaces continued to live in California, where Delos died in 1967. Maud Hart Lovelace died in Claremont on March 11, 1980, and is buried in Oakland Cemetery in Mankato, Minnesota. The excerpts

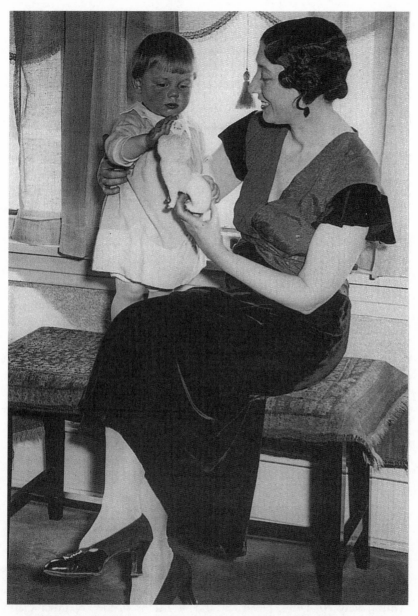

Maud Hart Lovelace and daughter, Merian, 1932. Used with permission of the Betsy-Tacy Society.

that follow come from her 1953–1955 diary and are reproduced with permission from her literary executor, Andrea Shaw, who acknowledges the assistance of Mary Thiessen in transcribing the diaries.

Monday, Nov. 2, 1953. "Betsy's Wedding" I started it today—with a prayer. . . .

Wed, Nov. 11, 1953. Armistice Day in Des Moines and the day mother died in 1947. Foggy. Our flowers from my windows are wreathed in fog. Worked on the article. Letters from Doris, Lillian Wakefield, Midge. Sun came out of course, as it always does. . . .

Thurs, Nov. 26, 1953. Thanksgiving morning. D and I sat at breakfast telling each other solely how much we have to be thankful for. That we have had such a wonderful marriage and love each other so dearly after 36 years; our great compatibility; our little income which permits him to write at last; our health; and so important our wonderful daughter and the fact that she is happy and well adjusted to life. . . .

Wed, Apr. 21, 1954. . . . I'm still reading thru the B-T [Betsy-Tacy] books but they make me cry so I can hardly read them. Wrote to Merian. . . .

Sun, Apr. 25, 1954. My birthday! And in honor of it (I'm sure) the fog left. It's like a midsummer day. I just went out and picked red and yellow roses for the vases and now must make spaghetti. We're playing Scarlatti Sonatas Delossy gave me for my birthday. I have Birds of the Pacific Coast coming too . . . A happy day although as always on such special days, missed our baby. . . .

Mon, May 17, 1954. I am struggling with the tape recorder. Got Chapter 1 of "Betsy's Wedding" recorded. Got my hair washed and nails done and tonight poured punch at Mrs. Engel's, where the St. Ambrose Woman's Guild was meeting. . . .

Thurs, May 20, 1954. Headache and all, I transcribed in bed that chapter I wrote last week, and Delossy and I sat outdoors a while enjoying our roses, and the birds. The big news today was that the Los Angeles Times which gave Delossy's talk of yesterday top place in its story of the event, and two paragraphs in contrast to everyone else's one. I am so proud of him. He's very good at this speaking business. . . .

Fri, May 28, 1954. A miserable morning at the Monster [tape recorder] which acted up altho my Chapter 3 is really ready to be written. I was very glad to dress and go to town to see Dr. Hartman (Dr. Hughes sent me to him) and get a prescription for new glasses incorporating the clip-ons I've found so satisfactory. . . .

Fri, June 4, 1954. Mulled over Chapter 5, typed notes, but nothing came. Delossy's Journey [to Bethlehem] is on Crowells juvenile (as well as adult, I feel sure) list for fall . . .

Sat, June 5, 1954. I had a big day on book. Dictated and transcribed Chapter 5. . . .

Sat, June 12, 1954. Dictated Chapter 6. Hooray! I'm getting on. Wrote to Merian, as I seem to every day. Wrote Annie, Katharine and Elizabeth the news [of Merian's upcoming wedding]. I want to write everyone we love. . . .

Tues, June 15, 1954. Chapter 6 was so good that I'm going to dictate it again. Didn't have much success, tho' . . . Wrote to Merian again. I've written every day since she 'phoned! . . . .

Wed, June 16, 1954. I brooded over Chapter 7, and the mail brought a letter from ER [Elizabeth Riley, Maud's editor] who is lunching with Merian. I read Delossy's Danny story again, and didn't think the revision entirely successful. He's going to put it on ice again. Callers again—this time a Mr. and Mrs. Clinton Laird—background, chiefly China, schools, and libraries—a second wife. She knows the Betsy-Tacy books and they've bought Journey so naturally they seem like nice folks. She suggested that I do a juvenile about the little girl with the Padua Hills Players.

Thur, June 17, 1954. I did a fine Chapter 7, before the letter came . . . The McCarthy hearings ended today. They've been shocking but entertaining. . . .

Wed, Jul. 21, 1954. A good day on Chapter 11. Tib came to life a little. . . .

Mon, Sept. 13, 1954. Today I must start full force on "Betsy's Wedding." (Don't feel like it either.) I'm now at my desk and how the mocking birds are warbling! One is stationed on the hedge, singing, twittering, warbling. He's so fat. Have been sitting out doors, trying to get story started. Crepe myrtle trunk peels, shows pole green beneath the grey. The mocking birds are trying to decide, with much talk, whether to nest in our hedge in a Cooper tree. Wrote to Merian today. Delossy heard from Colliers West Coast bureau, sounding him out on doing some work for them. . . .

Mon, Oct. 4, 1954. The most wonderful letter from Vera [Neville, illustrator for the teenage books] who loves the first chapter. Thinks it has a poetic quality. Her letter was very helpful, as she advises me not to be limited by the hard time I had getting out "Betsy and the Great World." Circumstances were so different then. She's right. I am so terribly impressionable that I never seem to forget, subconsciously, an ordeal such as that one was. Just "roll with the punches", she says. And tells me to let this book pour out just as it's started. Delossy and I put on evening clothes (the new tux) and went to the opening concert in Bridges Auditorium. A big audience for Robert Weede, the baritone, a natural singer who loves to sing. . .

Tues, Oct. 19, 1954. Back to chapter 4. Must have a big day today. I did.

Wed, Oct. 20, 1954. I finished Chapter 4 (Durans here) and Delossy read it aloud, and wept, and so did I. I think this is a pretty good sign. After coffee we went on my favorite drive, up to Padua Hills. From Via Padua up there, you see fold after fold, or layer after layer of hills. You are on a height, a dry river bed below, and hills—covered with brush etc— are beyond. They are mountains really. It is a superb view spot. Home for Scrabble, supper and an early bedtime. . . .

Tues, Nov. 9, 1954. I must and will finish Chapter 5—didn't but I certainly worked! Until 4 and then we had a ride—up into the mountains. . . .

Wednesday, Nov. 10, 1954. A hard day's work, and Chapter 5 was ready, by evening, to read to Delos. I hadn't even changed my dress. Put on a dressing gown for supper which he prepared. Chapter 5 too long but otherwise fine, he says, and I guess it's good as I wept when he read it. . . .

Fri, Nov. 19, 1954. Daddy's birthday! He's been gone almost 20 years and how near he still seems. Written later but I know I was shopping in Pomona and bought a pretty black dinner dress, neck outlined with pale pink and brilliants. . . .

Tues, Nov. 23, 1954. Woke with a headache but worked through it and got Chapter 6 mailed to Vera. It's good too. Headache so bad that Delos brought my supper to bed and I couldn't go to see the documentary film on Gandhi—Delossy says it was marvelous.

Wed, Nov. 24, 1954. When I finish a chapter it's like finishing a book. And a house cleaning goes on in my study. Paper sorted and thrown away, bills paid, letters answered. . . .

Fri, Nov. 26, 1954. Must and will now get a start on Chapter 7. . . .

Wed, Dec. 8, 1954. Today is the day I finish Chapter 7. I put in a full 8 hours at the typewriter, exclusive of lunch, and was dead. Delossy took me to the village on errands, got dinner and washed the dishes. I revived and we started on the Christmas cards. . . .

Thur, Dec. 9, 1954. Today is the day I really finish chapter 7. Cold. Overcast. I just went out to fill the metate. More Calendulas budded. I did finish it and Delossy read and cut it. Likes it, too. Rained most of the day. We got out to the village, though, on errands. Glanced fondly at the Betsy-Tacys and Journeys in Briar's window. Delos bought a Journey and took it to Mrs. Polos who mimeographed our Christmas cards—she wouldn't take any money for them because we had given her part of our paper! In the rain to the Oxford Inn to have dinner with our Hungarian friend. (Delossy got stuffed cabbage.) Home to address Christmas cards all evening. . . .

Thurs, Dec. 23, 1954. I stayed in bed until almost noon proofreading my Chapter 8 which Delossy mailed to Vera. Then dressed. Lots of excitement around here, mail twice a day and packages popping in. Delossy and I did a bit of last minute shopping and tonight had the Christmas tree and Louisa's candles lighted, and even opened a package or two. Libby Demp sent me a beautiful book on Venice with an inscription that brought tears to my eyes. Bickie had refilled the Knott's Berry farm jam glasses we sent her last year. Such a cute idea! Grace sent me beautiful hand work. We got Lebenkuchen, cookies and fruit. . . .

Sat Feb 19 [1955]. Chapter 14 please

Tues Feb 22 [1955]. Chapter 15, please. My prayer for today! I got a draft of sorts. And we had another sunshiny walk. I was too tired to go to hear Dr. Chew and Delossy went with Will.

Wed Feb 23 [1955]. . . . I got the good draft of Chapter 15 I wanted—got it in time so I could go over to Renaissance Room to hear the Litany and the Bishop's Lenten mediations. Hope our Merian is at Church! Home for lunch and to transcribe my chapter. This evening we go the first of a weekly Lenten series on the Eucharist. . . .

Thurs Feb 24 [1955]. Worked on Chapter 16. Did it. But exhausted . . . Delossy and I out tonight to hear the Budapest String Quartette.

Fri Feb 25 [1955]. Chapter 17 please. And it came. I was very tired. But went over my house, brought in flowers and made coffee and Alma and Miss Wiley came in. Miss W. is quite a person. A retired social worker who made a very famous exposure, years ago, of a watch factory where girls were being poisoned by working with radium. Deliberately poisoned, as the management took away their little cups of water so the girls had to moisten their brushes with their lips. They died of leukemia in a procession.

Sat Feb 26 [1955]. . . . Chapter 18. Didn't feel up to it so instead I did a mean job—corrections in Chapter 13.

Mon Feb 28 [1955]. Put correction in early chapters and transcribed chapter 17. A beautiful letter from our child loving the book, and what that does for me! I am so grateful and happy. . . .

Tues Mar 1 [1955]. 14 polished please. I got a start on it. Worked very hard.

Wed Mar 2 [1955]. Chapter 14 polished please . . . I think we moved a year ago today. Now chapter 14. It went marvelously but didn't quite get finished. We lunched out, for Durans were here. All full of warmth, sunshine, sweetness. Out tonight to hear Heifitz playing the Kreutzer Sonata and other things. Delossy very handsome in his tux.

Thurs Mar 3 [1955]. Chapter 14 finished please. It was. I worked until 6 and Delossy just as hard on his next-to-last chapter. . . .

Sun Mar 6 [1955]. Go to church to thank God, which I did. Early church and it was very beautiful. Delossy off to Sunday School and after my morning work I tried to write—but couldn't—except for a letter to Men'an. The day was divine. I walked around outside a bit, watering the calendulas, the nasturtiums, the budding freesias, the four or five inch high calla lilies and so on.

Mon Mar 7 [1955]. Chapter 15 today, please. I remember that after work we took a ride. The moon was rising in the East, full and beautiful, altho the world was still light. (In the morning we had seen it setting through the slats of our west window blinds.) The evening sky was like the inside of a shell.

Tues Mar 8 [1955]. Up at 5:10. A terrific day with one or two years rests in blue chair outside. But the chapter did not come clear until the end of the day. Oh, for tomorrow! After a rest, and a call at Mrs. K's for copy, we went to dinner at Lee's Shrimp House. Owner, a pretty young woman from New Orleans. She settled first in Pasadena, she said, but the doctor sent her here for sinus, and she's never had a bit since. The acacia trees, like drooping greenish, yellow faces, are still in bloom all over Claremont. And raspberry pink and light pink fruit trees, but not ours yet. Finches are circling over each other's heads.

Wed Mar 4 [1955]. Now to take Chapter 15 into my hands! Durans here but I barely saw them. Worked all day. And Delossy got dinner.

Thur Mar 10 [1955]. Worked all day, like a beaver. To dinner at Lee's Shrimp House and sat facing the mountains which are always balm to me. Our darling Claremont Courier has changed its shape and editor.

Fri Mar 11 [1955]. Worked until noon. Cleaned and polished and brought in flowers and Margaret Harding, charming ex-editor of Minnesota Press, her sister Betty and Ruth Nuhn came for cocktails. We took them to the inn for dinner. I like Margaret a lot and was glad to see her but I'm too tired and wound up for parties. Our mountains didn't show for her, but having visited this neighborhood a lot, she knew they were there. My manuscript came back from Merian, with a letter from our son-in-law. I was so pleased to get it.

Sat Mar 12 [1955]. A stunning draft of Chapter 16 dictated and transcribed. We got in a walk at noon. Mountains still hidden by mist but the blooming fruit trees everywhere are pleasant. Tonight we drove down to Yves for an excellent French dinner. Even had a cocktail. . . .

Mon Mar 14 [1955]. 17 Study 18. Make a rough draft

Tues Mar 15 [1955]. Chapter 17 done. A hard days work. Delossy usually takes me for a ride about twilight. He is working on his revisions now. Working very hard himself. Soon we'll both be free! . . . .

Tues Mar 29 [1955]. Oh how wonderful to have my book done! Although I still spend most of my day at the desk. This evening I went with Delossy to another of Dr. Chew's lectures. He spoke on the Psalms Proverbs and Book of Job. We look at Orion every night. Not all the constellations always visible.

Wed Mar 30 [1955]. Still busy at my desk but with a weight off my mind. Durans here. We went up to the Oxford inn for lunch . . . I believe it was tonight the Motion Picture Oscars were given out. Marlon Brando and Grace Kelly won. We were rooting for Bing and Judy Garland! . . . .

Wed Apr 6 [1955]. Felt very low today. Physically more than mentally. I'm still simply bushed. Had my hair done at Crystal's, but still look as tired as I feel. . . .

Sun Apr 10 [1955]. Our calla lily (one) bloomed for Easter. These are from bulbs we planted ourselves. Out early to the Easter service and stayed on to Sunday School. The children very sweet. Each mite box had a flower in it . . . Thought so much of Merian. Mrs Remington said she wrote to her for Easter. D and I both almost had tears in our eyes when she told us. I am thankful and happy that my book is done and everyone liked it. Now for Delossy to get in the same happy state! . . . .

Mon Apr 25 [1955]. Sixty three years old, as above! They've been good years and this was happy birthday. Delossy took me to Pomona and let me pick out a tea set for my birthday. (You can't live in Claremont without a tea set!) Packages were opened at coffee time. Anne Lindberg's lovely book from Merian and Bert. Merian knew how I love her writing. Helen and Frank sent a cute scratch pad with my name on a leather cover. Fosters book came later (Mormon Country and very good.) Bick sent a red and white checked cloth, and there were many cards, including cards from Midge and Libbie. One of the nicest presents was a wire from St. Catherine's College in St. Paul where they put on the musical version of Early Candlelight last night and tonight. "Happy Birthday. We play for you tonight The Candle-lighter." Delossy made a shortcake for a birthday cake. . . .

Wed May 4 [1955]. At last I am putting away "B's W" - although I still have letters to answer. Also am reading Ruth Suckow's delightful short stories. "Auntie Bissell" especially good . . . D and I took a walk. The gardens are at their loveliest. Of course pyracanthus everywhere is cascading white blossoms. Roses are so abundant and fragrant. Violets, violas, phlox make masses of color and fragrance. . . .

412

The Annals of the Sisters of St. Francis of the Holy Family (OSF), 1962–1973

The Sisters of the Third Order of St. Francis of the Holy Family, founded by Sister Mary Xavier (born Josephine Termehr), originated in Herford, Germany. On August 20, 1875, during the Franco-Prussian War, a group of the sisters sailed on the *Caland* for New York City. From there they continued west to Iowa City, Iowa. In December 1878, when an opportunity arose to move their order, the sisters founded a motherhouse in Dubuque. Soon the order began teaching throughout Iowa. The sisters arrived in the small northwest Iowa town of Granville in 1889, and they taught there until 1997, keeping "the annals," a record of convent life and work. In 1932 Sister Mary Leonice Martin wrote this observation in the annals: "We had many good times in our primitive living conditions. I have many happy memories of the place."

For twenty-two years, from 1962 to 1983, Sister Mary Merici Oehrlein, OSF, kept the annals for the convent community in Granville. During those years, she taught English and Latin and coached debate and speech at Spalding High School. Sister Merici describes her work as annalist in this way:

During the year, I would keep a notebook in which I jotted down what I believed were both ordinary and eventful happenings. I tried to be objective. At the end of the school year, I typed the notes, sent a copy to the archivist at the Motherhouse and retained a copy which was placed in a loose leaf binder in the convent library. This room was also the Superior's office. As the door was generally open, Sisters were free to enter at any time to read the annals. I don't recall consulting anyone about describing the events, although I'm sure we did discuss happenings; and thus I probably formulated decisions about what to write. As a whole, however, I would say these were individual situational decisions on my part. I was annalist from 1962–1983. (personal correspondence, September 20, 1998)

The annals kept by Sister Mary Merici from 1962 to 1973 mark a decade of great changes in the Catholic Church. After the Vatican II Council, religious services were in English rather than Latin; religious habits were changed; and many restrictions on nuns were lifted. In the face of declining enrollments and fewer

Sister Mary Merici Oehrlein, O.S.F., recorder for OSF Annals at Granville, Iowa, 1991

young women entering the convent to become teachers, Granville consolidated its parochial school system with those of the neighboring towns of Alton and Hospers and hired more lay teachers. Parents whose children attended St. Joseph Grade School and Spalding High School during this decade consistently voted in special school referenda against bond issues that would have funded the construction of a new public high school for the Floyd Valley School System. Political assassinations, the Vietnam War, and social activism influenced the lives and teaching of the members of the order during this period. All these events are recorded in the annals.

1962–63 annals . . . February 15 was "moving day" at Spalding High. Rooms 207, 209, and the Library were ready for occupancy. Other rooms were ready a few days later—the new wing was ready at last. . . . New chairs and tables were purchased for the library of the new wing. All the rooms in the new wing were ready for occupancy by April 8. . . . The Name SPALDING HIGH SCHOOL in raised black letters was placed on the south side of school; a new light was placed on the west side. . . . Graduation for forty-six seniors was held May 30 at 7:30 in the Spalding gym. An estimated crowd of 1,200 people attended the exercises. . . . This was the first graduating class of Spalding High School. . . .

1963–64 annals . . . Sister Mary Rosalita's feast day (Aug. 30) was celebrated on Sunday, August 25. A Mass was said for her intentions and a spiritual bouquet was given to her. Other gifts for Sister included vases for the chapel altar and a planter for the library. Sister was very pleased that the Sisters had decorated the library bulletin board for her. . . .

October 26 Sisters Mary Alcuin and Merici attended the Speech and Drama clinic at Spencer. . . . The grade and high school teachers attended the Annual Teachers' Institute at Storm Lake, October 9-10.

The following Sisters went roller skating in LeMars: Sisters Marie Bernadette, Felicitas, Matthew, Bernette. The rink was operated by Mrs. B. Soule, a sister of Sister Mary Brideen. . . .

Friday, November 22, faculty and students were shocked and saddened to hear of the assassination of President John F. Kennedy, the first Catholic president. Monday, November 25, school was dismissed as the nation observed a day of mourning. All school activities (basketball games, debate, etc., etc.) were cancelled this week-end. . . .

The first real winter weather, snow, wind and sleet came December 7 late in the afternoon. It continued to storm December 8. . . .

Graduation for Spalding's forty-seven seniors was May 24. . . . Final tests for high school students were May 25–27. Report cards were given out May 28 after a High Mass at 8:45. . . .

1964–65 annals . . . THE GOLDEN KERNEL, Spalding's first year-book, was ready for distribution August 12. Sister Mary Alcuin was moderator. . . .

At a Christmas Assembly Spalding students presented the faculty with gifts: the Sisters were given a fourteen-pound turkey and a bottle of Mogen David wine. Priests and lay members of the faculty were also given gifts.

Father George, Spalding superintendent, gave each sister of the high school and grade faculty a three-minute phone call as a Christmas gift. Father Becker's gift was a number of spiritual reading books.

The sisters at Granville decided to give their Christmas gifts to the new mission in Chile, South America, this year. A minimum was purchased in the way of Christmas gifts.

Many gifts were received from people of the parish: a Dutch oven, bakery goods, fruit, beer, pop, chicken, turkeys, ham, etc.. . . .

On Dec. 29, thirty-five sisters from Ashton, Larchwood, Sibley, Hospers and Granville met at Alton for a community meeting. Present also were Sister Mary Margaret Francis and Sister Mary Shaun. The meeting was both a business and a social one inasmuch as the financial drive for the EXPANSION PROGRAM was explained. Sister Mary Shaun, home from Cuernavaca, Mexico, modeled the slightly modified habit the missionaries will wear in South America. A dinner was served by ladies of the parish. In the afternoon, games were played. Many sisters toured Saint Mary's School for a final time as it will be razed in the spring. . . .

Sunday, Jan. 31, Holy Mass was said for the first time with the celebrant facing the congregation. The beautiful altar made by Father Becker was stationed just inside the Communion railing.

Monday, Feb. 1, the proper of the High Mass was sung in English for the first time by the Sisters at the 6:50 a.m. Mass. The proper was arranged to the psalm tones by Sister Mary Ancilla. . . .

A questionnaire or opinion poll was received from the Motherhouse concerning proposed changes in the veil, habit, coif, collar, cuffs, cord, etc. Changes were discussed during recreation and a tape recording was made of the discussion (of which most of the discussants were unaware). The sisters voted for their preferences and the poll was mailed to MSF [Mount St. Francis].

Feb. 11 the Spalding faculty and student body had a free day in honor of Our Lady of Lourdes, Spalding patroness. A blizzard that brought 12 inches of snow forced all schools in the area to close. . . .

1965–66 annals: . . . The Christmas Cantata, "The Song of Christmas," by Roy Ringwald was presented Sunday, Dec. 19 at 8:00 to a large and appreciative audience. Members of the Mixed Chorus wore the new choral gowns made by mothers of the students. The replica of a stained glass window on the stage was a very impressive background for the Nativity scenes pantomimed. Many of the audience commented favorably on the singing which was in charge of Sister Mary Celia, OSF. . . .

The Sisters found Christmas vacation a good time to house clean, sew, and prepare lesson plans and semester texts. In addition there was some time for recreation. On Dec. 27, "Mary Poppins" was shown at the Alton theater for Sisters of the area. A number of Granville sisters attended. [Another] was the film "Lord Jim" at the Palace theater, Remsen, Dec. 28.

Dec. 30 Sisters of Alton, Granville, Kingsley and Oyens met at Remsen for a showing of the new veils and a vote of preference. Modeling the new veils were Sisters Mary Bertille, Carl and Chabanel. Many Sisters tried on the veils before voting for their choice. After the style show, the sisters enjoyed a turkey dinner and then spent the afternoon playing games or visiting. . . .

A severe blizzard struck Granville and the surrounding area late in the afternoon of March 22. Electricity was cut off and remained off all that night. School was not held March 23–24 (Wednesday and Thursday) while all dug out from the steep drifts which were as high as ten feet in some places. . . . All over Iowa (for the blizzard hit all of the state) people were forced to find refuge against the storm. The storm did much damage in Minnesota and the Dakotas as well. The sisters used the free time afforded them by sewing, typing (the annals!), etc. . . .

March 27—More changes in the liturgy: English prayers at the Foot of the Altar, orations, preface, Our Father (new melody), the Pray Brethren, the Libera nos and all the responses. . . .

April 11. A sample of the new veil arrived and Sister M. Rosalita began immediately to measure and place orders for materials. Some sisters began work on trial veils, using old materials and wearing them in private in the convent. The new veil may not be worn in public until official approval is received from Rome. . . .

Word was received from the Convent April 29 that, although the new veil is not yet approved by Rome, still work could commence on the sewing of them. Some materials were received via Sacred Heart Hospital, Le Mars. The new veils will not be worn in public until Rome has confirmed the adoption.. . . .

Spalding presented its first Musical GREEN VALLEY, April 30. The musical production was directed by Sister Mary Celia. Father Walding was in charge of scenic effects and lighting. Sister Mary Bernette directed choreography. Sister Mary Constance was in charge of costuming. Sister Mary Merici gave some assistance in dramatics. A large and appreciative audience saw the musical. The seniors won the prize ($25) for having sold the most tickets. . . .

Father George's appointment was confirmed in the May 26 GLOBE. Father will study for a doctorate in theology and religious education at St. Paul's Seminary, Ottawa, Canada. Father Gerald Hartz will be the new superintendent of Spalding. . . .

May 31 The Catholic Daughters hosted a picnic at Lake Okoboji for the Sisters of Alton, Hospers and Granville. Fishing was not good, but the Sisters enjoyed the sun and the water . . . When they reached home the sisters found a message from Sacred Heart Hospital, LeMars, to the effect that Rome had finally approved the new veil and that it could now be worn in public. Final flurried finishing touches were made during the next days. . . .

June 4 the Sisters changed to the new veil and created quite a stir in the community. At 1:00 p.m., Sisters Rosalita, Jeanne Anne, Bernette, Beatrice, Felicitas, Celia, Lucretia and Alonzo left for retreat at Briar Cliff. Remaining at Granville for the week of June 4-11 to brave the stares of the laity were Sisters Mary Merici and Lumena. . . .

June 7 Sister Mary Constance returned from a home visit made in Portland, Oregon. While there Sister caught a 30 lb lingcod fish, an ocean perch, and two red snappers in the Pacific Ocean. She stayed at the Ocean cottage of the Sisters of the Good Shepherd, ferried over the Columbia River and went up to the point where the Columbia empties into the Pacific Ocean. . . .

1966–67 annals. School opened at Spalding and at St. Joseph Grade School August 29. New on the high school faculty were Mr. James Ell-wanger who was appointed assistant coach and assigned to teach biology and American history and Mrs. Donald Zwach, who contracted to teach dramatics and developmental reading. Returning lay teachers were Mr. Gerald Davies and Mr. Ken Kommes. Mrs. Mary Hodapp was retained as office assistant. . . .

Oct. 3 Spalding teachers attended the Annual Teachers' Institute at Carroll. Grade school teachers attended Oct. 4. Keynote address Oct. 3, "Christian Culture and the American Catholic High School" was given by Doctor John J. O'Brien of Saint Louis University. The Minimum Standards Act of Iowa was explained by Mr. Earl Miller of the Department of Public Instruction. Doctor Reginald Newwien explained "The Notre Dame Study: Catholic Schools in Action"—the results of the Carnegie foundation Study of Catholic Schools. . . .

October 16 the Granville sisters hosted a Chapter meeting on renewal and adaptations. "Up-dating Religious Life" was the subject discussed. Sisters from Alton and Hospers were entertained at dinner before the discussions were held. . . .

Dec. 21 Spalding students played Santa Claus to the faculty. The sisters were given table linen, a turkey and a bottle of Christmas spirits. . . . Many gifts of food and household articles were given the sisters from members of the parish at Christmas.

December 24 the sisters had their own Christmas party. Gifts of table linen, hood scarfs, coat linings, parlor pillows, a hair dryer, spiritual reading books were opened. A Holy Mass was offered for the intentions of the sisters. . . .

Jan. 2 the Sisters visited the sick and aged of the parish. . . .

Jan. 29 the Spalding Spartans won third place in the Diocesan tournament, and the cheerleaders won the trophy at the Tournament Finals held in the Sioux City Auditorium. Since the games were broadcast over the radio, the sisters were able to enjoy the victories with the teams. A free day was granted on Ash Wednesday in recognition of the victory. . . .

February 11 the varsity debaters took first place in the debate tournament at Hartley and brought home the A-division trophy. Sisters Mary Merici and Rosalita accompanied the team. . . .

Recommendations received from Mount Saint Francis state that the Sisters may take a week's vacation every year. Further, local communities are encouraged to experiment in the matter of silence. The use of TV is henceforth the responsibility of the individual sister. Daily necessities and food are to be available in a special place. Sisters may now assume personal responsibility for the disposal of worn-out clothing and articles of small value. They may eat outside the dining room. Sisters leaving the house briefly for business and/or visits to the sick may go without specific permission if they sign out. All sisters should be permitted to write, seal, stamp and mail their own letters. Flexibility in recreation is encouraged. Superiors should provide for the reception of the Sacrament of penance weekly, but the participation in a sacrament is the individual sister's responsibility. . . .

April 28 Sister Merici received a phone call from the Foreign Language League of Salt Lake City, Utah, that she has been selected as campus nurse and chaperone by this organization. She will study in Leysin, Switzerland, and Versailles, France, if she decides to accept. . . .

Word was received in May that Father Thomas Walding was being transferred to St. Mary's Remsen. The Sisters entertained Father at a Farewell. Father left June 7. . . .

In accordance with the renewal spirit, sisters were permitted to change their [religious] names to their baptismal name if they so wished, using with their baptismal names the family name so as to be able to distinguish from others of a similar surname. . . .

1967–68 annals: Position papers on the various facets of renewal were received from Mount Saint Francis. These were discussed by the Sisters in sessions with sisters from Hospers and Alton.

January 28 the Spartan Basketball team took first place in the CYO tournament at the Sioux City Auditorium by defeating Breda. A free day was granted Jan. 29. . . .

February 20 Sisters Margaret Francis and Georgia visited at St. Joseph Convent. Their purpose was to have meetings with Fathers Becker and Hartz concerning the withdrawal of Sisters from the schools and the hiring of lay teachers. It was decided that St. Joseph Grade School will lose one sister next year and hire one lay teacher in her place. Spalding will be given an additional Sister teacher in the next school year. . . .

March 31. Word was received at the convent that Gary Reichle, honor student of Spalding, class '67, was killed by a train at Ames. He had been a student at the university. . . .

Fifty-six seniors graduated from Spalding High School, May 26 when a layman, Attorney John Whitesell of Iowa Falls gave the Commencement address. . . .

Spalding teachers, St. Joseph faculty, and members of the Alton-Hospers-Granville parishes attended a special meeting held to discuss the Special School Referendum proposing a $1,875,000 central school for the Valley area of Alton-Granville-Hospers-Newkirk. Discussion centered on the tax increase, the present diminishing school population, the new reorganization proposed by the State which would make this very project obsolete. Speakers were Mr. Poppen, Floyd Valley superintendent, also a member of the architect firm, Father Becker, Father Hartz.

(The school bond was put to a vote and defeated by a very large majority, June 2). . . .

1968–69 annals: . . . A regional meeting of all Sisters of the Community from northwest Iowa was held at Briar Cliff October 12. Speakers were Sisters Mary Clotilde, Ruth Agnes and Viator. Discussion groups were held. Community Mass was at noon, followed by a sack lunch at Noonan Hall. Sisters Arnold and Brendan gave portions of their graduate recitals in organ and voice. . . .

Word was received that George Dehner of Alton, a 1967 graduate of Spalding, was killed in Vietnam, Oct. 19. There were no morning classes at Spalding October 28 so all could attend the funeral mass at Alton. In the sanctuary were Fathers Becker, Wendl, George, Boes, Walding and

420

Tiedeman. This was the first Vietnam casualty to affect Spalding and it had a profound effect on the student body.

The senior class play, "Charley's Aunt," was given November 1. . . .

Because of a slight error in executing the state report, St. Joseph Grade School was placed on the list of schools receiving a warning from the State Board of Education. After conferring with the State Board, Fr. Lafferty, superintendent of education in the Sioux City diocese, announced that the Board had retracted its statement.

For the second time, the vote on the Floyd Valley School bond was defeated in January. This time the margin was 3-1, somewhat closer than the first vote. . . .

1969–70 annals: Oct. 3 a special Vespers was said in preparation for the Feast of St. Francis and the charisms of each sister read by another sister . . . Oct. 4, the Feast of St. Francis, was observed with a dialog Mass, dialog homily, reception under two species in the convent chapel. . . .

Oct. 24 the Sisters' Shower was held at a Pot-luck luncheon at Spalding. The sisters were given money for wall-to-wall carpeting in the convent, totaling $704.88. The Guild promised to make up the difference of $175.00 as the total cost of covering the community room, dining room, back bathroom and corridor amounted to $879.88. The rug was purchased from the Moeller Furniture Co., Remsen. Snow tires were purchased for the car from the Conoco Company in Granville. . . .

Palm Sunday the new mass changes were observed at Granville. There was the blessing of the palms at the east entrance of Spalding and a procession back to the church. The prayers at the foot of the altar are now omitted and an examination of conscience is made instead. At the offertory there is a procession also. Water, wine, hosts and the collection are brought to the altar by a sister and a family of the parish. The first pew by the south confessional was reserved for this purpose. Other changes: the priest is seated and faces the people; a handshake symbolizes peace. . . .

July 28 Another Floyd Valley bond vote was cast by Alton, Hospers, Newkirk, and Granville. Voters decided in the third school bond issue in the last two years not to build a new public school at Alton. The proposal needed a 60% majority to pass. It got 52.1%.

At the Alton precinct, 69.9% of the voters approved a new school with 372 yes votes and 160 no votes. The majority of Hospers precinct voters also supported the issue with 57.9: 236 for and 171 against. Newkirk voted 73.4 percent yes with 166 for and 60 against. It was Granville who defeated the proposal overwhelmingly: only 7.5% of the precinct voters favored the new school with 28 for and 343 against. This was a total of 802 yes votes and 734 no votes.

1970–71 annals: At a house meeting August 23, the Sisters decided to adopt a budget of $18.00 per month. This would not include prescriptions nor gas for the car. Clothing, recreation, etc., would be included. It was also decided to return to a more structured recreation period (at 8:00 p.m.) and to have a house meeting each Thursday. . . .

The sisters attended a Sioux county institute at Rock Rapids September 22. The topic was individualized instruction. . . .

October 11 the Guild held a shower for the Sisters together with a pot luck luncheon at 1:00 p.m. in the Spalding cafeteria. Gifts of money totalled $300.00. There were also gifts of meat, fruit, etc.

1971–72 annals: In July, the Floyd Valley bond failed to pass for the fifth time. Since there was no sister appointed for domestic duties at St. Joseph convent, all the sisters planned to share cooking and laundry responsibilities. No superior was named. . . .

Sister Merici who had spent the summer studying at the Sorbonne in Paris, and traveling in Luxembourg, Germany, Ireland, Scotland and England, was several days late for school. . . .

About twenty Spalding junior and senior girls made retreat at the Holy Spirit Retreat House, Sioux City, Nov. 19-20. Sisters Nancy and Miriam accompanied the group. . . .

The sisters traded in their Chevrolet for a new 1972 Chevrolet, light green in color. . . .

The Spalding debaters were named Number 1 in the All-Iowa debate poll, January 16. . . .

Sisters Miriam and Nancy were involved in a grass-roots caucus of the Democratic party held on the precinct level during January and February. Other members of the Granville group were Father Kollasch and Mr. And Mrs. Jim Beck. . . .

1972–73 annals: Sister Mary Constance Herbers left by plane on a trip to California with her niece despite the pain she was suffering in her hip. Cards and letters received from Sister indicated that she enjoyed the trip very much. On her return from the west, Sister Constance went to a doctor in Dubuque who advised surgery on her hip. After making the August retreat, Sister entered Xavier Hospital, Dubuque. The surgery on August 14 was a complete success, but gall bladder and digestive disturbances seemed to keep Sister from making a complete recovery.

The Granville sisters wrote to Sister and phoned her several times during her hospital stay. Thursday, September 14, they chatted with her by phone, telling her of the feast day Mass being offered for her. All were greatly touched to learn that she died September 18 at 12:30 a.m. (Several months later it was learned that death had been caused by blood clots in the lung.)

The Spalding students and faculty members offered a High Mass for Sister Constance on September 19 . . . Sister Constance was greatly missed both in the convent and in school where she had been in charge of the library and the teacher of home economic. . . .

May 18 was Baccalaureate at Spalding . . . Twenty-six seniors were graduated from Spalding High School, May 20. Commencement speaker was sister Mary Elvira Kelley, a member of the Council at MSF. . . .

Much more freedom in sisters' apparel was accepted during this year: culottes, slacks, etc. were worn by the younger sisters when performing physical exercise—basketball, etc. During the winter months pant suits were sometimes worn in the school room.

The Diary of Carol Johnson, 1984

Carol Smith was born on August 9, 1953, in Mankato, Minnesota, to Bill and Betty Smith. She grew up in Mankato and graduated from Mankato High School in 1971. After her graduation, she attended Mankato State College until 1973, when she married Bob Johnson of Mankato. The young couple lived in New Ulm during the first several years of their marriage. Carol worked as a receptionist, and Bob worked at a flour mill. Their first child, Alice, was born in New Ulm on March 4, 1976. In 1978 the Johnson family moved to Mankato, where Carol and Bob's second child, Ted, was born on December 25, 1979.

Because Carol Johnson valued having the opportunity to be at home with her children while they were young, she began doing in-home child care during the late 1970s and continues this work today. She began keeping her diary on New Year's Day 1980 with the intention of recording important events in her children's development. As the 1980s progressed, Carol's yearly diaries began to record details of her child-care work, family travels, visits to and from relatives and friends, and responses to grief and loss.

The diary she kept during 1984 was a Christmas "stocking stuffer" measuring approximately four by five and a half inches and containing lined, dated pages, with one page allotted per day. She and her family members enjoy rereading her annual diaries.

Carol Johnson continues to live in Mankato with her husband

Bob. Their daughter Alice recently graduated from college, and their son Ted recently graduated from high school. In 1998 Carol completed her associate of arts degree at Mankato State University. She continues to operate an in-home child-care center, and she still writes in her diary, although she no longer writes daily entries. Instead, she writes periodic entries, and she is moving toward writing longer entries on a less frequent basis. Carol Johnson is a pseudonym, as are other names that appear in her journal.

1984

1–1 Happy New Year. 1984 already. Mom slept in cleaned up after party and took decorations off the Christmas tree. Dad and kids went to Jack's and rode snowmobiles. The weather has turned really mild, which is great after all the snow and cold we've had.

1–4 Alice back to school after a 2 week vacation. Ended it nicely by taking a walk to the park and building a snowman yesterday. She was so happy to see her friend she ran and gave her a big hug.

1–8 Fun family day. We went to Sibley Park and went sliding—had alot of fun until Ted scraped his face. Then Alice went ice skating—she does a great job. Ted slid on his boots and Dad pulled him on the sled on the ice.

1–13 Had fun reading many books with the kids. They have such good humor and memory—they amaze me.

2–9 Had a nice talk with Ted in the rocking chair in the afternoon, he's growing up so fast—smart little boy. Alice wrote her Valentines for school and read. We practiced writing and piano. She catches on fast.

2–11 Ted jumped off the picnic table and choked himself on clothesline—knocked back on table. Thank you, God for watching over him. His neck is bruised.

2–16 Acted out 3 Bears, 3 Pigs and Jack and Beanstalk with the kids— lots of fun. Piano for Alice. She's excited—talent show at school that she and friends want to rehearse for and audition—so pleased that she's excited and wants to do it.

3–2 Ted learned how to whistle and he skips really well now.

3–15 Alice was great in the play for the talent show. Gave classmate a ride home—dark house—said she was oldest one home—3 younger sisters—baby, 4 and 6 year old. Called and talked to kindergarden teacher—she suspects something also.

3–26 Dad and Ted went to Early Childhood—they used the gymnastic equipment and had lots of fun. Mom listened to Alice play the piano. She's doing great—has her 10 pieces memorized.

4–21 Dad and friend took kids to Jack and Jill's for an Easter egg hunt—fun. Mrs. Thomas had baskets for them—they took cupcakes over. Mom stayed home to stencil the living room—love the way it looks.

4–29 It's snowing and predicting 3–6 inches. This weather is absolutely crazy!

5–4 Took the boys to the park all morning, packed a lunch for Ted and he rode his Big Wheel—really goes fast.

5–6 Alice learned how to ride her bicycle—just like that she was doing it!

5–11 Irene brought me petunias yesterday. National Guild—Alice got all good marks and superior rating—proud! Alice's first piano recital—such beautiful songs. Tricia here for supper, to recital and overnight to make it special. A former student of Jewell's played—gave chills to imagine he started out just like Alice. Irene gave Alice piano scarf with Great Grandma's name—special!

5–22 Had a nice long talk with each of the kids, I love them dearly, thank you, God, for a good life. Precious times.

5–23 Went to mini series with Patti at MSU. Suzanne Bunkers spoke on "19th Centuries Diaries, Journals, etc.—What Midwest Women Were (Not) Saying."

5–24 Kids made a boat on the porch. Ted spent a special morning—went for ride in new truck and out for lunch, looked at the carnival and visited Irene. Skinned his knees and wondered how I knew how to take care of "big owies". Alice passed her 4's and 5's mult. test. They ate their picnic in their room because of rain, will go to the park next week.

5–30 Partial eclipse of sun today—saw it on paper through a pinhole—neat. At 11:30 it got very still and like late afternoon out.

6–6 Dad took Ted to Sibley Park to play and see animals—pretty peacock. Alice told us all about the party she attended. Nice talk. Alice let Ted wiggle her loose tooth—so cute.

6–14 Went to Little Cesaer's for pizza and got Ted a go-bot for giving up his pillow—hope he can get over sucking his fingers.

6–19 Read to Alice—had a nice talk—she told me about the Matchgirl from school movie—sad—she died because no one would buy her matches—precious time—Cupola House book—Mrs. Van Winkle called her diary her daybook.

6–22 Finished packing for out West with Dickinsons. It's so nice out there—a wonderful place to relax. We stopped with the girls in Walnut Grove to see Laura Ingalls Wilder museum—saw Laura's quilt.

6–23 Wonderful sunny day. Dads and kids fished, they had fun pulling in small walleyes. Moms relaxed in the sun. Bob grilled steaks and baked potatoes, Jane made strawberry shortcake. Mom and Jane stayed up until 4:30 am and talked. We needed it, felt so good, so much closer to each other—everyone needs someone they can talk to that intimately and touch base. A perfect day.

6–24 Dads went golfing, girls picked wildflowers and saw a deer. Kids are playing so nicely together, swung out on a rope over the lake—fun.

6–30 Went to the lake all day. People in MN wait all winter for days and weekends like this. So relaxing. Alice is swimming really well. To Rapidan for their fireworks. Some of the nicest in Southern MN. They lasted a long time and such different ones. Triple waterfalls that change colors.

7–8 Vacation—left for DeSmet, toured Ingalls homes, cemetary, homestead where Pa planted cottonwood trees, ate picnic in DeSmet Park. Good pageant, twisted prairie grass.

7–9 Badlands around noon—car turned 1000 miles in them—like castles or ruins—beautiful. Evening lighting ceremony at Mt. Rushmore just gorgeous.

7–11 Rapid City—Dinosaur Park and Storybook Island, fun, Ted's favorite. Sylvan Lake pretty walk, kids had pony rides on Silver. Nice fire—special times.

7–14 Home from vacation—Mom and Dad had mowed and weeded—great of them.

8–5 Left for vacation, Bearhead Lake State Park near Ely. The pines smell so nice, walked the trails and went down to the lake, sat around a fire in the evening.

8–8 Picked blueberries, told story of "Blueberries for Sal". Time at lake. Hailed and blew and rained like crazy. Talked with the kids and sang lullabys—camping is so nice for the precious family times it gives us togther.

8–21 Grandma and Alice had a special day, they went out for lunch together and shopping. Lucas came to stay overnight, special for Ted. Alice stayed with friends.

8–23 Special day for Ted. Grandma took him out for lunch in the Corvette and shopping.

8–26 We spent a nice afternoon at Minneopa—walked around the falls, thru the camping prairie area and thru Seppman's Mill. I will miss Alice so much—I love her dearly—hope 3rd grade goes great for her.

8–27 Alice got Mrs. White and all her friends, she's excited. Ted cut a big chunk out of the front of his hair, sometimes I just don't know what to do with him. (Is this a huge call for attention or what?)

8–28 Very hot, feel sorry for the kids in school. Bob and kids couldn't believe it—Mom jumped in the little swimming pool, clothes and all. Alice's teacher gave them paper icicles and told them to look at them when they get hot.

9–3 Labor Day marks the end of summer and I don't like it—have to get busy and into routines again.

9–17 Big decision to make, Bob was offered a job in Iowa—they know he's a good worker and dependable. Lots of talk and some big decisions ahead for us.

9–21 Happy birthday, Bob. "Rolling Stone" subscription. Kids helped Mom harvest the garden, big help, good job done. Did it a year ago to the day—last year predicted a freeze and did it outside in the cold and rain. What a difference this year—in the 80's. The folks were all over, then Bob downtown with friends. I hope he had a good day, needed a night with the guys.

9–23 Bud, Dorothy and Gordy here. Great to see him, it's been 11 years. His work situation isn't good either. Bud knew what the house and old garage looked like—strange because he's never seen them before. Gordy almost died flying a plane. Much more easy going now—he was resigned to dying.

10–1 Special day. Took Ted to preschool for orientation—met teachers, had cookies and donuts. Ted played, he loved it, so glad.

10–3 Special day. Ted's first day of preschool—said he was scared this morning—glad he can tell me. Seemed ok, but I'll never forget the look in his eyes when I left. I miss him, love the kids so much.

10–17 Cuddled and watched TV with the kids, nice evening. They got to stay up late because no school tomorrow or Friday.

10–18 Bob talked to boss today about his job. Boss told him not to worry, he was a talented young man. Good news, so proud of Bob.

10–20 West with Dickinson's. Kids took nice long walks—fresh air and open spaces just wonderful for them. Made a fort and built a fire while Dad's fished. Mom's went antiquing.

10–25 Watched Julian Lennon on TV. He talked about his dad saying he'd be there when a "feather floated across the room"—so sad—looks and sounds like a young John.

10–31 Happy Halloween, kids. Ted was a darling Superman, Alice a cute cheerleader. Bob and Nick took kids trick or treating. Gandhi was assassinated.

11–2 No school or preschool—nice to have the kids home and not have to go anywhere. Alice planned a picnic lunch in the living room. Her cursive writing is coming along very nicely. We practiced piano after supper, she works so hard.

11–5 Ted said his eyes get wet when he watches the end of "Annie"—glad he knows that it's ok to cry.

11–10 Dad and Ted had a special day. Went to Toys Plus to see He-Man in person and look at toys.

11–11 Alice and Mom had our special day—went to lunch and to see "Annie" play.

11–21 Jane told about getting a Christmas card from a woman dead 3 years and it disappearing—spooky!

11–22 Happy Thanksgiving—we have so much to be thankful for. To inlaws for dinner and the day. Grandpa took Ted for a walk and they played in the park all afternoon. Then everyone went outside and played football in the front yard—a beautiful day—quite a change from last year.

11–26 Harriet visited—brought darling nativity scenes for all the kids-she's so nice to us. Special time playing with Ted—house, parade and paper airplanes. Alice had a trick dog show at school.

12–5 Alice played school with the kids. Ted and Thea wrote their letters and numbers just great. Baked cookies. Played Construx with Ted—his imagination is wonderful.

12–12 Played cards with Ted, he's knowing numbers and which is larger. Read Christmas stories. Dad turned lights on outside trees—look really nice. Alice wrote about her family—so precious—what life is all about.

12–18 Ted knows the Christmas story so nice. Alice got thru the whole book of Christmas carols on piano.

12–20 Alice's Christmas program after lunch. Last night the Blue Birds sang at the hospital with reindeer hats and red noses—cute. Quick supper and to Ted's program. Alice got to hand out the programs and Ted was a darling shepard.

12–21 Alice made such beautiful gifts for us—precious card, notepad and really nice paper mache Santa. She really put alot of work into it.

12–22 Went for a ride to look at lights, nice to see people starting to decorate more. Alice is growing up, she didn't want to go. Enjoyed the manger scene.

12–31 Great to spend the night with our special friends, visited until 5 am. Thank you and goodbye, diary. You've served us well—goodbye 1984.

The Diary of Juanita Anderson Ahrens, 1992

Juanita Anderson was born on March 21, 1930, in the Anderson farmhouse at Kellogg, Iowa, to Maude (Milligan) and Andrew Anderson. Juanita had three brothers and three sisters. She graduated from Kellogg High School in 1946, then attended Central College at Pella, Iowa, and received a two-year teaching certificate in 1951. In the fall of 1948 she began teaching elementary school. She attended night classes at Penn College in Oskaloosa, Iowa, and received her bachelor's degree in 1963.

On December 22, 1950, Juanita Anderson married Paul Ahrens, and they have lived in Grinnell most of the time since then. Juanita and Paul Ahrens have two children, Michael Ahrens and Barbara Ahrens Bunkers. Juanita and Paul Ahrens also have four grandchildren, Justin and Andrea Ahrens, and Kimberly and Kelly Bunkers, whose diaries appear in Chapter 1 of this book. Excerpts from the diary of Paul's mother, Ruby Butler Ahrens, appear earlier in this chapter. In 1992, after a thirty-seven-year elementary school teaching career, most of it in Grinnell, Juanita Ahrens retired. Since then she has spent her time as a homemaker and a community volunteer. She enjoys photography and genealogy and has written two books of family history. The 1992 diary excerpts that follow, all short and descriptive, touch on daily work, family activities, community events, the weather, and deaths in the family. The diary remains in the possession of Juanita Ahrens.

January 2, 1992 Went back to work, 20 below 0. Kept kids in all day. Paul bowling tonite. Mike called. Got new boss. Barb called and chatted. . . .

January 12, 1992 Rained most all day. Went to 40th anniversary of Chick and Naomi. 200 there. Muddy! Elva and Nedra went with us. Church in town. . . .

January 15, 1992 Blowing snow. No school. Went to Betty Palmer's funeral. Paul bowling tonite. Worked on report cards. . . .

Juanita Anderson Ahrens, 1992

January 31, 1992 Girls had big fight today. Went to chili supper and ball game tonight. Called IPERS for retirement form. Paul painted living room. Peggy had back surgery 2 days ago. . . .

February 8, 1992 Sorted clothes all morning. Went to Des Moines in p.m. and ordered new bathroom cabinet and sink. Stopped at Barb's. Ate supper at "Choice". . . .

February 10, 1992 Nice day. 30 degrees. Davey was a pistol. Sore throat tonite. Paul paid off 1328 West Street today. Sent cards to Mike and Norma. . . .

February 17, 1992 Cloudy and rain in p.m. 46 degrees. Paul hauled in corn. Dahmer of Milwaukee to jail. Mike is 36 today. He played golf. . . .

February 22, 1992 Got perm this morning. Went to Des Moines to Home and Garden show. Ate at Nacho Mama's and went to civic center. No coat today!

February 28, 1992 Spring day! Showed the kids "Charlotte's Web" Marsha has Hepatitis C. Ruby Prince passed away. Changed the bulletin board. Had duties all day. . . .

March 2, 1992 Beautiful day. Church and breakfast. Cleaned bedrooms. Paul pruned some trees. Went to gpa's. Paul and gpa cleaned the lawn. 73 degrees. Set recordwarm in history.

March 12, 1992 Went to IPERS for retirement meeting and to Barbs. Went to Kim's school program. Kim played Zylophone solo and sang in trio.

March 13, 1992 Took Elva to Iowa City for treatment. Went to Monte and bought camper for $4500. Snowed an inch tonight. . . .

March 22, 1992 Went to Amana for dinner for Denny's birthday. Took Aunt Lucille and Gpa. Denny is 37 tomorrow. . . .

April 8, 1992 Went to Monte and got trailer. Julie had appendix out today

April 9, 1992 Spring program at middle school. Doug told the parents I was retiring and made me stand up. Supt. Bodensteiner there. . . .

April 20, 1992 Cold and wet. Went to visit Kim at school in third grade. At lunch at McDonalds. Omaha has 10 inches of snow. . . .

May 1, 1992 Went to school and worked tonight. It is 85 degrees. Paul rototilled gardens. . . .

May 3, 1992 Went to see building torn down by the State bank at 5 a.m.

May 5, 1992 Barb left for Virginia today. Sent flowers to Mike and Julie for #13 anniversary.

May 19, 1992 Took school kids to Des Moines zoo and science center. What a day!!!!!!!!!

May 20, 1992 Grandparents day and Retirement party at 3:00. Lots of people here. . . .

May 27, 1992 Cold and windy. Went to Kelly's graduation from pre-school.

May 28, 1992 Last day of school. Barb and girls came. Everyone cried. What a mess. Glad that is over.

May 31, 1992 Went to Kansas. Left at 8:30 and arrived at 3 p.m. Went to lake with camper. Mike and Justin and Andrea stayed, too. Mike and Julie gave me a beautiful diamond RING—a gift for my retirement!! Julie, Justin and I went to Walmart. Tonight we went to Justin's ball-game. . . .

June 3, 1992 Got big catfish. Paul cooked it for our lunch. Sun finally came out.

June 9, 1992 Checked out at school. Cleaned camper. Started on boxes. Paul worked at West Street all day. . . .

June 20, 1992 Went to Bunkers. Had pizza and home made ice cream and cake. Verna, Marilyn and Dick there. Home at 10:00. Got new door for Pearl Street at Menards. Chilly tonight. Kim is 9 tomorrow. Randy is painting his house. . . .

June 24, 1992 Becky is 52. Went to Elva's. Said she feels better. Went to board meeting tonight. Got plaque for 33 years of service to Grinnell schools Shorty will be 64 tomorrow. Barb and Denny are going to Black Hills in a couple of days. . . .

July 8, 1992 Chick had massive stroke this morning in a motel in Kansas. He cannot possibly live very long. This has been a long day. They had to call Don to find me as we were working at 1022 Pearl.

July 9, 1992 Chick passed away this morning at the hospital in Kansas. Went to Naomi's and Shorty's for a short while tonight. . . .

July 27, 1992 Took Wanda to bus at 9:00. Cried all day. Paul worked at 1022. I stayed here.

August 4, 1992 Played golf at 6:30 this morning. Paul worked on camper and I helped hold the outside up. Went to Altoona tonight for Kelly's birthday. Dick and Marilyn there. Called June.

August 10, 1992 Kids are all here. Built a tree house. Had fun. Went to movie at night, "I Blew Up the Kids" Paul mowed West Street. Got corn from Shorty. . . .

September 4, 1992 Took Elva to Iowa City for regular treatment. She had to stay in hospital. I slept on floor. . . .

September 28, 1992 Elva has been hospitalized all month. I have been with her alot. She is getting blood. I called David. June is here.

September 29, 1992 Elva passed away this morning. Jill and I were there. Called June, Barb, and Grace. Went to Toledo and stayed till tonight. . . .

October 14, 1992 Beautiful day! Bond issue for 12 million failed yesterday. Vote was 1800 to 1100. Went to Mar's with gpa. Picked apples in top of tree. Paul home at 2:00. Had supper with Williard and Mildred. Hazel Oltrooge died today. . . .

October 26 , 1992 Worked in extra bedroom. Dinner at gpas. Paul did Marys garden and Lindas. Watched "Salute to Minnie Pearl" tonight. Toronto won the World Series. . . .

November 13, 1992 Paul went to Salina, Kansas at 9:30. Is very windy and -5 degrees wind chill. I cleaned more cupboards. Had dinner with gpa. Barb and Denny came and we had spaghetti. . . .

December 19, 1992 Had Christmas dinner here. Gpa came and we had turkey. Mike cooked. Paul and I went to Ruth Wells funeral. We had pie at 5:00. . . .

December 30, 1992 Took gpa for lunch at club and he stayed. We tore up carpet at 1014 Pearl and 1531 Hobart. It is icy and cold today. We went to Sally's to see Cheryl tonight.

The Diary of Sandra K. Gens, July 1992

Sandra K. Gens was born on October 20, 1958, and grew up on her family's farm in southern Minnesota, where she lived with her parents, Marvel (Schultz) and Waldon Gens, her older sisters, Judy, Deb, and Zoe (Lo), and her younger brother, Scott. She began keeping a diary when she was eight and in the second grade at Madelia Elementary School. After graduating from Madelia High School in 1977, Sandra completed an associate of arts degree in music at Golden Valley Lutheran College in Minnesota. She then helped found StayWell, a company that provides wellness programs for corporations. She has recently moved on to another position managing customer care for UroMetrics.

She has kept a diary for most of her life, and she feels that it was unfortunate that she did not during the seven years she was married. After her divorce, she began to keep a journal on her computer rather than in a formal diary or blank book, and she prints out the pages of her computer-diary once a month so that she has a hard copy. She now lives in Eagan, Minnesota. The excerpts from her journal that follow deal with a major turning point in her life. In a letter accompanying the typescript of these diary excerpts, Sandra told me, "I was somehow surprised to find that, when I re-read it in preparation for sending it to you, it still made me weep and laugh and feel that time so acutely again."

Friday, July 3, 1992.
    Didn't have to work today because of the holiday, so I mowed the lawn and trimmed and weeded. At 8:10pm I was weeding the lilac bushes when Cindy came outside to tell me I had a phone call. It was Tami and she said Dad had a heart attack and had been taken to the Madelia Hospital. "It's pretty bad—you better come." I threw some stuff in a suitcase (even took a black dress, thinking that if I had it, I wouldn't need

435

Sandra Gens, 1997

it). I stopped at Judy's on the way but she said she'd come later if she decided to. I FLEW out of there and prayed for God to clear the way—I just wanted to hold his big, strong hands one more time. 80-90mph all the way to Madelia and got there at 10pm. All the way I kept saying, "Dad, your soul knows what to do—if you want to go, go. But I wish you could have a little more time here." I didn't know any of the cars in the hospital parking lot, but I ran in and the nurse told me Dad had passed away!!! I did 105mph all the way to the farm, sobbing the whole way. Aunt Donna & Uncle Ken, Pastor Turnmeier, and Auntie Val were already there. Lo & Pete rolled in about 15 minutes later-they'd been at a movie and Kathy had walked over right away to tell them. Judy got there at 10:45!! Everyone was surprised. (Tami didn't even know who she was!) We all stayed up and cried and talked till 2am. It's so hard to see Scotty <u>wracked</u> by sobs! Judy & I stayed at Mom's—talked till 3am and slept fitfully.

What happened was, Scott & Dad had been moving a sow into a farrowing pen & Dad said he wasn't feeling quite right, so Scott told him to sit down and rest a minute. Next thing Dad was walking to the house which was unusual because he never left until the job was done. (7:30pm) Dad went in and took a blood pressure pill and sat down on the couch. Mom was reading a western and she heard him kind of gurgle. She tried to pat his cheek and get him to respond but it wasn't working, so she called Scott & he was there in a flash. He called to Tami and the two of them gave Dad CPR for a half hour, while Mom called the ambulance and waited for it at the end of the driveway. The ambulance got lost on the way, but it didn't matter because the doctor said he was dead before he got laid down.

I can't believe it—my beautiful Daddy is dead! I'll never see his twinkly eyes, and hear his giggle, or see him stand at the door welcoming me in again.

Saturday, July 4 Independence Day.
Got up at 7:30 and had visitors all day bringing food and sympathy . . . Gert Kassube, Virgie Bergemann, Dolly & Herman, Ann & Erv. Erv told hunting stories and it was very obvious that he was as shocked and broken up as the rest of us. When they left, we all hugged him and said he could tell those stories anytime—such special memories!

At 1pm, Mom, Judy, Deb, Lo, Tami, Scott & I went to Olson Funeral Home in Truman. The funeral director (or furniture director, as Lo called him) was Dennis Boro and he couldn't have been better!! He let us talk and cry and he was very professional, but he made it comfortable too. We decided how we wanted the service, then we picked a casket. Tami just sobbed. We picked a beautiful light oak one with wheat on the inside.

Got back at 4:30. Judy left at 7pm. I stayed at Lo's—Mom wants to do her crying in private. Lo made a little shrine to Dad—special pictures of him, a sympathy card with a beautiful verse, a bottle of his Old Spice and a couple of origami pieces that Aaron Nelson had brought over with a little card that said "I'm sorry" written in pencil in his little-boy hand-writing—so sweet! Got back to Lo's at 9pm—I let Adam drive—he loved that! I wanted to yell at the people on the highway to get home and cry for my Dad!!

We decided to go to the fireworks in Mankato—it's simulcast with special radio music. When we turned it on the first thing we heard was "Taps" & "America the Beautiful—always makes me cry. Buster met us there—he took my hand and couldn't say anything, but his eyes said how sorry he was. Lo & I both recalled the beautiful sunset last night—like Dad's spirit was filling up the <u>whole sky</u>!! Lo recalled seeing a fox STANDING on the side of the road yesterday morning—like he was on his way to go pick up Dad's spirit!

Sunday, July 5, 1992
We all went to church (and communion) together—VERY HARD!! (The only thing that we could smile about was that Robin still plays the organ just terrible!! Lo said she was sent to us as a gift to make us smile.) During the prayers, when the pastor said, ". . . our dear departed brother, Waldon Gens, was called home . . ." Mom put her face in her hands and sobbed. Harold & Marion hugged me—it was the first they'd heard! Gary & Ardis came over for an hour after church. We all told stories and laughed and cried. We went back to Lake Crystal at noon. Tom & Kay C came over to convey their sympathy. Lo & the boys & I went to Mankato to buy them some clothes for the funeral and visitation. I drove on to Faribault and met Steve there—he had picked up some clothes for me and met me halfway. Got back to Lo's at 5:15 and we all drove back out to the farm for supper. The pastor came over again—I wanted him to understand about the great person Dad was—since he's only been at this church for 8 months he didn't know him very well, and I want him to do a good eulogy—so we told more stories and things we cherished about Dad. Home at 11:30.

Monday, July 6, 1992
Nancy called this morning—we talked and cried for an hour. SO good to hear from her—I want everyone to miss him as much as I do. The morning went by so quick—we got to the farm at lunchtime and put together some pictures for a display at the Funeral Home. We went there at 4pm. (Mom wanted to watch me put gas in my car because she's never done it before. "I'm going to have to learn this kind of stuff now.")

Scott put out the Swift, the 30.06 and the 6MM as well as a bunch of Dad's awards. Tami put out a deck of cards . . .

To see Dad lying in the coffin was AWFUL!!!! I sobbed and cried but finally calmed down. He looked good—like he was just going to grin. I touched his hands and his permanently-bent little finger, and his hair . . .

The pastor had a devotion before everyone came & he stood and sang a hymn a capella to us—it was terrible—his shirt was too small and his buttons were popping and Lo almost started to laugh because it was such an emotional situation.

There were SO MANY people—friends and relatives—Cal & Donna Jean Glaman, Harriet & Gordy Haglund, people from Wood Lake area— I almost fell over when my work people walked in (Becky, Sue, Jill & Diana). Was great to have Nancy there—Lynn Samlaska came too. The flowers were stupendous!—from my work, Class of '77, the Golden Girls, Nancy, Fairmont Trap Club, and the flowers Lyle Hohenstein did for us (husband, father, grandfather (even had a fishing lure in it), uncle, brother) were magnificent! He even sent one from himself!! The time went by so quickly—I couldn't talk with everyone—the place was PACKED! Kathy Nelson packed a whole cooler full of pop and fruit and sandwiches for us-can't believe how thoughtful and great everyone has been!!! We all went to Auntie Val's afterwards. All SO tired. July & Alisa stayed at Auntie Val's. Got back to Lo's around 11pm— Steve was waiting for us and stayed overnite. Buster brought three roses—one for me, Lo and Mom for tomorrow. He bought them from "some religious group"—he said, "Those people must have been sent!"

Mom is really being a rock and keeping our spirits up. We were standing by the casket toward the end of the evening, silently crying, when she suddenly stuck her hand in Dad's suit pocket and said, "You didn't leave $10 in here, did you, Dad?" It was so mortifyingly irreverent that we all started laughing. Deb said, "Mom, if you start going through his pants, I'm walking away!"

Tuesday, July 7, 1992

I didn't think I'd have to think about this day coming for another 30 years—Grandpa lived to be 101—Aunt Lil and Aunt Ella, 103 & 104!

We all got to the church an hour early for the final visitation—it was really pretty with all the flowers up in front. We all cried really hard—it was the first time Judy actually went up to the casket. It was difficult to tear myself away because I knew that as soon as I went downstairs they'd close it and I'd never see him in the flesh again. Lo kissed him and so did I.

A breaker blew before the service, so Erv had to run home and get another one—Dad would have appreciated a small mechanical problem, I think.

The church was packed! Del & Karen & Kris were there (they had gotten here so early and drove in to Lewisville. There were a couple guys sitting on the bench on main street who looked them up & down and said, "You here for the Gens funeral?" Only in small-town America . . .) Also Sue & Becky from work. It was so nice to talk with Deb & Deann Arndt too! The hymns were all the great one—"Asleep in Jesus" (Judy really lost it on that one—I'm sure she could still hear Dad leaning over her shoulder and singing it), "Beautiful Savior," "I Know That My Redeemer Lives," and "For All The Saints." I sang as good as I could. Sharon played the organ and Rich played his cello—absolutely beautiful. Rich did a beautiful solo on "I'm But A Stranger Here"—Dad would have LOVED it! They did Saint-Saens' "The Swan" for a prelude—SO touching! The pastor's sermon was called "His Hands—really good. Steve taped it for us. Karen said that none of them had ever been so touched by a funeral! Mom carried Buster's rose all morning. When we walked out on the last hymn, I grabbed five roses out of the bouquet from us kids and gave one to each to lay on the casket at the end. Erv drove his car with me, Lo & the boys in. He tried to think of stuff to say, but he was really grieved by this all. The line of cars was so long that cars were still leaving the church when we had already gotten to the cemetery 2 miles away! Scott wanted to be a pallbearer so badly—everyone told him it would be too hard, but he walked right by the casket as they took it to the grave. Tami really cried during the "ashes to ashes" part. Talked to a lot of people when we got back to the church for the lunch. Holly even flew home from North Carolina (— she's still weird though). Aunt Darlene had a migraine headache through the whole thing so she was out in the car most of the time! We all talked to people till about 2pm when it all kind of broke up. Lo saw two foxes on the way home tonite—IT'S GOT TO BE A SIGN!!!!

There are so many things to be thankful for—I'm so glad he died at home, and in the summer, and that he didn't have to go through all that hospital humiliation or a long sickness. He lived his whole life doing things he loved—being his own boss, farming, hunting, fishing, dancing, playing cards with good friends. He was a good person with a strong faith. I'm so happy he'll be buried on the farm's cemetery—he'll always be close.

I'm so glad that I don't have regrets—I had started hugging him and saying I loved him, even when it felt goofy. I wish I had gone out in the boat with him & Pete the last time up north—they asked me every time they went if I wanted to go, but it was SO cold. I'm happy for the times I DID go though—when it was just him & me and we sat in the boat together without talking—just enjoying the sunset and scenery.

I was thinking how Deb, Lo & I played the piano after dinner last

Easter and sang all the favorite hymns. Everyone else left, but Dad just sat on the couch and closed his eyes and listened and kind of sang along. And how, last time we were all up north, we all sat around the breakfast table for a LONG time and Dad told stories of his childhood, and we all told our favorite "Dad-ism"—like a living epitaph!

I remember Scotty & I going to the trap-shooting club with Dad every Wednesday night all summer long when we were kids—we'd catch fireflys. There's a million fireflys this year, and LOTS of white clover. I think that will always remind me of this time now.

Afterword

Why do diaries have such staying power? This difficult question is one that I do not believe can be answered definitively, either by a diarist or by a reader of diaries. Yet, like many others who read (and perhaps keep) diaries, I know that diaries do have staying power. After I have read someone's diary, I find myself replaying specific memorable entries in my head, imagining what the diarist might have been like, wondering what feelings and circumstances might have created her need to begin and maintain a diary. And, as I have worked on this project for fifteen years, I have been captivated not only by what makes a person keep a diary but also by how an individual's diary survives.

In several cases, such as those of Sarah Gillespie and Martha Furgerson Nash, the diarist herself donated her diaries to the archives of a historical society. In other cases, such as those of Maranda Cline and Sarah Jane Kimball, the author's diary was passed on to a descendant who saved it, perhaps keeping it in the family's possession, perhaps donating it to an archive. In still other cases, such as those of Linda B. Kennedy, Carol Johnson, Juanita Ahrens, and Sandra Gens, the writer herself has held onto her diary, saving it for years or decades. On occasion, as in the case of the diary of Elspeth Close, a diary was "rescued" by someone who had no idea who the diarist was but who recognized her diary was worth saving. On rare occasions, one comes upon a diary that has been saved without anyone's even knowing the diarist's identity.

That is what happened to the diary of an unidentified woman from Iowa who, according to her file in the State Historical Society of Iowa Archives, "appears to be a school teacher in Vernon Springs, Howard County, area." The diary was donated to the SHSI so long ago that no accession records exist, but I continue to

442

search for the identity of the woman who kept this diary. It is a small diary that measures about three by five inches; it has no cover and consists of only forty or fifty yellowed pages, many of which are dog-eared; some pages are even falling out of the loosely sewn binding. The diarist's handwriting is very hard to read; in fact, some words are illegible. As was the case with many diaries written during the middle of the nineteenth century, the diarist's spelling, punctuation, capitalization, and sentence structure are very fluid. Despite everything, this diary has captivated me not only because it seems to embody all the reasons a midwestern American girl or woman might have kept a diary but also because it draws me into the life of the unidentified diarist. Ultimately, that is what this project is all about:

Monday, Oct. 22, 1860. Well well, my pledge was soon broken—I have not writen in my Journal very long, but I do mean write every day now— And still another year has passed, and I am one year older, one year less to toil in this very changfull wourld. Yes I am still near my home than I was one year ago and oh! In three years that has passed, am I and more prepared for the grate final day of accounts, oh! How much one can do to sustain them in the hours of temtation. Oh if it was not for this one sin of yielding, we might pass along in life with less of the bitter and any much more of the sweet. I do know that I want to live to some purpose and to serve him and then my self. I have started once more with a full determination to keep a daly rechord of all that is of importents to write, this is ~~my~~ again my birth day. ah aim I do improve fore the better as not, but I do mean to try to do more as I ought, with these very promises I will say ~~good~~ good night.

Archival Sources
Bibliography

Archival Sources

Abbreviations for Archives

IWA	Iowa Women's Archives, Iowa City, Iowa
SHSI-IC	State Historical Society of Iowa, Iowa City, Iowa
SHSI-DM	State Historical Society of Iowa, Des Moines, Iowa
MHS	Minnesota Historical Society, St. Paul, Minnesota
SHSW-M	Wisconsin State Historical Society, Madison, Wisconsin
SHSW-ARC-EC	SHSW—Area Research Center, Eau Claire, Wisconsin
SHSW-ARC-LC	SHSW—Area Research Center, La Crosse, Wisconsin
SHSW-ARC-RF	SHSW—Area Research Center, River Falls, Wisconsin
SHSW-ARC-WW	SHSW—Area Research Center, Whitewater, Wisconsin
OSF	Sisters of the Third Order of St. Francis Archives, Dubuque, Iowa
SSND	School Sisters of Notre Dame Archives, Mankato, Minnesota
BECHS	Blue Earth County Historical Society, Mankato, Minnesota
BHS	Berlin Historical Society, Berlin, Wisconsin
KOS	Kossuth County Historical Society, Algona, Iowa
OCHS	Olmstead County Historical Society, Rochester, Minnesota
PH	Privately held by diarist

Locations of Diaries

Ahrens, Juanita Anderson	PH
Ahrens, Ruby Butler	PH
Andrews, Jennie Blair	SHSW-ARC-RF
Barland, Dorothea	SHSW-ARC-EC
Brackenridge, Blanche	OCHS
Brewster, Martha Smith	BECHS
Bullard, Marjorie	MHS
Bullard, Polly Caroline	MHS
Bunkers, Kelly	PH
Bunkers, Kimberly	PH
Bunkers-Harmes, Rachel	PH
Cairns, Gertrude	SHSW-ARC-RF
Carpenter, Lillian Stephens	MHS
Call, Etta Luella	KOS
Cline, Maranda J.	PH
Close, Elspeth	SHSI-IC
Fowler, Gwendolyn Wilson	IWA
Gens, Sandra	PH
Griffin, Abbie T.	MHS
Griffith, Mary	SHSI-IC
Grout, Jane F.	MHS
Hamilton, Eliza and J. Talmai	SHSW-M
Holdredge, Margaret Vedder	BHS
Holton, Lucinda and Edward	SHSW-M
Huftalen, Sarah Gillespie	SHSI-IC
James, Ada L.	SHSW-M
Johnson, Alena	PH
Johnson, Alice Gortner	MHS
Johnson, Carol	PH
Kennedy, Megan	PH
Kesselring, Megan	PH
Kimball, Sarah Jane	SHSI-IC
Lovelace, Maud Hart	PH
King, Antoinette Porter	MHS
McDaniel, Agnes Barland	SHSW-ARC-EC
McKinnon, Isabella	WSHS-M
Madigan, Mary	PH
Merrill, Maria Morton	SHSW-ARC-LC
Miller, Edythe	SHSI-DM
Nash, Martha Furgerson	IWA
OSF Annals	OSF
Petersen, Pauline	SHSI-DM
Pratt, Sarah	SHSW-ARC-WW
Quiner, Emily	SHSW-M

SSND Chronicle	SSND
Tripp, Addie	SHSWB–RC-LC
Zuckerman, Ruth Van Horn	PH

Contact Information for Archives

IOWA

Sisters of the Third Order of St. Francis Motherhouse Archives
3390 Windsor Avenue
Dubuque, Iowa 52001
319-583-9786
<http://www.osfdbq.org/>

State Historical Society of Iowa in Des Moines
600 E. Locust Street
Des Moines, Iowa 50319-0290
515-281-5111
<http://www.culturalaffairs.org/shsi/library/library.htm>

State Historical Society of Iowa in Iowa City
402 Iowa Avenue
Iowa City, Iowa 52240-1806
309-335-3916
<http://www.culturalaffairs.org/shsi/library/library.htm>

Iowa Women's Archives in Iowa City
100 Main University Library
3d Floor South
University of Iowa
Iowa City, Iowa 52242
319-335-5068
<http://www.lib.uiowa.edu/iwa/>

Kossuth County Historical Society
Algona, Iowa 50511

MINNESOTA

Blue Earth County Historical Society
415 Cherry Street
Mankato, Minn. 56001
507-345-5566
<http://www.internet-connections.net/reg9/bechs/>

Archival Sources

Minnesota Historical Society
Manuscript Collections
345 Kellogg Boulevard West
St. Paul, Minn. 55102-1906
612-296-2620
<http://www.mnhs.org/library/index.html>

Olmstead County Historical Society
County Road 122 S.W.
P.O. Box 6411
Rochester, Minn. 55903
507-282-9447

School Sisters of Notre Dame Motherhouse Archives
Mankato Province
170 Good Counsel Drive
Mankato, Minn. 56001-3138
507-389-4200
<http://www.ssnd.org/>

WISCONSIN

Berlin Historical Society
Berlin, Wis. 54923

State Historical Society of Wisconsin
816 State Street
Madison, Wis. 53706-1488
608-264-6460
<http://www.shsw.wisc.edu/archives/index.html>

State Historical Society of Wisconsin Eau Claire Area Research Center
William D. McIntyre Library
University of Wisconsin–Eau Claire
Eau Claire, Wis. 54702-5010
715-836-3873
<http://www.shsw.wisc.edu/archives/arcnet/eauclair.html>

State Historical Society of Wisconsin River Falls Area Research Center
Chalmer Davee Library
University of Wisconsin–River Falls
410 S. Third Street
River Falls, Wis. 54022
715-425-3567
<http://www.shsw.wisc.edu/archives/arcnet/riverfls.html>

State Historical Society of Wisconsin La Crosse Area Research Center
Murphy Library
University of Wisconsin–La Crosse
La Crosse, Wis. 54601
608-785-8511
<http://www.shsw.wisc.edu/archives/arcnet/lacrosse.html>

State Historical Society of Wisconsin Whitewater Area Research Center
Harold Andersen Library
University of Wisconsin–Whitewater
800 West Main Street
Whitewater, Wis. 53190
414-472-5520
<http://www.shsw.wisc.edu/archives/arcnet/whitewtr.html>

Bibliography

Abell, Mrs. L. G. 1853. *Woman in Her Various Relations.* New York: R. T. Young.

Adams, Kathleen. 1990. *Journal to the Self: Twenty-two Paths to Personal Growth.* New York: Warner.

Aptheker, Bettina. 1989. *Tapestries of Life: Women's Work, Women's Consciousness, and the Meaning of Daily Experience.* Amherst: University of Massachusetts Press.

Association pour l'autobiographie et le patrimoine autobiographique et amis des bibliothèques de Lyon. 1997. *Un journal à soi: ou la passion des journaux intimes.* Lyon: Bibliothèque municipale de Lyon.

Baldwin, Christina. 1990. *Life's Companion: Journal Writing as a Spiritual Quest.* New York: Bantam Doubleday Dell.

Begos, Jane DuPree, ed. 1989. *A Women's Diaries Miscellany.* Weston, Conn.: MagiCircle.

Bernstein, Basil B. 1971. *Class, Codes, and Control: Theoretical Studies Toward a Sociology of Language.* Vol. 1. London: Routledge and Kegan Paul.

Blodgett, Harriet. 1989. *Centuries of Female Days: English Women's Private Diaries.* New Brunswick, N.J.: Rutgers University Press.

Blodgett, Harriet. 1991. *Capacious Hold-all: An Anthology of English Women's Diary Writings.* Charlottesville: University Press of Virginia.

Bloom, Lynn Z. 1996. " 'I Write for Myself and Others': Private Diaries as Public Documents." In Suzanne L. Bunkers and Cynthia Huff, eds., *Inscribing the Daily: Critical Essays on Women's Diaries,* 23–27. Amherst: University of Massachusetts Press.

Brackenridge, Blanche. Unpublished diary, 1876–1880. Rochester, Minn.: Olmstead County Historical Society.

Brent, Jonathan. 1997. "The 1918 Diary of Tsaritsa Alexandra." In Vladimir A. Kozlov and Vladimir M. Khrustalev, eds., *The Last Diary of Tsaritsa Alexandra,* xlvii–lx. New Haven, Conn.: Yale University Press.

Brodzki, Bella, and Celeste Schenck, eds. 1988. *Life/lines: Theorizing Women's Autobiography.* Ithaca, N.Y.: Cornell University Press.

Broughton, Trev Lynn, and Linda Anderson. 1997. Preface to Trev Lynn Broughton and Linda Anderson, eds., *Women's Lives/Women's Times: New Essays on Auto/Biography,* xi–xvii. Albany: State University of New York Press.

Brumberg, Joan Jacobs. 1997. *The Body Project: An Intimate History of American Girls.* New York: Random House.

452

Bunkers, Suzanne L. 1987. "'Faithful Friend': Nineteenth-Century Midwestern Women's Unpublished Diaries." *Women's Studies International Forum* 10, no. 1: 7–17.

Bunkers, Suzanne L. 1988. "Midwestern Diaries and Journals: What Women Were (Not) Saying in the Late 1800s." In James Olney, ed., *Studies in Autobiography*, 190–210. New York: Oxford University Press.

Bunkers, Suzanne L. 1993. "What Do Women Really Mean? Thoughts on Women's Diaries and Lives." In Olivia Frey, Frances Zauhar, and Diane Freedman, eds., *The Intimate Critique: Autobiographical Literary Criticism*, 207–21. Durham, N.C.: Duke University Press.

Bunkers, Suzanne L. 1996. "Whose Diary Is It, Anyway? Issues of Agency, Authority, Ownership." Paper presented at Modern Language Association Convention, 27–30 December, Washington, D.C.

Bunkers, Suzanne L., and Cynthia A. Huff. 1996. "Issues in Studying Women's Diaries: A Theoretical and Critical Introduction." In Suzanne L. Bunkers and Cynthia A. Huff, eds., *Inscribing the Daily: Critical Essays on Women's Diaries*. Amherst: University of Massachusetts Press.

Buss, Helen M. 1993. "Pioneer Women's Diaries and Journals: Letters Home/ Letters to the Future." *Mapping Our Selves: Canadian Women's Autobiography in English*, 37–60. Montreal: McGill-Queen's University Press.

Butruille, Susan G., ed. 1995. *Women's Voices from the Western Frontier*. Spokane, Wash.: Tamarack Books.

Butruille, Susan G., and Kathleen Petersen, eds. 1994. *Women's Voices from the Oregon Trail*. Spokane, Wash.: Tamarack Books.

Carter, Kathryn. 1997. *Voix feministes, Feminist Voices: Diaries in English by Women in Canada, 1753–1995, An Annotated Bibliography*. Ottawa: CRIAW/ICREF.

Carter, Kathryn. In press. Introduction to Kathryn Carter, ed., *The Small Details of a Life: Twenty Diaries by Women in Canada, 1830–1996*. Toronto: University of Toronto Press.

Coburn, Carol K., and Martha Smith. 1999. *Spirited Lives: How Nuns Shaped Catholic Culture and American Lives, 1836–1920*. Chapel Hill: University of North Carolina Press.

Cole, Charlotte, ed. 1998. *Between You and Me: Real-Life Diaries and Letters by Women Writers*. London: Livewire.

Conrad, Margaret, Toni Laidlaw, and Donna Smyth. 1988. *No Place Like Home: Diaries and Letters of Nova Scotia Women, 1771–1938*. Halifax, Canada: Formac.

Cott, Nancy. 1977. *The Bonds of Womanhood: "Woman's Sphere" in New England, 1780–1835*. New Haven, Conn.: Yale University Press.

Culley, Margo, ed. 1985. *A Day at a Time: The Diary Literature of American Women from 1764 to the Present*. New York: Feminist Press.

Davidson, Cathy N. 1998. "Preface: No More Separate Spheres!" *American Literature* 70, no. 3 (September): 443–63.

Dunaway, Philip, and Mel Evans, eds. 1957. *A Treasury of the World's Great Diaries*. New York: Doubleday.

Egan, Susanna. 1999. *Mirror Talk: Genres of Crisis in Contemporary Autobiography*. Chapel Hill: University of North Carolina Press.

Bibliography

Engel, Susan. 1998. *Context Is Everything: The Nature of Memory*. New York: Freeman.

Fairbanks, Carol, and Sara Brooks Sundberg. 1983. *Farm Women on the Prairie Frontier: A Sourcebook for Canada and the United States*. Metuchen, N.J.: Scarecrow.

Faragher, John Mack. 1979. *Women and Men on the Overland Trail*. New Haven, Conn.: Yale University Press.

Fothergill, Robert. 1974. *Private Chronicles: A Study of English Diaries*. New York: Oxford University Press.

Frankenberg, Ruth, ed. 1997. *Displacing Whiteness: Essays in Social and Cultural Criticism*. Durham, N.C.: Duke University Press.

Franklin, Penelope, ed. 1986. *Private Pages: Diaries of American Women, 1830s–1970s*. New York: Ballantine.

Friedman, Susan Stanford. 1998. *Mappings: Feminism and the Cultural Geographies of Encounter*. Princeton, N.J.: Princeton University Press.

Fulmer, Constance M., and Margaret E. Barfield, eds. 1998. *A Monument to the Memory of George Eliot: Edith J. Simcox's Autobiography of a Shirtmaker*. New York: Garland,

Gag, Wanda. [1940] 1984. *Growing Pains: Diaries and Drawings for the Years 1908–1917*. St. Paul: Minnesota Historical Society Press.

Gannett, Cinthia. 1992. *Gender and the Journal: Diaries and Academic Discourse*. Albany: State University of New York Press.

Gilmore, Leigh. 1994. *Autobiographics: A Feminist Theory of Women's Self-Representation*. Ithaca, N.Y.: Cornell University Press.

Gingko. *Dreaming Among the Jade Clouds*, on-line journal <http://www.jade-leaves.com/journal/journal_index.shtml>. 15 August 2000.

Graves, Mrs. A. J. 1841. *Woman in America: Being an Examination into the Moral and Intellectual Condition of American Female Society*. New York: Harper.

Gristwood, Sarah. 1988. *Recording Angels: The Secret World of Women's Diaries*. London: Harrap.

Gwin, Minrose, ed. 1992. *A Woman's Civil War: A Diary, with Reminiscences of the War, from March 1862*, by Cornelia Peake McDonald. Madison: University of Wisconsin Press.

Halpern, Daniel, ed. 1988. *Our Private Lives: Journals, Notebooks, and Diaries*. New York: Random House.

Hampsten, Elizabeth. 1982. *Read This Only to Yourself: The Private Writings of Midwestern Women, 1880–1910*. Bloomington: Indiana University Press.

Heider, Hazel Rahn. 1981. *Along the Waterloo Road*. Sparta, Wis.: Graffix Design.

Hinz, Evelyn. 1992. "Mimesis: The Dramatic Lineage of Auto/Biography." In Marlene Kadar, ed., *Essays on Life Writing*, 195–212. Toronto: University of Toronto Press.

Hogan, Rebecca S. 1991. "Engendered Autobiographies: Diaries as a Feminine Form." *Prose Studies* 14, no. 2 (September): 95–107.

Hornbostel, Julia. 1996. *A Good and Caring Woman: The Life and Times of Nellie Tallman*. Lakeville, Minn.: Galde.

Huff, Cynthia. 1989. "'That Profoundly Female, and Feminist Genre': The Diary as Feminist Praxis." *Women's Studies Quarterly* 17, no. 3–4 (Fall–Winter): 6–14.

Johnson, Alexandra. 1997. *The Hidden Writer: Diaries and the Creative Life.* New York: Doubleday.

Kadar, Marlene, ed. 1992. *Essays on Life Writing.* Toronto: University of Toronto Press.

Kagle, Steven E. 1988. *Late Nineteenth-Century American Diary Literature.* Boston: Hall.

Kerber, Linda K. 1997. *Toward an Intellectual History of Women.* Chapel Hill: University of North Carolina Press.

Klemperer, Victor. 1998. *I Will Bear Witness: A Diary of the Nazi Years, 1933–1941.* Trans. Martin Chalmers. New York: Random House.

Kozlov, Vladimir A., and Vladimir M. Khrustalev, eds. 1997. *The Last Diary of Tsaritsa Alexandra.* New Haven, Conn.: Yale University Press.

Lejeune, Philippe. 1996. "The 'Journal de jeune fille' in Nineteenth-Century France." Trans. Martine Breillac. In Suzanne L. Bunkers and Cynthia A. Huff, eds., *Inscribing the Daily: Critical Essays on Women's Diaries,* 107–22. Amherst: University of Massachusetts Press.

Lejeune, Philippe. 1997. "Exposer l'intime." In Association pour l'autobiographie et le patrimoine autobiographique et amis des bibliothèques de Lyon, *Un journal à soi: ou la passion des journaux intimes,* 7–13. Lyon: Bibliothèque municipale de Lyon.

Lejeune, Philippe. 1997. "Tenir un journal: histoire d'une enquête." *Poétique* (September): 359–81.

Lensink, Judy Nolte. 1987. "Expanding the Boundaries of Criticism: The Diary as Female Autobiography." *Women's Studies* 14:39–53.

Lensink, Judy Nolte, ed. 1989. *"A Secret to Be Burried": The Life and Diary of Emily Hawley Gillespie.* Iowa City: University of Iowa Press.

Lionnet, Francoise. 1989. *Autobiographical Voices: Race, Gender, Self-portraiture.* Ithaca, N.Y.: Cornell University Press.

McKenzie, K. A. 1961. *Edith Simcox and George Eliot.* London: Oxford University Press.

Mallon, Thomas. 1984. *A Book of One's Own: People and Their Diaries.* New York: Ticknor and Fields.

Marcus, Jane. 1984. "Invisible Mending." In Carol Ascher, Louise DeSalvo, and Sara Ruddick, eds., *Between Women: Biographers, Novelists, Critics, Teachers, and Artists Write About Their Work on Women,* 381–95. Boston: Beacon Press.

Motz, Marilyn Ferris. 1983. *True Sisterhood: Michigan Women and Their Kin, 1820–1920.* Albany: State University of New York Press.

Olney, James. 1998. *Memory and Narrative: The Weave of Life-Writing.* Chicago: University of Chicago Press.

Pascal, Roy. 1960. *Design and Truth in Autobiography.* Cambridge, Mass.: Harvard University Press.

Patterson, David. 1997. "The Summons of the Word and the Speaking of the Spirit in the Holocaust Diary." *a/b: Auto/biography Studies* 12, no. 1 (Spring): 37–51.

Pennebaker, James W. 1990. *Opening Up: The Healing Power of Expressing Emotions.* New York: Guilford.

Pipher, Mary. 1994. *Reviving Ophelia: Saving the Selves of Adolescent Girls.* New York: Ballantine.

Radner, Joan N. and Susan S. Lanser. 1993. "Strategies of Coding in Women's Cultures." In Joan Newlon Radner, ed., *Feminist Messages: Coding in Women's Folk Culture,* 1–29. Chicago: University of Chicago Press.

Rainer, Tristine. 1978. *The New Diary: How to Use a Journal for Self-Guidance and Expanded Creativity.* Los Angeles: Tarcher.

Rainer, Tristine. 1997. *Your Life as Story.* New York: Tarcher/Putnam.

Riley, Glenda. 1981. *Frontierswomen: The Iowa Experience.* Ames: Iowa State University Press.

Riley, Glenda. 1996. *Prairie Voices: Iowa's Pioneering Women.* Ames: Iowa State University Press.

Romero, Lora. 1997. *Home Fronts: Domesticity and its Critics in the Antebellum United States.* Durham, N.C.: Duke University Press.

Rosenbaum, Marcus D., ed. 1998. *Heart of a Wife: The Diary of a Southern Jewish Woman* by Helen Jacobus Apte. New Brunswick, Del.: Scholarly Resources.

Rosenblatt, Paul C. 1983. *Bitter, Bitter Tears: Nineteenth-Century Diarists and Twentieth-Century Grief Theories.* Minneapolis: University of Minnesota Press.

Schiwy, Marlene A. 1996. *A Voice of Her Own: Women and the Journal Writing Journey.* New York: Simon and Schuster.

Schlereth, Thomas K., ed. 1985. "Material Culture and Cultural Research." In Thomas K. Schlereth, ed., *Material Culture: A Research Guide,* 1–34. Lawrence: University Press of Kansas.

Schlissel, Lillian. 1981. *Women's Diaries of the Westward Journey.* New York: Schocken.

Schlissel, Lillian, Vicki L. Ruiz, and Janice Monk. 1988. *Western Women: Their Land, Their Lives.* Albuquerque: University of New Mexico Press.

Shandler, Sara. 1999. *Ophelia Speaks: Adolescent Girls Write About Their Search for Self.* New York: HarperPerennial.

Showalter, Elaine. 1986. "Piecing and Writing." In Nancy K. Miller, ed., *The Poetics of Gender,* 222–47. New York: Columbia University Press.

Simons, Judy. 1990. *Diaries and Journals of Literary Women from Fanny Burney to Virginia Woolf.* Iowa City: University of Iowa Press.

Smith-Rosenberg, Carroll. 1986. "Writing History: Language, Class, and Gender." In Teresa de Lauretis, ed., *Feminist Studies, Critical Studies,* 31–54. Bloomington: Indiana University Press.

Solly, Richard, and Roseann Lloyd. 1989. *Journey Notes: Writing for Recovery and Spiritual Growth.* New York: Harper and Row.

Spelman, Elizabeth V. 1988. *Inessential Woman: Problems of Exclusion in Feminist Thought.* Boston: Beacon.

Stanley, Liz. 1992. *The Auto/biographical I.* Manchester, U.K.: Manchester University Press.

Stratton, Joanna. 1981. *Pioneer Women: Voices from the Kansas Frontier.* New York: Simon and Schuster.

Temple, Judy Nolte, and Suzanne L. Bunkers. 1995. "Mothers, Daughters, Diaries: Literacy, Relationships, and Cultural Context." In Catherine Hobbs, ed., *Nineteenth-Century Women Learn to Write*, 197–216. Charlottesville: University Press of Virginia.

Thomas, Trudelle H. 1984. "Women's Diaries of the Westward Movement: A Methodological Study." *Forum: A Women's Studies Quarterly*, 10, no. 3 (Spring): 7, 9–11.

Ulrich, Laurel Thatcher. 1990. *A Midwife's Tale: The Life of Martha Ballard, Based on Her Diary, 1785–1812*. New York: Random House.

Welter, Barbara. 1966. "The Cult of True Womanhood, 1820–1860." *American Quarterly* 18 (Summer): 151–74.

Wilber, Jessica. 1996. *Totally Private and Person: Journaling Ideas for Girls and Young Women*. Minneapolis: Free Spirit.

Wink, Amy L. "She Left Nothing in Particular: The Autobiographical Legacy of Nineteenth-Century Women's Diaries." Ph.D. diss. Texas A&M University, College Station, 1996.

Woodman, Marion. 1996. Foreword to Marlene A. Schiwy, *A Voice of Her Own: Women and the Journal-Writing Journey*. New York: Simon and Schuster.

Zelinsky, Wilbur. 1994. *Exploring the Beloved Country: Geographic Forays into American Society and Culture*. Iowa City: University of Iowa Press.